Also by Patrick McCarthy:
Céline (1976)

CAMUS

CAMUS
Patrick McCarthy

Random House   New York

Library of Congress Cataloging in Publication Data

McCarthy, Patrick, 1941-
Camus

Bibliography: p.
Includes index.
1. Camus, Albert, 1913–1960. 2. Authors, French
—20th century—Biography. I. Title.
PQ2605.A3734Z72135   848′.91409 [B]   82-437
AACR2
ISBN   0-394-52459-4

Manufactured in the United States of America
2 3 4 5 6 7 8 9

For Veronica

Contents

CAMUS

Introduction

Camus' posthumous existence has been odd. During the last ten years of his life he was not merely admired as a great writer but he was also worshipped like a film-star. Since his death, however, he has been neglected. In Anglo-Saxon countries his reputation has not fallen but young Frenchmen have almost ignored him. There is hardly a novelist or dramatist working in France today who has been influenced by Camus. Moreover men who were twenty years old in the 1960's disagreed with his stand on the Algerian War and turned away from the writer who had been the conscience of their parents' generation.

In part this has little to do with Camus. It is now clear that a great change took place in French and perhaps European culture around 1960. A literature of moral and political questioning, flavoured with rhetoric and polemic, gave way to a literature that was more obviously aesthetic and set out to investigate language. The now not so new novel made Camus, who had prepared the way for it in *L'Etranger*, seem obsolete. The theatre experiments of Beckett, Ionesco and Arrabal eclipsed plays like *Caligula* and *Les Justes*. The great writers of the Liberation – Sartre and Malraux as well as Camus – fell into disfavour.

Camus' case is special because he was so much a part of that age. *La Peste* exalted the values that had enabled men to combat Nazism – courage and fraternity. Camus was acclaimed as the writer who stood firm in the Cold War, denouncing both capitalist and marxist utopias. An idealized Camus was created, which made it all the easier for the next generation to dismiss him as a saint who had betrayed.

Camus was no saint and the first task of anyone, whether biographer or critic, who writes about him is to cut through the myths that surround him. Although he wrote a great deal, only a small part of his work remains alive. He was a bad philosopher and he has little to tell us about politics. His plays are wooden even if his novels are superb. As a man he was more interesting and less heroic than his legend. He was vulnerable and quick-tempered, his honesty could be devious and he was insufferably self-righteous. Yet he was also humorous, immensely popular and incapable of taking himself seriously.

The best way to approach him is to look at his childhood and at the now vanished world of French Algeria. In recent years Camus' first adolescent writings, an unpublished novel called *La Mort Heureuse* and his pre-1939 journalism have all been published. They reveal an Algerian Camus: a pied-noir whose main preoccupation as he grew up was to explore his territory. His life and writing were shaped by a few images of his childhood – the Mediterranean, the sudden silence of the Algiers evening and, above all, his mother. During the Second World War Camus left Algeria and never returned there to live but his closest friends remained the men he had known in adolescence. Algeria became, rather dangerously, a golden age which contrasted with the complicated 1950's. Then came the Algerian War which tormented Camus who could not face the fact that the French must leave. His attitude was not very heroic nor very moral; it was a matter of instinct and emotion – he was a proud pied-noir.

Not that Camus' childhood was as happy as he would have us believe. He created a legend of sunshine and carefree poverty but there was a darker side. His father was killed shortly after he was born, his mother was poverty-stricken and backward and he had a grave attack of tuberculosis when he was sixteen. His first marriage to a drug-addict ended in divorce and he was jobless and poor until he was thirty. These experiences shaped him, inspiring him with his sense of death and confirming his cold, pessimistic vision. Camus could be wonderfully happy: his friends relished his vitality and women flocked to him. But the edge of what he called indifference remained: nothing seemed real to him except his mother's silent toil; the universe was beautiful but it was empty.

So the triumphant Camus of the '57 Nobel Prize was never more than a part of the whole. Retrospectively the tributes paid to him seem ridiculous. No man could have lived up to them and Camus less than most. He was not, for example, the Resistance warrior his admirers thought him. He did not enter the Resistance until eight months before the liberation of Paris. Behind the façade of triumph his post-war life might be seen as an exile from Algeria and as a string of failures. His newspaper,

Combat, which was to be the model of truthful journalism, collapsed and his dispute with Sartre ended in a painful defeat, at least in the eyes of French intellectuals. He never resolved the contradictions of his private life, although he shows his best and certainly his happiest side in his affair with Maria Casarès.

It is the unsaintly, anguished and curiously indifferent Camus who is the subject of this book. As one discards the legend of his life and looks more closely at his Algerian upbringing so his writing looks different too. He was not the universal philosopher-moralist he sometimes tried to be. But his lyrical essays on Algeria remain fascinating. In *L'Envers et L'Endroit, Noces* and *L'Eté* the struggle to live and the need for beauty clash with the sense of mortality; Camus' vision is uncomplicated and barbaric.

In his novels he curbs his lyrical impulse, cutting it back so painfully that it leaves a scar. To present-day readers the value of *La Peste* lies in its deliberately incomplete point of view. Rieux tells us a story about a plague but, since he does not understand the plague, there are gaps in his story. Meursault had tried in *L'Etranger* to explain how he killed the Arab but he could not.

In *La Chute* Camus went still further and allowed his narrator, Jean-Baptiste Clamence, to tell a story that is quite false. Like the other two novels *La Chute* offers a religious view of the world, for Camus was haunted by the absence of God. Determined not to believe, he catalogued the traps which a religious temperament sets for a man – the temptations of guilt, purity and harmony. He told his readers not to pursue the illusion of oneness but he could not help feeling that without God the world was a tragic place. This inspired him to experiment with narrative technique: if there was no God then clearly there could be no omniscient narrators. So Camus wrote the ironic, deliberately ambiguous novels that were his greatest achievement.

This book is, then, an attempt to re-evaluate. It asks the questions: what remains of Camus and how do we look back on him? The first five chapters deal with his experience up to the departure from Algeria and the writing of *L'Etranger*. One whole chapter is an introduction to French Algeria. The last chapters depict the Camus of *La Peste*, the quarrel with Sartre, the Algerian War and the 1960 car crash. Biography is unashamedly mixed with literary criticism because Camus' vision was more autobiographical than it seems. He was not a novelist who created plots and characters; he toiled to make his books objective but they all lead back to him. Conversely the way his work was interpreted shaped his later life. He was trapped in the roles of lay saint and moral conscience of his generation. In a similar way he shaped and was shaped by his age. Long before the Algerian War he had depicted, however ambiguously, the murder of an Arab by a French Algerian. When that war broke out it plunged him into a depression that left him unable to write.

So this is a book about Camus' life, work and times. It pursues him in his various roles as Algiers street-kid, Communist militant, Maria Casarès' lover and so on. Camus was elusive and few of his many friends really knew him. He must be the most photographed writer of the century but most of the photographs show him turning away as if to flee. A lover of the theatre, he acted in his daily life and in his books he hides behind his uncertain narrators. Somewhere behind Meursault and Clamence lurks the remote, secretive figure of Camus.

1

Camus' Early Years

In 1934 when he married Simone Hié Camus was twenty-one years old. He was mature because he had endured much hardship. Jean Grenier, the schoolteacher who had such an influence on him, had guided him towards literature. Now Camus was studying philosophy at the university and he had started to write. He had a circle of friends with whom he discussed Gide, God and the Communist Party. He was starting to reflect on the French Algeria in which he had grown up.

The next years would bring great changes. His marriage would break up, leaving a wound that hurt all the more because he was too proudly masculine to mention it. Algeria would alter as the Popular Front came to power and as Arab protest grew. Camus would undergo a long, difficult apprenticeship as a writer. Yet the most important events were already past: the childhood in Belcourt, the impossible dialogue with a silent mother, the presence of the Mediterranean. All his life Camus would puzzle over the figure of his mother and over his memories of the Algiers streets and the sea. His last, unfinished book, *Le Premier Homme*, is an attempt to depict how he grew up in Algeria. He is a writer whose work is dominated by a few intense images of childhood.

One must glance at his boyhood and adolescence and ask the difficult question: what did Camus himself make of them? One must discover not only what they were 'really' like but how he lived through them. Then one may be able to draw the portrait of the twenty-one-year-old Camus.

He was born on November 1, 1913 at Mondovi, a village in the Algerian interior. Situated in the fertile Bône plain, Mondovi was lined with beech and eucalyptus trees and surrounded by vineyards. Camus' father worked on a grape farm not outdoors tending the grapes but helping in the manufacture of wine. Camus believed that his father's family had come to Algeria from Alsace-Lorraine after the 1870 Franco-Prussian war. In fact this was not so. They had arrived not long after the 1830 Conquest of Algeria and from a different part of France.[1] Since Camus never knew this, it is as if his father had come from Alsace-Lorraine. This was important to him because it confirmed two strands in his identity. The men of his family had chosen to remain French rather than to become German and they had arrived as pioneers in Algeria. Thus Camus was authentically French and Algerian. Third and fourth strands were provided by his mother's family which came from Minorca. Camus was equally proud to be Spanish and to be, like so many other Algerians, of mixed racial descent.

He was the younger of two sons and, when he was less than a year old, his father was called up and went off to war. Badly wounded at the Marne, he was transported hundreds of miles to Saint-Brieuc hospital where he died. Thirty years later Camus' friend, Louis Guilloux, who lived in Saint-Brieuc, sought out Lucien Camus' tomb and took Camus to visit it. Of his father Camus knew little. The one detail, which his mother recounted and which stuck in his mind, was that his father once attended an execution. He saw nothing wrong in capital punishment and this was a particularly horrible crime: a labourer had murdered an entire family and stolen their money. Yet, when Camus' father returned from the execution, he threw himself on the bed and began to vomit. A silent man, he never explained exactly what had shocked him.

His silence was a trait which his wife remembered; industriousness and obstinacy were two others. Camus inherited the obstinacy and, when he displayed it, his mother used to tap her forehead. 'Hard-headed,' she would say, 'like all the Camus.'[2] Otherwise she rarely spoke of her husband and Camus remembered him only for the Marne and the guillotine. The Marne explains Camus' loathing for bloodshed and his sense that he belonged to a generation cursed by wars. When he started school his teachers were kind to him because he was a war-orphan. In 1939 he could think only of how to avoid a second cataclysm. Otherwise his father was present in his life as a painful absence. Camus was forced into a precocious maturity yet he kept looking for substitute fathers like Grenier.

After her husband's death his mother fell back on her family.

She went to live with her own mother and her brothers in the Algiers suburb of Belcourt. Belcourt was working-class and it resembled Bab-el-Oued, where Camus would go to grammar-school, except that it was further from the centre. Camus' newspaper, *Alger-Républicain*, would run a local column headed 'From Belcourt to Bab-el-Oued'. Belcourt housed a mixture of Italians, Greeks, Spaniards and French and the French looked down on all the others. It was an industrial area, dotted with warehouses, workshops and small factories; the workers were artisans rather than proletarians accustomed to the conveyer-belt. Belcourt was full of crowded apartment buildings where the flats were small and consisted of two or three rooms. Camus' family lived in such a flat on the rue de Lyon. In Belcourt the people knew one another. They hung their washing in the windows, shouted across the narrow streets and went to the same small shops. Politically Belcourt was left-wing and the Communist Party did fairly well in the elections of the mid-1920's. This is a far too gloomy picture of Belcourt, painted by a novelist who was Camus' friend:

'Belcourt stretches out on both sides of the rue de Lyon which is lined with bars, cafés and Arab restaurants. Towards the rue Sadi Carnot and the port there are only factories, engineering workshops, joiners, cement works and depots of metal products, paints and dyes . . . In the winter the dusty streets turn into rivers of mud which wind amidst the gloomy walls and the stretches of waste-ground. Everything is littered with rusty metal sheets, broken bottles and planks . . . On the other side of the rue de Lyon, towards Boulevard Bru and the European cemetery the hovels climb up the side of the incline and present their leprous fronts to the sea . . . This is an industrial suburb, stifling and over-populated, ugly and grim.'[3]

There was also an Arab section because Belcourt possessed a mosque and an Arab graveyard. While Camus was growing up, more Arabs moved in and formed a slum behind the cemetery. This was 'a poor, cramped area'. The roads were unpaved and, when it rained, they turned into 'sticky, slimy slopes'. Most Arab families were 'crowded into hovels without light or air'.[4] So, if the Europeans were poor, the Arabs were much poorer and, when Arab nationalism grew in the 1930's, it found supporters in Belcourt.

Belcourt influenced Camus in two ways. Living on the streets, he had to fend for himself. He enjoyed the company of other boys but he also knew how to fight them off. He acquired that mental boxer's stance which his friends would notice; he learned to be wary and to counterpunch. He also acquired a sense of community. There was a warmth about Belcourt which went beyond the taunts which the French and the Spanish hurled at each other. Camus' friend, Charles Poncet, who grew up there at the same time felt it too. He had spent part of his childhood in France and he found Belcourt much more friendly.

The curious Camus considered Belcourt his territory and he explored it. As a young boy he knew all the café-owners and the shopkeepers. Long after he left Belcourt he would seek out the working-class neighbourhoods in the cities he visited. He loathed New York but enjoyed Chinatown in lower Manhattan because he rediscovered there the 'teeming street life' which he had known in his childhood.[5] Camus was proud of being a child of Belcourt. It was both a role he enjoyed and a genuine part of his character.

His early life revolved around his mother, Catherine, who herself came from a matriarchial family. Photographs show a fine-boned woman, rather beautiful in an austere way. After working in a factory she became a charwoman and cleaned houses. Care of the children was left to her mother, a strong-minded, talkative lady who ruled over the household like a queen. She had remained very Spanish and Camus absorbed this. He felt his grandmother's pride. All Spaniards were aristocrats, he believed, even or especially working-class Spaniards. As a young boy Camus himself was grave and dignified; he was also touchy and quick to take offence.

Although he admired his grandmother he feared her too. She did not hesitate to beat him or his brother and they could not look to their mother for help. Catherine never stood up to her mother who berated her for having married a man who had died young and had left her with two fatherless children. One of Catherine's brothers, Joseph, had moved out of the flat but the second, Etienne, remained. He had been deaf and dumb until adolescence when an operation left him still very deaf but able to speak. He worked as a cooper in a small workshop that made barrels. Camus had the same mixed feelings about his uncle as about his grandmother. He admired in Etienne the silent, stoical artisan who worked hard and did not complain. But he disliked the Etienne who was rough with Catherine. Camus tells a story of how his mother had a love-affair with a neighbour; when he discovered it Etienne threw the man out of the apartment and poured a torrent of abuse on Catherine.

Camus' mother had no formal education and could not read. She seldom spoke and she too was partially deaf. How backward she was is a matter of dispute. Camus' friends describe her variously as 'full of nobility' and 'incapable of thought'. His brother, Lucien, feels that both Catherine's backwardness and their poverty have been exaggerated; they were badly-off, he says, but never hungry. A schoolteacher remembers that both boys came to school neatly dressed and that the family made a point of being tidy.

Lucien himself was three years older than Camus and had been born in Algiers before the family moved to Mondovi. He spoke and heard normally but had none of his brother's intelligence. When the two were at elementary school Camus seemed the older and he used to protect Lucien who had little to say. Lucien did not go beyond elementary school and went to work as his uncles had done. He lived the normal life of a Belcourt man: he did his military service, had various jobs as a labourer and lived at home until he married. Camus felt close to Lucien because he was his brother but the two boys were too unalike to be friends.

A photograph of the family, taken around 1918, shows Camus, a stubby child in a black smock, surrounded by adults unused to being photographed and dressed for the occasion. The men are embarrassed in their stiff collars and suits, while the women wear long, formal dresses.

This is a working-class family yet there was in the household an emotional poverty that was exceptional even in Belcourt. Catherine toiled all day and was exhausted in the evening. Since her husband was dead she was doubly the object of her son's affections but she was unable to respond in the ways most mothers do. When he went one day to a friend's house, Camus was amazed to discover that the friend's mother chatted and joked with them. Never had his own mother done this. Later she would be unable to read his books and she would distrust his success. He had exaggerated, she felt, he had strayed too far from Belcourt. She possessed, instinctively, the fatalism of the poor: a charwoman's son should not turn into a famous writer; it was a crime of hubris. When Camus told her that the French president had invited him to the Elysée palace she showed no enthusiasm: 'That's too much, you've already risen far too high.'[6]

Camus could tell this story with a certain pride. He usually added that Etienne had intervened to say that presidents and politicians were all idiots. As an adult Camus was proud of his working-class family and saw in their lives virtues that he cherished. They were tough, stoical and sceptical. Their silence contained a greater truth than the rhetoric of politicians or the theorizing of intellectuals. But the adult Camus painted too rosy a picture of his childhood. There was in his family a special loneliness born not merely of poverty but of his father's death and his mother's backwardness. As a child Camus suffered from this. It caused him pain which he could not express and had to hide. He turned in on himself, locking himself in some private prison.

At elementary school he had the good fortune to meet a dedicated teacher, Louis Germain. Germain's depiction of the young Camus makes amusing reading today because Camus appears as the model pupil, the teacher's pet.[7] One is tempted to believe that this is the young Camus' first seduction. Like so many French schoolteachers, Germain believed that the education system was both just and democratic; its task was to create a generation of good republicans. Camus responded as many working-class pupils did: he admired the rituals of the school and he seemed aware of the difference between school and home. When he arrived he was behind the other pupils but he soon caught up. Already he was industrious: 'He worked diligently all day long ... without ever being told to.' He became especially good in French and mathematics which were the key subjects for the examinations. Without realizing it, he was showing his ambition.

Germain picked up two other traits in the young Camus. When he worked, 'his attention never strayed'. Camus' university friends would stress his ability to concentrate and to work quickly. When they first met him, they realized that his concentration could be focused on people too; he weighed everything that was said. Secondly Germain comments on

Camus' sense of privacy: 'he thought a great deal, he spoke rarely and slowly,' he was 'very reserved and serious'. Because he had to juxtapose home and school, the child was wary. He liked school, he welcomed the kindness which Germain, his first father-substitute, offered him, but he kept a separate domain where no-one was allowed to penetrate. This distance was another trait which Camus' university friends would perceive. Already young Camus was self-possessed. Another photograph, taken around 1924, shows him in a sailor suit and sandals, surrounded by classmates. The other children look embarrassed or excited at being photographed, but Camus is impassive.

During 1924 Germain prepared him for the entrance examination to the grammar school. Towards the end of the year Madame Camus came to see Germain. She thanked him for his help but added: 'Unfortunately I am not well-off and I shall not be able to afford the fees.' Germain assured her that her son would get a scholarship, which he duly did. In 1925 he entered the Bab-el-Oued grammar school as a 'boursier'. The 'boursier' is a familiar figure in the Third Republic: the boy of poor background, whose studies are paid for by the state and who rises through and because of the education system. Camus' ambition, industry and admiration for the education system itself are characteristic of the 'boursier' mentality. He had been given a chance and he was grateful. Unlike French writers of middle-class background who castigate it, Camus praises the teacher-pupil relationship. This is the first huge difference between him and Sartre. Of course, the Algerian school system, which was provincial and whose standards were lower than in France, imposed no great strain on a boy as intelligent as Camus. He could excel and yet not feel trapped. The Bab-el-Oued school was light-years away from the Lycée Henri IV which Sartre attended.

Entry to grammar school also marked the end of Camus' religious education. Neither of his parents had been practising Catholics. He was baptized at Saint Bonaventure's church in Algiers and received some religious instruction because his grandmother believed in it. Her view of religion was conventional: she simply wanted her grandson to make his first communion. She quarrelled with the priest who was instructing him because she wanted to get it out of the way before Camus went to grammar school. Nothing in all this explains the deep religious sense which is already manifest in Camus' adolescence.

As Camus grew up, he drew closer to an uncle whose exuberance counterbalanced the silence of his home. His mother's sister, another withdrawn woman, had married a butcher, M. Acault, who was exactly the opposite. They had a shop on the rue Michelet, one of the main Algiers streets. It was much frequented because M. Acault sold 'French' meat which, characteristically, enjoyed great prestige in Algeria. Since M. Acault's meat was particularly good, he became 'the object of a kind of veneration'.[8] Dressed in a huge, white apron, he cut up the joints like an artist, making graceful gestures with long, vicious knives. He was a fat man who always wore a cap and, as he cut, he delivered interminable monologues to his customers. His wife sat ever silent near the cash-register and paid absolutely no attention to her extrovert husband's opinions on literature and politics.

Most of all he liked to abandon the shop and drag his favourite customers to the Café de la Renaissance across the street. While drinking pastis, he would tell them about his life. He had lived in Lyon, where he had acquired a taste for sausage and become an anarchist. He issued diatribes against the right, the Communists and all political parties, while the other pastis-drinkers listened open-mouthed. M. Acault was self-taught and had read widely. He liked Joyce, who wrote such gloriously scabrous pages, and Gide, who was such a daring heretic. The Acaults, more prosperous and installed in the centre of Algiers, offered Camus an outlet. He liked his uncle because he could joke with him.

Camus was turning into an outgoing youth. He loved to tramp the streets and often walked all the way home from school. He liked the port with its smell of tar, its ships coming and going and its brawny dockers, who joked and swore as they carried off barrels of wine or bales of grain. Most of all Camus liked two other physical pursuits: soccer and swimming. Soccer was played in the schoolyard during the two hour lunch-break. Friends remember Camus racing up and down in the blazing sun. He could dribble well and the ball seemed a part of him.[9] But, because he was small, he was put in goal for the regular matches. When he was fifteen, he used to play for a junior team from the RUA – Racing Universitaire d'Alger.

Camus never lost his love for soccer. After the war he supported the Paris team, Racing, and was pleased that they wore the same colours, blue and white, as the RUA. He used to get excited at the games and would shout so loudly that people turned around and recognized him. When he went to Brazil, he delighted his hosts by asking to go to a football match. As a boy he enjoyed the sense of the team and the comradeship of the other players. The RUA offered him his first taste of the male friendship and fraternity which he would rediscover in journalism and the theatre. Yet the goalkeeper is less a part of the team than any other player: he remains something of an outsider.

Camus also welcomed the idea of the game itself. The rules were arbitrary but they permitted intensity, as does the artifice of the theatre. In *La Peste* there is a discussion of soccer, where the men agree that the centre-half controls the game. But none of them plays centre-half, so the order is beyond their reach. What remains is the thrill of running and tackling and the moments of harmony that occur during a dribble.

Swimming was an even more frequent pastime. Camus used to take his bathing-suit to school and, since Bab-el-Oued was near the sea, he would slip away with other boys. He would swim and then lie on the beach to roast. Even after his illness he continued to brave the sun and to stay out in it until it almost bleached him. He made regular pilgrimages to the numerous Algiers beaches and afterwards consumed sardines and white wine in restaurants near the port. Like soccer, swimming was a matter of rhythm. Camus tried to swim with regular even strokes that enabled him to feel a part of the ocean.

Swimming, too, has its place in *La Peste*, where it is Rieux's moment of relief and the setting for his comradeship with Tarrou. Even as a boy Camus felt that swimming offered more than just a physical delight. While swimming he felt liberated from his family and carried off into the purity of nature. Camus had his first taste of beauty while swimming and walking. As he roamed the hills, he looked down on the Algiers bay and was struck by its splendour. The rich, barren Algerian countryside corresponded to his own restrained but fervent sensibility. Sensuous experience led on to aesthetic, which in turn became religious. The countryside seemed to belong to a different realm from Belcourt and perhaps it had a different creator. 'God is a question of beauty,' Camus told a friend.[10]

His career as a goalkeeper was cut short by his first attack of tuberculosis which occurred in 1930, just before his seventeenth birthday. It appeared in one of his lungs and he was reduced to coughing and spitting up blood. He had to remain in bed and the doctor came repeatedly to the house. After a while he moved out to his uncle's house which was larger. M. Acault looked after him, gave him steak and made him drink glasses of blood in order to build him up. But the illness was severe and Camus had to repeat a year in school. Moreover the treatment, which consisted of pumping air into the lung, was itself painful. Worst of all, Camus never really recovered. He continued to have treatment and a few years later he discovered he had tuberculosis in the other lung.

He rarely talked about his illness, either then or later. He was too proud to reveal what he considered a weakness. To be poor was already bad, to be ill was unforgivable. He refused to acknowledge his disease and he grew angry when doctors told him to rest. Living in Algiers he and his friends could often get work on cargo boats and they did so in order to travel. Camus set out on a boat to Tunisia but he was racked by fits of coughing and had to return home. Yet he continued to walk and to cycle. He talks of 'the concentrated effort of walking; the air in my lungs is like a red-hot iron or a sharpened razor'.[11] Despite his sense of privacy he sometimes had to confide his fears. At the age of nineteen he told a friend that he would soon die, that he had only four years to live.

His disease, which he was never allowed to forget, weighed on him. It strengthened his awareness of death, because it came and went in a seemingly haphazard way. When it retreated, as it did after the first attack, he returned to life with the heightened pleasure which is common among TB patients. Then came a fresh bout and he relapsed into gloom. These periodic crises formed the rhythm of his existence. In 1937 he had an attack during a troubled summer which also saw him break with the Communist Party and his first theatre group. When he was ill, he would grow irritable and withdraw into himself. From his earliest years he had had to battle against deprivation; now he had a new, mysterious enemy which made him battle all the harder. Not long before his death he told an old friend that TB was catching up with him, that he had not long to live. Yet during those last months he was more cheerful than he had been for years. Tuberculosis made him oscillate between extremes of despair and happiness.

The contemplation of death and the burden imposed by his mother's silent poverty accentuated Camus' sense of stoicism or indifference. It was first noticed by Jean Grenier.[12] When he realized, during the winter of 1930, that Camus was absent from school Grenier made the long, forty-five minute bus trip to Belcourt and arrived at the shabby flat. He found a sullen Camus who scarcely said hello and replied in monosyllables when asked about his condition. Grenier tried to make conversation but his pupil was taciturn. A visit from a teacher was an unusual event and Camus was being impertinent.

Grenier was too subtle not to see beyond the rudeness. He detected Camus' sense of privacy and his pride. This pride was an energetic refusal: Camus would not disguise his poverty and illness; they were ugly things and he would confront them. Actually he was delighted by Grenier's visit. The act of friendship was important to a boy who treasured friendship. Yet he grasped the limits of Grenier's kindness: when Grenier left, Camus remained there, poor and ill.

Camus never moved back to his mother's home after his illness. He lived with his uncle until he married and after his divorce he lived with friends or in a room of his own. He returned frequently to Belcourt, sometimes for months at a time. But the break with his mother was made. In some ways, however, Camus never left her. She dominates his first book *L'Envers et l'Endroit* and he invokes her in his most important statements on the Algerian War. In 1930 he was weighing the new world, into which he was moving and which was made up of Grenier, friends and books, against the old world of his home. Much as he liked the opportunities which were opening up to him, they could not obliterate his earlier experiences. Only rarely could middle-class friends be as close as working-class friends and the yardstick by which he measured his new life was the value which he perceived in his mother's hard toil.

In part this is the dilemma of the working-class boy. The middle-class family, because of its wealth and social connections, retains its importance as the child grows up. His task is to escape it. The working-class boy has no such difficulty, since he leaves his family behind as he rises socially or culturally. His task is to retain contact with it. Camus did this by seeing in his mother's silence the aristocratic virtues of dignity and honour.

When he later wrote about his childhood he stressed its happiness: 'Poverty never meant unhappiness for me . . . I lived without much money but in a kind of joy . . . in Africa the sea and the sun cost nothing.'[13] Such statements, made during the '50's, should be treated with care. As Camus' dislike of literary Paris grew because of the quarrels over *L'Homme Révolté* and the Algerian War, so he looked back with ever greater nostalgia on pre-war Algeria, which was both his childhood and the inspiration of his writing. He tended to forget the hardships he had known. He could not complain about them without being retrospectively disloyal to his mother.

Her daily fatigue and the absence between them of conventional affection brought Camus much suffering. During his first bout of TB he was surprised that she was not more worried about him. Yet he chose to perceive in her apparent coldness an act of revolt against her life. His own task was to participate in the act by not complaining about his condition. This in turn was the contact between them. They did not need words of affection, books or teams; their bond lay in their joint indifference, the badge of the suffering and the knowledge that they shared. Clearly this view involved pain because Camus had to live with silence. Grenier felt that Camus was 'locked up, he had shut himself away in some dungeon'.[14] Camus himself felt the need to break out of his prison and it cannot be an accident that Meursault in *L'Etranger* is tried for symbolic matricide. But the decision to turn emotional poverty into a value was the only way he could remain in contact with his mother. This was how he lived through his boyhood.

The bond between them was a kind of illness. Much later, Camus talked of 'my profound indifference which is like a natural infirmity'.[15] The long hours spent with his mother were a death where Camus ceased to be a separate person and was merged with her. Yet her mute suffering also sharpened his desire to write. Since she could not speak he would speak for her. His writing would be tough and concise because it would contain her silence. Finally her suffering assumed a religious form. Her stoicism was not merely a rebellion; it was an ascetic rejection of the things of this world. 'A God is present in her,' writes the young Camus.[16] This God was remote and uncaring; He was the God of beauty but not of love. This and not his few

21

hurried catechism lessons was the source of Camus' strong, ever frustrated religious impulse.

Much in Camus goes back to his childhood experience of death. It was an awful but valuable reality to which he clung tenaciously. Not that the seventeen-year-old had reached this understanding. But the indifference which struck Jean Grenier was the mark of the years spent in the house with the deaf uncle and the backward mother. The core of Camus' character was taking shape: an indifference which masked a vulnerability, an edge of distance, a strong vein of ambition, a stubborn pride. Through all this ran a flair for happiness, physical pleasure and beauty which made Camus an attractive boy. His friends remember him as thin and emaciated by tuberculosis but with broad shoulders and a Spanish touch to his face. One said – with a theatricality that Camus would have loathed – that he had the concentration of the bullfighter who stares at his death in the bull's black head.

When he recovered from his bout of TB, Camus formed his first group of friends. Throughout his life he would be a man of groups, gregarious as well as private. Now he teamed up with boys who were exploring, as he was. The most complex of these friendships was with Max-Pol Fouchet, who was himself to become a well-known writer.

Fouchet already knew Camus by reputation. His father was one of M. Acault's customers and he had heard much about the brilliant nephew. There was a tension in the friendship from the start. Fouchet's family were not pied-noir.* They were from Northern France and had come to Algeria because M. Fouchet, who had been gassed at Verdun, found the climate healthy. Although the family had been financially ruined by the war, it was solidly middle-class by background. In both respects Fouchet was the opposite of Camus who seemed to him 'the

---

*In writing about French Algeria one encounters grave problems of terminology. 'Pied-noir' is the word which Camus' friends use about themselves. Of uncertain origin, it means a Frenchman or a European born in Algeria. In post-independence Algeria the term 'Algerian' is reserved for those who live under the present Algerian government, i.e. Arabs. The term is often used retrospectively in this way. It can be extended to include Europeans who live or have lived in Algeria and who accept or accepted Algerian independence. Is Camus an Algerian? Controversy reigns. In this book the language used in French Algeria has been retained both because it is simple and because it was Camus' language.

archetypal pied-noir'. In return, Camus, showing an inferiority complex vis-à-vis the metropolitan Frenchman, refused to believe that Fouchet, who was not 'born here', could know anything about Algeria. Camus felt that Fouchet was soft, whereas he himself was a tough street-kid from Belcourt. Fouchet also had a desirable girlfriend, Simone Hié, with whom the whole group was half in love; this added to the tension. Fouchet found Camus cocky and difficult; Camus considered Fouchet affected. Yet the two boys had much in common, especially since there were not many people in Algiers who were interested in writing or left-wing politics.

They were joined by other friends like Jean de Maisonseul, Louis Miquel and Louis Bénisti. De Maisonseul, who came from the top ranks of colonial society, was dignified and polite. Bored with his social equals, he sought his friends among poorer boys. He was studying architecture and drawing and he subscribed to the magazine, *Plans*, which defended Le Corbusier. Corbusier's vision of vast blocks of popular housing had a left-wing slant which appealed to the group but De Maisonseul was more interested in aesthetics than in politics. Corbusier's skyscrapers were the creation of the twentieth century, audacious and anonymous like Greek temples. De Maisonseul had a religious yearning which was another link with Camus. He admired the asceticism of Arab life and especially the bare Arab houses which opened outward onto the sky. A piece by Camus called *La Maison Mauresque* (1933) shows he welcomed De Maisonseul's ideas: the patio is 'wide, horizontal and infinite, bathed in perfect light'.[17]

At the fine arts school, De Maisonseul met Louis Miquel who came from a poor Spanish family. He, too, was studying architecture and was supporting himself by working as a draughtsman. The shy Miquel felt overshadowed by the others but he shared their interest in Le Corbusier, in the *Nouvelle Revue Française* and in things Arab.

Louis Bénisti, who was ten years older than the others, had worked for years as a jeweller until a worker had robbed him and forced him to give up. He took to sculpture instead and met De Maisonseul. This was his first encounter with someone of higher social background. Bénisti's family was part-Jewish and part-Berber, which meant that, although they had come to Algeria long before the Conquest, they were not accepted by the

French. He was thus pleasantly surprised to discover that De Maisonseul was willing to be friendly. Once more the sense of class was important: Camus, Miquel and Bénisti were all from the working class. At first, Bénisti found Camus arrogant and sarcastic – 'he always seemed to be making fun of us'. One day he told Camus this to his face. Camus took it well and Bénisti realized that Camus was distrustful rather than arrogant.[18] Camus has left a portrait of Bénisti in *La Mort Heureuse*: the sculptor Noël 'thinks in shapes and clay';[19] he is good-natured and straight-talking. Camus preferred men who were straight.

On Sunday afternoons Camus and Fouchet went to the popular dance-halls of Bab-el-Oued; their favourite was called the Bains Padovani. The local boys and girls first went swimming and then came in to dance; music blared out, while the sea rushed against the wooden planks at the base of the building. Camus and Fouchet pursued the girls from the Bab-el-Oued factories. Some, who worked making cigarettes, still smelt of tobacco; all smelt of salt from the sea. The two eighteen-year olds joked with each other, half-laughing but half-serious, that in dancing with these girls they were embracing the teeming peoples of the Mediterranean. Camus tried to lure the girls outside onto the sand, while Fouchet wrote poems about the dance-halls:

> 'good men, not rich at all,
> workers burdened with cares;
> rundown and penniless
> they court Jean and Margot;
> they laugh and care not for
> motorcars, wealth and pearls'.[20]

The Bab-el-Oued cigarette girls were Camus' first experience of the opposite sex. He was still timid, hesitating between purity and brothels.

Camus and Fouchet talked much of politics. Fouchet's father, who died in 1929, had been anti-clerical and Fouchet was a left-winger. In 1930 he founded a Young Socialists group in Algiers. Membership was not strict and Camus, who was not a member, came to their meetings. They never rallied more than a few people but they were enough to irritate the much stronger right and fighting often broke out. In the interior of Algeria there were even fewer socialists, sometimes only the village schoolmaster, and here the pro-Fascist Leagues were much too belligerent. The Young Socialists obtained some revenge on May Day, when they marched along the port in Algiers and were joined by the dockers. One day they went into the interior to visit an old man called Lefèvre, who had fought in the Paris Commune and had retired to this remote spot. Before they left, he showed them a red rag taken from the sacred flag of the Commune.[21] Other moments were less exalted: a French comrade crossed the Mediterranean in order to bore them with long ideological harangues which they could not understand.

Camus was a left-winger from the moment he first thought about politics. This did not mean that he embraced any party or doctrine and, although he read Marx, he was not impressed. To be a left-winger meant that he was committed to intangible but emotionally-charged things like justice and freedom. More important, it was an instinctive choice which allowed him to assert his working-class upbringing and his dislike of the rich colonials.

Belcourt is not, however, an adequate explanation for Camus' interest in Arab affairs. From their earliest conversations he and Miquel were agreed that Arab poverty was intolerable. Few working-class Europeans shared their concern or saw any link between their own struggles and the Arabs. Not that Camus had a political programme. He believed that 'you had to be generous' and that assimilation could work. Although he knew some Arabs in Belcourt, he seems to have had no Arab friends. Retrospectively, Miquel describes their concern as 'platonic' but it is important to situate it. They were well ahead of the crowds who thronged to the 1930 centenary of the Conquest but they had not gone beyond puzzled expressions of sympathy.

Camus did not join the Young Socialists. He was more interested in writing than politics and he did not become an activist until the mid-30's. He disliked the Socialist Party, which he considered tepid, prone to inaction and inclined to rely on progress. Too pessimistic to believe in progress, Camus was a doer and he felt that the Communists were more likely to act. Once more, he was different from Fouchet. Nor did he hide his contempt for the Socialist Party. In 1934 Fouchet brought the Young Socialists into the Amsterdam-Pleyel movement and the party leadership denounced him for joining a pro-Communist front.* But this did not impress Camus who denounced Fouchet himself as a 'social traitor' and declared that all Socialists were reformists and were merely preparing the way for Fascism.[22] At this point Camus was suspicious of all parties, as was Bénisti who, though a left-winger, distrusted politicians.

Usually the group forgot politics and went tramping around the city. They were taking possession of their territory. They used to visit the Casbah and look for the cafés where Gide had sat during his stays in Algiers. They drank mint tea and listened as the muezzin called the people to prayer at the mosque. At other times they caught the bus up to Bouzaréah, a village in the hills above Algiers. From there they looked down on the bay and the sea. Walking back down the hill, they stopped at cemeteries which Camus loved. 'They are such lively places,' he used to say. He laughed hilariously as armies of red ants marched, in military formation, out of the graves. There was in Camus a touch of gallows humour which his illness had strengthened. He also studied the different inscriptions on the graves – Spanish, Maltese and old French names, soldiers who had died during the Conquest, whole families who had been wiped out by the plagues of the nineteenth century. Camus brooded on these but he said nothing; he simply went running down the hill.

Another favourite spot was the neighbourhood of the Marine. It was dark and dubious, there were shady cafés and prostitutes stood on street corners with their pimps. Camus' band would buy glasses of pastis and eat olives or chickpeas, spitting the pips at one another. Camus particularly liked a café which had a guillotine in one corner and a skeleton in another; the skeleton had a large penis, and when you pulled a string, it leapt up. In the evenings they sometimes went to the cinema, where they liked horror films and westerns; they had a vague interest in America, especially in New Orleans jazz. Often they ended their walks at the port, where they watched the cargo boats and listened to the dockers. Camus encouraged the others

*Amsterdam-Pleyel was a movement of intellectuals who were opposed to Fascism and war. Formed in 1933 it was part of the trend towards committed writing and towards the involvement of writers in politics. It was closely linked with the French Communist Party.

to pick up the slang of the streets, which was particularly rich in a city of diverse races and little formal education. Camus felt that it expressed what the working class felt – their limited but lived wisdom. He liked to listen to conversations on buses and in cafés; they seemed to him to fall out of the skies.

The group continued their own conversations throughout their walks. De Maisonseul spoke in long, complex periods with frequent pauses, Bénisti said what he had to say and then stopped. Miquel usually listened and Fouchet, so they felt, talked too much. Although ten years older, Bénisti never felt older than Camus. Camus' attentive silences were imposing and, when he spoke, everyone listened.

From the very start, Camus thought in moral terms. He was aware of the difference between his home and the world in which he now moved and he sought to work out a code of behaviour. The group's aim must be to live intensely: 'to store up as much life and experience as possible until they realized that the experience was useless.'[23] But, in order to live with such lucid intensity, they needed rules. Camus repeated what he had learned in Belcourt: a man must be honest and proud, generous and masculine. But he also drew on the French heritage of moral thinking which was enshrined in classical literature, imparted by the education system and renewed by the *NRF*. Louis Germain's influence remained strong. While he instinctively felt that the world made no sense, Camus kept returning to reason as a tool. In particular he used it to check his own tendency to go to extremes. When he became famous, Camus was perceived and perceived himself as the moralist of an age plagued by wars and nihilism. This is correct, but the origins of his moral thought have little to do with Hitler. They lie in the adolescent's attempt to understand this exciting Algeria in which he was growing up.

Another topic of discussion was precisely 'to situate oneself in Algeria'.[24] They brooded on the desert, the new society that had emerged from the Conquest and on the Mediterranean. The theme of the Mediterranean 'came from the guts'. It was inspired by the port where they ended their walks and by the mixture of Greeks and Neapolitans on the streets. Since Algiers possessed few famous writers or painters, the group felt, correctly or not, that it was cut off from the past. Its task was to shape an Algerian identity. Algeria was different from but linked with France; it was also linked with Italy and Spain and it had to include the Arabs, even if their place was unclear. The group did not wish to remain provincial or local for they saw in the Mediterranean a form of internationalism. 'Already Camus was a Greek,' says Fouchet. But Algeria had its own identity within the greater confines of the Mediterranean. It was more barren than Italy, less refined than France. Its primitivism was valuable but it had to be scrutinized by the most sophisticated moral thinking.

The lesson that experience is useless was a thoroughly Algerian one. Camus had learned it through his brush with death and he imparted it to the others. Bénisti remembers a tomb bearing the name of a monk who had come from another country. This intrigued Camus: the monk had come from elsewhere for some unknown reason; he had prayed and died in Algeria and that was all. The beautiful countryside around showed that the Grecian sense of harmony between man and nature was a matter of a few moments only.

Clearly there could be no natural or historical laws. Society was as arbitrary as death. Justice, Camus kept repeating, was a 'lottery': some were born rich and others poor. Yet this was unacceptable. The task of the moralist and the left-winger was to introduce order where none previously existed. A man's life took shape as an act of protest.

Meanwhile the deeper interrogation continued. Camus read the Bible, brooded on medieval mystics and talked about the figure of Jesus. Bénisti insists that Camus was no atheist and perhaps not even an agnostic; he believed in 'a God of whom we can ask nothing'.[25] Fouchet tells an anecdote to illustrate this. One day, as they were walking down from Bouzaréah, they found a crowd of Arabs gathered together. A child was dying, knocked down by a bus-driver who, since the child was an Arab, had not bothered to stop. The mother's lament rang out and eventually Camus and Fouchet, having looked on helplessly, turned to leave. Camus pointed up at the perfect Algerian sky: 'See, He is silent'.[26]

Camus found his God in the cruelty of Algerian life – in his mother's backwardness or Arab suffering. This is the problem which Paneloux will face in *La Peste*. Once more Camus was in conflict with Fouchet, who had a strong but different religious sense. Fouchet's poems have a Franciscan motif: the universe is full of birds and blessings; grace flows from God. Where Camus was determined to confront mortality, Fouchet was sentimental. He was half-converted to catholicism and drew closer to the *Esprit* group, inspired by Emmanuel Mounier.* Camus remained aloof, although he once described himself as an 'independent Catholic'.[27] Yet by repeating that the divinity was harsh and absent he was separating the things of God from the things of man. The only course was to rely on man: the moralist and the left-winger. Camus did think about possible intermediaries like Jesus and the Church. He considered Jesus 'an extraordinary philosopher', meaning that Jesus taught and lived out an admirable code of behaviour. But he had no sense of Jesus' divinity. The line 'all is consummated' recurs in *L'Etranger* and *Caligula* but it signifies human mortality. As for the Catholic Church, Camus felt there were 'very few Christians'. The Algerian Church seemed to ignore the injustice committed against Arabs. Yet Camus, who avoided the anticlericalism so characteristic of the pre-1939 left, was drawn to monks; he liked to visit monasteries and he admired monks who had taken vows of silence. God remained in his thought as man's dream of oneness, his sense of his own inadequacy. No moral thinking or left-wing politics could fill the void left by God's absence.

Writing and painting, however, interested the friends more than politics. Their taste was not always advanced because Algeria was a thoroughly provincial city. Bénisti was drawn to Picasso's sculpture but he was afraid that Picasso had gone too far in abandoning representation. He clung to Maillol and his favourite painter was Cézanne. Camus, too, liked Cézanne but the first time he saw an abstract painting he was shocked. The group ignored surrealism and knew little of Miró or Kandinsky. Bénisti knew the artists who came to Abd-el-Tif, a villa near Algiers where painters resided on government grants; but they were usually landscape painters. As for music Camus listened to Ravel and Debussy, Mozart and Wagner. He seems to have known little about contemporary music except for Stravinsky.

---

*Mounier revitalized '30's French catholicism with the doctrine of personalism which held that the individual's need for God was the starting-point of all religion. The Church itself was secondary. A group of people gathered in Algiers as in other French cities to discuss and read Mounier's magazine, *L'Esprit*.

His favourite writers, when he was eighteen, were Dostoevsky and Nietzsche. Indeed Dostoevsky cast his shadow over the entire group. Camus pondered on the extravagant passions of his characters and on their eternal self-analysis. He imitated their mannerisms and considered them models of how to live. He also quoted Nietzsche 'in season and out of season'.[28] In *Zarathustra* he discovered his own problem: were there limits placed on man's aspirations and, if there were, how could he live intensely? Camus was looking for moral lessons: could Nietzsche and Dostoevsky help him as he grew up in Algeria? In reading Joyce he showed his caution; he thought there was too much disorder in *Ulysses*.

When he turned to French writing Camus admired the *NRF*. Later he told the story of how his uncle gave him *Nourritures Terrestres* and how he could see nothing of interest in it.[29] Gide, the heretic, did not seem audacious to a boy who had grown up near the Algerian beaches. Camus did not find in him the passion which he liked in Dostoevsky. He could not imagine Gide loving completely and he could not imagine him on his deathbed. Yet he admired him for his un-Dostoevskian and un-Algerian qualities. Gide was the model of a writer who had explored his temperament and preserved its various strands. Even as it exalted sensuous experience, *Les Nourritures Terrestres* remained intellectual. Gide weighed moral values and pitted them one against another. In *L'Enfant Prodigue*, which Camus was to stage as a play, he demonstrated the charms of a return to tradition as well as of rebellion. As he began to write Camus saw the aesthetic advantages in Gide's habit of thinking against himself. The writing could be most lyrical if it was restrained.

The *Nouvelle Revue Française* was not and never had been a really avant-garde magazine. It occupied a place in the mainstream of French writing and it set out to be both innovative and traditional. Its very title reveals this. It had a flair for taking what was new and examining it critically; intelligence and subtlety were the *NRF* watchwords. It had a strong moral slant and yet it defended the purely aesthetic value of good writing. Such contradictions suited Gide who was the enemy of all orthodoxies, whether religious or political.

He had started the review with a group of friends in 1908. Then Gaston Gallimard took over the publishing both of the magazine itself and of books by the authors who wrote in it. By the 1920's the *NRF* had become a web with the review and the Gallimard publishing house as its centres. Around them clustered many writers who argued and debated with one another. The *NRF* was the sum of its contradictions and it offered no set dogmas. It continued to occupy its central place behind the surrealists, who were the avant-garde, and it continued to suggest rather than decree that moral values, good writing and heresy were the most important things in life.

This attracted the sophisticate in Camus who devoured *NRF* writing. He liked Jacques Copeau whose theatre experiments influenced his own. He read Proust who disturbed him. Perhaps Proust had already said everything leaving him nothing to say? Camus was already worried about sterility and was showing his lifelong fear that one day he would be unable to write.

The *NRF* writer he liked best was Malraux. He and his friends felt that Malraux was more their contemporary than Gide. *La Condition Humaine* (1933) offered a tragic vision of the human condition. Camus inherited both the concept of 'condition', which explained man in metaphysical rather than psychological terms, and the tragic sense. He also admired in Malraux the committed, anti-Fascist writer. Malraux was then engaged in another of the *NRF*'s complex debates and was trying to push the magazine towards political commitment. Its editor, Jean Paulhan, was resisting and Gide was, characteristically, both pushing and resisting. Jean Grenier would have his say in this debate and Camus himself would brood on the concept of committed writing. But in the early '30's he admired the bold way in which Malraux' adventurous heroes engaged in action in order to give shape to their lives.

Dostoevsky, Nietzsche and Gide were favourite authors of Jean Grenier who arrived at the Bab-el-Oued school in 1930. Grenier had visited Algeria before and it fascinated him. A Breton who grew up in a large, lonely house near the sea, he was conscious of being a Celt. He talked about a melancholy called 'the Breton disease' and he, too, liked cemeteries. He saw the Mediterranean as an outsider and could reveal to Camus what Camus knew instinctively but had not yet articulated.

Grenier came to Algiers with a certain prestige because he had published with Grasset an essay called *Interiora Rerum*. In the same book Malraux had published *D'une Jeunesse Européenne* which was a meditation on East and West. Not long afterwards Malraux recruited Grenier for the *NRF*. This was appropriate because Grenier's writing draws on Gide, whose blend of fervour and scepticism he shared.

To the Algerians Grenier seemed 'a being astray on our planet'.[30] He prowled the city, drank pastis with M. Acault and puzzled over the Arabs. He was secretive and curious, convinced that the world offered hidden miracles which he would never discover. 'I would like to write a novel,' he said one day, 'but I know nothing about life.' He was amazed that he had married and even more amazed when his children arrived. No orthodox schoolmaster, he treated his chosen pupils as disciples and watched their reactions to him. He quickly divided his philosophy class into the dunces and the clever; the cleverest of all was Camus with whom Grenier carried on long discussions while the dunces played games in the back seats. Any connection between Grenier's classes and the syllabus for the 'baccalauréat' was purely accidental. He talked about his own favourite philosophers like Bergson.

Grenier's relationship with Camus is often misunderstood. Camus acknowledged his debt long and openly, referring to Grenier as 'my master'. He certainly felt this but he may have known that admitting it did not detract from his originality and added to his reputation for generosity. This was an example of Camus' dubiously angelic nature: honesty could become a strategy.[31] If he had cared more for Grenier, he might have publicized his gratitude less, for it mortified Grenier who saw himself robbed of his own originality and reduced to an appendage of Camus. The post-war Camus-Grenier relationship was full of concealed hypocrisies which lay behind the master-pupil effusions and by the end Camus was thoroughly sick of him. Meanwhile Grenier fought back by telling everyone that he had done little for Camus, no more than for other students. This was a way of saying that his originality lay elsewhere, perhaps in his own books. *Les Iles* and *Inspirations Méditerranéennes* were important in their own right and not merely because they influenced Camus. At all events the Camus-Grenier relationship in the early and mid-'30's contained both an influence and a reaction by Camus against that influence.

Grenier provided Camus's group with ideas and he influenced other students like Fouchet. In particular he imparted to a Camus who was ready for it his sense of death and of man as an 'amputated being'.[32] This was the theme of Grenier's own writing. Man was incomplete, a traveller in search of hidden miracles. *Les Iles* (1933) begins on the Breton beaches which are immense and lonely. By contrast the Mediterranean is rich and its towns – Naples, Palermo and Algiers – are teeming with life. Yet Grenier does not stop at the banal contrast between North and South. The Mediterranean may offer a harmony between man and nature but it promises no escape from mortality: 'the sun creates a void and man finds he is alone with himself.'[33] Grenier, too, talks of indifference but, ever the Celt, he looks in it for further secrets.

In Algeria he discovers the desert: 'the immensity of the desert is like an abyss for the mind . . . it is an intoxication and man cannot do without it.'[34] In the silent villages of the interior and in the Arabs Grenier saw the glimmer of immortality. More religious than Gide, he wonders whether man might not attain it. This would require that man be transformed, that he cease to be human and become a 'something'. For Grenier Algeria was Eastern as well as Southern. Like Malraux, he delved into Oriental philosophy and encouraged his students to read the *Bhagavadgita*. Yet he retained the sceptical *NRF* strain. The 'something' that man might become could not be codified; there were moments of insight but no total understanding.

Grenier's thought had a metaphysical starting-point that appealed to the young Camus. He stated, correctly, that the various fragments of *Les Iles* receive their unity from the pervading sense of death. Grenier brought to Camus the revelation that the amputation, which he had felt during his illness and in the silence of his home, was an important experience. It was the mark of man's condition, as was the desire to remedy it through some sort of oneness. Next Grenier showed Camus that the Mediterranean might offer a solution. The intense pleasure of the beaches might be more than physical. The pieces which Camus wrote in the early '30's revolve around these themes.

But Camus was to resolve them differently. He was a barbarian where Grenier was sophisticated; he was tougher and he could enjoy soccer and swimming for what they were. Moreover he distrusted the metaphysical urge, even though it obsessed him. Grenier failed to interest him in Arab religion or Eastern philosophy. There was a vein of caution in Camus who did not wish to be transformed into a 'something'. When he went into the desert he felt that he might lose himself in it. So he quickly asserted himself against it. This reaction of defiance led him back to more practical moral and social questions which interested Grenier less.

The mystical strand in Grenier's thought was taken up in Algiers. He became the local leader of the *Esprit* group and he drew to it the more religious of Camus' friends like Fouchet. He tried to convert others not to any one religion but to his own fascination with religion. To a girl who was resolutely atheist but who admired the *NRF*, he said: 'How can you be interested in Gide if you are not interested in God?'.[35] He looked on as Camus plunged into the theatre and into politics. Sometimes he encouraged him, trying to live via Camus; at other times he made fun of him. 'When will you understand', he asked during one particularly chaotic rehearsal, 'that there is a difference between action and agitation?'

A piece that Grenier wrote reads like another rebuke to Camus: 'some people throw themselves blindly and frantically into action but they do not believe in it ... in their lucid moments they know perfectly well that they have exchanged one kind of nothingness for another'.[36] Grenier felt that Camus' caution was exaggerated: a working-class boy exposed to the strange world of Indian philosophy, he remained on the defensive, crouched in his Belcourt boxer's stance. But Grenier was underestimating Camus' need to believe. Even after the early writings it remains his central theme, although the form it takes changes.

In 1932 Camus began to write and reaffirmed the difference between himself and Fouchet. Fouchet's earliest pieces possess the fluency which marks his entire work. Some of his poems are mock-simple and humorous. He punctures an utopian flight of fancy with the lines: 'All the world is so good/perhaps even my poems are good.' Camus had greater difficulty in finding a style and his early pieces are full of rhetoric and sentimentality. A true Mediterranean, he was attracted to the grand manner: flowing periods and abundant adjectives, but he tried to write concisely and objectively. Writing was a struggle and a part of his ambition. 'For Camus the will to write and the will to succeed were the same,' says Fouchet. But the struggle was directed against himself. If he was to speak for his mother, he had to incorporate her silence.

He wrote four pieces for a little magazine run by a group of his schoolmates, one of whose fathers was a printer. *Sud* was proudly Algerian: 'As from now North Africa has an artistic and intellectual life of its own,'[37] proclaims the first number. Bénisti wrote a piece which rejects Rodin and praises Maillol because his sculpture is so Mediterranean, while Fouchet contributed a fluent article on jazz. Grenier persuaded the printer's son to publish a series of essays written by the students in his philosophy class. Not surprisingly this brought about the financial collapse of the magazine which had to change its format and start publishing articles on Paris fashion.

Camus' pieces show the immaturity of the schoolboy. He talks about 'the clammy hand of experience' and about 'vague, inexpressible melancholies'. He also shows his addiction to rhetoric: 'the Poor Man wanders forth, brooding on his poverty, swallowing down his distress. Hidden desires, dark revolts well up in him. No one can penetrate the secret of his heart hidden behind his sordid rags.' A sentimental view of social injustice runs through this piece, as does the theme of violence; the beggar talks about 'gunning down the nearest bystander'. Yet the main motif is that man can occasionally find refuge in a dream of love.

Camus was wondering whether art might not offer a superior dream, one that could be pitted against reality. Music 'hides from us the horrors of the world we live in' and tragedy is the creation of a beauty that lies beyond pessimism. Camus makes a sharp distinction between ordinary life and art, philosophy or religion. When he writes about philosophy, he condemns reason which is another enemy of the dream and he looks to Bergson for support. He praises him for emphasizing intuition but criticizes him for his caution and asks whether intuition might not become the basis of a new religion. He talks about 'the philosophy, the religion, the gospel of our century for which contemporary thinkers are waiting'. Such a gospel would illuminate the insights which flicker in *Les Iles*.

A troubled religious urge runs through other early pieces. Camus talks of 'my so mystical soul which demands an object for its fervour and faith'. Even God laments that he has no God to turn to. Rephrasing his remark to Bénisti, Camus writes: 'God created the world in a fit of madness and then forgot about it.' Yet man persists in searching. Camus is already aware of the traps which man's religious urge creates for him. If he gives himself up to happiness, that happiness triggers off the desire for immortality. If he turns his back on the world, his silence is a microcosm of eternity. And there remains his sense of imperfection, of a personal lack or guilt. Revolt, which is briefly mentioned, is nothing more than the dislike of the shabby, godless universe.

The possibility that the Mediterranean might offer an answer is raised in *La Maison Mauresque*. Inspired by the Arab, man can forget his flawed existence and be at one with the purity of nature. If Algeria mocks any kind of transcendence, it offers its own brand of eternity. One of Camus' rare poems depicts death as part of some greater Mediterranean ritual:

'Alone, naked, without secrets, your sons await their deaths,
Death will return them to you purified at last.'[38]

Even as he laughed at the armies of ants in the graveyard, Camus could write longingly of this pantheistic death. The problem of the Mediterranean is presented: is its beauty sufficient to embrace human mortality? In these pieces Camus thinks it might be.

Before the poem was written he had completed the *baccalauréat* and had decided to remain in school for one more year. This year was called a 'khâgne' and was supposed to prepare pupils for the examinations which led to the élite universities of France. In Algiers, however, it was nothing of the kind. It was a small group of about ten students, organized by Jean Grenier and Paul Mathieu, who taught French and Classics. There was no programme and no discipline; Grenier simply taught what he liked. This infuriated the austere Mathieu who complained that Camus 'philosophised crazily even in his French essays'.[39] Although outstanding, Camus was no orthodox student. He liked philosophy but refused to erect systems; he enjoyed literature but never divided it into periods or genres.

Two of the other students were to become close friends. Even as Camus was exploring the Algiers streets with Fouchet, André Belamich and Claude de Fréminville were spending their

36

evenings wandering around Oran. They walked in the square near the cathedral and through the old Spanish town. Like Camus, they disliked the rich businessmen and were friendly with the small shopkeepers and the artisans. Like Camus, they relished the popular language of Oran, which was a mixture of French and Spanish. They even had their own Jean Grenier, a philosophy teacher called Choski who was a socialist and a pacifist. He, too, admired the *NRF* and encouraged them to read Gide and Claudel.

Belamich and De Fréminville were very different boys. Belamich was Jewish, working-class and shy; De Fréminville, who dominated the friendship, came of an aristocratic French family. His father had served in the colonial army and, when he died, his wife retired to Oran. She despised the coarseness of the French Algerians and dominated her son. The problem of the mother, although posed differently, was a link between him and Camus.

'Frémin' was not at home in the Bab-el-Oued school. Unsure of himself, too eager to please and too easily rejected, he did not take to Grenier who considered him 'an eternal adolescent'.[40] He did, however, impress Camus with his enormous energy. The two were opposites. Frémin was tall and blond, his gestures were nervous and he could not remain still; Camus was 'phlegmatic, very sure of himself . . . he kept his distance'.[41] Camus saw in Frémin a great creative talent. Belamich had felt the same as he listened, during their Oran walks, while his friend talked novel after novel. De Fréminville had already published some poems, if only in privately-printed editions. One has an Algerian ring for it depicts 'Midday . . . like primitive creation'.[42] Ever doubtful of his own ability to create, Camus maintained throughout the '30's that Frémin was the most talented of all his friends because of his abundant energy. Ultimately Camus was wrong and Grenier was right, because De Fréminville's energy vanished the moment he picked up a pen.

He and Camus read Baudelaire together and imitated him. Frémin was attracted by the satanic, perverse Baudelaire, Camus by the dandy. Camus, too, tried to be a dandy. A photograph shows him in a grey-flannelled suit with highly-polished shoes and a white tie. His friends remember the care he took with his ties and the little felt hats which he affected. M.

Acault was generous and Camus did not lack pocket-money. He tried to be elegant, as befitted a young aesthete. By Parisian standards he looked thoroughly provincial but the attempt is revealing. Dandyism was a mark of his determination to hide his emotions. 'Nothing touches me', he used to say. He also compartmentalized his friendships for Belamich never knew Fouchet or Bénisti well.

At first De Fréminville dominated their friendship, the only one of Camus' friends who did. Belamich was too shy to say much and Camus treated him like a younger brother; Belamich felt that Camus was indeed much older and that he was in control of every situation. De Fréminville talked about jazz, negro spirituals and the American novel. They went to Russian films and saw the *Battleship Potemkin* over and again.

Russian films were linked with politics for Frémin was thinking of becoming a Communist and Camus was moving with him. Frémin shared his mother's contempt for the French Algerian middle-class. Coming from a once rich French family, he sympathized with the working-class Camus. He, too, had discovered the Arabs. If the French Algerians kept saying they were lazy and vicious, then there must be something good about them. Troubled by their poverty, Frémin looked to the Parti Communiste to remedy it. He flirted with the Young Socialists but they did not satisfy him. When the 'khâgne' ended in 1933, he went to study in Paris and watched, as French intellectuals gathered to combat Fascism.

Seeing Gide and so many others support the Communist Party, Frémin did the same. He was swept along by the anti-Fascist current. But he had a more secret motive: the desire to belong and the dream of fraternity. 'I want to feel in my cell the promise of a different humanity,' he exclaimed lyrically.[43] He had the zeal of the convert who sets about making other converts. In September '34 he was planning to start a magazine in Algiers. Belamich would write about music, Camus about Gide, he himself about Malraux; there would be much talk of Marx and Arabs; readers would be steered towards the PC. The magazine came to nothing but De Fréminville kept pushing Camus towards Communism. Already in 1933 he was sure that Camus was 'mentally' a Communist and he described to him the joys that awaited him when he obtained his party card. He had some influence but not very much, for Camus' temperament was different from his. As late as May '35 Camus said that he was approaching Communism 'slowly and prudently'. This was a gamble and he was trying to ensure that the odds were on his side.

His friendship with Frémin broke down the distance which Camus tried to maintain. Already Jean de Maisonseul had detected his vulnerability and his fear of death. To De Fréminville Camus poured out his misery in unashamedly sentimental language. His tuberculosis was flaring up again and he did not have long to live. He needed to write quickly, to say what he had to say. But he had to scrape his living. He had no money, no possessions, nothing. He was obsessed, despite his friendships, by loneliness. Usually Camus hid all this but in his letters to De Fréminville his sense of being abandoned comes flooding through.

During the year 1932–33 he began attending lectures at the university of Algiers, where Grenier also taught. The following year he and Belamich went there, Camus to study philosophy and Belamich literature. Neither found the work difficult. The chair of philosophy had been started by René Poirier who came from Montpellier and had fallen in love with the Algerian countryside. The university, Poirier remembers, was small and isolated from the city. This is important when one remembers that Camus' activity centred around the university for the next several years. The faculties of law and medicine had ties with the town because the professors practised there; but the faculty of letters did not. Most of the professors came from France and considered Algiers provincial.

Yet the faculty had some interesting men during Camus' years. The dean, Gernet, was a left-winger who watched with dismay the rise of Fascism and who encouraged Camus' political activities. In 1930 Jacques Heurgon had arrived as professor of history and he too liked Algeria. Although Camus never studied with him, he went to his lectures on the Augustine Age, which strengthened his interest in the Classics. Moreover Heurgon had known Gide, because his wife was the daughter of Gide's friend, Paul Desjardins.

Camus and Heurgon became friends, showing yet again Camus' ability to consort with older men. They observed a formal politeness, which was part of any student-teacher contact but which also suited Camus' sense of privacy. With

Poirier relations were more difficult because Poirier was, on his own admission, more of the 'Herr Professor'. His lectures did not treat any of the philosophers whom Camus had or would read – Nietzsche, Husserl or Heidegger. Poirier taught Camus old-fashioned philosophy: the methodology of logic, psychology and the like. There was no history of philosophy, no Marx, none of Grenier's socratic questioning and much discussion of technical problems. Poirier covered all the material on his own, helped only by Grenier who gave an occasional lecture on any topic that interested him.

Anticipating Sartre, Poirier had a low opinion of Camus as a philosopher. He was too literary, he never learned enough methodology and he had too many outside interests. Poirier was not surprised by the philosophical naivety revealed in *Le Mythe de Sisyphe*. He also thought Camus was unbearably arrogant. The portrait he leaves of him is interesting because it does not contradict more favourable impressions.[44] Poirier admits that Camus showed no resentment of his poverty; to have done so would have been a sign of weakness. Moreover Camus was scrupulously polite. But, when Poirier argued with him about an essay, Camus simply paid no attention. He was insolently sure of himself. There was indeed a touch of the aristocrat in him and he felt superior to the other students who accepted this. Even the right-wing students grudgingly admired Camus.

This mixture of pride and concealed vulnerability stemmed from Camus' early struggles. Even Grenier found him difficult and so did Heurgon. In a group, if Camus disliked something that was said, he just walked off. Once he quarrelled, he rarely forgave. After one such incident Heurgon told him he was difficult and Camus replied: 'I just cannot overcome the violence that wells up in me and prevents me from being fair.'[45] His self-control was great but it occasionally slipped.

Meanwhile he made his way through the university without difficulty. He failed the examination in classical literature in June '34 – this was the month he married – and had to retake it in the autumn. In the philosophy examinations he did fairly well on the written and improved on the oral – Camus could always talk, says Poirier. He was the outstanding student of his year and he worked with the concentration for which he was now famous. In the university library 'he never looked up, he would sit there for hours without once being distracted'. The

40

'boursier' was still alive in Camus, even if he had none of the 'boursier's narrowness.

After one year at university Camus married Simone Hié. This was an enormously important event, both because Camus loved her and because the break up of their marriage made him bitter towards women, reinforced his loneliness and helped shape his early writing. And Simone was a personage in her own right: beautiful, difficult and genuinely tragic. She and Camus fell in love and tried to help each other; they failed.

When Camus met Simone she was Fouchet's girlfriend. Fouchet had met her during the 1930 centenary of the Conquest; they chatted and planned to meet again. They were both very young – Simone just sixteen – and hid their meetings from her family. But the persuasive Fouchet succeeded in convincing Simone's mother that he was a suitable and serious young man and so they were soon able to meet openly. He showed her off to his friends. Some disliked her and one declared that she was as affected as Fouchet himself. But Miquel and De Maisonseul were fascinated by her, as was Camus who, characteristically, hid his admiration.[46]

Simone was certainly striking. She was tall with wavy hair, large eyes and regular features. She wore long black dresses and white make-up and looked like the heroine of a silent film. In Algeria, where everyone went to the beach and was tanned, Simone had decided to look different. Her mother gave her ample pocket-money so she bought big hats and was the envy of the other girls. They gossiped about her and called her a 'vamp' or worse. Fouchet thought her a character from Baudelaire or Dostoevsky and she acted the part: unfathomable and tormented, prone to long silences and outbursts of enthusiasm. In particular she loved to shock. She sang obscene songs on the street, pulled out banknotes to pay taxi drivers and boasted about her love affairs. She was also generous and intelligent. After she married Camus she attended some of Poirier's lectures, although she never troubled herself with the methodology of philosophy. But she joined in the conversations about writing for it was she who persuaded the group of friends to read André Breton and who made them a present of his books. Neither Fouchet nor Camus felt superior to her; she was their equal.

Her eccentricity was not a Dostoevskian pose but grew out of her life. Her father, M. Hié, had left her mother when she was a little girl. Simone had fond memories of him because he used to take her bathing, but she never forgave him for leaving and she rarely saw him afterwards. Her mother, Marthe Sogler, was a doctor, dedicated to her practice, devoid of any practical sense and too busy to be a wife. She was well-connected for her sister was married to the dean of the law faculty and she was well-known in Algiers, where people gossiped about her supposedly debauched life. Such gossip may have had no foundation. Algiers was a town where brothels abounded and where the cigarette-girls were allowed to live freely but where the middle-classes locked up their daughters. There were two standards of morality and scant respect for privacy. But Simone certainly knew that her mother was a subject of gossip. She also suffered because her mother, although an attractive woman, dressed carelessly. So Simone resolved to be outrageously elegant and to defy the tittle-tattle.

She was just starting to grow up when her mother remarried a M. Pianezzi. It was a bad choice because Pianezzi did not work, lived off his wife and was a womanizer. He was no stepfather for a young girl and he made advances to which Simone may or may not have responded but which further troubled her. Fouchet claims that Pianezzi was jealous of him and tried to prevent him from seeing Simone. At all events the marriage was not happy and after a few years Marthe got rid of her husband.

But the tragedy of Simone's life began when she was fourteen. Her first periods were painful and her mother gave her morphine. Simone quickly became addicted and began to forge her mother's signature on the prescription forms. Marthe, absorbed in her work, failed to notice and, when she did, it was too late. Drug addiction was uncommon in 1930's Algeria and doctors had little idea how to treat it. Simone could not break the habit and Marthe, conscience-stricken and indulgent, helped her obtain the doses she needed.

Drugs gave Simone the dangerous fascination which drew Fouchet and Camus. She needed to seduce, as if to compensate for her father's desertion. She flaunted her readiness to sleep with Fouchet or with other boys and he called her a 'tease'. He also wrote a poem, where she is depicted as sulky and gay, happy and tearful. Without knowing the full story, De Maisonseul sensed in Simone a little girl who knew she was trapped. She had moments of purity where she would speak of trees, water and countryside. She sensed that her beauty might not last and that she must fascinate while she could. At parties she would turn away from the conversation and retire to the bathroom. When she returned her eyes were bright with the drug and she was triumphantly seductive.

Simone incarnated that intense existence of which Camus spoke. He was delighted by her beauty and he forgave her affectations. That many men desired her made her all the more attractive. Camus was proud of his masculinity and he strove to win her. He began to see her secretly, apart from the group. In 1933 Fouchet went into the interior to organize a Young Socialists meeting and he arranged to meet Simone on his return. She did not turn up in the park where they used to walk and instead he received a note from Camus. Rather melodramatically Camus told him that Simone had chosen: she was now Camus' girlfriend.

This was the end of the Camus-Fouchet friendship. They continued to see and to write to each other but they were never again close. Perhaps they were in any case too dissimilar to be friends. The severe Camus decided that Fouchet was really too affected. He was playing at being the humble Franciscan and he paraded around Algiers like a wandering friar. Not surprisingly Fouchet felt that Camus, the cocky pied-noir, was flaunting his victory. The quarrel lasted for the rest of Camus' life, although the two met occasionally after the war.

Once they started to see each other openly, Camus and Simone moved quickly. His family was less enthusiastic than hers. Marthe Sogler liked the strong-minded young man and believed that he would help her daughter. M. Acault thought that Marthe and Simone were a pair of harlots and that his nephew was making a mistake. Camus himself both liked and disliked the upper-class society in which he now began to move. After their marriage he found a flat near the Parc Hydra, not far from Jean Grenier. From Paris De Fréminville fretted: 'Tell Camus to write to me,' he said to Belamich, 'Camus has changed completely.'[47]

Camus was hoping for change. Simone had told him of her addiction and he was to help her fight it. He knew little about drugs but he was accustomed to battling with tuberculosis and he thought that morphine addiction would involve a similar struggle. Simone herself had not chosen lightly. She continued her extravagances, for in the days before the wedding she toured the Algiers shops with Jean de Maisonseul and told everyone that he was her future husband. But she had decided that Camus possessed a strength of character which was lacking in Fouchet. By marrying him she hoped to save herself. For his part Camus hoped that marriage would offer a relief from loneliness. He had lived through his childhood in silence and now he was marrying a woman who was the opposite of his mother. Simone offered him beauty, a stimulus to write and real affection. Both she and he were gamblers and they were betting that they could overcome his sense of abandonment and her addiction.

It was a brief moment of happiness for Camus. His passion for life seemed to have overcome his indifference. But the change was not decisive and both strains persisted. There was nothing simple about the twenty-one-year old Camus. After the war he would be exalted as a model of honesty: 'in a world where everyone cheats, Camus alone does not cheat.' Camus himself knew better: 'nothing is more difficult than to separate in a man the parts he is playing and the deeper instincts which dictate them.'[48] Camus was a man of many parts: the swaggering Belcourt street-kid, the aristocratic dandy, Fouchet's cold-blooded rival and De Fréminville's miserable friend. He was distant with most people yet gave himself passionately to Simone. All these selves go back to the boy who had grown up in the tiny flat and who used to escape from school to go swimming. But even as he sought his way Camus was being shaped by the country in which he lived. One must glance next at the vanished world of French Algeria.

2

The Ambiguities of French Algeria

In 1930, Camus' friends joined half-heartedly in the celebrations which marked the centenary of the Conquest. Fouchet and Simone watched the military parade from a balcony, while Miquel still remembers the dust and the horses. Jules Roy,* who would not meet Camus until after the war, was now a sub-lieutenant in the artillery; he filed past President Doumergue's podium with thousands of other soldiers. The enthusiasm was immense, as the pied-noir's liking for bands and uniforms merged into his joy at the consecration of his Algeria. The tone had been set in France by articles like this one:

'Since France appeared, tranquil and powerful, in Algeria, peace has reigned there and prosperity is growing ... Destroying nothing France is pursuing her mission of civilisation, respectful of the past and mindful of the future ... The forthcoming centenary is an excellent occasion to take stock of France's effort: it is a subject of pride and glory ... North Africa is on the verge of an era of prosperity so great that it will outshine the most optimistic forecasts'.[1]

Eight years later, Camus wrote that the conquest of Morocco was 'nothing to be proud of'.[2] Already he felt that there was something indecent about flaunting victory before the vanquished. Fouchet was disgusted by the swarm of French dignitaries who devoured couscous and carried back to France the fantasy of a primitive, sun-baked paradise. De Fréminville wrote to his uncle about the exploitation of Arab labour and Fouchet even wondered when the next Arab revolt might come.

But Camus' friends were a tiny minority. The Communist

*Jules Roy was a soldier, airman and writer who grew up in Rovigo in the interior of Algeria. His view of Camus is discussed in Chapter 9.

Party had launched a campaign against the centenary and had watched it fail. The Arabs themselves were hesitating. Some of their leaders attended the banquet for President Doumergue but resentment of the centenary hastened the rise of cultural and religious if not political nationalism. Messali Hadj, who was then a Communist and was to become the first important nationalist, chose 1930 to visit the Soviet Union. Yet there were no doubts among the Europeans. Their Algeria was secure for ever and their pastis-filled toasts to Bugeaud, the general who had completed the conquest of Algeria, were lavish.

Here one is faced with a problem. One is tempted to reconstruct the whole of French Algerian history in the light of the independence war. Yet this runs against the testimony of Fouchet, Miquel and all of Camus' friends who repeat that in the '30's no European dreamed there could ever be an independent Algeria. No one who studies Camus' place in Algerian history should make such a reconstruction. Yet the rumblings of rebellion were present in events Camus lived through: the distress of Arab farmers or the failures of the Algerian Communist Party. The attempt by French Algerian writers to wedge Arabs and Europeans into a box called Mediterranean culture was the sign of a half-recognized problem. The menace of Arab revolt was present and, because it was not faced, it emerged obliquely in the tensions which ran through Algeria. Anti-semitism, which is always a distorted expression of real troubles, was rife. French Algeria did perceive that it was not secure for ever but it hid that knowledge from itself. Camus' vision was clearer than almost anyone's but he, too, fell into ambiguity.

No uncertainty had ever touched the conqueror Bugeaud and the rhetoric of 1930 would not have impressed him. His vision of the colony was crude: there had to be more Europeans than Arabs. If there were, the conquest was safe; if not . . . Bugeaud did not worry about niceties like assimilation. In 1830 there were three million Arabs so he wanted to bring in more than three million Europeans. In 1930 the population stood at nine hundred thousand Europeans and six million Arabs.

Even historically the conquest was not as solid as it looked. Arab rebellion had flared up sporadically for much of the nineteenth century. After the Dey surrendered in 1830 the Emir Abdelkader continued the struggle. In Kabylia, a mountainous area not very far from Algiers and the home of the Berbers who had been living in North Africa when the Arabs arrived, fighting went on until 1864. After 1870 the flood of immigrants from Alsace-Lorraine triggered off another uprising. In the Aurès mountains, which would be a stronghold of the Front de Libération Nationale during the 1950's, fighting went on for years. The annexation of Tunisia in the 1880's caused fresh disturbances. Then the Arabs seemed to give up. Their leaders co-operated with the French and pursued the goal of assimilation. There were, however, fresh riots at Tlemcen in 1911 when young Arabs were drafted into the army, while resistance to conscription continued throughout the war. So the notion of an armed insurrection was not quite as remote as it seemed.

Yet the European population had indeed established itself. Jules Roy's family was even more typical than Camus'. They had arrived in Algeria in 1854 and had moved into a new settlement called Rovigo. They had struggled with the sun, the infertile soil and the sicknesses. Malaria was endemic in Rovigo and plagues were frequent. To Camus, too, plagues were not a mere allegory; he knew about the recurrent plagues in Mondovi and about the great 1849 plague in Oran. The interior of Algeria was dotted with villages like Rovigo. There were fewer Europeans than on the coast; there was a church, a school for the French children and a monument to the conquest; a second monument was added after 1918. Arab caravans came through from the South and the sense of the desert was strong; the Arab farmers lived alongside but separate from the Europeans.

There was a legend about the colonization which was current in both the literature and the popular mentality of the 1930's. Such myths are important to an observer of Camus' Algeria because they explain the way that his contemporaries saw themselves. French Algerians thought they were a tough frontier people like the pioneer Americans. They had brought civilization and prosperity to their country; Algeria had not existed until they arrived.

After 1880 Algeria had gone through a period of rapid change. The new wave of colonizers was transforming the country. By 1900 there were more than six hundred thousand Europeans. Of these three hundred and sixty thousand were French or naturalized and there were one hundred and fifty thousand Spaniards – a quarter of the European population. Already farming was changing and large-scale cultivation of wheat and grapes was being undertaken. Camus' father had worked on such a farm. The gulf between poor and rich farmers widened and the term 'colon' was introduced to designate the rich farmers who had the largest share of power in the colony. In *La Mort Heureuse* Camus, who loathed the colons, satirizes a certain Moralès who buys a Bugatti and wants to expel all foreigners. Politically Algeria was gaining an identity of its own. In 1898 it was given an elected assembly and in 1900 a special budget. This led to a tension between the political interests of French Algeria and those of France and hence between the governor-general, appointed by Paris, and the elected officials. Algiers itself expanded rapidly in the 1890's. The old fortifications were torn down and the city spread out to the West. The first telegraph poles and cars appeared. From being primarily a garrison, Algiers became a commercial city.

Out of this period grew a second legend which one might call the Mediterranean medley. Popular novelist, Paul Achard, describes it well in *L'Homme de Mer*, where he depicts the flood of immigrants from every shore of the Mediterranean. The Catalonians, Neapolitans and Maltese had reconquered North Africa and were building a new Mediterranean nation which was also to be French, endowed with the Marseillaise and free elementary education. The mixture of races became the most popular theme of Algerian folklore. There was even a cookbook which demonstrated that Algerian cooking was particularly good, because it was a blend of several national styles.* There remained the problem of the Arab. He could, of course, be included in the Mediterranean medley but often the earlier legend of the conquest was maintained. The shrewd Achard describes a Maltese who has an Arab servant; treating the servant badly is the Maltese's revenge for the long centuries during which the Arabs occupied Malta.

The political development and the mixture of European races, even as they gave Algiers its special flavour, also created difficulties. Sections of the city were reserved for the various

*It was written by a rather pretentious lady called Constance Raffi-Mallebay whose father Ernest Mallebay had been the most distinguished journalist in Algeria. Her son, Paul Raffi, was Camus' friend and her family ran the *Revue Algérienne*, which offers much information about '30's Algeria.

groups: Bab-el-Oued was Spanish, la Marine was Italian. The centre, which lay around the Place du Gouvernement was French, most of the rich people were French and the French felt themselves superior to the others. Anti-semitism was endemic in Algeria because it was the cement of the new Mediterranean nation. The Dreyfus Case had enormous repercussions. The anti-semitic leader, Drumont, came to Algiers to join forces with the know-nothing mayor, Max Régis, who was a forerunner of Camus' great enemy, Maximin Rozis, mayor in the late 1930's. To cries of 'Long live France' thousands of Spaniards and Sicilians smashed the Jewish shops in the centre of Algiers. Achard describes the dilemma: 'The true France was made up of these . . . Maltese, Italians, Spaniards, whether they were French citizens or not, and they were going to exterminate all the Jews, whether they were called Cohen or Durand.'[3] Achard's hero is anti-semitic instinctively, because it is good for business and, most of all, because it shows he is French; yet he knows France is entirely Jewish for Drumont has told him so. Hence the only true France is Algeria . . . one is already not so far from the OAS.

Not surprisingly, anti-semitism persisted. Jean Daniel, future friend of Camus and today editor of the *Nouvel Observateur*, felt the threat when he was growing up in Bône in the 1930's. He remembers a fist-fight on the street between his father and an anti-semitic bully. There was also an Arab anti-semitism which went deep in Moslem culture, flared up when the Crémieux decree of 1870 gave French citizenship to the Jews and was assiduously cultivated by the Europeans. French Algeria, facing France, its own mixed races and the Arabs, needed anti-semitism to strengthen its fragile sense of identity.

The development of Algeria continued between the wars and Algiers grew ever more modern as blocks of flats replaced houses and the suburbs crept further out. Yet the economy faltered and went into a slump which lasted until 1940. Camus was growing up in a period of economic distress which turned into political turmoil. Agriculture first went wrong with the bad harvest of 1920, when there was a drought and the animals died. Yet the real reason lay, of course, in the world-wide depression which was felt more severely in an underdeveloped colony like Algeria. Agricultural prices dropped and a dreary cycle set in.

49

Smaller farmers lost money and were obliged to borrow and then to sell; larger farmers hung on and bought up land cheaply. Economies in scale then enabled them to survive. Mixed farming gave way ever more to the cultivation of a few large crops, although these, too, were vulnerable on the world market.

Agriculture could save itself only by such centralization and specialization; yet this meant ruin for poorer farmers and especially for Arabs. Camus' articles on Kabylia do not describe an exceptional situation. By then the depression had cut prices still more and the Raffis were lamenting 'the appalling crisis which has devastated the country since 1930.'[4] Kabylia was special only in that the land was not suitable for grain so the farmers relied on olive oil, a commodity whose world price was especially low. Stories of Arab famine are common enough in the 1930's, although not in the Algiers press. 'The Arab is at the end of his tether; he has no money and no food; his debts are crushing him and his land is mortgaged to the hilt,' runs one government report. Another investigation in Constantine discovered hardships which Camus would recount: Arab children arrived at school without having eaten for twenty-four hours. Similarly, Camus' campaign to defend Michel Hodent is part of a general battle. Hodent, a conscientious civil servant, was applying the government's policy of buying grain at fixed prices in order to protect poor farmers. He was attacked by wealthier farmers who wanted to force the poor off the land and buy up their farms. Usually this meant a transfer of land from Arabs to Europeans and by 1940 Arabs, although twenty times more numerous than the European farmers, owned only three times as much land. Much of this, as in Kabylia, was the poorest land.

A traditional Arab solution lay in emigration, which was blocked in the 1930's. Another lay in moving to the cities but here, too, the depression was damaging and the volume of industrial exports and imports went down in the early 1930's. Algerian industry meant primarily the port, mining and those enterprises that were close to agriculture – flour, biscuits and distilleries. Although the port of Algiers grew, industry could not possibly expand fast enough to meet the flood of people from the countryside, whether European or Arab. The Casbah was overcrowded, so Arabs spilled over into shanty neighbourhoods throughout the city. This did not escape Camus' attention and he noted an increase of Arab poverty in his own Belcourt.[5] Meanwhile development brought fortunes to a few and increased the lopsidedness of Algerian society.

It was not necessarily in French interests to help Algeria solve its problems. Economic relations with France were often bad, which encouraged the Europeans to believe that France was exploiting them. This in turn revived their old distrust of France and the inferiority complex which they felt vis-à-vis the metropole. One remembers Camus and Fouchet. In part French interest lay in keeping Algeria under-industrialized so that it could not compete with France. Minerals were exported in a raw state and refined in Marseilles. Tariff barriers were imposed on agricultural products, in order that French producers might be protected. Camus attended a meeting of the Algerian chamber of agriculture and noted the irritation with France. He did not grasp the economic issues but he picked up the call for the removal of tariffs.[6] Meanwhile French manufacturers dominated the Algerian market for consumer goods and prevented the rise of domestic industry. This was a classic colonial economy and the Europeans were right to feel that they were trapped. Their standard of living was lower than that of equivalent Frenchmen and public services, whether in health or education, were poorer. Yet they had to accept French discrimination in order to obtain French military protection against the Arabs. If they lived less well than the French, they were far better-off than the Arabs. To this were added the enormous differences within the European population, for the big landowners were a race apart.

Algerian politics were confused. When Maurice Viollette was governor in the 1920's he made himself unpopular with the Europeans because he wanted them to pay a larger share of the military budget; they retorted with attacks on France's economic discrimination. But this was not the gravest source of friction. The French Republic professed to live by the ideals of equality and fraternity and, although it did not in practice do so, the very existence of such heresies increased Arab demands. If they were, as the Republic kept telling them, French, then why should they not vote like Frenchmen? Moreover when social legislation was passed in France Arabs demanded that it be extended to Algeria. Camus joined in this campaign when he called for subsidized medical care for Arab workers. Civil servants like Michel Hodent tried to implement such laws but they quickly discovered that the colons would not permit this and that their fellow civil servants lived ambivalent lives. The republican Hodent had thought naively that French officials were 'intelligent, understanding and progressive.' He discovered the opposite when they threw him into prison.[7]

The gulf between the French government and the European Algerians could usually be bridged. It might widen, however, if the French elected a left-wing government which would take seriously the policy of assimilation. The May 1936 elections returned to power the Popular Front and for the first time France had a socialist prime minister, Léon Blum, who wanted to implement Viollette's plan to give the vote to a larger number of Arabs. At once French Algeria moved to the brink of revolt.

The weapons which it used were its own elected officials and its press. Camus discovered the power of the Algiers town hall when he tried to put on his first play, *Révolte dans les Asturies*. The governor-general gave permission but the mayor, Rozis, refused. This was a tiny incident but it said much about Algerian mayors. The press was perhaps an even more important weapon. When the Popular Front supporters rallied, they realized that they had to have their own newspaper, *Alger-Républicain*, because their opponents controlled the main Algiers dailies, the *Dépêche* and the *Echo*. Not that Algiers was a great newspaper-reading city – once more its cultural poverty is revealed. The circulation of both papers was quite small – around thirty thousand each. But they were read by people interested in politics and their influence was felt by people who did not read them. The *Dépêche* was resolutely right-wing and belonged to a rich landowner, Maurel. The *Echo* had some lively journalists and its drama critic, Gustave Mercier, praised Camus' theatre. Several of Camus' friends worked as type-setters for it. Yet the *Echo* belonged to a mine-owner, Duroux, who rejected the Popular Front and flirted with Fascism.

Duroux was no exception. Although the supposedly left-of-centre Radicals were strong in Algeria, party labels were misleading. The country was volatile and prone to right-wing extremism. In the '30's it was fertile ground for the pro-Fascist Leagues. 'For months we have had to put up with the insolence of the Fascist bands,' sighs the Communist Party paper.[8] In 1936 the Popular Front won in France but remained a small minority in Algeria. The right was in control and it was strong enough to defy Blum.

Throughout the '20's and early '30's the left – Socialists, Communists and a few Radicals – could get no more than 20% of the vote. It did best in the cities where it was helped by the high unemployment. In 1932 the official figure for European workers reached 12%. The number of strikes grew too – in 1929 there were twice as many as 1927. The left's base lay in the European working class, as the trade union membership shows. In 1933 there were ten thousand members, of whom nine thousand were Europeans. Labour was well-organized in the railways and in the port of Algiers where the Communists were fairly strong.

The left grew in the '30's, helped by Hitler's rise to power and by the events of February 1934. On February 6, when the right-wing leagues, outraged by the Stavisky scandal, rioted in Paris, Algiers did not move. But on February 9 the call for a general strike was answered and on February 12 the left's counter-demonstration was well-attended – one thousand people. The police arrived with their batons and Camus' friend Charles Poncet, a pacifist who took part in all anti-Fascist demonstrations, remembers that he received a crack on the head. This did not dampen the hopeful mood and many Arabs joined in the singing of the Internationale. In October the Socialists and Communists signed an agreement which was to grow into the Popular Front.

Alongside the traditional parties grew what one might call the new left of the '30's. This was the plethora of little movements, animated by Camus and his friends, of which the *Commune* group and Amsterdam-Pleyel were only two. These were small: Poncet remembers drawing no more than fifty people to a *Commune* meeting in Belcourt.* Moreover, their memberships overlapped both with one another and with the parties. They were intensely active but they did not have much influence. Their inspiration had to come from France because Algeria provided little.

*Like Amsterdam-Pleyel, *Commune* was an organization of fellow-travellers which defended the German Communists imprisoned by Hitler and which also tried to set up 'maisons de culture'.

Yet even this provincial colony was drawn into the anti-Fascist struggle. Jean Daniel remembers that in Blida the school was divided between the sons of the army officers, who were right-wing and read the newspaper *Action Française*, and the smaller left-wing group which read Barbusse's *Monde*. The two sides fought pitched battles in the park, quite aware that this was the European conflict in miniature. Daniel, too, looked in *Monde* for the pictures of Stalin with his arm around Gorki's shoulder or of Gide announcing his conversion to Communism.[9] The left was pacifist; party divisions were blurred in the resolve to form a common front; Algerian issues took a second place to the international struggle; economics was less important than morality.

Nor were the cultural battles neglected. In June '35 the 'Congrès international des écrivains pour la défense de la culture' held its grandiose meeting in Paris, presided over by Gide and Malraux. The following month Malraux visited Algiers as the guest of the *Commune* group. According to a partisan newspaper, the atmosphere was not at all like a lecture. There was 'an intense feeling of communion which grew stronger and stronger throughout the evening'. Malraux talked about the role of the intellectual: he would fight for the working classes by 'helping them to attain an awareness of their situation which capitalist society denies them'.[10] This facile notion, so characteristic of the period, delighted Malraux' listeners. These were, very roughly, the same people as would come to Camus' plays and subscribe to *Alger-Républicain*.

But the weakness of the Algerian left is demonstrated by the failures of its supposedly hard core, the Communist Party. These are of special interest because they help explain Camus' entry into and departure from the party and because they reveal the ambiguity of French Algeria.

The Algerian delegates at the Tours congress of 1920 voted to accept Lenin's conditions and joined the Communist Party. The Parti Communiste Français (PCF) continued the old socialist policy of assimilation until around 1925 when it turned anti-colonialist.* At once membership of the Algerian section plummeted from one thousand to two hundred and fifty. The

*This decision, which reflects the PCF's determination to shake off the influence of the Socialists, was made by the French party. In general Paris treated Algiers as Moscow treated Paris.

reason was obvious: 'If you scratch lightly at a Communist, you find a European conqueror underneath.'[11] The European worker might vote communist in spite of the anti-colonialist stand, but he did not vote for it. Yet the party needed the Arab masses, if it was ever to become a force. It tried to arabize its leadership but without much success. The only outstanding Arab of the '30's was Amar Ouzegane, who would clash with Camus in '37 and who later joined the FLN. The PC was slow to accept Arab history or the Arab language. Even its Arab spokesmen talked about 1789 and the Commune. In short, the base of the party as well as its voters resisted the anti-colonialist line. By 1934 the PC was down to one hundred members and had only a few dozen Arabs, who made up 'a tiny group of outcasts'. The party seemed scarcely to count – in the 1932 elections it had won only three hundred and seven votes in Algiers. It was too Arab for the Europeans and too European for the Arabs.

Yet it staged a comeback in the mid-1930's and, when Camus joined in 1935, it was nearing the peak of its influence. Alarmed, internationally, by Hitler and, in Algeria, by the strength of the Leagues, the PCF leaders made a fresh effort. Although party secretary Thorez at first opposed the idea, they decided that the Algerian section should become independent. So the Parti Communiste Algérien (PCA) was founded and given separate membership in the International. A new fraternal delegate was sent from Paris and told to re-organize the party. The choice was excellent: Jean Chaintron, known by the pseudonym of Comrade Barthel.

After the February riots and the October agreement with the Socialists Chaintron had something to work with. Membership had already gone up to seven hundred. Against the background of the international anti-Fascist campaign Chaintron built the new PCA which held its first independent congress in 1936. Camus joined as part of a flood of new members. By the time Chaintron left Algeria in 1937, membership had gone up to five thousand, of whom one thousand were Arabs. In the 1936 elections the PCA won 9% of the vote in Algiers and in areas like Bab-el-Oued and Belcourt it was back up to 20%.

Chaintron's success in increasing the number of Arab members explodes the myth that the PCA softened its anti-colonialist position after the Stalin-Laval agreement of May

1935.* This would have been logical, independent of Stalin and Laval, because the PCA was now in alliance with the Socialists, who were pro-colonialist, and to some degree with the Radicals, who were the champions of colonialism. Indeed this tendency was present and it grew stronger as the Popular Front developed and as the French Communists saw themselves more as a national force. But Chaintron was too good an organizer not to see the chance of making headway among the Arabs. Indeed the Party had tried this strategy for a decade and would not give it up lightly. Chaintron advanced on both fronts: Arab rights and anti-Fascism. His good fortune was that there was no conflict between the two. In 1935 the victory of the left in France could be presented as the first step towards increased political power for Arabs. Arab movements outside the PCA agreed, so the Party was able to form alliances, which in turn won it more support. Only later, when the Popular Front failed to enact the Blum-Viollette plan, did the PCA's strategy disintegrate. By this time Chaintron was gone and his successor was less skilful. The PCA found itself facing its old dilemma: its Arab members demanded a stronger anti-colonialist line, its Europeans objected. In 1937 it made the opposite decision from 1925, but it was no more successful.

Camus joined during the Party's happiest years. He himself stated that he became a Communist in 1934 and left in 1935, because the Party switched its pro-Arab line after Laval's trip to Moscow. Both dates and the reason are wrong and one can only wonder whether Camus was not trying to minimize his Communist past.[12] From the PCA's viewpoint, Camus' entry in 1935 reflected the Party's increased strength and showed that it could attract able recruits. Similarly his departure in 1937 reflected and anticipated the Party's decline. In 1935 Camus was welcomed and he was both more and less important than he would have been in France. The PCA was different from the PCF in that it did not have battalions of intellectuals who could be tossed into the fray. Its social composition was more limited. It was, naturally, a working-class party with a tendency towards skilled workers; some members were government employees, usually at the lower levels, and there were groups of elementary

*Stalin and Pierre Laval, who was then the French prime minister, agreed that France would work with Russia to contain Germany and that in return the French Communist Party would take a more responsible line.

schoolteachers. There were few intellectuals because Algiers was a provincial city. The party needed recruits who could implement its cultural policy, yet it did not attach very much importance to culture.

The PCA's brief success and subsequent decline is crucial because this was the hardest test of European-Arab relations. The Communists appealed to the segment of Algerian society where the two communities met – the urban working-class. This was where they had the most in common – the struggle for better working conditions – and where there was the greatest friction – competition for jobs and different wage-levels. The PCA's failure to reconcile the two groups, either by making assimilation credible or by becoming a vehicle for nationalism, is the failure of French Algeria.

In the mid-30's this failure was demonstrated by the growing dispute between the Communists and Messali Hadj. Messali, formerly a Communist and married to a Communist, had founded the 'Etoile nord-africaine' in order to campaign for Algerian independence. It was a front organization for the PC and membership-cards were interchangeable. There was no conflict of interest and Chaintron's double-pronged offensive suited Messali well. But Messali had doubts about the Popular Front's ability to carry out its promises. In 1935 he was arrested for showing the Algerian flag. As soon as the Popular Front took power, he criticized the Blum-Viollette plan and pointed out, correctly, that it would give the vote to no more than twenty thousand Arabs. As Messali's protests grew more strident, his split with the PCA widened and this provoked the 1937 dispute within the party.

In the mid-1930's Messali's Arab following was small and other Arab organizations were more important. The 'Fédération des élus', founded in 1927, drew on Arab notables, who were working with the French but felt they were achieving little. The ulemas set out to reform the Moslem religion and they advocated a return to a more ascetic brand of Islam. This had political implications, since it led the Arabs to take pride in their religious heritage. The French authorities were quick to realize this and ulema leader, Cheik El Okbi, was banned from preaching in the mosques. These Arab movements overlapped with the European left: Arab notable Ben Badis was the Algerian representative of the 'Congrès international des écrivains'. In 1936 Arabs joined with Europeans to celebrate the victory of the Popular Front. They too chanted the slogan 'des soviets partout', although a few, perhaps the most sensible, called for 'des souliers pour tous'. Their leaders petitioned the government to introduce the Blum-Viollette plan as the first step towards assimilation.

Assimilation is a term that crops up everywhere in 1930's Algeria and its ambiguity is symptomatic. Until 1939 it was the accepted policy of protest, whether in Algeria or elsewhere in the French Empire, and only slowly did the new language of nationalism replace it. The local populations appealed to the supposedly democratic republic over the heads of the colonists. From the standpoint of the French government assimilation would have been difficult, since, if carried through, it would have meant that Arab members representing six million Arabs would have sat in the Paris parliament. From an Arab viewpoint it was no easier, since it would have meant giving up the Arab past, language and culture.

The problem was illustrated by Ferhat Abbas, a long-time believer in assimilation and during the 1950's a belated convert to the FLN. In 1936 he stated that the future lay with France because there was no Algerian nation. 'I have looked into history,' declared Abbas, 'I have questioned the living and the dead; I have visited the cemeteries. No one has spoken to me of an Algerian nation.' This statement became famous and was repeated countless times, usually by Frenchmen. Less well-known is Ben Badis' more sensible reply. The concept of the nation, he declared, was inseparable from religion and customs. Here the Algerian Arabs did possess identity of their own.[13] El Okbi agreed and was strengthening this identity by his religious teaching. Both felt that the entity of Algeria could not be abandoned as easily as Ferhat Abbas suggested. So, while campaigning for assimilation, Ben Badis asserted that Algeria was very different from France and would need 'a considerable degree of independence'.

Probably most Arab leaders believed that assimilation was a useful weapon and a stepping-stone towards an as yet undefined and unattainable goal. Certainly the Arab working classes never felt themselves to be French and were never encouraged to do so. Even after the wage increases of the Popular Front an Arab

58

worker earned less than a third as much as a European worker. The economic aspect of colonialism was brutally clear.

Yet ambiguity persisted and it runs through the thought of Camus' future friend, Mouloud Feraoun. If ever there was an example of assimilation, it was Feraoun. He was steeped in the culture taught by the Third Republic schools and was himself a village schoolmaster. The Arab past, he had learned, was shameful but it could be redeemed. He should become a good Frenchman; hard work and the French language would liberate him. In particular he should become a republican, for the republic had, after the Revolution, created the universal values of equality and fraternity. The teacher who taught him this was a Berber, a socialist who believed firmly in France. But, as the years went by, he saw that young Frenchmen were always promoted ahead of him, so he gradually lost faith in France and his influence over his pupils declined.

Yet Feraoun did not think this through until the Algerian War. Only then did he undertake a critique of assimilation which caused him much pain and taught him that part of his life had been a lie. In the 1930's the young Feraoun had not reached this understanding. So it would be wrong to see in every Arab either an unfulfilled Frenchman or a future FLN gunman.

What then of the pied-noir's view of assimilation? Jules Roy says that until he met Camus in 1945 he did not think that Arabs had a soul. Roy sums up the Rovigo opinion: 'The Arabs were always considered like oxen; we treated them well but there could be no question of feeling sorry for them.' Since they were Arabs, Arabs were inferior beings; it was only natural that they should live in huts, that too was part of being an Arab. Certainly the Europeans felt no guilt.[14] This testimony is suspect because Roy was writing during the Algerian war, when past mistakes were clear. But already in the 1930's Michel Hodent said that assimilation was in practice nonsense and that the Arabs were just being kept in their place. Numerous Communist militants could testify with chagrin that the European workers thought primarily of the economic advantages of colonialism. Amar Ouzegane concludes that 'the European labour aristocracy found life in the colonial system easy and privileged'.[15] Already in the 1920's an Arab novelist had depicted a left-wing trade-unionist who was friendly with Arabs; at the first quarrel he flew into a rage about Arabs who wanted to throw all the Europeans into the sea.[16] Yet it would be equally wrong to see in every French Algerian a future OAS gunman. Opinions ranged from the very few like Camus, who attacked the practice of assimilation and even wondered about the concept, to the openly hostile like Maximim Rozis. Most Europeans came somewhere in between, closer to Rozis than to Camus but paying lip-service to equality.

The key years in Algerian history were 1936 to 1940. It was during this period that the tensions became clear and that the ambivalences began to be resolved. The economic situation did not improve and the international crisis worsened. Like France itself, Algeria was split between left and right. But this was less important than the split between the two communities. Camus reached maturity just when the fabric of French Algeria was starting to unravel. Already the pressure of famine and unemployment was building up into riots. Once more these took the form of anti-semitism. In Constantine in 1934 and in Sétif in 1935 the Arabs attacked Jewish families and property, while the French authorities looked on. Camus' theatre, journalism and early writings are an integral part of this period.

But the sorry tale of economic and political woes is only one half of French Algerian history. Jules Roy puts it crudely: 'At the time none of us, I especially, gave a damn about justice . . . Our country was the sun.'[17] Camus was a characteristic pied-noir in his feeling for his own neighbourhood and in his love of the sea and the mountains. Frenchmen who came to Algeria felt its seduction: Grenier was no exception. Fouchet, whose feelings were so mixed, talks of the pied-noir's determination to enjoy life. Even the FLN leaders do not deny this. They recognize in the European community a passion for Algeria, which led, precisely, to aberration. Fouchet says that French Algerians 'clung to their happiness with a blind, ferocious rage'.[18] They were themselves convinced by the legend of a primitive, sun-baked paradise.

Algiers was brashly and proudly ugly. Its setting between the mountains and the sea was so spectacular that it did not need to be beautiful. As the centre of the new Mediterranean nation it had no use for history: 'What does this city owe to its past? Almost nothing. What does it expect from its future? Almost everything.'[19] It distrusted culture too. Camus disliked opera

60

but he complained that he had the entire city against him. Algiers liked flamboyant opera with tirades, duels and costumes. It also liked, as the Centenary showed, bands, parades and military music. They suited the capital's liking for strength and barbarity. A contributor to *Sud* was typical when he picked up the 'insatiable appetites' of Algiers.[20]

Of course, since the strands of Algerian life were interwoven, the cult of military music led back to politics. Jean Daniel notes the special prestige that the children of army officers enjoyed in Blida. Their parents were less wealthy than the colons but their social status was high. French Algerians were proud of their record during the First World War when they had gone back, like Camus' father, to fight. This was a proof of their Frenchness and the Marne, where many died, became part of their mythology. It was the union of North and South; France had summoned her barbaric children and they had responded; the Marne and the Mediterranean were fused. Yet the army was also the force which protected them against the internal enemy. Achard puts it simply: the European Algerians owed everything to the army because they lived in a country 'where every Duval was surrounded by ten Ahmeds'. The sense of defeat, which Bugeaud would have understood, lingered on. It was a secret fear, not a guilt but a fear.

It remained well-hidden, emerging only in such distorted forms as this love of bands. Algiers was absorbed in its daily life. Its social structure was as simple as its history. On the top were the rich colons who lived on their farms but had flats in the capital. Their only peers were the relatively small group of businessmen. Both distrusted the French civil servants and admired the French officers. They squabbled over invitations to the governor's balls and spent their summers in Vichy. But their snobbery was not subtle, for they were no refined aristocracy. Their level of education was low and their tastes earthy. They liked to eat, drink and swim and they displayed their wealth without inhibition. They ran their farms efficiently and Algeria just as efficiently.

Underneath them was a European population which stretched down through small businessmen and minor civil servants to labourers. This was a mixed urban populace rather than a factory proletariat. Camus' uncle, the barrel-maker, was typical. There was not enough heavy industry in Algeria to create a solid mass of factory workers – the docks alone came close. So the sense of class was, if not weak, then at least diffuse. Artisans, shopkeepers and town-hall clerks felt a bond; they did not possess the militant class-consciousness of coal-miners or steel-workers. This was even more true of the rest of Algeria. 'I was not well-prepared for the doctrine of class struggle,' says Jean Daniel.[21] Neither was Camus.

The Algiers streets had that savour which Camus and his friends loved. It was made up of markets, Arab cafés, different dialects, urchins selling and stealing and old men talking politics on street corners. It was the usual Mediterranean brew, but spicier and with its Arab flavour. Camus' uncle, the butcher, was one of many who preferred pastis and philosophy to work. On Sundays the entire European population spilled out onto the beaches. The *Revue Algérienne* is full of advertisements for bathing stations, one being the Bains Padovani which Camus used as a theatre. Along the coast from Algiers the beauty-spots made easy week-end trips and Tipasa was already a tourist resort. Physical pleasure was everything. Algerian men were, so they felt, more virile than all others and Algerian girls were prettier. Sport had a larger and more vociferous following than in France and middle-weight, Marcel Cerdan, was starting his climb to the world title. His career, as much as Camus', would be a parable of the North African sense of death which was present in the Algiers streets. In every carnival one float contained a man stretched out on his coffin, acting the corpse. Death was brutal but familiar.

'The Marseilles temperament is bad enough,' says Achard, 'but people in Algiers are frenetic.'[22] The urchins were more cunning, the shops more colourful and the conversations more heated than anywhere on the Mediterranean. Camus was cautious and reserved; Algiers was quite the opposite. Yet it was monotonous as well as rhetorical because it was half-dead already. Moments of silence were a counter-point to the frenzy. The hush of evening descended suddenly and froze the noisy streets. Achard describes a peanut-seller: 'He stands there for hours without moving, he can hardly be bothered to serve his customers ... You never see him eat, drink or run ... he doesn't read or gamble. He has no wants and no master, except tobacco.'[23]

In this brew of sun, street slang, young girls on beaches and tense moments of silence there was another ingredient. Caught up with the swagger of seduction was the 'instinct for violence which has broken out so often among North African peoples'. Algerian newspapers lavished space on robberies and murders. Fouchet writes that 'Algerian virility turns easily into blood-letting'.[24] Jean Daniel tells the story of an old woman who lived only to hate the man who had brought the news of her son's death. Like the peanut-seller she neither talks nor moves; but it is the immobility of hatred.

Put more crudely, Algeria was indeed a primitive society, a place to make babies and fight with knives. It did not have enough Louis Germains and enough moral thinking. It drew on cultures which had known centuries of bloodshed and had turned fighting into a ritual. Then too Algeria was a frontier country. Whenever he could, Daniel's father abandoned his shop and escaped into the mountains, where he had an unprofitable farm which he loved. Fighting was a part of the frontier mentality. But the main cause of violence lay, inevitably, in the colonial situation, in that secret, unavowed fear. Algeria was becoming ever more a frontier country because the European population was retreating into the coastal cities. Algiers, Oran and Constantine were a toe-hold in Africa and even they were being invaded by Arabs.

Camus inherited all this and he used it in *L'Etranger*. Meursault is the French Algerian who buries his mother, goes off to the beach and gets into a fight. He is even more indifferent than Achard's peanut-seller. But Camus saw the danger of violence and he depicted it, however ambiguously, in *L'Etranger* where the murder of the Arab is caught up with sunshine and virility. In *Le Mythe de Sisyphe* he stressed the need for limits and measure. His aim was to correct French Algeria's view of itself. The pieds-noirs must learn that killing the messenger is no use and that paradises cannot be perpetuated by murder. During the Algerian War Camus would try to expound his lesson of limits but by then it was too late. French Algeria paid him no attention and the crowds he loved turned against him. But in the '30's the beauty of Algiers was deliberately thoughtless and the sun could seem innocent.

These problems had already been considered by other writers. Bénisti was correct when he said that the theme of the Mediterranean came 'from the guts'. But it was the main preoccupation of three generations of Algerian writers. They too wanted to 'situate themselves in Algeria'. Camus knew this and his Algeria both continues and refutes theirs.

The fountainhead of French Algerian writing was Louis Bertrand, who was not Algerian at all. Like so many other colonizers, he came from Lorraine. He arrived in Algiers in 1891 and fell in love with the country. He stayed nine years, wandered the Algiers streets, pressed on to the South and explored the Roman ruins of Tipasa. Bertrand was a classicist with a touch of the barbarian in him. *Pépète et Balthazar* is one of the best novels about Algiers street-life and Bertrand also felt the lure of the desert. He loved the way the hard lines of rock merged into a haze; solid objects vanished into the emptiness of the sand. Bénisti sets *Pépète* and the desert apart in Bertrand's work.

As Bertrand grew older he began to distrust the desert, source of mirages. Instead he concentrated on the Mediterranean. Despite his touch of barbarism, he had very Western ideas about who should run it. 'Mare nostrum', he pronounced and added warningly, 'May it be ours for ever.'[25] The mixture of races is to be fused into the latin nation. The 1830 Conquest was the revenge of the Latins and the reversal of the defeat suffered centuries before during the Arab occupation of Spain. The Greeks are discarded and the Romans are exalted because they were warriors. The descendant of the Roman legions is, of course, the French army. The tension which existed in Algeria between the French and non-French Europeans is resolved in favour of the French. The task of the Maltese and the Neapolitan is to become French as quickly as possible.

Naturally enough, Bertrand had scant use for Arabs: 'what interests me in this country is what we have created.'[26] Algeria was to become latin again, as it had been during the Roman period. Bertrand made great play with Saint Augustine, the North African and Christian. Indeed after Bertrand, Augustine became a hero of Algerian culture and, although not much read, he could be trotted out in the most implausible circumstances. Even Maurice Thorez talked about Augustine when he came to Algiers in 1939. The problem of the irritating Arabs is thus disposed of; they are not really Arabs at all but latins. They should shrug off Islam and assimilate.

But Bertrand had no faith in the Arab's ability to emulate

64

Saint Augustine. Spinning out his argument of conquest and reconquest, he saw an inevitable struggle between the Arabs and the French. Good colonials, he said, must have 'a sense of the enemy'. The civilizing mania of the Third Republic was dangerous: 'the more we enrich them, the more we educate them, the more they will turn against us.' Bertrand grew ever more racist and talked of a 'fundamental, essential and irremediable inequality among the human races'. A true Lorrainer, he began to confuse the Arabs with the Germans: they were a threatening, barbaric horde with a 'fanatically aggressive temperament'.[27]

But Bertrand had no faith in the French Algerians either because he felt they were fascinated by the Arabs. Pépète loves to go to the Casbah, where 'his laziness is mingled with the indolent life of the natives'.[28] He is fatalistic and silent; the Arab personifies both traits. Many other writers, like Jean Grenier, dwell on the fascination of the Arab who incarnates a mystical indifference which the European seeks in vain to emulate. Isabelle Eberhardt spent her life trying not to penetrate Arab culture but to participate in what she perceived as its spirituality: 'the Arab nomads trudge, indifferently, towards the fulfilment of their destiny.'[29] The danger is that the European might resent either the fascination itself or his inability to satisfy it. Certainly Bertrand felt that he had to destroy it before it destroyed him. By the perverse logic which characterizes this brand of right-wing thinking, he personified in the Arab the side of himself which he disliked. The Arab was draining the European of his latinity; he must be destroyed so that Pépète could become a Roman warrior.

Not surprisingly, the FLN spokesmen castigate Bertrand. His books are, says Ouzegane, a catechism of hatred.[30] True enough, but Ouzegane might have added that they are also a catechism of defeat. Bertrand felt that, when the French and the Arabs fought over Algeria, the Arabs would win. He kept saying this during the centenary. He published an idealized account of the French victory called *Le Roman de la Conquête* but he also noted that the Europeans were withdrawing from the interior. Even more than the violence, it is the fear of French Algeria which Bertrand reveals. His books are full of warnings, vague but dire. He keeps repeating that the Arabs' indifference is a trap:

'They seem to be asleep but they are not; they are laughing at the vain efforts of civilized man. They know that eventually they will get rid of him or dominate him, that one day or another they will get the upper hand. They have a faith, they believe in themselves and they despise everything that is different from them.'[31]

Despite his dislike of Germany, Bertrand flirted with Hitler; similarly he loathes and admires the perfidious Arab. Fear takes strange forms in this admirer of imperial Rome. And his portrayal of the Arab was repeated by Achard:

'The others, the conquered, looked on with guileful indifference. They displayed that passivity which is either a menace for men or an adoration of God. They live parallel, mysterious lives alongside the conquerors.'[32]

All this was anathema to Camus, who stressed Greece in order to correct Bertrand's emphasis on Rome. Paradoxically, Bertrand's thought had been cast in an openly Fascist mould by the Italians, rival claimants to the Roman succession. Mussolini threatened Tunisia and had a certain following among French Algerians who felt that he would be a bulwark against Islam. So the Algerian left makes fun of latinity, although even Camus describes the Mediterranean as a 'latin pearl, radiant as a lily'. [33]
However, Camus sought to combat the violence of French Algeria rather than to flaunt it and he preferred the Greeks, traders and tragedians, to the Roman legions. The murder of the Arab in *L'Etranger* contains themes reminiscent of Bertrand. Meursault, another fatalist, kills the Arab who is even more indifferent than he; if he had not killed him, he would have been struck down by the sun; the Arab is more authentic and hence must be dispatched. The dark side of Camus' imagination showed him that the French Algerians would ignore his lessons about limits.

The generation which followed Bertrand produced floods of novels: descriptions of colonial society, studies of Arabs and adventure stories about the desert. The best-known of these books was Robert Randau's *Les Colons*. Randau wrote for the *Echo d'Alger* and contributed at least one piece to *Alger-Républicain*. Camus met him in the '30's. By this time *Les Colons* was a landmark in Algerian writing and it was helping to foster the legend of the new nation. The French Algerians are depicted as tough, energetic settlers. The parallels with the United States are explored and frontier society exalted. The hero, Jos, lives in the countryside, runs his farm efficiently and despises Algiers. His brutality – he tries to rape his niece and murder her fiancé – is presented as a virtue. During the novel he gives up his farm, buys more land and starts over again as a pioneer.

Jos, who laughs at priests, philosophers and ideas, knows that he will soon die. This does not trouble him for he 'believes in Algeria not in God'.[34] He also laughs at cemeteries and funeral masses. The counterpoint to his swagger is provided by his friend; Jean Cassard is a silent man 'into whom the desert has instilled its remote impassibility'. As in the Algiers carnivals, death is familiar and unceremonious.

Bertrand deigned to approve of Randau but there is one important difference between them: the Arab is a brother not an enemy. The colons 'cultivated the soil on which the battles had been fought, they exploited their victims and then discovered that they had much in common with them'.[35] Jos, who despises the metropolitan Frenchmen, considers his Arab neighbours as fellow-barbarians and equals. Here one returns to the realm of ambiguity. Arab critics dismiss *Les Colons* as the glorification of colonialism: the European-Arab friendship was merely a fiction that concealed the economic oppression of the colonized by the colonizer. This is partly true, but Randau was willing to go beyond Bertrand's concept of conquest and to abandon latinity in order to find a place for the Arabs. He mocks assimilation and calls for a fusion of the two races, although he has no idea how this could be achieved.

Camus and his friends disliked Randau's provincialism. He wanted to break with France and create an Algerian literature. Steeped in the *NRF*, Camus wanted to draw on the technical innovations of modern French writing. He felt that the adventure-story format of *Les Colons* was too simple. Moreover, his group was more pessimistic than Randau, more in harmony with the depression and less confident of Algeria's future. Yet they, too, felt that Algeria was barbaric and they, too, tried, with scarcely greater success, to find a place for the Arab.

So when *Sud* announced in 1931 that 'as from now North Africa has a literary and artistic life of its own', it was exaggerating its own importance. Camus and his friends were the third generation of Algerian writers. When another young contributor talked of 'our sky, our sea and its shores: Andalusia, Provence, Italy and Greece', he was echoing many voices.

The first book which Camus recognized as the work of his generation was Gabriel Audisio's *Jeunesse de la Méditerranée*, 1935. Firstly, it was published by the *NRF*, which meant it was not provincial. Indeed Audisio was not even a pied-noir for he had arrived from Marseilles in 1910, when his father became director of the Algiers opera. His themes are not new for he too waxes eloquent about the unity of the Mediterranean race: 'We are all brothers, from Algeciras to Messina, via Marseilles.'[36] The Arab is part of the Mediterranean medley; he must be included because alongside its latinity the Mediterranean has seen centuries of Islam. In fact the old, dangerous theme of authenticity recurs: the Arab with his kif and his immobility is the model Mediterranean type. Here again is the unavowed fear of French Algeria. But it is buried beneath the joyful assertion of Mediterranean unity which receives new vigour from the language. Audisio's originality seemed to his contemporaries to lie in his technique: *Jeunesse* is half-essay and half-poem in prose. Retrospectively it seems wordy but to Camus' friends it was bold and fresh.

The picture which Camus paints of Algeria, in a lecture which he gave at the Maison de Culture and in his early books like *Noces*, reiterates many of these themes and only once goes beyond them. The Algerians are barbarians: 'a race born out of the sea and the sun.' They have no culture and they do not 'grow, learn or improve'.[37] They live in emotional poverty for 'there is no love in their existence'. But in compensation they are rich in vitality. They may also be artists for creation is a primitive act; they are 'not without poetry'. The tough men and the pretty girls on the beaches live more intensely than other nations.

Camus disposes of Bertrand: 'It's a great mistake to confuse the Mediterranean with latinity or to attribute to Rome what came from Greece.'[38] The exaltation of the Roman legions leads to false brands of Mediterraneanism like Mussolini's invasion of Ethiopia. Camus next distinguishes between two Greeces: the one contains pre-socratic tragedy and comedy, the other post-socratic philosophy. The latter is a second form of false Mediterraneanism because it ignores limits. It abandons the concrete realm of sensuous experience and art in order to construct vast, abstract syntheses. True Mediterraneanism offers a harmony between man and the world. Here Camus is fighting on several fronts. The mania for speculative reason has shifted to North Europe and become a German heresy, against which Camus pits his brand of Mediterraneanism. But he has another, unnamed enemy who is closer even than Mussolini. The harmony between man and world can only be brief and it cannot be prolonged by illusions about a sun-baked paradise. From the silence of the Algiers evenings, the pieds noirs must learn that they will die. They should not resign themselves; they should return to life with the zest of a prisoner who awaits the guillotine. Yet they should not live blindly and should not try to postpone their own deaths by slaughtering others. The moralist in Camus rebukes excess; pride leads man to face his condition lucidly.

This was also a matter of style. Bertrand, who ignored his own warning, had noted that Algerian writers 'tend to go too far and lapse into bombast'.[39] Camus realized that the primitive force of Algeria could best be expressed in a form that was antithetical to it. He himself had an un-Mediterranean side which his friends remarked: he was phlegmatic and distant. In his writing he fought the tendency towards rhetoric which he showed in his first pieces. *Noces* is more concisely lyrical than Audisio.

Camus' originality is clear here but he is less innovative when he takes up the theme of the mixed races. The Algerian nation exists only as a part of the Mediterranean, which extends from Greece to Morocco. In this melting pot the Arab has his place: 'In Algiers there is no difference between the way a Spaniard or an Italian lives and the way the Arabs around him live,' says Camus who ignores the difference in average wage. The Mediterranean is the meeting-point of East and West and it embraces 'the great Eastern cultures'. Yet the chief sign of its unity is the Latin language – latinity creeps in through the back door. This is no different from the Mediterranean medley and offers no fresh definition of what the Arab's place is to be. Not that this is a full statement of Camus' views. In his journalism he campaigned for economic reforms and in *L'Etranger* he half-spelled out his fears. But he did not avoid falling into the ambiguity which pervaded French Algeria.

The vitality of Camus's early writing comes from Algeria. The invitation in *Le Mythe de Sisyphe* to grasp hold of life is the wisdom which he had learned on the Algiers beach. His was a special voice among French writers because he felt swimming was at least as important as philosophy. When placed next to Camus, Sartre seems very much a writer of Northern France – of Le Havre, the rain and the mud. This still does not explain why *L'Etranger*, a short novel about a North African town, should become one of the most influential novels of the Occupation and should circulate in the prison camps of Hitler's Germany. Yet the sense that life is an unsolvable puzzle, which drew readers to *L'Etranger*, came from Algeria. Camus' pessimism was deepened by the seemingly unsolvable Arab problem. It dramatized the gulf between man's aspirations and the world in which he lived.

It may be no coincidence that another great writer of the 1940's, George Orwell, was also a colonial. Certainly Orwell could have discovered newspeak in the French Algerian pronouncements on assimilation. He had depicted in *Burmese Days* a colonial society that lived on alcohol and hatred; the one Englishman who reaches out to the Burmese is unable to help them or himself. In the 1940's Europe was to go through a period of madness and cruelty and the colonies were rich in both. They showed the cracks in their culture before the mother countries. But Orwell's situation was easier than Camus' for he could demand an end to empire, whereas Camus was bound to his people who had no home but Algeria. There seemed to Camus to be no solution, no way to cut through the ambiguity and violence. These merely confirmed his vision of an amputated existence; the world was beautiful but it was not made for man. Meanwhile, as if to offer a prelude to the '40's, Algeria laid its tensions bare in the late '30's and Camus participated in its conflicts.

3

Marriage, Friendships and Plays

When Camus finished his degree in the summer of 1935 he was
not thinking primarily of Algeria's troubles. Ever the diligent
student, he decided to take his 'diplôme d'études supérieures',
which was the next rung on the university ladder. He hoped to
go on to the 'agrégation', the passport to university teaching.
Although he was determined to write, he had no intention of
relying on writing to make a living. Coming from a poor family,
he had no use for bohemianism. He wanted to get a teaching job
in France which would allow him money and freedom to lead
his own life. Once more Grenier was the model. So the next step
was the diploma, for which he had to write a thesis.

He discussed the topic with Grenier, who suggested that he
write about Indian philosophy. Without much thought Camus
agreed and went to see Poirier who was to supervise him. But
Poirier ridiculed the notion. The university of Algiers library
had no books on Indian philosophy and no one in Algiers, least
of all Poirier, knew anything about it. He suggested a different
topic. His friend, Jean Guitton, had just published a book on
Plotinus and Saint Augustine. Camus should read it, select a
theme and re-treat it. Drawn to the Greeks and to the North
African Augustine, Camus agreed. Poirier thought little about
the thesis. The diploma was not very difficult to obtain and
Camus was not a good enough philosopher to write anything
outstanding. Poirier was sure that Camus would spend too
much time on politics and too little on Plotinus. He was mildly
surprised when he read the completed work. Camus had been
conscientious and the thesis was, if not outstanding, then at
least competent.

The marks of the good student are evident: footnotes,
bibliography and a clear line of argument. Camus did not go
deeply into Augustine and he relied heavily on other people's

interpretations – Etienne Gilson as well as Guitton.[1] Yet he reveals his personal interests. When he writes that reason is 'only a weaker form of intuition', he reminds us of his enthusiasm for Bergson. He looks for the sensibilities which lie behind the various philosophies. He explains that, if Plotinus writes so well, it is because 'he accepts discipline';[2] one remembers that Camus was disciplining himself in his own writing. At certain moments of the thesis the style alters, the sentences grow more urgent and the argument leaves Guitton behind.

Many of the themes echo Camus' own religious debate. They were foreshadowed in his remarks about Jesus and in his sense of an absent deity. He dislikes socratic Greece because the wise man becomes a God; the world is interpretable and the tragic is banished. By contrast early Christianity fascinates him because it possesses not merely the Algerian mixture of races but also the Algerian sense of death. Camus describes vividly the early Christian belief that the world will soon end and that knowledge is vanity. The Church is dominated by the 'physical horror of death'; the only hope is redemption through Christ's suffering but redemption is gratuitous and there is nothing man can do to earn it. Meanwhile the Church's law is harsh. Camus depicts a tough Jesus who tells his followers that they must leave behind mother and son. This is the opposite of the Jesus whom he discussed with Bénisti and yet the two Jesuses are closer than they seem. In each case the dual nature of Christ, man and God, is denied. Camus liked the early Christians because they struggled after a remote God, as he himself did.

Christianity had to be transformed in order to penetrate the world of socratic Greece. Camus runs through the various attempts and dwells on the Gnostics. He singles out Marcion who explains that sin comes from the simultaneous existence of two Gods, the more powerful of them evil. This intrigues Camus who detects 'in the pessimistic view of the universe and in this proud refusal to submit to the accents of a really modern sensibility'. It is, of course, Camus' own sensibility. Man is partially innocent; he is condemned to mortality but he strives for totality.

Yet Camus is not content with the gulf between man and the universe. He wonders whether it might not be spanned, whether there might not be some fragile Jean Grenier-ish bridge. He admires Plotinus because the bridge is made by intuition and by art rather than by reason. Plotinus becomes Bergson's forerunner and the creator of the dream.

An even more fragile bridge is present in Augustine, as Camus interprets him. Augustine takes Plotinus' theme of intuition and adds to it faith, which may, like grace, be withheld. Without faith man cannot know good and evil and is left to die. Camus admires a pessimistic Augustine who is almost certain that man is damned and yet urges him to struggle for his salvation. He ignores the more orthodox Augustine, for whom the notion of sin is inseparable from the notion of grace. Conversely Camus' and Marcion's sense of innocence is absent from Augustine who felt that man was doomed to sin, unless God redeemed him.

Throughout the discussion runs Camus' peculiar sense of a flawed universe from which God is not quite absent. He admires the dualism of the early Christians and of his pessimistic Augustine but he cannot give up the dream of oneness which he finds in Plotinus. It is present in the Algerian mountains and it inspires man with his metaphysical urge. Camus' treatment of Augustine anticipates his treatment of Marx, Hegel and Husserl. In each case he accepts the demolition they carry out but he demolishes their constructions. Husserl is allowed to criticize the neat Cartesian universe but not to construct a new theory of knowledge. Yet Camus builds skyscraper constructions of his own, founded on the unsatisfied but admirable longing for totality. He is a Gnostic or a Manichean rather than an Augustinian.

Meanwhile Camus' marriage to Simone was turning sour. At Christmas Camus presented her with some pleasantly precious fairy-tales which he had written for her. They are populated by religious cats and arrogant knights but the main character is the fairy who by her dance creates the dream. Once again the dream quickly yields to silence. 'It's a pity fairy-tales cannot consist solely of beginnings,' said Camus.[3] He was discovering that drug addiction could not be cured by strength of character. His friends noticed that Simone continued to take morphine. At a party at Jacques Heurgon's house she ignored the charades and then went outside to dose herself. Camus had hoped that marriage would break her dependence, both physical and psychological, but it continued. Simone still needed to seduce.

De Fréminville, invited to Hydra, watched her wander around in long, transparent dresses.[4] He was shocked and Camus said nothing, although he was too Mediterranean and too masculine not to be hurt. In the summer of '35, after he had finished his degree, the two spent a holiday in Minorca but Camus returned just as worried. Yet he loved Simone. In her happy moods she delighted him with her vivacity which made him feel more alive. The two discussed her addiction and decided that she should have it treated. She had never sought medical help before but in the autumn she entered a private clinic in Algiers.

Camus had already been feeling his old loneliness. After his marriage, he had withdrawn somewhat from his group of friends. Then he began going from his own house over to Paul Raffi, who also lived in Hydra.[5] The Raffis were a tribe, for Paul had two brothers who invited their friends. The gang of young men would sit around and tell stories. Pierre Raffi was melodramatically worried about Fascism. 'It will plunge the world into chaos,' he would declare, throwing open his arms. Camus used to laugh and encourage him to fresh outbursts of rhetoric. Paul's father was a sea captain who told yarns about ships and ports; these too intrigued the attentive Camus. He never talked about Simone and the others never asked: you did not intrude on Camus. But they felt that he needed the company and the male conversation. Paul's mother considered their noisy evenings crude and remained upstairs in her bedroom.

Camus still hoped that his marriage could be put right. He visited Simone regularly when she was in the clinic. He gave up the Hydra house and moved in with her mother. Marthe was pleased that Camus had persuaded Simone to seek treatment and they arranged that, when she was discharged, she and Camus would live in Marthe's house. But the treatment did Simone little good. The doctor seems to have given his patients drugs in order to placate them and to make his clinic popular and profitable. He made no attempt to wean Simone from morphine. She may also have slept with him, either to assure regular supplies or else out of her need to seduce. She certainly used any method to get hold of the drug. It was more difficult now because Marthe and Camus were watching her, so she resorted to seduction. Marriage seemed to have worsened rather than improved her condition; she disliked the intimacy and felt trapped. The brilliant, vivacious girl appeared only at ever rarer moments. She took little interest in Camus' life, either in his studies or in his increasing political activity.

Camus had joined the Communist Party just before his trip to Minorca. His reasons were complex but one of them, according to Jean Grenier, was ambition. Grenier advised Camus to join because the Communists were the hard core of the Popular Front and party membership would help him publish his books and get work as a journalist. But Grenier had his own, more subtle reasons for offering such advice. He was taking a different road and three years later he published *L'Esprit de l'Orthodoxie*, which criticizes the 1930's mania for commitment. Ever the *NRF* writer and ever fascinated by contradictions, Grenier steered Camus in the opposite direction in order to study him. As his disenchantment with the PC grew, Camus understood what Grenier had done and resented it. Once more their relationship took the form of influence and reaction against the influence. But in '35 it made sense for an ambitious young man to join the PC. There was nothing ignoble about this for Malraux almost did the same. Once he joined Camus worked hard and began to rise in the party.

The second reason lay in Camus' background. Joining the PC was a return to 'my origins, my childhood companions, everything that I feel and know'. It grew out of his poverty, his sense of class and his upbringing in Belcourt. Yet he was not simplistic about this. He knew that, while the PC claimed to be the party of the working class, working-class people distrusted all politicians – 'lots of cruel experiences have taught them to be wary'.[6] Camus was wary himself. Like Bénisti, he felt that politics was a shoddy affair and that parties enslaved their militants. Yet the PC provided him, as it did the more naive De Fréminville, with a comradeship.

Moreover, Communism suited the tough Camus. One remembers the argument with Fouchet: Camus felt that the Socialists were weak but that the Communists would act. He toiled as a militant. He organized his own cell, represented the PCA in the Amsterdam-Pleyel movement and started the Maison de Culture. Although he disliked them, he carried out the tedious chores of selling newspapers and sticking posters on walls. He resigned himself to making speeches and attending meetings, both of which he loathed. The Popular Front was growing stronger and Camus wanted to serve it. He was attracted to the figure of the Communist militant: dedicated and self-sacrificing.

Yet this led to the heart of his dilemma: he both liked and disliked the religious strain in the PC. He complains about 'the marxist claim to construct a morality where man is his own end'. The PC offered its militants absolute truth: history made sense when interpreted through the class struggle; no metaphysics were needed because history had replaced them; the party's interpretation of the class struggle was infallible; therefore the militant was always right. This simple catechism was repeated and doubt was banished. But Camus did not believe a word of it, just as he did not believe in the Catholic catechism. It contradicted his own religious sense of the absent God. Even Communist militants were not always just and virtuous; their lives were amputated too. Yet Camus welcomed the nihilistic part of Communist religion. God was indeed absent, history was chaos and it was vanity to talk of progress or reforms. The PC mocked what Camus calls 'pseudo-idealisms and instant optimisms'. It corresponded to his sense of a world that could not be changed by socialists. The Communist militant is, like Camusian man, a tragic figure whose abnegation stems from his pessimism. He has to work harder because life is so impossible.

It was no accident that Camus joined and left the PC. This was not the usual '30's flirtation, wedged between the February riots and the Moscow trials. It was a chapter both in the saga of Camus' religious struggles and in the meditation on politics which culminates in *L'Homme Révolté*. Already Camus was objecting to the concept of revolution. Ideologies were superstructures and religions were opiums; but the classless society gave order to the universe. Revolution was a redemption which rewarded the militant for his toil. It was an absolute value to which all else should be sacrificed. Beyond its Manichean-Augustinian pessimism Communism reconstructed a socratic universe. But Camus did not believe in absolutes, or rather he doubted them. He agreed with the PC's absolute nihilism and he half-admired the Communist militant's absolute dedication. He was not willing to say that, since the human condition could not be transformed by revolution, only a tepid, Socialist Party-style militancy was possible. Man's need for oneness was admirable and could be channelled into moral and political action. Yet it could not be satisfied by the absent revolution.

Of course the PC disagreed. The militant's dedication springs from his belief in revolution without which there is no spur to action. The certainty of revolution justifies whatever tactics the party employs. This is the old debate about ends and means. In Camus' eyes the impossibility of revolution imposes another and different moral code, which retains the Communist themes of abnegation and dedication but suggests other values such as lucidity and limits. Attraction and repulsion are inseparable in Camus' attitude towards Communism because he is not pitting relatives against absolutes, laicism against religion. Rather he is defending his own brand of absolutes against a rival brand.

Not surprisingly Camus was an excellent Communist: zealous and tough. Initially he had no success but he persisted and formed a solid group. It has been said that his task within the PCA was to organize Arabs but this is untrue.[7] The party lacked intellectuals and Camus was supposed to recruit them. They in turn were to influence working-class people, in practice Europeans. This was the usual Communist method in the '30's.

So Camus recruited his friends into a study-group. Miquel, the Raffi brothers and others were persuaded to meet and discuss marxist texts. Then they organized lectures for workers, who were sent by the unions. The subjects of the lectures ranged from industrial law to art history; propaganda was not encouraged. This first group did not flourish. Paul Raffi left and Miquel moved to a more active cell outside Algiers. The members seem never to have had the party card and they knew little about the party leadership. The few workers who came rarely came again.

Camus, who was the only one in touch with the PCA leadership, persisted. He was the party's representative in the Belcourt section of Amsterdam-Pleyel and he was a member of an anti-Fascist group within the university. Dean Gernet, Grenier and some students met to discuss how they could combat the right's overwhelming influence in Algiers. Camus frequently showed his intransigent character: he remained haughtily silent while the others talked; then he would castigate them for their weakness and lay down the line to follow.

Nor was he always persuasive. The university students were divided into two associations: one was right-wing, the other smaller one, left-wing. Camus wanted the left-wing *Union fédérale des étudiants* (UFE) to enter the PCA. A meeting was called to discuss the proposal and about seventy people turned up. There was a noisy debate but the opposition had a clear majority. There seemed no reason why students could not be left-wing without becoming communist. Camus spoke for a long time and was shouted down; he had only a handful of supporters in the hall. Finally he stalked out furiously and never returned to the association.[8]

Throughout 1936, as the Popular Front came to power, Camus recruited his second, larger group. They were not necessarily party members and, when they were, they were not zealous. But they joined in activities which had a pro-communist or at least a left-wing slant. Without the PCA Camus might not have formed this group or put on his plays.

Some of his henchmen were friends from schooldays, like Bénisti and Belamich. But his closest collaborators were Jeanne Sicard and Marguerite Dobrenn, whom he recruited in the autumn of '35. Both were from Oran and both were of middle-class families. Indeed Jeanne Sicard's parents were wealthy and owned the cigarette firm Bastos. They were horrified at their daughter's friendship with Camus and appalled when she entered the PC. There were angry scenes, Jacques Heurgon was asked to intervene and Jeanne's allowance was cut off. Undaunted, she finished her degree in history and supported herself by giving lessons. She had the self-confidence of her background and she stood beside Camus on the platform when he was booed out of the UFE meeting. Marguerite Dobrenn's parents, who had left-wing sympathies, were more understanding and they continued her allowance.

Although the group revolved around the university it was not made up exclusively of students. In '35 Camus met Charles Poncet, another working-class boy from Belcourt. Poncet was born in France but, unlike Fouchet, he had acquired the pied-noir accent and the pied-noir sense of territory. By now he had become a *Commune* militant and a member of Amsterdam-Pleyel. Although he considered himself a fellow-traveller Poncet did not join the PC. He had read Boris Souvarine's book on Stalin which prepared him for the Moscow trials. He took no part in the group's theatrical experiments, whereas others were interested only in putting on plays. Marie Vitton, who did the costumes, was from France and enjoyed a grudging prestige because she spoke with a Paris accent. Louis Miquel was enlisted to do the sets and Paul Raffi publicized the plays in his mother's *Revue Algérienne*.

While brooding on Gide, the theatre and communism the group liked to walk and swim. They made pilgrimages to Tipasa where they bathed and wandered around the Roman ruins. They were agreed in their barbarism and their love of the Mediterranean. Pretension was anathema to them and, while they did not want to seem provincial, they distrusted sophistication.

The exception who proved the rule was René-Jean Clot. Born in Algiers, Clot rejected everything Mediterranean. Where the Algiers citizens lived for pleasure, Clot was ascetic, drawn to the Middle Ages and a prophet of doom. He was convinced that the Barbary pirates would return and that Algiers would be burned to the ground. His paintings, influenced by Expressionism, were the antithesis of popular Algiers taste and sold well because of it. He did a series of nuns which were much appreciated. Camus was drawn to Clot's talent and to his sense of death. One day they went to a museum to see the remains of a slave who had been tossed into a pit of quicklime centuries before; bits of his skeleton had attained a bizarre immortality. But Camus also felt that Clot, like Fouchet, was affected and flaunted his religious faith. Clot, too, paraded around Algiers with the spurious naivety of a wandering friar. Yet Grenier was interested in Clot and introduced him to the *Esprit* group.

In '36 Camus needed friendship more than ever because his marriage broke up. It did not improve after Simone left the clinic but the break did not come until the following year. In the summer she, Camus and another friend, Léon Bourgeois, set off on a long trip. This time Camus abandoned the Mediterranean and plunged into the alien, German-speaking world. He liked Salzburg and Innsbruck, which seemed like a toytown; but he felt that Breslau had 'a tragic quality of its own'.[9] He loathed Vienna – 'the most unnatural city in the world', a place where 'beauty has given way to civilisation'.[10] Meanwhile he listened anxiously to the radio because the Spanish Civil War had broken out and Hitler had sent troops into the Rhineland.

But Hitler and Franco troubled Camus less than Simone. During the journey he opened a letter written to her by a doctor: it was clear that she was continuing to take drugs and was paying for them with sex. Camus abandoned her and Bourgeois and took the train for Prague.[11] He had almost no money, scarcely enough for the cheapest restaurants. He visited the Jewish cemetery and tramped the streets of this half-Slav, half-German city that was so different from Algiers. He was lonely, depressed and furious. 'I am living like a madman,' he wrote to Marguerite Dobrenn.[12]

But he quickly showed his tough side. He wrote that his marriage was over and that he never wanted to talk about it. When he returned to Algiers he took up his work as if nothing had happened and moved into a room on the Rue Michelet. His masculine pride was shocked at Simone's betrayal which was an affront to his virility. He had suspicions about her relationship with Bourgeois and he soon broke with him. All his friends agree that Camus loved Simone and that the break-up left a mark. He had hoped to change his life by this marriage and he had not succeeded. He was more alone than ever. Conversely he now became a Don Juan. De Maisonseul and De Fréminville, who had known him at school, saw the difference: the shy, pure Camus was no more. The easily-shocked De Fréminville used to sit with Camus in cafés while Camus 'sized up the girls and stared at them with a strained, contemptuous smile'.[13] Seduction was a revenge for Simone and a demonstration of his power over women.

Simone continued her tragic existence. She went off to Saint-Tropez and to Paris where she was still pretty enough and intelligent enough to win admirers. In 1941 she married a French doctor, Léon Cottenceau, who had some of Camus' moral courage but who failed to cure her. Simone continued her extravagances. In the cafés of the Liberation she introduced herself as Madame Camus and she turned up in the '50's at the Gallimard publishing house where she announced herself as Camus' wife. A Swiss clinic had succeeded in stabilizing her craving for morphine and she lived as a registered addict. Fouchet met her once on the Paris streets; she was holding a flower in her hand and talking to herself in the crowd. He was shocked because her beauty was gone. There was no trace of the young girl he and Camus had loved.

Camus almost never talked about Simone. At the Liberation he met Fouchet and the conversation turned to her. 'I loved her,' said Camus, 'but it was hopeless.' He broke off and began to talk about the war. Camus, who was nothing if not loyal, had not lost all sympathy for Simone and her mother after the marriage broke up. When Simone, who had had ballet lessons, gave a dance recital in Algiers Camus went along himself and dragged Jeanne Sicard with him. Marthe felt that Camus had done all he could and was blameless. She and he agreed that Simone's life was destroyed by the impersonal evil of drug-addiction. When Simone spoke to her second husband about Camus she said that he had been patient and strong. She did not describe what had happened on the Prague trip but she never criticized Camus.

After the break-up Camus' friends supported him as best they could. They were practical people and, if they had little money, they did not indulge in a cult of bohemianism. You needed, Marguerite Dobrenn says, two thousand francs a month to live. Camus pieced them together by giving private lessons and by holding a multiplicity of jobs. He had no regular post from the time he finished his thesis in the summer of '36 until the moment he joined *Alger-Républicain* in late '38. He had already worked at the Algiers town hall issuing driving licences. In '37 he found work at the meteorological office. He was supposed to do a survey of the three hundred and fifty weather stations in Algeria. This confirmed his scepticism and provided the material for endless stories. The results never corroborated and the weather was always different from the forecasts. The town hall had been less fun: its monotony exhausted him and he came home too tired to write. He may also have worked selling spare parts for cars and he certainly acted in a semi-professional troupe. But his most reliable source of income was the lessons he gave on philosophy and literature.

Camus had learned that poverty corrodes. If he had to get up an hour earlier to walk to an appointment because he had no money for the bus, that was an hour lost to writing or swimming. When he travelled he used cheap train tickets, which meant that he had to stay several days in one town before he could move on. Because he was limited to certain trains, he used to wait hours in the station. He could eat only one meal a day and had to tramp the streets looking for the cheapest restaurants. Understandably, he felt that travel was an ascetic experience. He continued to find in the forced frugality of poverty an aristocratic virtue; but he well understood how the tedious tasks of working-class life turned men into robots. He writes well about the way poverty dulls the sensibility: 'If he earned a few bob a week and worked in a factory, Tristan would have nothing to say to Isolde.'[14] His own life was precarious because he never knew where the next private lesson was coming from. This strengthened his gambling instinct but it made him prudent. He thought long and hard before risking a job or a contact. Despite the effort he had made, he had not succeeded in escaping from his mother's poverty. Later, when he did become wealthy, he did not spend lavishly; he was merely pleased to be free of money worries. In the '30's poverty reinforced his need for comradeship: in a group there was always someone who had a flat or knew of a job.

Camus dominated his group, asserting his power over men as well as over women. His air of certainty impressed them, as it had his schoolmates. He continued to compartmentalize and often his friends knew him well but not one another. Now he banded most of them into a Communist cell which was nicknamed 'the intellectuals' cell'. Jeanne Sicard and Marguerite Dobrenn took the party card but those who did not – Bénisti and Poncet – did not feel left out. It was Camus' group rather than the PCA's and anyway this was '36 and there were no enemies on the left. The cell had no Arabs and was left by the PCA leadership to its own devices. Jean Chaintron came to only one meeting. Amar Ouzegane came several times and was pleased at the way Camus handled the business: he had started a number of little cultural organizations – cinema and discussion groups as well as the theatre troupe. As far as Jeanne Sicard and Marguerite Dobrenn were concerned, their ties with the party were solely with Camus. They joined and left when he did. Camus ran the cell energetically. Each member had his own tasks. Marguerite Dobrenn was prodded into running a series of social studies: her sub-group read extracts from nineteenth-century thinkers. There were no splits within the cell or within the group. Trouble only came because the larger Théâtre du Travail troupe, which grew from this group, contained experienced Communists from other cells. For the moment, Camus was still the only member of his cell who was in touch with the PCA leadership. He knew Ouzegane fairly well and attended meetings at federation level.

In the autumn of '36 the group fused its projects into a

Maison de Culture. It began modestly for the first meeting consisted of a session on jazz to which Camus, Jeanne Sicard and Poncet each invited a few friends. As a member of the *Commune* group, Poncet was well-qualified to organize the Algiers branch of the national, Maison de Culture chain. This was a good example of Communist cultural policy in that it was not to be sectarian. It was to attract the largest number of people possible and, if cultural agreement led to political allegiance, then so much the better. Of course there were limits to the PC's tolerance and Poncet encountered them when he wanted to hold a debate on Gide's *Retour de l'URSS*. It had been published to howls of rage from the Communists who denounced Gide as a traitor. From Paris the *Commune* leaders told Poncet that a debate would be 'untimely'. But Camus encouraged Poncet to go ahead. The debate was held in the basement of a café, a hundred people attended and the Communists looked on glumly as Grenier teased them. Camus' attitude was characteristic: he was often hardline but never dictatorial.[15]

The Maison's aim was to create a 'cultural Front that will be an integral part of the Popular Front' and 'to give to popular culture the place it deserves'. This meant a different role for the intellectual: 'The bourgeois order has separated culture from life. The intellectual is a man who thinks and does not live. This division is false;'[16] by involvement in the workers' struggle the intellectual will overcome the alienation which springs from capitalism. Camus welcomed this conventional notion but it never satisfied him and his theatre soon ran into contradictions which it could not explain. But in the meantime the Maison offered debates on popular language and concerts of popular music.

Along with these went tributes to Russia. On May 1, 1937 the Friends of the Soviet Union organized a huge demonstration with a Pushkin Gala, for which Camus' troupe did *Don Juan*. Ciné-Travail put on the inevitable *Battleship Potemkin* and a wildly pro-Russian documentary called 'A month in the land of the Soviets'. However, the Maison de Culture admitted that not all its spectators were pleased with the string of Russian films and that, alas, the level of the Russian cinema was going down. How this could be possible in a country where socialism was growing, the Maison could not explain. But recent Russian films were simply 'a load of clichés that bored everyone'. The comrades should return to the 'bold virile' films that they had been making in the '20's. Unspoken is the thought that this was before Stalin consolidated his rule.[17] Camus' own enthusiasm for the Soviet Union seems to have been strictly limited. He explains in his lecture that the Mediterranean is better suited to socialism than Russia and that Algerian socialism would be very different from Stalin's.

Meanwhile the Arabs were not forgotten. Camus and De Fréminville were active in an *Union franco-musulmane*, another flanking organization which was linked with both the Congrès musulman and the PCA. The Union worked hard to organize the petition in support of the Blum-Viollette project and Marguerite Dobrenn was sent to collect the signatures of the university lecturers. In May '37 the Union announced a lecture on 'Rome and the Berbers', which sounds like a variant on the Mediterranean medley.[18] There were also discussions of Arab comedy and Arab popular songs. De Fréminville hoped to decentralize the Union and root it in the different neighbourhoods of Algiers. Out of the contact between Arabs and Europeans was to come support for reforms in the Arab condition. But, although one section was founded in Belcourt, the Union had scant success. Few Europeans came to the meetings and those who did were prejudiced. The PCA had not resolved its central problem and the '37 split was implicit in the Union's failure.

The most successful of Camus' projects was his theatre. His long-standing interest in the theatre sprang less from what he had seen than from what he had read, especially Copeau. It also sprang from more private sources such as his love of groups and his sense of game-playing. His edge of remoteness made him see even the most earnest conversations with friends as unreal. From here it was a short step to turn his team into a troupe. The actor is the man who incarnates unreality and hence he is the only true man. As a director Camus was fascinated by the moment when the actor has not fully learned his part, when he is neither man nor character. This is a painful moment and Camus was able to be sympathetic. But, even when the role is learned, the actor retains an edge of Camusian indifference. The reverse is also true: since he has only a few hours to become Hamlet, the actor must live intensely. Camus encouraged a flamboyant style of acting.

The aim of the Théâtre du Travail and the Théâtre de l'Equipe was to explore this private vision. Yet they had to work within the Maison de Culture and the concept of commitment. At first Camus followed the mainstream of '30's left-wing theatre. *Monde, Vendredi* and other papers analyse how the theatre can be a weapon in the class struggle. Themes from working-class life must be chosen and political didacticism is no longer to be despised. Changes in technique will follow: the play's message might, for example, be expressed through a chorus. Clearly the committed theatre will not be limited to such simplistic innovations. Camus talks often of violence, which also reflects his period. Conventional theatre seeks to please and to reassure its audience; revolutionary theatre shocks. The spectator is to be jolted out of his habits, exposed naked to the cruelty which is present in 1930's Europe. The relationship between play and playgoer will be altered. But, after being shocked, the specatator will be stirred; he will be isolated and then swept up into the group.[19]

Camus' aim was not limited, when he founded the Théâtre du Travail, to choosing kitchen-sink or political themes. He wanted above all to establish a more intense relationship with the audience. Of *Révolte dans les Asturies* the group writes: 'We have made the action more direct and more immediate by breaking with the traditional methods of the theatre.'[20] The words 'direct' and 'immediate' recur in most of the group's statements. By abolishing the division into acts or scenes, by making the spectator a passerby on the street and by scrapping scenery, Camus wanted to involve the audience in the work. The Théâtre du Travail stress that they are 'a group without stars, where the actors do not take bows, where they are also painters and electricians, where they put up posters and make costumes'.[21] This encourages the audience to view the troupe not as a race apart but as ordinary people, artisans like themselves. This sense of fraternity does not, however, exclude a radical subjectivity. In *Le Temps du Mépris* the lighting was repeatedly switched so that the play looked different from each part of the theatre. Camus wanted to be lyrical rather than realistic.

Le Temps du Mépris was performed in January 1936. The choice was excellent: Malraux's anti-Fascist appeal for the freeing of German Communist leader Thaelmann. Camus wrote to Malraux for authorization and was delighted when he received a telegram 'Go ahead, André Malraux'. Not only had Malraux given permission but he had used the familiar 'tu' form. The group presented the play in the Bains Padovani before fifteen hundred people and *Lutte sociale* noted proudly that all social classes were present. The tide washed up against the pillars on which the building rested and the sound of the waves echoed through the room. The spotlight switched from one character to another and the scenery had been cut into blocks so that it could be moved quickly. Off stage drums were beaten and marching feet marked the presence of the masses. As Camus hoped, tension built up in the hall. The actors themselves grew excited and Belamich remembers feeling terrified, although he had only three words to say. The spectators were turned into the audience at Thaelmann's trial and, identifying with an orator who stood up among them, they demanded aloud that Thaelmann be freed. Finally they burst into the singing of the Internationale and gave the clenched fist salute of the Popular Front. It was a glorious piece of political theatre: melodramatic, unashamedly partisan and rousing.

The next play was to have been *Révolte dans les Asturies*, written by Camus, Jeanne Sicard and two friends. They discussed it during long evenings and the collectivity of authorship was another statement of fraternity. How much of the play Camus wrote is not clear; but one character, the 'Père éternel', is certainly his. The play was designed to continue *Le Temps du Mépris* and the revolt of the Asturian miners was an eminently suitable subject. *Révolte* should have been performed in March and Camus had obtained permission from the Governor-General. But the mayor, Rozis, objected, claiming that the play's revolutionary theme would cause trouble in a pre-election period. It was the first round in the Rozis-Camus battle and a straightforward example of political censorship. The strong Algiers right could override the decisions of the French civil service and was determined to make no concessions to the weaker left. Camus took some slight revenge by staging readings from the play, now renamed *Espagne '34*.

Révolte would have made excellent Popular Front theatre for it is quick-moving, sentimental and didactic. There are at least three themes which recur in Camus' work. The first is the problem of political violence which is resolved simply. 'You can't make revolutions with a ladies' fan,' says one of the miners.[22] When the counter-revolutionaries make trouble, they are executed and no one protests. This theme becomes more complex in Camus' work as he broods on the need for limits. The 'Père éternel' is vintage Camus and could have come from *L'Envers et l'Endroit*. An old tramp, he has lived in poverty but he has felt the beauty of the world. He says nothing but 'thank you' and 'goodbye' and seems to be mad. To contemplate the beautiful, empty world is, Camus feels, to risk silence and madness. The third theme is personified by Antonio, who joins the revolution because he wishes to end injustice and who is haunted by the memory of the snow in his native mountains. The revolution, he feels, will recreate the innocence of the natural world. Camus himself knew that revolution and innocence were not synonymous and would confront this problem the following year.

There is a conscious naivety in *Révolte* which reflects the early enthusiasm of the Popular Front. Bénisti's posters depict a Spanish miner bearing the tidings of revolution. He is bearded, curiously gentle and is meant to look like Christ. The audience was to have become the crowds on the Oviedo streets and to have participated in the struggle. The miners' defeat is shocking but it encourages the spectator to join the long march of the left.

After the banning of *Révolte* the Théâtre du Travail could offer nothing before the autumn, because it had to begin rehearsing a new play. Despite the break-up of his marriage, Camus pushed resolutely ahead. He realized that the Théâtre du Travail had to evolve, that it could not keep repeating the same message-laden plays. Techniques of audience-involvement must be refined and fresh subjects must be attacked. In September he started the rehearsals for Gorki's *Lower Depths*, which was performed in November. A friendly critic said that the first act was jerky and that the actors were amateurish, although they improved later.[23] Next came even more difficult plays – Ben Jonson's *The Silent Woman*, Pushkin's *Don Juan* and Aeschylus' *Prometheus in Chains*.

Camus liked Jonson's sheer theatrical flair, which offered the troupe a chance to learn. He also arranged for some old English music to be played, which was another attempt to create a mood and draw in the audience. Moreover Jonson was supposed to counterbalance the political plays. More successful, however, was *Don Juan*, which was presented at the Maison de Culture as part of the Pushkin gala. Jacques Heurgon gave a lecture and Bénisti contributed a picture of Don Juan. In the *Revue Algérienne* Paul Raffi wrote that the acting showed improvement and that the scenery was excellent. Instead of cluttering the stage with furniture or with lavish backdrops,the troupe had built simple, stylized scenery. It remained the same for most of the play, so that the few changes – the presence or absence of a crucifix – made an impact. Raffi also noted that the play was 'far removed from politics'.[24] This is not entirely true for the tribute to Russia had a political intent; but Camus was trying to go beyond the simplistic, committed theatre advocated by *Monde* and *Vendredi*. He was willing to do light comedy and found time to put on Courteline's *L'article 330*; but his interest lay elsewhere.

The troupe's boldest venture was *Prometheus in Chains*, performed in March 1937. Once more a loudspeaker poured philosophical discourse onto the audience to ensure that they grasped the message of revolt. But, as Jeanne Sicard pointed out, the revolution was not solely a marxist or political one. There was a general problem: 'the presence of the inhuman at the core of life'; the drama lay in Prometheus' display of grandeur: 'his greatness lies not in his submission to suffering but in his defiance of the injustice and irrationality of what he calls Fate.'[25] Prometheus is a brother of the Asturian miners, but he is also a universal symbol and an unashamed hero. This is emphasized by the production, for the actors wore masks which were designed to eliminate their individual psychology and to fix them as examples of the human condition.

Actually there had been a dispute about the masks. They were made by Bénisti who wanted them to be brutal, more Algerian than Greek; they were to stress the simple fact of man facing death. But Marie Vitton argued that Bénisti's masks were too crude and, exploiting the prestige of her Frenchness, she convinced Camus. So the masks were altered, which annoyed Bénisti who felt that Camus was not being Algerian enough. There was a touch of the barbarian in Bénisti too. But the stylization of the masks was retained and the break with the topicality of *Le Temps du Mépris* was deliberate.

Camus was heading towards a very different kind of drama.

The more intense bond between spectators and troupe was to engender in the theatre those exceptional moments of insight when man confronts his existence. If human activity was, as Camus felt, a series of games played out in the presence of death, then the theatre, sanctuary of game-playing, could freeze this presence. So Camus' concept has a 'philosophical' aspect. It is not philosophical in the usual sense of the term, for there is nothing much to understand. In the 1950's Camus would grow angry when his plays were dismissed as abstract or speculative. The moments of insight reduce themselves to the central, monotonous experience of death. 'Philosophical' – once more 'religious' would be as good a word – means the absence of diversity, of individual psychology. Such theatre tends to become heroic because it stresses the conflicts and the exceptional. Camus does not talk openly about heroism but he does use the term 'virile'. Indeed it is a code-word within the group and even the women use it. Jeanne Sicard says that Prometheus is virile because he does not concern himself with suffering or pleasure, does not treat himself as a person. He transcends his own character when he confronts the eagle. Stylistically, this leads to rhetoric and Camus' own plays will be rhetorical. Politics is not absent for, to reverse Jeanne Sicard's statement, the marxist revolution is one part of Prometheus' own. But Camus' concept was closer to traditional tragedy than to the committed theatre of the day.

This in turn led to clashes with the PCA and the break came in mid-1937. There were three overlapping quarrels: between Camus and Prédhumeau, between Camus and a faction of the group led by Jean Degueurce and between Camus and the new PCA leader, Deloche. Of these the last was the most important and it shaped the other two.

Prédhumeau was an exuberant, voluble man, a camper who organized youth groups for the PCA. No great thinker, he was a born agitator and street-corner debater. He was a member of the Théâtre du Travail and had acted well in *Prometheus*. In June 1937 he deliberately picked a quarrel, when he accused Camus of helping himself to the Maison de Culture's funds. The accusation was preposterous, if only because the Maison had no funds. It lived from day to day and, if anything, Camus and Jeanne Sicard were putting their own money into it. Yet there was a furious scene where Prédhumeau hurled insults at

Camus. An astonished crowd gathered and Camus turned white. After listening to the harangue for some minutes, he leapt at Prédhumeau. There was a moment of silence and then Prédhumeau backed off. Much bigger than Camus and considered something of a brawler, he did not want to fight and was frightened by Camus' cold fury. Camus went for him again and had Prédhumeau by the throat but the others intervened and dragged him away. Only at rare moments in his life did Camus reveal the violence which he felt and disliked in himself. Now he was angered by the attack on his integrity and by the split within the team. The crowd that was watching made him resolve in his masculine, Spanish way not to back down. After he and Prédhumeau had been separated, he recovered his control but he was intransigent. Expulsion, he declared, was the only way to deal with people like Prédhumeau. A meeting of the Maison de Culture's council, dominated by the PCA, was called. It condemned Prédhumeau and expelled him from the Maison, although not from the party.[26] Camus was not a man to forgive and he had both his friends and the party behind him. He had won the first round.

But his position was weakened by a split within the Théâtre du Travail. Already there was tension between Camus and Thomas-Rouault, nephew of the painter. Rouault had his own theatre group but he had joined forces with Camus to produce *The Silent Woman*. He found himself taking second place to Camus and resented it. When an intermediary was sent to placate him, he burst into a rage and declared that he felt for Camus 'a hatred that would follow him to the ends of the earth'.[27] The dispute was theatrical and Algerian but it grew more serious when Thomas-Rouault allied himself with another painter, Maurice Girard, and with Jean Degueurce. Degueurce came of a Protestant and anarchist family which had discovered its true vocation in communism. He was precisely the kind of dedicated militant whom Camus half-admired and half-disliked. Degueurce believed that he had been placed on earth to spread the gospel of marxism.[28]

He and Girard opposed the direction which the Théâtre du Travail was taking. Their definition of proletarian theatre was narrow: the play should have a direct, useful message. They were pleased by *Le Temps du Mépris* and by the fragments of *Révolte* in which Degueurce acted. They accepted Aeschylus and

Gorki but Ben Jonson was too much. When they demanded a return to the earlier style, Camus refused and his closest friends like Jeanne Sicard and Marguerite Dobrenn supported him. They were at best half-hearted Communists, more interested in Jonson than in Marx. They considered the Maison a useful vehicle for their various projects but no more. As for Camus, he was determined to press ahead with a theatre that had the human condition as its subject. Ever mobile, he wanted to explore the techniques which his group had discovered.

But Degueurce's criticism stemmed from a purely political split within the PCA. By now its tightrope act between Arabs and Europeans, anti-colonialism and anti-Fascism had grown perilous. It was talking of a Russian-style solution for Algeria: a Moslem republic within the Communist French state. Such nonsense was a sign of desperation. The PCA's position could become credible, only if the Blum-Viollette project were introduced. But the Popular Front had many other battles to fight and the Algerian right was too strong. From Paris the PCF reiterated the line that France and Algeria must stand together against the common enemy – Fascism. Independence was indeed a goal but the time was not ripe; later perhaps, after Hitler's overthrow ... Messali's protests grew stronger and Arab discontent increased with the riots of Sidi-bel-Abbès in February 1937. By now Chaintron was gone. He saw *Lower Depths* in November '36 and left shortly afterwards. His successor Deloche was, in Poncet's phrase, 'less than brilliant'. Anyway, his task was difficult. The party was growing restive and some of the European members were frightened by the influx of poor Arabs whom Chaintron had won over. Little had been done to change the mentality of the Europeans; little could have been done.

In January 1937 Blum dissolved the 'Etoile nord-africaine'. Messali promptly rebaptized it Parti Populaire Algérien (PPA) and continued his agitation. This was taking place within the wider splits caused by the Popular Front. The mayors denounced any talk of Arab reform and the administration obstructed the government. Never had it been so clear that France did not control Algeria. In March the unions went on strike at Kouif and the police fired at them. As the split between right and left widened, so Blum gave way to the right. This in turn made the PCA's position more difficult. The rift within its ranks grew along with the rift between the two communities. Once more the PCA's crisis was the crisis of French Algeria.

On July 14, 1937, just as Camus' aesthetic dilemmas were at their height, Messali organized a huge PPA procession in Algiers and was arrested again. By now relations between Communists and nationalists had broken down. The nationalists claimed that the Communists had not only failed to protest against the banning of the Etoile but had even denounced its members to the police. The Communists denied this, but unconvincingly. Many people felt the PCA was pleased that its rival had been banned and that it had less competition.[29] In turn the Communists denounced the nationalists as provocateurs who were dividing the two communities and playing into the hands of the right. *Lutte sociale* was virulent, if unoriginal, in its attacks on Messali.

Camus was drawn into the polemic. His instinctive sympathy for Arabs made him disagree with the PCA's line. He began to argue with the leadership and he was not without support. De Fréminville, of course, sided with him and Arab leaders like Ouzegane felt that the party had gone too far and sacrificed too much for the tepid policies of the Popular Front. Broadening the debate, Camus argued that the PCA should never have entered a coalition with the Radicals, who were the champions of colonialism. The debate raged in *Lutte sociale* and Camus' position was shared by a minority within the party.

During the summer Camus was called to a federation meeting at Belcourt. A friend of Poncet, who was present, remembers that Camus was extremely angry. He repeated the view that the PCA should have helped the arrested PPA militants and that it had betrayed the Arab cause. He refused to tone down his statements and seemed determined to get himself expelled. Deloche, showing none of Chaintron's tact, dismissed Camus as a Trotskyite. Camus left the party and took his friends with him. The Maison de Culture collapsed and the PCA's cultural policy was ruined, although it continued to support Camus' ventures. On the Arab question no concession was made to the minority. Ouzegane submitted to the majority and remained on the central committee, although he was demoted. Today he feels that the form which Camus' protest took was '*gauchiste* and revolutionary' but that he was right on the issue itself.[30]

Certainly the PCA declined after '37. By the following year

Arab membership in Algiers was down and Messali did better among Arab voters in the cantonal elections. This caused fresh polemics, during which the epithets of 'provocateurs' and 'informers' were once more bandied around. The PCA's Arab leaders tried to prevent a complete break between the party and the Arab masses but they were unsuccessful. From this time on the nationalists, slowly and inexorably, drew ahead of the Communists. To mask its weakness the party launched a huge campaign of support for Republican Spain but the Arabs were, understandably, unimpressed. By now Camus was gone, as were De Fréminville and Girard, who disagreed with Camus about Ben Jonson but agreed about Arabs.

Camus left the party as a left-wing rebel who criticized the compromises of the Popular Front and the Arab policy. Yet it is wrong to take Deloche or Ouzegane literally and imagine that he proposed policies that were revolutionary. On the Arab issue, he defended the nationalists when they were banned and persecuted by the police. His main criticism of the PCA was that it showed no solidarity, no fraternity. But this did not mean that he supported Messali's bid for independence. Camus' stand remained, as his *Alger-Républicain* articles show, assimilationist and very close to the PCA.[31] Communist policy, as defined by Thorez who came to Algiers in 1939, was based on the concept of the Mediterranean medley. Like Camus, Thorez talked about the Romans, the Berbers and the Maltese and he made the obligatory mention of Saint Augustine. Algerian identity was made up of these many strands, one of which was Arab. There was no question of a clash among them and certainly no sense that Arabness could win out. All this was reminiscent of Camus' Maison de Culture lecture.

In reality Camus was leaving the party for a variety of reasons. He had never been a very orthodox Communist and he was too much of an outsider to accept party dictates for long. He came to feel that Bénisti and Poncet had been right after all. The daily round of organizing meetings, signing petitions and selling newspapers was a tedious chore; but the demand that he sacrifice to the party his theatre and his sympathy for Arabs was quite exorbitant.

He began to feel that Grenier had advised him badly and this feeling grew stronger when he read *l'Esprit de l'Orthodoxie*. Grenier condemned the 1930's demand for absolutes and messiahs. Anticipating the main theme of *l'Homme Révolté*, he declared that marxist messianism 'justifies in advance every kind of massacre'.[32] Grenier was engaged in one of the *NRF*'s complex debates. Political commitment destroyed, he felt, the key *NRF* values of doubt and complexity. The intellectual should not ignore politics but he should not substitute political judgements for moral and aesthetic judgements.

Grenier's position was close to Gide's. Having admired the Communists, Gide had recanted in *Retour de l'URSS*. He had visited Russia which had appalled him. But *Retour* is as much a book about the *NRF* as it is a book about Russia. Gide had supported the Communist Party as an act of heresy. But by 1936 pro-Communist sentiments were so strong among French intellectuals that they constituted a new orthodoxy. This was one reason why Gide abandoned the party.

Grenier understood him and he attacked Malraux who was taking the opposite stand. In *L'Espoir* Malraux had, so Grenier maintained, shown that he was willing to accept Communist domination in order to act. Malraux' need to act and to undergo the transformation of self that comes only from facing death was so great that he exalted 'Bolshevik man', the Communist militant who sacrifices his life to his actions. But Grenier reiterates that the intellectual's role is to doubt and not to convert, to ponder and not to act.

Although Camus was a doer, he agreed with Grenier. He must also have noticed another theme in *L'Esprit de l'Orthodoxie*. Grenier discusses the 'boursiers' who join the PC because they wish to remain in touch with the working class from which their education is separating them. This was nonsense, writes Grenier, both because no party could speak for the working classes in all their sceptical diversity and because the 'boursiers' were intellectuals. They might be ex-workers but they were not workers. Grenier had learned this from watching Camus and Camus knew that Grenier was right.

Camus was also brooding on another book. Aldous Huxley's *Ends and Means* was published in 1937 and translated immediately into French. In it Camus discovered his own dislike of totalitarianism. Huxley castigates the Soviet Union and the belief that history has some absolute meaning. As well as advocating pacifism and criticizing violence, Huxley makes a plea for moral values. They are not a luxury because the

94

methods used are themselves a part of history: 'the end cannot justify the means, for the simple and obvious reason that the means employed determine the nature of the ends produced.'[33] This delighted Camus who encouraged his friends to read the book. Huxley was giving substance to the moral sense which Camus had possessed since his boyhood.

For his split with the PCA was a matter of morality rather than politics. His code of honour demanded that he defend the persecuted nationalists. The PCA argued that the nationalists could be discarded because they were an obstacle to the goal of revolution; the absolute nature of revolution justified such surrenders. Camus, equally absolutist, argued that the PCA must defend the nationalists. It might not do them or the party much good but that was unimportant; the militant's duty was to try his hardest. A pragmatist might argue that the PCA should have defended the nationalists a little while pursuing its alliance with the Radicals. But Camus would not agree: there could be no compromise.

So he was not as close to Grenier as he seemed. The intellectual's role was not merely to doubt and to criticize; the *NRF* was falsely neutral and needlessly complex. Camus was of Malraux' generation in believing that the intellectual must risk and fight for his brand of truth. The trouble was that Camus' intransigence prevented him from acting. Malraux was willing to pay the price: if action meant rubbing shoulders with Stalinists or supporting the repression of the May riots, then so be it. But Camus refused to dirty his hands because efficacy was less important than morality and the end mattered less than the means; indeed morality and means were absolute things. This might have led Camus to abandon the political arena but it did not. He disagreed with Grenier and Gide that there was a separate domain of morality and aesthetics. Politics and morality ran together: the militant must be just. Art could be revolutionary, as Camus would try to demonstrate in his *Alger-Républicain* articles.

The break with the PCA left a scar on Camus. He kept until his death that incurable suspicion of Communists which is the mark of the ex-Communist. When *Doctor Zhivago* was published in the West, Camus immediately began organizing a collection for Pasternak because he was certain the Russians would expel him. Of course, he had real disputes with the PC after the war but they do not in themselves explain his distrust. Moreover, Camus never worked out a coherent political position, never resolved the dilemma of the moralist in politics. This would be crucial at the Liberation and during the Algerian War.

In '37 the break with the PCA was yet another defeat which followed his divorce. Yet Camus, the battler, turned it into a liberation. If the Théâtre du Travail was finished, the Théâtre de l'Equipe would replace it. If he could not be a Communist, he would be a crusading journalist. His life was a series of such struggles, carried on to the rhythm of his tuberculosis. His friends often noticed that he was ill but they did not inquire further. If they did, Camus said he had 'flu.

In the summer his illness flared up again and he went with De Fréminville to Savoy, where the mountain air was supposed to do him good. The countryside was strange and he treated it like an adversary; he wrestled with it, trying to impose himself on it. Outside their chalet there was a solitary pine which defied him until he laughed and accepted its strangeness. One night he coughed blood for hours, while De Fréminville stayed up to tend him. Next day the sun was shining and Camus felt better.

As if to celebrate his recovery, he went off to Italy with Jeanne and Marguerite. They visited Pisa which Camus liked: 'Pisa, alive and austere ... stretched out along the severe Arno.'[34] In Florence they realized how little money they had so they stayed in a very cheap boarding-house and ate great mounds of spaghetti. They tramped the city and went to the museums. Camus liked Giotto just as he liked early Greek sculpture. Giotto did not attempt to explain the world or to explore its diversity. The barbarian Camus ignored what is, after all, the main theme of Florentine culture: the emphasis on human beauty and harmony which is found in Botticelli or Michelangelo. Instead he stressed the clear contours of the Tuscan countryside, its bareness and brownness. His Florence is narrow and uncomplicated like Algiers.

The same applies to Fiesole to which he made the obligatory pilgrimage. He liked the monastery and the Franciscan monks. Despite his unkind comments about Fouchet, he often imagined himself a monk – it was a pose that amused his friends who teased him about the vows of chastity. In the *Carnets* he calls the Fiesole Franciscans 'men of my race' because they welcomed poverty and opened themselves to nature.[35] To the Franciscans the world is beautiful because it is a map of God; without the divine presence it would be hideous. To Camus its beauty is caught up with its emptiness and yet there might still, he felt, be monks and saints.

He himself saw the Italian trip as a rebirth: 'Today I feel free of my past and of everything I have lost.'[36] Without Simone and the PC he would face the future. Other battles and other attacks of tuberculosis awaited him but he felt, if not optimistic, then hopeful. He returned to Algeria and to a teaching job that he had been offered at Sidi-bel-Abbès.

Earlier he had received another blow: he would not be able to take the 'agrégation' because he could not pass the physical examination. This meant that, while he might still get a job teaching at a grammar school, he could not hope to rise high or to teach at a university. For the ambitious Camus this was a setback. He had virtually no alternative but to accept a post at Sidi-bel-Abbès. In October he went there, stayed one day and caught the next train back. The ugliness of the town, the school and his work bothered him less, so he told Jacques Heurgon, than the mediocrity. If he stayed he might grow accustomed to it, for it was more insidious than ugliness; he might in a few years turn into a provincial hack.[37] Rather than be stranded in a remote village with dreary colleagues and pupils, he preferred to stay in Algiers and continue forecasting the weather or selling spare parts for cars. Jeanne Sicard, who had been appointed to Tlemcen, did the same. They both received much admiration from their friends, who felt that they had been bold and had risked their future. It was the gamblers' choice.

Yet Camus was a prudent gambler. He thought once more of leaving for Paris so he wrote to Gabriel Audisio, asking him whether he could get a job. He listed his qualifications: diploma, actor, apprentice-writer. Audisio replied that he could promise nothing definite but that Camus would almost certainly get something. Camus hesitated and then decided not to leave. He explained why: the risk was too great. Poverty, he repeated, was never fruitful. If he had to scrape a living on the Paris streets, he would be ground down as surely as in Sidi-bel-Abbès. Better to remain in Algiers with the meteorological office and his friends.[38] So he continued his useless calculations and did not get a real job until *Alger-Républicain* was started one year later.

But in autumn '37 he and his friends were full of plans. Jeanne and Marguerite were now living in the Maison Fichu, a big house which stood on a hill outside Algiers. The rent was low, there was lots of space and the balcony overlooked the sea. Everyone who needed a place to live moved in for a while, including Camus. De Fréminville came and painted the wall of the living-room bright red so that it would clash with the blue sky. There was a stray dog which Camus christened Kierk after Kierkegaard because it looked mangy and anguished. There were also two cats called Cali and Gula; Gula was a thin black question mark prone to fits of madness, while Cali was white and sulky. The house looked less like a dwelling than a stage-set so it was a fine headquarters for the troupe.

It was always full of people and Camus wrote a poem about it which shows his ambivalent need for friendship: 'Where the world stops/a friendship is born.'[39] But soon the world would begin to move again, spinning towards death and leaving the friendship behind. Camus felt that the 'world' was present in the Maison Fichu so he christened it 'the House-in-front-of-the-world'. Because of its exposed site it was radiant with light. Algerian nature was personified and seemed to be watching the group. While sunbathing there, Camus lived intense moments of pleasure and of communication with nature. In *La Mort Heureuse* he describes the Maison Fichu: 'Abandoned to the world, it hung in the dazzling sky above the glittering dance of the countryside'.[40] It was a part of the pantheistic universe and it reawakened in Camus his old sense that God was a question of beauty.

With Jeanne and Marguerite lived Christiane Galindo, another Oran girl with whom Camus had a relationship. Almost none of the group knew that Christiane was more to Camus than a friend; the two concealed their intimacy. Christiane delighted him because she was pagan and natural, a welcome change from Simone. She went swimming with him, visited Tipasa and walked for miles over the hills. Camus leaves this portrait of her in *La Mort Heureuse*: 'She had a solid, well-shaped body, skin the colour of brown bread and an animal sense of what is important. No one grasped better than she the secret language of the trees, the sea and the wind.'[41] Jeanne Sicard treated Christiane like a younger sister and Camus felt in part like a brother to her. But along with their friendship went a tenderness. Christiane typed Camus' manuscripts and he talked to her about his writing. They remained close long after their most intense relationship had ceased.

Camus' male friends thought that he was merely a seducer. During the years after he broke with Simone he slept with dozens of girls. He was good-looking and he encountered little resistance. In part he was no different from other swaggering young men in Algiers and, like them, he boasted of his conquests. But he was also sensitive to the sheer beauty of women – the lines of the body, the grace of a movement. Again and again he uses the language of ballet to describe them. Nor is it a coincidence that Christiane was frank and natural. Women were a part of the nature which Camus so loved. Contact with them involved a dehumanization which suited the seducer and the pantheist: 'in a body which I draw close to me, I discover that strange joy which descends from the sky towards the sea.'[42] Love-making was less a moment of intimacy between two people than a participation in natural beauty. But, just as nature was indifferent, so love-making was cold. When women drew close to Camus, he moved away.

Love, according to Camus, could scarcely exist and yet he pursued it at least as much as he pursued seduction. Only the women who succeeded in drawing close to him perceived the secret side of Camus' nature and they are, naturally, reluctant to discuss it. But it is clear that he needed and revelled in women's tenderness. To Christiane and others he revealed far more of his vulnerability than he showed his male friends. This does not mean he was quite sincere with them: sentiment is an excellent weapon of seduction. But Camus hid his very strong emotions so well that they had to break out somewhere. So he fell in love and conducted affairs of passion that ran alongside sexual affairs.

Tenderness and indifference ran together in Camus, and both are revealed in a friendship which he began in the autumn of '37. Blanche Balain was the pretty, vivacious daughter of a cavalry officer who had retired to Algeria. She met Marie Vitton who introduced her to Camus. He promptly brought her into the Equipe troupe and gave her a part in *Le Paquebot Tenacity*.

She showed him her poems and he helped her to publish them. By her own admission Camus dazzled her with his Spanish good-looks, the breadth of his reading and the way he dominated the troupe. He showed her his favourite Algiers cafés, took her to the port and admired her. For a few months they were close and then they quarrelled. Blanche wanted the lead role in *Karamazov* and Camus would not give it to her; she felt snubbed and refused to be one of his many interests. Yet Camus clearly did not consider her just another woman. They continued their friendship and he told her about his illness, his poverty and his hope of finding work at *Alger-Républicain*. She felt that he needed her, although she knew better than to exaggerate this.

Blanche's poems *La Sève du Jour* were published by Edmond Charlot, another member of the group. The talkative, energetic Charlot ran a bookshop which doubled as a lending library and turned into a publishing house. This was another piece of teamwork because Camus was the chief reader and De Fréminville the printer. They decided to publish a series called *Méditerranéens*, which was to offer specimens of new Algerian writing. Camus contributed *L'Envers et l'Endroit*, Jean Grenier *Santa-Cruz*, De Fréminville a prose piece called *A la Vue de la Méditerranée* and Fouchet and Clot volumes of poetry.

Another project was the magazine *Rivages*, also published by Charlot. This, too, was designed to preach the gospel of Mediterranean unity and Algerian primitivism. '*Rivages* is born out of an excess of life,' Camus exclaims in the introduction, 'it is the first fruit of the welling sap.'[43] Actually *Rivages* had a short life because Charlot was too fond of books and writers to be a commercially successful publisher; he ran into financial troubles and *Rivages* died after the second number. Camus had contributed a chunk of *Noces*, De Fréminville the fragment of a novel, Gabriel Audisio some poems and Jeanne Sicard a translation of Cervantes. Translations were an important part of a magazine that stressed the unity of the Mediterranean. *Rivages* published translations of Eugenio Montale, of Lorca, who was much admired by these supporters of Republican Spain, and of Andalusian folk songs.

Meanwhile Camus was working at his own writing, conducting a deeper meditation on the Mediterranean and on his own life. Many of the experiences of these years find their way into his early books. The rebirth of Italy is described in *Noces*, the jealousy he felt for Simone is obliquely present in *La Mort Hereuse* and the debate about absolutes animates *Le Mythe de Sisyphe*. But Camus says less in his writing than in his life. The Camus who wrote was not the gay companion who conversed in the House-in-front-of-the-world. The love, which he had felt for Simone, is present in his writing only as a painful absence. Even as he threw himself into politics, theatre and friendships, even as he dispensed his energy and demonstrated his mobility, Camus pursued in his work the few, old Manichean images that haunted him – his mother, the bay of Algiers, the silence of evening on the streets.

Of course he evolved. *L'Envers et l'Endroit* offers ambiguous images of oneness; *La Mort Heureuse* forces man to confront death but depicts this as joyous and innocent; *L'Etranger* strands man in a dualistic universe, although the urge to oneness is as strong as ever. By now the reaction against Grenier is clear and Camus has decided there are limits which he cannot transgress. Meanwhile an apprenticeship in writing has taken place. Camus has struggled to strip away the rhetoric, to talk of others and not of himself, to be concise. He was demonstrating his ascetic nature. Writing, he once said, was an act of violence against himself.

His faithful troupe, now rechristened the Equipe, allowed him, even as he was starting *Caligula*, to deepen his vision of the theatre. Thomas-Rouault and the rival band struggled to put on one play and then gave up. Camus went ahead, reiterating the concept of the team. The Equipe hoped to form an association of spectators who would be considered part of the troupe. The innovations of staging were to be maintained, as were the goals of directness and immediacy. The insistence on joint creation should not, however, blind one to Camus' leading role. He was the one who talked of group endeavour; the others felt they were followers.

If he was exacting, he had the example of Copeau before him. The two agreed that 'it is precisely technique which frees the emotion'.[44] There were no short-cuts to lyricism; author, director and actors must subordinate themselves to the work itself. Reacting against the facile brilliance of the pre-1914 Paris theatre, Copeau insisted that the play was more important than the staging or the stars. In a characteristic *NRF* manner, he battled for austerity. Camus, reacting against the ostentation of the Algiers opera, agreed.

He decided that technique was important because it reversed the perceptions of ordinary life. During rehearsals the director dominated the actor but, once the play opened, he was eclipsed by him just as the actor was eclipsed by his role. There remained only the work which was a genuine and false fountain of emotion. This upside-down world was to Camus a mirror of the death-ridden universe. Since it was false it contained that inhuman quality that Jeanne Sicard had mentioned. Since it was a common creation of the audience and troupe, it embraced the heroic struggle against the inhuman.

Camus looked more and more to other periods, he selected difficult plays and he searched for pure game-playing. He continued to put on the Courteline farce *L'Article 330*. The Equipe did it so often that they began to invent their own lines and by the end there was nothing of Courteline left. But Camus also turned to the periods of great tragedy – Greece, Elizabethan England, the Spain of the Golden Age. He thought of putting on *Hamlet* and *Othello* but his own vision was different from Shakespeare's. For him there was no Fortinbras who might arrive after Hamlet's death to announce some order, however dubious. The Equipe talks little about order and much about violence. The theatre must shock, must demonstrate the arbitrariness of the upside-down universe and must set its Prometheuses against the sterile Algerian countryside. Clearly such a concept is less grand and more ironic than traditional tragedy.

The Equipe's first production was Fernand da Rojas' play *La Célestine*, performed in December '37. The *Echo d'Alger* reported that Marie Vitton's costumes, made to look like playing cards, were gloriously unreal but that the play was too long and too difficult.[45] The more popular *Paquebot Tenacity* by Charles Vildrac was counterpoint to da Rojas and pleased the Algiers audience more. It was also Jeanne Sicard's great triumph for, playing the café-owner's wife, she transformed herself into an ugly hag and gave a performance which her friends still remember. Next Camus returned to more difficult plays and put on Gide's *Retour de l'Enfant Prodigue*. This was an acting triumph for Camus himself. 'He has made great progress as an actor. He is a tormented, uncertain prodigal son and he declaims his lines with great power', said the *Echo*.[46] The play was slanted to emphasize not the resignation of the prodigal but the departure of his younger brother. When the brother left, he passed through a high, narrow door which Louis Miquel designed to illustrate the splendour and miseries of freedom. This was a good example of the Equipe's stylized scenery. Decor was not important as a lavish display nor as a realistic setting; it should not be applauded, Miquel felt, when the curtain went up. But it could be used freely to emphasize a mood or a theme. Miquel liked bright expanses of colour. In *Prometheus* he had used red against grey to emphasize the hero's struggle; now his door was orange against red.

Retour was an apprenticeship for the group's most ambitious productions – *Karamazov* and *Playboy of the Western World*. Dostoevsky's novel had already been adapted for the stage by Copeau, whose notebooks Camus had read. He was even more exacting than usual during the rehearsals but then there was a last-minute hitch. When the costumes, which for once had been made to order, arrived they were too opera-ish. Once more cursing the Algiers obsession with opera, Camus sent out for old-fashioned frock-coats, which were at least sober. The one in which he was to play Ivan was far too large and he went around telling the others that Ivan had clearly never gone hungry. He chose to play the part in a subdued, frozen style. While the other actors flaunted their Dostoevskian wildness, Ivan-Camus stood in the centre of the stage, impenetrable and remote. It was a part that Camus would remember with joy. In the '50's he would play it in restaurants or during meetings at Gallimard and he would watch his friends to make sure they were watching him. It seemed to him the epitome of the theatre because it stressed both the part and the act of acting.

Playboy was supposed to demonstrate the cruelty of the theatre. A series of advertisements in *Alger-Républicain*, probably written by Camus himself, claim that the play is 'bitter and disenchanted', a 'virile, hardheaded lesson' and 'a pitiless study of human stupidity'.[47] The primitivism of Western Ireland intrigued Camus and reminded him of Algeria. He liked the farcical scenes and the gambler, Christy Mahon, whom he played himself. It was a flamboyant performance, quite different from Ivan. Wearing a green shirt with wide sleeves, Camus rampaged around the stage. Between acts he was as excited as the spectators but he still laughed at himself. His production was designed to emphasize movement, which in turn was to indicate the arbitrariness of the action. Camus noted that the crime of parricide is committed once by passion and once by calculation; in neither case are there scruples and each time the villagers are full of admiration. Camus loved the scenes where Christy boasts of his crime. Society scarcely exists and its only rules are those of the games at which the Playboy excels. All this is presented without the solemnity of traditional tragedy and with a black humour.

The starting-point of Camus' own plays was already present. He had moved from the naively committed *Le Temps du Mépris* through *Prometheus* to *Karamazov* and *Playboy*. Repeated talk of fraternity and directness should not blind one to the complexity of this evolution, which runs from the singing of the Internationale to the mock-heroism of murder. The spectator is still drawn into the play but he enters a shifting, upside-down world where morality and logic, left and right are absent. Camus was hesitating between a theatre which would pit man against the inhuman and resemble traditional tragedy and a theatre that would strand man in an universe of nonsense, leaving him to lament, fall silent or be furious. This is the more modern kind of theatre but Camus had not given up the traditional kind. The contradiction would plague him throughout his career as a dramatist. Still *Caligula*, with its horrified sense of human limits and its gallows humour, follows naturally on *Karamazov* and *Playboy*.

The Théâtre de l'Equipe is important because it shows Camus moving beyond the Maison de Culture and the PCA and because it also shows a happy Camus. The people who worked with him remember these productions with pleasure, as he did himself. In the '50's, when he looked back longingly on pre-war Algeria, the Equipe seemed an image of carefree fraternity. During the mid and late '30's Camus' best moments were spent rehearsing and making scenery. The theatre consoled him for disappointments in his private and political life and it gave him the strength to battle on. But by mid-1938 a job was opening up that would turn into an adventure: Camus began work on *Alger-Républicain*.

4

The Adventure of Alger-Républicain

The founding of *Alger-Républicain* was announced during a Théâtre de l'Equipe performance and was applauded by the audience. Many subscribers to the plays were shareholders in the new paper and conversely it would publicize the Equipe. Bénisti and Poncet were both shareholders and felt that *Alger-Républicain* was not just another paper; it belonged to them and was their mouthpiece. It was the expression of the Popular Front and a response to the right-wing *Dépêche* and the moderate yet sporadically pro-Fascist *Echo*.

It was founded by Jean-Pierre Faure, a businessman with interests in property whose father was art historian and left-winger Elie Faure. Jean-Pierre Faure had the right contacts and could turn for advice to men like Aragon or Malraux. He gathered around him collaborators who came from the liberal middle-classes of Algiers – lawyers, architects and teachers. They in turn reached out to the unions. Roger Menicucci, an official in the postal union, would write for the paper. There were also Arab supporters: K. Mackaci, A. Turqui and Lechani Mohammed were on the board.[1]

The paper's aim was to unite. Like the Popular Front itself it was to bring together Socialists, Radicals and Communists. This was even more difficult in Algeria than in France because few Algerian Radicals supported the Popular Front. While welcoming *Alger-Républicain*, the PCA stood aloof. It was afraid that the paper would be tepid on the Arab question and it was still deluding itself that it could recapture the support of the Arab masses. The Socialists were the strongest group within the *Alger-Républicain* board but the paper was determined not to become the voice of any one party. When obliged to discuss the issues which divided the parties of the Popular Front it lapsed into vagueness and it published few editorials for fear they might widen the splits.

The paper's general line was stated in the first few numbers. It expected to have as enemies 'the feudal barons of industry, agriculture and banking'. It was the foe of international Fascism, of anti-semitism, of Italian designs on North Africa and of Franco. It condemned the Algiers right and conducted a special campaign, led by Camus, against the mayor Rozis. Conversely it would defend the gains of the Popular Front, especially the forty-hour week and the wage increases. Following the strategy of the period, it talked less of the 'working class' than of the 'masses' and less of 'socialism' than of 'democracy'. It was to stress the Arab question and to work for 'political equality' for them. The goal, clearly stated, was assimilation: 'the complete fusion of minds and hearts in this our overseas France'. Actually this programme was less simple than it seemed and there was a foreign policy dilemma. While condemning the Munich agreements, the paper advocated peace because war or threat of war would destroy the hope of social reform. This meant coming to some sort of agreement with Hitler, yet *Alger-Républicain* criticized the policy of non-intervention in Spain and kept warning against Fascist aggression.

It was supposed not merely to advocate different policies from the *Dépêche* or the *Echo* but to be itself a different kind of newspaper. It dismissed the rest of the Algiers press as the mouthpiece of the big colons and it lamented the corruption of the French press, which served vested interests by providing distorted information. *Alger-Républicain* was to be owned by its readers. Jean-Pierre Faure assembled five thousand people who bought shares at one hundred francs each. However many shares one person bought, he received only one vote at shareholders' meetings. This was to prevent special interests from taking over the paper. No share could be bought except under the holder's own name and no share could be sold without the board's permission. The board itself was chosen from the shareholders; its members were unpaid and were not allowed to hold political office. When one of them, Zévaco, decided to campaign for the senate, he had to resign from the board.

All this was to enable the paper to be objective. Partisan in its support for the Popular Front, it professed the strictest objectivity in its presentation of the news. In practice its organization was neither as complex nor as rigid as it seemed. Faure was appointed as the spokesman for the board and he gave complete freedom to the editor. Most of the shareholders had no say in how the paper was run.

This did not much matter but *Alger-Républicain* laboured under a more important handicap – the moment at which it appeared. Its origins go back at least to 1937 when Faure discussed the project with his friends. But firstly there were delays in raising money and then the man who was responsible for the printing was killed in a car crash. So the first number did not appear until October 6, 1938. By this time Daladier and the Radical Party were in power, the Blum-Viollette project had been defeated in the senate and the Munich agreement had been signed. The Popular Front was finished and the paper's role was to be 'a prophet of disaster'. It announced the bombing of Barcelona, the oppression of the Czechs, Daladier's rule by decree and the policy of deflation. It was an organ of protest and of defiance rather than of cohesive support.

This role suited the editor, Pascal Pia, who was to become, after Jean Grenier, the second great influence on Camus. When Faure went to France to look for an editor, Aragon suggested Pia who was working at *Ce Soir*, not as a reporter but as news-editor. He was dissatisfied with his job and was feeling restless, so he agreed at once to come to Algiers.

Pia was much more than a journalist. He came of a working-class family and his father was killed during the 1914 war – already a link with Camus. Pia had to do all kinds of jobs while he got some education and for a while he was in the merchant navy. But his passion was for books and in the early 1920's he worked for little publishing houses, spying out first editions, precious binding and erotic works. He met Malraux who was doing the same and the two became friends. Malraux shared Pia's love of erudition, a personally-acquired and savoured erudition that was closer to luxury than to pedantry. He also liked Pia's bluntness and independence. The two spent hours in art galleries and museums, discussing Eastern art and African sculpture. There was a vagabond strain in Pia and he almost accompanied Malraux on the trip to Indo China where Malraux ended up in prison. Clara Malraux was suspicious of Pia, fearing that he encouraged her husband to wander, but the friendship persisted.

Pia had already plunged into dadaism. As early as 1921, before he was twenty years old, he began writing in *Disque Vert*, a little Belgian magazine that was tinged with dadaism and surrealism. 'For us happiness lies in anarchy,' he proclaims, 'out of anarchy will come a new physics and a new poetry.'[2] There is a preciousness, characteristic both of adolescence and of the early 1920's, in these pieces; some of them are prose-poems, full of artificial twists of language, others are fragments, sketches of novels that lead nowhere. But Pia was no dilettante and his anarchism was genuine. He praises Jarry because Ubu's logic is rigorous to the point of absurdity and he criticizes Thoreau, because he is too cautious and does not unleash his imagination.*

Pia's truculent independence soon led him to break with the surrealists. He denounced Breton for turning the bold innovations of dada into a clique. Pia, who gave up *Disque Vert*, had no patience with slogans or dogmas. Politically he was left-wing by temperament but he believed in nothing, never read Marx, never joined a party – political parties were anathema to him – and so far has voted only once in his life. He was drawn to prisons, hospitals and barracks, centres of outsiderness. But he had no political creed beyond a conviction that all states and societies are oppressive. Generous, energetic and much-liked, Pia lived the absurd. If Camus had not felt the absurd on the Algiers beaches, he could have learned it from Pia who carried it further than he. Pia had none of Camus' caution or ambition and he was too sceptical to be a moralist.

In the '20's Pia's passion for the forgotten, the hidden and the banned grew stronger. He devoured German mystics, medieval heretics and eighteenth-century pornography. He became a man of encyclopedias and dictionaries. This sceptic remains one of the most erudite French critics. His special interest was in books that have been banned as pornographic, books which the authorities have consigned to a special hell in the national library. Recently he completed a catalogue of this hell, a huge task which had last been undertaken by Apollinaire.[3]

Pia combined a phenomenal memory with a gift for mystification. If a friend told him he had just been to Rome, Pia

*Pia loved Jarry's *Ubu Roi* which seemed to him the best depiction of the absurd universe. When he was irritated by the chaos of *Alger-Républicain* Pia used to call Algeria 'Ubu country'.

would launch into a description of the Trastevere where every detail was correct. Had he ever been to Rome or had he read about it? Legends surrounded his life: had he fought in the Rif war and had he been to the East? Like Malraux, who allowed it to be believed that he had met Mao-Tse-Tung and been on the Long March, Pia did not explain. His love of invention extended to his researches. He 'discovered' a Rimbaud manuscript but one poem, *La Serveuse*, may have been his rather than Rimbaud's.* He discovered other poems by Rimbaud and his friends but Breton, who watched Pia with his usual malevolence and an unusual respect, said that one of Rimbaud's friends must have been called Pia.[4]

Pia was unfathomable, a true Florentine from the Renaissance. That he should become a journalist was in itself ridiculous. The young Pia denounced journalism as 'a banal occupation for careless people'.[5] Yet the reason may lie in his scepticism which extended to language itself. 'You can do anything with words,' he once wrote. Steeped in Lautréamont, Jarry and Apollinaire, he loved the magical freedom of language; but he went further than they. Language had no links with anything, it was arbitrary and wayward. Pia gave up his own writing and limited himself to criticism. He was drawn to journalism because it makes no pretence of validity. Journalism sets down facts in their abrupt disorder and does not, like poetry, reshape the world. Because of its crudeness it attracted Pia. Yet it also appealed to his sense of honour. Believing in nothing and delighting in invention, Pia was ferociously honest. It was a matter not of morality but of freedom. No one was going to prevent Pia from telling the truth; since few journalists ever told the truth, this was the trade for him.

He brought to it his restless passion for perfection. He loved the craftsmanship – the copyroom and the hours at night when the paper is being readied. He grew ever more meticulous about the veracity of the news he printed. In short he behaved as if journalism were the highest art-form. At the same time he mocked it and insisted that the press had no influence at all or else did harm. Not surprisingly, he was never content with his jobs. He worked on *Le Progrès* at Lyons, on *Ce Soir* and on many other papers. Often he did not write at all but preferred

*This fact haunted me throughout my long conversation with Pia. Perhaps he was now inventing *Alger-Républicain* . . .

the technical task of a news-editor, where he sifted the agency reports and corrected their biases.

When he arrived in Algiers, Pia was shocked. About half of the five thousand shareholders had not paid up so the fledgling paper had no money. He could not hire professional journalists, the equipment was so bad that the first numbers were smudged and the distribution was poor. 'If I had known what it was like,' says Pia, 'I would never have gone.' This is another piece of self-mockery, for the chaos suited Pia's temperament. He hired one journalist from the *Echo*, Lucienne Jean-Darrouy, who did investigations into schools and hospitals, he arranged to share a Paris correspondent with *Oran-Républicain* and he brought in a team of amateurs, part-timers and enthusiasts, of whom the most important was Camus.

Pia and Faure do not remember precisely how Camus was hired, but Faure knew him already. He was aware that Camus had left the PCA which pleased him. Camus seemed to Faure a free-thinking intellectual, uncluttered by parties or dogmas but sincerely left-wing. At first Camus was merely one of many helpers but then Pia recognized his talent and made him his chief aide. The office of *Alger-Républicain* consisted of one large room, where most of the staff worked along a long table, and Pia's study which was separate. Pia used to call Camus into his study and discuss with him the lay-out of the paper. He gave him important assignments like the El Okbi trial or the Kabylia investigation as well as a regular column on books. When the war broke out and *Alger-Républicain* became *Soir-Républicain*, Camus became Pia's main and often only collaborator.

Alger-Républicain changed Camus' private life by providing him with a steady income. From the autumn of '37 to the autumn of '38 he had been waiting for the paper to start up. Its delays had irritated him and had forced him to continue scraping a living by giving private lessons and working at the meteorological office. He was heartily sick of both but he had no alternatives. He never regretted his flight from Sidi-bel-Abbès but he was too proud to be content with part-time, mediocre jobs. Camus was not modest about his ability and he wanted to see it recognized.

In the summer of '38 Christiane Galindo introduced him to her brother Pierre who had come to Algiers for a visit. Camus was delighted because Pierre was exactly the kind of pied-noir whom he was trying to depict in his writing. Galindo worked for an export firm and he knew the Oran docks intimately. He had the shoulders of Marcel Cerdan and he wasted no energy talking. The intellectual Camus was fascinated by this tough guy. Certainly Galindo was a man of action for he would take part in the Oran resistance during the war. Even better, he had an air of mystery about him because he had been involved in a fight on the Oran beach with a group of Arabs. No one seemed to know exactly what had happened and Pierre himself was not telling. But there was a hint of violence in his long silences.

Camus had found both the model for Meursault and the central incident of *L'Etranger*. Pierre was a living proof that Camus was right when he talked about the silent, tough pieds-noirs. He told his friends about Pierre and they laughed. This was a meeting of opposites: the fragile Camus and the brawny Galindo. Pierre was impressed by Camus' sophistication; he had never met anyone so articulate and so widely-read. When *L'Etranger* was published he recognized himself with enormous pride and he began acting the role of Meursault. Having become a character in a famous novel he transformed the novel into real life. This amused Camus who himself played Ivan and the Playboy in real life.

Galindo helped distract him from the political situation which was growing worse. Republican Spain was drifting towards defeat while Hitler was menacing Czechoslovakia. When news of the Munich agreement reached Algiers Camus had an angry argument with a friend called Robert Jaussaud. Jaussaud, who had known Camus since schooldays and had helped with the Equipe theatre, was anti-Munich and was disappointed when a protest strike, called for November 30, collapsed. He turned to Camus for consolation only to discover that Camus was pro-Munich. To go to war was folly, declared Camus, the last war had solved nothing and this one would mean the massacre of the French working class.

Despite his gloomy prophecies Camus was well-pleased with *Alger-Républicain*. He was paid two thousand francs a month which was the union rate and the amount which Marguerite Dobrenn considered sufficient to live. Camus arrived at the *Alger-Républicain* office at about four o'clock in the afternoon and stayed until eleven. He often worked in the day too, covering trials or city council meetings. He learned to write quickly and he finished his own articles in a couple of hours before going to help Pia make up the paper. When he had worked at the town hall he had been told that his style was not bureaucratic enough; his sentences did not contain enough jargon. He was relieved to work for Pia who encouraged him to write simply.

Camus was still living in hotel rooms which he rented by the week or the month. A friend who visited him in one of them was struck by the lack of belongings. There seemed to be only one piece of furniture – a long chest. Camus kept his clothes in it and threw a mattress on it at night. There were piles of books on the floor and nothing on the walls. Camus moved frequently, went back to his mother's flat and, when he was especially tired, spent the night with the Jaussauds who lived near the *Alger-Républicain* office.

He had no place to work in his bed-sitting rooms so he carried his books and his writing-paper around with him. When he had half a day free he would go to the House-in-front-of-the-world. He would sunbathe and then settle down at the large kitchen table. His ability to concentrate continued to amaze Marguerite Dobrenn. At other times Camus worked in cafés or at other friends' houses. He liked this gypsy routine and he was never displeased when his friends entered the cafés and distracted him.

As usual he was doing several things at once. He was running the rehearsals for *Playboy* which was performed in March '39. He was acting as a reader for Edmond Charlot's little publishing house. His weekly book-reviews meant still more reading. At *Alger-Républicain* there were the extra chores which the exacting Pia piled on him. Finally there was his own writing. In early '39 he was toiling at *Caligula*, striving to depict his mad dictator while the threats of real dictators grew ever louder.

Despite or because of its handicaps *Alger-Républicain* remained an adventure. The under-paid staff worked well together and Camus rediscovered in the newsroom the sense of the team. Paul Balazard, who wrote about soccer, remembers the Sunday evenings. They would sit around the long table as the results came in from all over Algeria; Camus knew all the teams and followed the struggles for relegation or promotion. When the RUA won he would go round the room boasting and when they lost the other men teased him.[6] Sport was lavishly covered in *Alger-Républicain* for it would be a mistake to imagine that the paper's readers looked solely for news of the Popular Front. Out of four pages most of one went to soccer, racing and boxing. Every bit as serious as the discussion of Munich was a long article asking whether Algeria should take up rugby union or rugby league. More space was devoted to the rise of Marcel Cerdan than to the decline of Léon Blum. Nor was that other Algiers pastime, crime, neglected. The paper described with gory details the string of knifings and robberies that took place each week.

The credit for the team spirit shown in the office goes chiefly to Pia who was enormously admired in Algiers for his professionalism and his humour. He worked sixteen hours a day, twelve of them at the printing press. Smoking innumerable cigarettes he organized every line of the paper and then reread all the copy to check for mistakes. When he wrote himself he liked to attack the Algiers town hall. There was a touch of the pamphleteer in Pia who heaped abuse on Rozis and described one of Rozis' friends as 'the puppet of big capitalism'.[7]

Such abuse was, however, exceptional and Pia's prime concern was precision. Reacting against the biased reporting of the *Echo*, he wanted to be objective. Having worked so long on papers he knew how the news can be deformed and he explained in a series of articles how papers obtain their information and how much credibility it has. Pia did not confuse news and opinions. He insisted that *Alger-Républicain* not present the reports from Spain as more favourable to the Republic than they actually were. As an editor he encouraged sober, accurate journalism.

He imparted to Camus his precision, his liking for facts and details. He also imparted his love for the craftsmanship of the press: the smell of ink, the gossip of the printers, a well laid-out page. Most of all Pia strengthened Camus' penchant for irony. Feeling that the precision of facts was unreal, Pia gave to *Alger-Républicain* a subtle air of absurdity. It is found in Camus' articles on the trials where the decorum of the courtroom is mocked. It grows stronger after the outbreak of war, when the battle against censorship becomes the paper's main theme. Objectivity and irony were the twin poles of Pia's concept of journalism and they would later become the hallmark of *Combat*. Certainly they are present in Camus' best articles.

His writings on French and Algerian politics may be read as a protest against what he perceived as a counter-revolution. 'The working classes are certain,' he states, 'that they are faced with Fascist-style policies of oppression.' Daladier's economic and political decisions were reversing the conquests of the Popular Front. Camus pointed out in October that the salary increases, granted by Blum, had been swallowed up by inflation. Salary increases were worthless, unless accompanied by price controls and profit taxes; inflation was a class-based phenomenon which hit workers hardest.

Camus did not pursue the economic arguments but he excercised his gift for satire, when he attacked Daladier for circumventing parliament and ruling by decree. 'He loves democracy so much that he is strangling it,' says Camus, 'he says "I" all the time and, and when he tries to say "us", what comes out is "me".' Future author of *Caligula*, Camus shows a good understanding of the psychology of power. There is a link between mediocrity, fear of diversity and the need to control; Daladier is a little man who cannot tolerate other opinions. Switching to a moral condemnation, Camus argues that mediocrity turns into arrogance. The working class will respond to Daladier's arrogance not with resentment, which is a sign of mediocrity, but with the aristocratic values of dignity and pride.

Daladier's ally in Algiers was Rozis, a virulent enemy of the Popular Front who would turn into an enthusiastic Vichyite. Because of men like Rozis the Vichy laws against the Jews would be applied in Algeria although there were no German troops present. Camus joined Pia, Menicucci and other reporters in championing the unions who were waging their daily battle against the town hall for welfare benefits, pensions and the like. While doubting political parties, Camus supported trade unions because he felt they were closer to working-class people. His town hall pieces are solid and muck-raking. He gives facts and figures about the city budget and juxtaposes them with portraits of idle councillors doodling during the debates. In order to be useful, Camus had to delve into tedious but necessary detail. When there was a gas explosion on the rue Blanchard he worked out the position of the pipes and the state of repair in order to decide whether the municipality was responsible.

Elsewhere he resorts to satire because the Algerian left is weak. During the senatorial election of '38 there were three candidates: Mallarmé, backed by the municipality, Duroux, owner of the *Echo*, and Zévaco, who had resigned from the *Alger-Républicain* board. Naturally Zévaco had no chance and the other two went into a run-off. It prompted one of Camus' funniest pieces where he describes how the feeble and the infirm were wheeled up to the voting booth to cast their ballots for Mallarmé, who duly won. Politics, Camus exclaims, is what most people think of as theatre. 'It is a huge swindle where everyone tries to cheat and to be cheated.' Once more he condemns the election according to an aristocratic morality: the candidates are humiliating themselves and the voters by their intrigues.

This moral condemnation does not usually conflict with politics, as it had done in the summer of '37. If *Alger-Républicain* had been expounding a particular plan of action, then a conflict might have arisen. Since it was an organ of protest, Camus had chiefly to criticize. Yet there were potential dangers in his view of power. It can, after all, be used creatively and the quest for it is not necessarily ignoble. Camus' criticisms reveal his familiar moral intransigence which was reinforced by his work as a journalist. Power was used against Arab militants or striking workers; it seemed never to be used for them. It was Daladier's prerogative not Blum's. Camus was so accustomed to being in the opposition that the pursuit and attainment of power seemed an evil thing. So he tended to ignore the uncomfortable fact that social change entails the conquest of power. Like Pia, he was better at fighting dictators than at spelling out new programmes.

This is why he campaigned for Michel Hodent, El Okbi and the Auribeau labourers: they were all innocents threatened by arbitrary authority. Power was being used to destroy human dignity and the political apparatus was clearly evil. So Camus' habit of pitting pride against arrogance, the individual against the state and morality against realpolitik gives him the correct insight, except in one important respect.

Hodent's trial was held in rural Tiaret and *Alger-Républicain* was the only newspaper to send a correspondent. Even the Tiaret paper, mouthpiece of the local colons, paid scant attention. Hodent was really being tried for political reasons.

He was accused of cheating the Arabs who brought him their grain but his real accusers were the rich colons and the Arab caids, who wanted to undermine the Office du Blé's work and ruin the poor farmers. Since the Office had been set up by the Popular Front, this one incident had wider meaning. El Okbi's trial was more sensational. Three years before he had led a Congrès Musulman delegation to Paris in order to plead for Arab reform. Blum's government had received him favourably and on his return he planned a huge meeting for August 2, 1936. The muphti of Algiers, an ally of the French administration, protested and shortly after he was murdered. El Okbi was charged, along with *Alger-Républicain* supporter Abbas Turqui. They were brought to trial, cleared and then tried again. By this time their accusers' motives were clear: they wanted to get rid of a leading Arab spokesman. The Auribeau trial in July 1939 was the most shocking of the three and it aroused Camus to fury. The farm labourers had been striking for higher pay when a building in the village was burned down. They were arrested, tried without any pretence of fairness or even evidence and ignored by most of the Algiers press. In all three cases the real issue was the colonial system itself.

Camus stresses the local and personal themes. If he does not turn Hodent's trial into a test case for the Popular Front, it is because his aim is to get Hodent released. Journalism, as he perceived it, dealt with real people and the crusading press was supposed to help the weaker members of society. He describes the contradictions in the accusations and the confusion among the witnesses. He won his battle for Hodent was released. El Okbi was also released, although his supposed henchman, Akacha, was condemned to life-imprisonment. The Auribeau group were packed off to jail. Morally Camus showed how the accused were dehumanized by the authorities. Hodent had a friend who tried to help; the friend was tossed into prison, which deprived Hodent of any comradeship. The Auribeau group was tortured, as were minor figures in the El Okbi trial. If Camus abhorred torture, it was less because of the physical pain than because it broke down the individual. It turned him into a coward or a liar, anything the torturer wanted him to be. It was the most brutal onslaught on human dignity.

Of course Camus could not and did not avoid the political aspects. Hodent was 'guilty of having protected the Arab farmers and of having irritated their masters'; his case was not exceptional but reflected 'the unbelievable chaos which reigns in certain parts of Algeria'. Camus describes at length how the Arab witnesses are egged on to lie and how the prosecution lawyer makes speeches about French culture and national defence. During the El Okbi trial he stresses that the government's aim is not so much to prove that the Sheikh is guilty as to depict him as anti-French. All three cases are fresh battles in the long struggle which Camus has been waging for Arab rights.

Hodent himself considered his trial purely political. He wrote an autobiographical novel, *Des Charognards sur un Homme*, which Camus and De Fréminville published. It repeats Camus' theme that the trial was an affront to human dignity, but it lays the blame not on an aberration of the colonial system but on the system itself. Hodent debunks the myth of assimilation: 'the rich colons have all the rights, they do whatever they like ... it's always been like that and nobody cares.'[8] Camus criticizes the application of assimilation but implicit in his argument is the sense that, if the laws were applied as they should be, institutions like the Office du Blé would work. According to Hodent, it could not work because it does not serve the interests of the rich colons. In his journalism, as in his attempts to define Mediterranean culture, Camus refuses to confront the colonial system itself, although he analyses its manifestations.

What remains is to attribute injustice to some universal cause. The Auribeau trial is an 'inadmissable and deeply disgusting matter' but it is attributed to 'human stupidity'. Camus leaps from the individual plight of the labourers to eternal human nature while passing over the political. He tends, like Pia, to see in such cases fresh reasons for scepticism and to dwell on their absurdity. He describes with glee how the judge admitted that Hodent could prove he had not cheated; this, added the judge, was the final proof of Hodent's villainy – he had deceitfully covered up his tracks.

The El Okbi trial provided Camus with many more examples of absurdity, because there was a genuine mystery. The murder has never been solved. The most probable explanation is that the Muphti was killed by Messali's cohorts, either because his pro-French stance infuriated them or else because they wished to discredit El Okbi and polarize the two communities. But the suggestion has been made recently that El Okbi was indeed guilty and even Camus seems to have had doubts.[9] He calls the murder 'an obscure, fascinating affair' and 'a tissue of contradictions and mysteries'. He picks up strange details, like a typewriter which the defence wish to examine and which has mysteriously vanished. He notes the arbitrary outcome: El Okbi rises to shout 'long live French justice'; Akacha, condemned to forced labour, repeats the cry ironically. It is rather like the two parricides in *Playboy*.

Indeed Hodent, El Okbi and the Auribeau labourers resemble characters from the Equipe. Like Prometheus, they stand for justice and are defeated by the contradictions in the universe. The theme of the courtroom fascinates Camus who uses it so well in *L'Etranger*. He loves to depict the trappings of justice – the judge's robes, the flowery language – because they are mere forms without content. He uses indirect speech, now inserting the 'he said' and now omitting it; it makes the proceedings colder and more remote. He blends facts with ironic asides. This is exactly the kind of journalism he was learning from Pia.

Its merits and limitations are demonstrated in his series of articles on Kabylia. Kabylian poverty was usually ignored in the Algiers press and, when it was mentioned in the *Dépêche*, it was explained away by the 'Kabylian mentality'. Camus went beyond his compatriots in analysing at least some of its political and economic causes. He knew the region well for he often travelled into the interior. He had camped there in 1937 and he returned in the spring of 1939 in order to gather material. To save money he stayed with the subscribers to *Alger-Républicain*, many of whom were Arab schoolteachers. He therefore had better information than most journalists and he was independent of the French administration. To his texts Pia added photographs of crippled and blind Arabs and of families waiting hopelessly in line for free distribution of grain. This was to be a model of *Alger-Républicain*'s crusading journalism.

Kabylia was starving, Camus writes, because the land produced only figs and olives which were in surplus on the world market. Wheat, although also cheap, cost more so the farmers could not afford to buy bread. There was scant employment outside agriculture and credit was both expensive and difficult. The economic substructure – roads and skilled labour – was inadequate, as were the social services. Most children did not attend school, the houses had no hygiene, doctors were scarce and infant mortality high. Camus' solutions to these ills reflect the newish, Keynesian thinking of the 1930's: the government should advance loans to the farmers and finance public works. Decrease in unemployment would mean higher wages and, with technical assistance, the farmers could learn to diversify their crops.

Camus knew this was impossible without political change and he shows at least some understanding of how power works. In order to be economically active, the Kabyles would have to take political control over their lives. This could be done through a decentralization, which would transfer power from the French civil service to the elected officials in the villages. Kabylia would become 'a sort of federal republic based on a really genuine democracy'. Camus' dealings with the PCA had strengthened his distrust of authority and he was a foe of centralized parties, churches and states.

The flaw in all this is that Camus, while discussing political solutions, was avoiding the key issue of the colonial system. He suggests, for example, that the government set up co-operatives in order to refine Kabylian olive oil, which was now being refined by European middle-men who charged exorbitant prices. He does not suggest how the economic and hence political influence of these middle-men is to be overcome. Moreover, decentralization could not take place within the French administration and the large sums of money needed for the Kabylian new deal would certainly be blocked by colon pressure.

Camus' understanding of power was still inadequate, although he does show his suspicion of the colons: 'It's no good expecting them to undertake these tasks, we are not sure that they want to.' He even raises doubts about the French administration. He wonders why France builds a few expensive schools instead of many cheap ones. At first he attributes this to human stupidity but he notes what an Arab friend tells him: the Third Republic does not want to create a race of Arab 'boursiers'; it simply wants to exploit.

If this were true, then conclusions might be drawn but Camus does not draw them. He was proud of his Kabylia pieces and he included most of them in *Actuelles 3*. He felt, correctly, that he had been in advance of his contemporaries. Yet these articles do not go much further than the stands he had already taken within and without the PCA. He could foresee no future except assimilation and, if the Third Republic was not fostering it, that could only be because of universal stupidity. Camus could not perceive that the colonial system was a matter of domination and could be changed only by a power-struggle. The Arab fight for power would certainly be bitter but it might be fruitful too. This Camus could not admit. Did his dislike of power blind him to the necessity of Arab rebellion or was it the other way around?

What remains in the Kabylia pieces is a more private vision. Camus heaps up the details of squalor, which are heightened by the Kabyles' traditional dignity. For Kabylia is 'Greece in rags': its people used to live close to nature, they had no prisons and their cemeteries were bare. So they, too, are images of the human condition and characters from the Equipe. Investigating their downfall is also a private matter. Camus is not merely a crusading journalist but a searcher who wishes to absorb Kabylian poverty. 'One must fill oneself with this misery,' he writes. Of course the moralist argues that poverty, like torture, humiliates and that it must be remedied. As Camus' indignation rises, sonorous phrases like 'abject logic', 'fraternal comprehension' and 'profound generosity' recur.

Yet 'filling oneself with distress' is more than a moral act; it is also a self-transformation. 'I have to admit I wasn't proud to be there. I didn't want to start asking questions.' If the issues are political or moral, then the investigating reporter can maintain his distance. But Kabylian poverty corrodes every moment of people's lives and embraces the investigator too. He is humiliated by it, rendered stupid, shown that his intelligence and generosity are worthless. Both statistics and rhetoric stop, so the journalist's only recourse is to give up *Alger-Républicain* and begin writing *L'Etranger*.

This is foreshadowed in what is perhaps Camus' best piece: a visit to a prison ship. The crusading journalist intervenes to protest against life-imprisonment. The moralist notes that jails, like slums, rob men of their dignity. There is a sentimental note as Camus watches a rainbow rise over the ship. But for most of the article the prisoners' suffering is presented as a normal, dreadful fact. Dehumanized, they become merely figures and shapes so Camus describes the length of the cells and the movement of the light. Once more the journalist feels guilt – 'I am not proud to be here.' There is no question of action for there is nothing he can do. His sense of inadequacy is revealed in the flat language. The absence of rhetoric and satire is a kind of self-destruction which the journalist undergoes. By not commenting, he suppresses his own vision and leaves his writing incomplete.

The inadequacy of journalism is another theme which Camus learned from Pia. If governments were always oppressors and humans always stupid, then it made no sense to publish newspapers. The journalist must try his hardest, whether out of Camus' moral sense or Pia's paradoxical honour; but his writing must contain irony which is a form of self-criticism. Camus twice depicted journalists in his novels. In *L'Etranger* the reporter stares at Meursault; each is aware of the other but there is no bond between them. When Meursault is condemned to death the reporter looks away. In *La Peste* Rambert is the only one of the leading characters who does not write about the plague. Journalism is not able to penetrate death as Tarrou does in his diary.

All writing should contain an incomplete note because the writer is an amputated being. This is one of the themes which Camus discusses in his weekly book columns. His reviews are simple and are meant to inform. His critical technique is traditional: he distinguishes between 'form' and 'content' as the education system had taught him. Algerian books are praised if they are earthy: Blanche Balain's poems are full of roots and sap. Abstraction is the artist's cardinal fault. Gide's theatre is too abstract, so is Giraudoux' and so are Aldous Huxley's novels.[10] Camus condescends to discuss popular novels but he prefers to talk about Greek classicism. Pia thinks that few of *Alger-Républicain*'s readers ever read Camus' book column. Yet his reviews are sensible and they include a few outstanding articles on Ignazio Silone, Paul Nizan and Sartre.

Camus returns to the theme of committed writing and raises the problem of 'saying less' which he will discuss in *Le Mythe de Sisyphe*. Paul Nizan was Sartre's boyhood friend who became a novelist and an enthusiastic Communist. Silone had been a high-ranking member of the Italian Communist Party before he quarrelled with its leader, Palmiro Togliatti, and left the party.

In his piece on Nizan Camus affirms that a book should not be judged by the political views of its author. Political commitment is like getting married; it is something writers do but it cannot be the yardstick by which their work is judged. Camus praises Gide, who, while taking political stands, retains a personal and aesthetic independence. Yet, while admiring the old *NRF*, Camus is still not of it. Aesthetics, morality and politics must run together and the best example he can offer is Silone's *Vino e Pane*. In reviewing this book, which describes in fictional form how Silone left the Communist Party after the expulsion of Trotsky, Camus is reliving his own break with the PCA. He even says that Pietro Spina, the Communist militant, abandons the party in order to be true to his working-class background. Spina is not working-class at all: Camus is thinking of himself.

He and Silone have much in common: a sense of their roots and a moral impulse. Silone joined the Italian Communist Party out of moral revulsion against the injustice he had seen in the Abruzzo countryside. His decision was 'a conversion, a total commitment' which soon clashed with the moral impulse that had provoked it.[11] Trotsky's expulsion played the role which the nationalists' arrest played for Camus; Silone broke with Togliatti's realpolitik and began to write. Like Camus, he had a religious temperament. In *Vino e Pane* the poverty of the Abruzzo countryside mocks the PCI and its revolution, just as the Algerian hills do. But Silone gives free rein to his religious urge, allowing Pietro Spina to dress as a priest and work mock-but not so mock-miracles. Camus traces this evolution with sympathy but he exaggerates when he calls *Vino e Pane* a 'revolutionary' work. It has no political meaning at all, aside from the rejection of Communism. Pietro Spina's protest against the Fascist invasion of Abyssinia arouses no more support in Abruzzo than the PCI had done. Moreover Silone never found a coherent political position after he left the party. Writing was precisely an act that replaced political commitment. Camus is right, however, when he speaks of Silone's ability to criticize his own enthusiasms. The narration of *Vino e Pane* is ironic, while the concision of the language is reminiscent of Camus. This is what Camus meant when he described the book as 'revolutionary'.

He realized the problem was not merely concision. His articles on Sartre show the kinship as well as the even greater differences between the two men. [12] Camus is fascinated by the revelation of otherness, which Roquentin undergoes in *La Nausée*. He follows the aberrations which this revelation provokes and which are catalogued in *Le Mur*. He states his own view when he writes that life is less appalling than Sartre claims and that man might have the strength to assert his innocence against the universe. Then the discussion of technique leads back to the need to say less. Camus praises the shifting points of view in *Le Mur*; if there is no order in the world then there can be no conventional narrator and the novel can be only a partial viewpoint. But he criticizes the verbosity of *La Nausée* because it betrays too great a trust in language. It is a sign that Sartre has fallen into a new Cartesianism: 'I write therefore I am.'

This rebuke, which anticipates the self-criticism of *Les Mots*, demonstrates Camus' dilemma. He felt that modern writing contained a critical consciousness which was its special characteristic. But he persisted in believing that this was akin to the act of political protest. One remains unconvinced: *Le Mur* is no more and no less 'revolutionary' than *Vino e Pane*. There is nothing very political about offering a partial viewpoint.

In 1939 *Alger-Républicain*'s headlines grew gloomier as war drew nearer. The paper seemed to be hypnotized by the cataclysm and it laid bare its contradictions. It condemned Munich but opposed rearmament. Distrusting Daladier it suspected that he was using the Nazi threat to increase his own power. If France went to war and won, capitalism would be strengthened. If Hitler won the hope of socialism would vanish. Yet peace meant betraying the Czechs.

Camus grew more and more agitated as the French government re-armed and French generals boasted about the Maginot Line. In the early summer he went to the beach with Jaussaud. Camus was frenetically gay. 'Let's enjoy ourselves,' he kept saying, 'it may be the last time.' 'Is there anything you have wanted to do and never done?' he asked Jaussaud. 'If there is, better do it now.'

Camus was nervous and exhausted. He flew into a temper whenever Jaussaud talked about the betrayal of the Czechs or the need to defend Poland. It was nonsense to talk about defending Poland when France was allowing Republican Spain to be crushed. Cassandra-Camus kept prophesying wars and bloodshed; the moral thinker in him kept repeating that it was his duty to prevent them.

In this bright summer of '39 he was hoping to go to Greece. Now that he had a little money he could visit the land he loved but had never seen. The sea voyage would give him a chance to rest; there would be days of blessed silence unbroken by Hitler's harangues. He would tour the Greek temples and go out to the islands. He went to see Jacques Heurgon who lent him some books on architecture. Yet Camus was half-convinced that his dream would not be realized. Any day the war would start and men would cease to be men. They would be turned at worst into cannon-fodder and at best into robots who chanted patriotic slogans. Camus was hoping to set out for Greece in late August but the war came too close and he gave up the trip.

The day after war was declared he wrote a lament on the first page of *Alger-Républicain*. 'Never have left-wingers had such reason to despair,' he declared. He was in despair himself and he could see the future only as a suicidal orgy of bloodshed. His article outraged Jaussaud who wrote him a furious letter; Camus, equally furious, broke off the friendship.[13]

This was no isolated incident. Another friend was called up and came to a café wearing his uniform – trousers only because the jackets were in short supply. 'I'm off to kill hundreds of Boches,' he yelled in pure jest.[14] Camus, usually so willing to joke, gave him a harsh lecture. When Blanche Balain wrote to him in August saying that war was now inevitable Camus rebuked her for her fatalism: she was wrong to submit to an imaginary inevitability. His letter was, she felt, harsh and silly because by the time he wrote it war had been declared. However, the invasion of Poland did not change Camus' view. His duty was still to prevent bloodshed.[15]

During the months following the invasion *Alger-Républicain* campaigned against Hitler and against the war. The Allies should not accept the occupation of Poland but they should offer peace. Hitler was not completely in the wrong for the Versailles treaty was unjust; some concessions could be made and a plebiscite could be held in the Polish corridor. Camus placed much hope in Neville Chamberlain.

His articles are very different in tone from the exultant

Combat editorials of '44 but they are entirely in character. Along with many European left-wingers he refused to support a second world war. It would be long, working men would be slaughtered and nothing would be resolved. His moral sense rebelled against the fatalism of which he accused Blanche Balain. War was no more inevitable than revolution and acts of violence could not be justified. 'There is no fatalism in history unless we decide there is,' he wrote.

Politically, Camus' view was ridiculous. Despite his anti-Fascist stand, he had not grasped the nature of the Hitler regime. Not until after the Fall of France did he realize that it was especially virulent. Moreover, he chose to ignore that France could not fight Hitler while parading her readiness to negotiate with him. While insisting that he was rejecting fatalism in the name of action, Camus was condemning himself to passivity. Yet the problem of efficacy did not really interest him. As in 1937 he asserted absolute moral principles. He was continuing his battle with the PC.

In the *Carnets* he jots down his impressions of the war. It was curiously absent from Algiers where there was no fighting but it was suggested by the dimmed street-lighting, which had been turned down to save electricity and which veiled the city in a murky twilight. War was a pervasive something which heightened the banal absurdity of each day.[16] It was a part of the universal stupidity and the two combatants resembled each other. Camus tried to join the army but was refused on health grounds. Had he been accepted, he would have campaigned in the barracks for a negotiated peace. To submit to the war was like submitting to tuberculosis.

Meanwhile *Alger-Républicain* battled with the military censorship. The war had dealt several extra blows to the struggling paper. Conscription robbed it of its distributors and it quickly ran short of paper. Some of its backers were themselves called up. Jean-Pierre Faure went to join his regiment, leaving Pia with full powers. When Paul Balazard went off to the army, the others clubbed together to buy him a football. More than ever Pia and Camus ran the paper themselves. Then Pia had a brilliant idea. Since distribution was so difficult, he would give up the morning edition and concentrate on Algiers and the suburbs. *Soir-Républicain* could be sold by vendors during the rush hour. Pia even managed to find a huge supply of paper which he carried off before the army could requisition it. Once this was exhausted there would be no more and the paper would have to close. This thought was always at the back of Pia's mind and it made him even more uncompromising than usual.

Two more of Camus' friends had been enlisted for *Alger-Républicain*. Robert Namia had been in the Young Socialists with Fouchet, had been beaten up during February '34 and had passed to the PC. He had learned his trade as a bookbinder from an Italian anarchist, who forged false papers for other anarchists and who inspired Namia with a loathing for governments. When the Spanish Civil War broke out, Namia did not hesitate. An admirer of Malraux, he believed that you had to be a part of history; you could never understand the whole but you could participate in it. He was wounded, returned to Algeria and broke with the PCA. He had already criticized the choice of Jean Chaintron as unofficial head of the party and had argued that an Arab should have been chosen. Camus, who disagreed with Namia about history but agreed with him about governments, Spain and Arabs, recruited him for *Alger-Républicain*. Namia, future news-editor of *Le Nouvel Observateur*, learned a second trade under another anarchist, Pia.

Camus had met Emmanuel Roblès while he was rehearsing the Da Rojas play. Roblès was not only of a Spanish family but knew the language and tried to teach it to Camus. He also knew Belcourt, which he describes in his novel *L'Action*. He showed the manuscript to Camus who was struck by a passage about death: 'The presence of death in all its stupid simplicity inspired in Astore a strange shudder, a terrible but entrancing anguish.' Camus told Roblès that he, too, felt each day the fascination of sudden death. The friendship grew and Roblès, who was stationed at a barracks outside Algiers, used to visit Camus both at the bare room which he rented on the rue Michelet and in the *Alger-Républicain* office. Camus welcomed in Roblès, whose family was working-class, his own sense of Algeria and even their writing is not without parallels. Camus encouraged Roblès to contribute pieces for *Alger-Républicain* on the Algiers slang as well as on the war.

Roblès remembers the battle with the military censorship.[17] Pia and Camus were determined to publish accurately all the news they could find on the war. If they learned that the Finns were collapsing, they intended to say so. Pia listened to the BBC and had a secretary take down the broadcasts in shorthand so that he could use the material for his articles. The censorship retaliated by striking out whole paragraphs. Even when the news had been announced on the French radio, they made cuts. Led on by their own logic, they censored everything. But, since they did not wish to appear authoritarian, they asked Pia not to publish the paper with blanks. Naturally Pia refused. Censorship is always stupid, he says, but in a backward country like Algeria it was unusually stupid.

Camus enjoyed the battle. Relentlessly polite, he made fun of the officers who were sent to the *Soir-Républicain*'s offices. He would hand them a text full of long words which they did not know so that they had to return to the barracks and consult their dictionaries. He inserted into his articles quotations from Voltaire and La Fontaine, which were erased as secret military information. He included chunks from school text-books and these too were censored. One day the uniformed officers struck out statistics on the soldiers killed during the 1914 war. Ironically the paper, with its reduced costs, began making a profit for the first time. Perhaps the frequent blanks made it seem more interesting. One evening the censors demanded that the paper be withdrawn after it had been put on the streets. The quick-witted newsboys sold extra copies to the cry of '*Alger-Républicain*, read special banned edition'.

Pia and Camus took their absurd task very seriously. They had always maintained that the war would lead to greater authoritarianism; now they had been proved right and they must fight back. In *Le Manifeste du Conformisme Intégral* Camus shows how the refusal to doubt and the acceptance of jingoism lead to persecution. His own role was to be a model of dissent and he had recourse to his artist's weapons. He adopted various pseudonyms: Jean Meursault was cynical about official statistics, Irénée was hopeful of peace, Zaks informed readers about National Socialism, Néron delved into the moral issues. By parading his various selves Camus was pretending that *Soir-Républicain* had more journalists than it did and was a more powerful champion of freedom than it was. He was also multiplying the different viewpoints, opposing diverse heresies to the military orthodoxy and asserting that there was no one truth. The Equipe had had to give up but Camus was still acting.

Naturally all this could not last. The censorship grew ever more strict and the *Alger-Républicain* shareholders told Pia that he was going too far. Some had obtained favours from the military authorities – a contract awarded or a call-up deferred; in return they wanted Pia to compromise. But Pia refused. He knew that he would soon have to close down because paper was running out and, in any case, he was enjoying the game. First the military authorities imposed sanctions and then in January 1940 – a few days before the supply of paper was exhausted – they banned *Soir-Républicain*. There was an angry row with the shareholders who accused Pia and Camus of 'consciously and deliberately sabotaging the paper' by taking 'an anarchist line'.[18] They were furious because their investment was lost; a compromise, they felt, would have been possible.

Pia treated such comments with contempt. He had done what he thought right, he had provided the only kind of journalism he believed in, he had behaved rationally in an absurd world. Now that he had to look for another job he was happy to leave Algeria. He wrote to friends and was offered work at *Paris-Soir*. So he left, telling Camus that he would find something for him too. Camus' career in Algeria was over and his political battle was lost. The war was going to continue and Algeria was ripe for Vichyism. Although no one, not even Camus, realized it, the last hope of a reconciliation with the Arabs had vanished with the Popular Front. Camus' personal situation had also deteriorated. For years he had made ends meet by his various odd jobs; now he had lost the only steady, if ill-paid, post he had ever had. He had often thought of going to France and he no longer had any reason not to go. He waited a few more weeks until he heard from Pia.

He had, however, become an excellent journalist. The *Alger-Républicain* articles are the best pieces of journalism he ever did, better than the more famous *Combat* editorials or the *L'Express* series on the Algerian War. They contain the germs of a weakness: the tendency towards moral rhetoric, towards empty, sonorous antitheses. In the *Combat* editorials the moralist will run amuck but here he is checked by a careful, scrupulous reporter. Camus heaps up statistics, conducts investigations and checks his facts. If he advocates a new kind of health care, he explains exactly how much it will cost.

This caution did not prevent him from becoming a crusading journalist. Muck-raking, unpopular causes, innocents wrongly accused, these are his main preoccupations. But he is practical as well as zealous. Throughout the Kabylian series he appeals to common sense; in the Hodent articles he seems to be writing for the jury. He hoped to educate rather than overwhelm his readers for he was still Louis Germain's pupil as well as Pia's. His headlines are not flamboyant and he uses 'a minimum of words' because protest must be precise and solid.

A more private vision is also present and it looks forward to the books he would soon publish, especially to *L'Etranger*. Camus wrote about Daladier's success, Kabylian poverty and Hitler's victories. Small wonder that the world seemed Augustinian to him. The violence of *Caligula* was all around him and the despair of *Le Mythe* had taken over the streets. Camus could do nothing about this so he turned it into universal stupidity. The journalist's last weapon was irony. The portraits of Daladier and Rozis are the work of a Camus who can do nothing but mock. Did Rozis really intend to demonstrate his patriotism by taking down the red danger flags and putting up tricolours instead? One is not sure because Rozis has become a Camus character.

Beyond irony there could lie only the depiction of inadequacy. When he describes the gas explosion on the rue Blanchard, Camus lists the ordinary, incongruous details. A ceiling is festooned with table napkins, a basket of eggs remains intact, the walls have fallen in but on the table is a portrait of a child wearing an unblemished lace-shirt. These are 'the important, indifferent signs of the recent catastrophe'. The curious journalist cannot be indifferent but he can occasionally suggest that there are no explanations; there is an emptiness at the end of such articles. The journalist can go no further but the novelist might.

The adventure of *Alger-Républicain* had run its course from false hopes to real catastrophes. The moments of friendship around the long table remained as happy a memory as the rehearsals of the Equipe. The paper never returned to the newstands and Camus had to set about scraping a living.[19] He began to give lessons again. For a brief moment he hoped to get a job with a printing firm. But the firm did not have enough business to take on an extra person. Or else it was afraid to antagonize the authorities who had put Camus and Pia on an enemies list. Camus had no alternative but to wait and see what Pia could find for him in Paris. His real task, as he prepared to leave Algeria, was to finish writing *Caligula*, *Le Mythe de Sisyphe* and *L'Etranger*.

5

Camus' Early Writing: Beyond God and Algeria?

Throughout the years he worked with the Equipe and at *Alger-Républicain* Camus toiled at a series of six books: *L'Envers et l'Endroit*, *Noces*, *La Mort Heureuse*, *Caligula*, *Le Mythe de Sisyphe* and *L'Etranger*. These works cannot be well understood if one begins with the concept of absurdity because Camus had a different starting-point. He wanted to probe the experience of oneness which he had discovered in his mother's indifference and on the Algerian beaches. So his writing has a lyrical impetus and his first three books revolve around a few central images such as sea-bathing or the sudden silence of the Algiers evening. He reveals the primitive quality that his friends admired because he wants to seize that oneness directly and will tolerate no intellectual subterfuges. Moreover this is religious writing because Camus wants to depict a state of innocence or goodness where man is freed from the divisions of his fallen, sinful state and where he is reconciled with himself.

Yet Camus cannot believe in this reconciliation because the stark fact of human mortality is emphasized by the bare Algerian mountains. The awareness of death remains in man's consciousness as a division or an otherness. This is the experience of the absurd, which will be discussed more fully later but which must be understood as a failure to attain the oneness that was Camus' prime concern. From *Sisyphe* onward he depicts absurd man who is acutely aware of his contradictions: the Meursault of *L'Etranger* keeps asking questions about the world around him, although he can discover no answers.

These books may also be read as part of Camus' attempt to situate himself in Algeria. Like his friends he was writing about the Mediterranean, the Algiers streets and death. He offers various insights into Algeria and his task as a writer was to find a way of setting down what he had learned as he was growing up.

A brief glance at two of his friends will help us to appreciate Camus' originality. De Fréminville describes a cold harmony between humans and the universe: 'man slumbers in the world's indifference'.[1] This is interesting but indifference quickly becomes mere decadence, which leads De Fréminville to a banal discussion of impotence and desire. *Buñoz*, which is his attempt to write the Algerian novel, presents an Oran that reminds one of Meursault's Algiers. But the novel is as wordy as *L'Etranger* is concise because De Fréminville has not been able to find a language for indifference.

Roblès fares better in *L'Action* which is a rousing, popular novel about the Algiers streets. The leading characters are tough, soccer-loving busdrivers who live thoughtlessly and greedily. There is a political motif because the busdrivers go on strike when the Popular Front takes over. But then the strike fails, the hero Astore is shot by a jealous husband and the novel fades out. 'Death poisons life and drains it of meaning,' says Roblès.[2]

From this emptiness violence spills out. Hadj, whose father was killed by European farmers, is the first Arab rebel. He decides to avenge his father by killing the owner of the bus company but he fails and kills himself instead. As in Camus, murder runs close to suicide. Astore, the strike-leader, feels the lure of death for he is often tempted to turn the wheel of the bus and crash it over a cliff.

Despite his role in the strike Astore remains a remote figure: 'he had learned to be silent and to listen to himself living'. This reminds one of Meursault, who listens to his heartbeat and whose indifference Astore shares. But Roblès has written an adventure novel which is told from a conventional and traditional viewpoint. Emptiness is present around the edges but Roblès does not reconstruct the world around the experience of emptiness as Camus will do in *L'Etranger*.

Yet Roblès may be read as a kind of popular Camus. Most of these young Algerian writers felt that beyond the frenzy of Mediterranean life there was a silence, whether blissful or horrible, and that their task was to explore it. Only Camus grasped that he must give up the realistic trappings of street-urchins and slang and that he must practise the un-Algerian virtues of concision and stylization in order to do

132

so. And even he had to undergo an apprenticeship of several years as he tried out various styles and genres: the essay and the realistic novel, lyricism and irony.

L'Envers et l'Endroit (1937) is a book of five essays which draw on Camus' childhood as well as on his 1936 stays in Prague and in Vicenza. Since the essays are written in the same kind of language they may be considered together. At their core lies the two-sided experience of the loss of self into something that is greater than the self. In part this is terrifying because it is a kind of death: 'Now the streets were darker and more deserted. Voices still went by. They grew more solemn in the strange calm of the evening. Behind the hills which stretched around the city there were still glimmers of daylight ... The old man closed his eyes. The rumble of the city was being carried off and the smiling sky was vacuously indifferent. He was alone, lost, naked, dead already.'[3] But it can also be glorious because it is an onrush of happiness: 'I walk along the road towards the crickets which I can hear from far away ... I advance slowly, overwhelmed by the weight of beauty ... One by one the crickets grow louder and burst into song: a mystery in this sky, from which indifference and beauty rain down.'[4]

Occasionally Camus makes his familiar distinction between North and South Europe, setting the terror in Prague and the happiness on the Mediterranean. But this is a superficial contrast because the two moments are complementary. Each presupposes the loss of individual awareness and of contact with other people or with the tangible world. The eye and the look are in Camus' writing the sign of man's divided condition: he can only stare at the hostile universe. But in these privileged moments they disappear as man is reconciled with the universe.

Frequently death is seductive: 'I understand that men sometimes wish to die because, when life is revealed in all its transparency, nothing is important any longer.' Transparency means the way in which the concrete world dissolves into near-emptiness. This tempts man and fills him with a death-wish which may take the form of suicide. Such a death-wish haunted Camus but it disgusted as well as tempted him. When he describes his stay in Prague he depicts the disintegration of human character. Habit protects man, as do friends and, most interestingly, words. But travel breaks down such things and compels man to face his emptiness. He is not a journalist or an office-worker or whatever he thought he was. The various traits of his character such as bravery, generosity or kindness crumble and leave him without any personality. This frightens him and he may plunge into violence or madness in order to escape from the anguish which is the mark of his condition.

Conversely man may live most intensely in such moments because he participates in the beauty of the universe. One remembers the occasions when Camus emerged from bathing and greeted his friends: he was saturated with delight and bleached by the sun. Disintegration of self may be a liberation from the tedious ties of everyday life. At these moments the primitive in Camus exulted in the beauty he felt around him. It is no coincidence that he should write about the crickets' song. The harmony of the Vicenza experience is an aesthetic order which spurs the artist to create. Camus' task was to find a lyrical language with which to render his joy.

So the above-quoted passages are characteristic of his early writing where people and objects give way to shapes and sounds. Although Camus was not interested in ballet, images of dance recur. New shapes emerge which are different from those of the physical world. The smiling sky, the strange peace and the disembodied voices are fragments of a greater whole. Man's individual consciousness is lost but he is a part of the ballet and the ballet itself is eternal. Here is another mystical moment where the narrator sits in a café alone except for the Arab proprietor. As so often in French-Algerian writing, the Arab helps the narrator to enter his trance: 'The world sighs out to me long and rhythmically and it brings me the indifference and tranquillity of that which does not die ... A kind of secret melody is born of the indifference. Once more I am at home.'[5]

The origin of the experience lies in the narrator's relationship with his mother, which explains the reference to 'home'. The mother's indifference is the source of the world's and only by denying his own individuality can the narrator reach out to her. Clearly love has scant place in this scheme of things although the tie with the mother is crucial and Camus' mother hovers behind every page of *L'Envers*. The only other people who interest the narrator and who make up the band of minor characters are those who incarnate some aspect of the quest for oneness.

These characters, who foreshadow the minor characters of Camus' novels, are a motley crew. First come the old, who are stripped of the distractions that constitute ordinary life and are forced to brood on death, and the mad, who have gone deeper into the trance than Camus' narrator and are unable to come back. A second group might be the athletes, whose rhythmical movement reflects the universal harmony, and their counterparts the cripples, who are excluded from it. In general Camus is drawn to the disinherited because they are exposed naked to transparency. He is interested in Arabs, who are more contemplative than Europeans, in working-class men, whose silence is a simple form of meditation, and in prisoners, who have been condemned to death and who feel an exhilaration simply because they are alive.

The two-sided experience which *L'Envers* depicts is the wisdom of Algeria, the midday eternity which De Fréminville and Roblès both understood. They also understood the price to be paid: the destruction of what makes a man – his individual awareness and his friendships. In order to pursue this theme Camus would have to delve deeper into the mystical moments. Having started with a rudimentary pantheism he could now explore the ecstasy it offered. For Camus' starting-point was religious. If man accepts the dissolution of self into a greater whole, then that whole must be some sort of God. Camus uses the language of catholicism but there is nothing catholic about this vision, if only because it rejects intermediaries like the Church. Moreover transcendence is unnecessary because the world's beauty needs no ulterior justification. Yet Camus sees in the natural world a harmony which is more than the regularity of a line of cypress trees. Similarly death is more than extinction, even if the eternal is dimly perceived.

Camus could have pursued his mystical quest, as Jean Grenier did. Yet Camus was cautious. He was Louis Germain's pupil as well as Grenier's and he was wary of all mysticisms, whether catholic or pantheistic. Alongside his death-wish he had a much stronger revulsion against death. So he would not pay the price of losing individual awareness even if it bought a revelation of innocence. Instead he defends the most traditional of French values – 'conscience' – and he introduces a contradiction into *L'Envers*.

He notes that the universal ballet is only a metaphor for the transformation of self: 'to be the glow in which my cigarette is consumed' is to feel 'an extreme emotion which frees me from all else.' This offers the narrator a kind of knowledge because he is feeling his way into the harmony around him. But Camus feels that knowledge entails a distinction between subject and object. There is in *L'Envers* an 'I' who warns against the perils of totality. Entry into the mother's world is too easy and the death-wish is an evasion. The severe Camus stresses that man cannot know his condition without accepting certain limits. The 'I' will lend but not give itself to the Prague-Vicenza experience. And as individual awareness re-asserts itself, the dualism of man confronted with an alien world enters the book.

Camus' uncertainty is present in the writing itself. He tried to make *L'Envers* more objective, he omitted a few very personal passages and, when the mother appears, he tries to let her speak for herself. Yet he admitted to Jean de Maisonseul that he had not succeeded and that the book remains too personal. The contemporary reader might feel that it is either too personal or not personal enough. It hovers unsatisfactorily between the prose-poem and the essay.

The language is always on the verge of lyricism. It can also lapse into sentimentality – 'the young man listened with an enormous mysterious pain that throbbed in his breast'. There was a sentimentalist in Camus, carefully hidden behind the ironic indifference. But the special weakness of *L'Envers* lies in the long passages about Algiers or Vicenza. They are not convincing as prose-poems but they swamp the rest of the essay. Nor is this merely a matter of bad writing. Camus has not yet learned how to depict the vision that obsesses him. Are these moments of insight all-embracing? If so they should be explored more fully from within. If not, then the essayist's point of view is better. Unable to decide, Camus oscillates between the diary and objective description and frequently strands the 'I' of his narration in some midway point. Such switches are artificial and *L'Envers* has no coherent point of view.

Noces, which was written in '37 and '38 and published in '39, is another series of essays which have a common theme and may be treated together. Although it continues Camus' meditation on Algeria and presents the same few, tenaciously-held images of the desert and the sea, *Noces* seems a very different book from

L'Envers. Where the latter was uncertain, *Noces* depicts a resolute will to happiness. Instead of the glimmers and fragments of *L'Envers* Camus uses boldly erotic language – 'the sea sucks the rocks with the sound of kisses'. Camus' life had now changed. He had recovered from his divorce, asserted his power over the Equipe group and was demonstrating his ability as a journalist. He had learned from his discussion with Jean de Maisonseul and he now wrote more objectively. *Noces* is a better book than *L'Envers* and yet it contains the same contradiction. Camus still did not know how to depict his vision of oneness.

The same two-sided experience dominates these essays. Camus describes the desert wind: 'I was a little part of that force which carried me along ... The wind shaped me, stripping me as it stripped everything around me.' Once more this is a deprivation as well as an ecstasy because man loses his individual character. Camus feels, however, that this is a small price to pay for the anonymous pantheistic upsurge. This is the characteristically Mediterranean brand of sensibility: crude, violent and intense. In one essay Camus even crosses the sea and annexes Italy, barbarizing Florence and comparing Fiesole, home of Renaissance culture, with the Algerian desert village of Djémila. Italy, says Camus, is indeed the land of supreme intelligence but it is also the land which demonstrates the inadequacy of intelligence. Faced with the bare Tuscany hills man finds himself as if in the desert. When he writes about Italian painting Camus admires Giotto's expressionless figures and dismisses Raphael's portraits where individual psychological traits dominate. Psychology, refinement and learning are secondary things to the barbarian Camus.

Exulting in the joy of the Mediterranean he introduces the theme of reconciliation: 'I understood that at the heart of my revolt lay a consent.' One might turn this around for consent precedes revolt which does not become a theme until *Le Mythe de Sisyphe*. Consent means that Camus is at one with the universe although it teaches him each day that he will die. Yet Camus dismisses the death-wish and refuses to believe that death might be good or that it can be accepted without jealousy. So the contradiction of *L'Envers* recurs and the concept of reconciliation remains unsatisfactory.

If man can confront the fact of his extinction, argues Camus, then he can be at one with the beautiful, alien universe. The

137

trouble is that, in order to confront that fact, man needs to believe in some sort of eternal life. It need not be the traditional Christian heaven but it must be some revelation. Camus seems to promise this through his pantheistic upsurge in which death is no more important to a man than it is to a stone. The desert stones, which are broken into fragments by the wind, are not destroyed but change their shape while remaining a part of the desert. Yet Camus cannot convince himself that men should or could view their deaths with the same calm. The extinction of awareness is frightening and man looks upon it with jealous rage.

The contradiction that is present in consent is revealed in the point of view from which *Noces* is written. The moments of abandon are presented and then a commentary is woven around them. Camus writes like an *NRF* essayist who is sifting his experience and who knows that totality is merely the sum of contradictions. Camus even writes about the violent, mindless Algerians as an outsider. He is not one of them; he follows behind the throng and interprets them to the reader. Yet if the experience of oneness is to be man's goal, then the task of the Algerian artist will be to compose a work that will depict the world from the viewpoint of that oneness. Such a viewpoint is present only in the lyrical passages around which the essayist weaves his commentary. So *Noces* does not contain in its language the consent of which Camus writes and the oscillation between lyric poem and essay, which was present in *L'Envers*, recurs here. Camus knew that he had to reconstruct the world around his vision of consent and he set out to do this in his first novel *La Mort Heureuse*.

Although it lay unpublished until long after his death, *La Mort Heureuse* is an important landmark in Camus' development. It spells out more fully than the essays the initiation which man must undergo in order to attain the state of oneness. Camus chose not to publish the book because he had still not resolved the problem of how to depict that oneness. But, having made this serious attempt, he could then give up the pursuit of consent and he could write his next three books which depict a divided universe and are written from the viewpoint of a fractured, incomplete consciousness. So *La Mort Heureuse* both reveals to us the religious vision which was Camus' starting-point as a writer and explains why he abandoned it for the vision of the absurd.

The book is set in Algeria and depicts some of Camus' favourite spots: the docks, the 'House-in-front-of-the-world' and the Tipasa hills. Its hero, Patrice Mersault (who will acquire another 'u' in his name in *L'Etranger*) begins by killing a cripple Zagreus and stealing the money that will liberate him from the crushing routine of his office. At the end Mersault, who is living alone near the sea, dies a death that is a kind of suicide. In between these two acts of violence he has a love-affair which involves jealousy, he travels to Prague, he lives with his friends in the House-in-front-of-the-world and then he retreats into solitude in order to die. *La Mort Heureuse* is what the Germans call a 'Bildungsroman': a novel where the main character grows and learns. But instead of opening to diverse experiences, Mersault pursues the one intense, narrow ecstasy of innocence. He is an apprentice mystic.

His journey has the shape of a circle: the murder of Zagreus sets in motion his own death. Camus uses the motif of the circle frequently because he is always hoping to recapture something that was present in his childhood. But this circle is shaped by the acts of violence because both the elements in his two-sided vision of consent lead men to kill. The anguish of confronting death may inspire a death-wish; conversely if death is a necessary transition in the pantheistic upsurge, then men will think little of killing others or themselves. These two motivations overlap so that the pursuit of primeval innocence is a dangerous matter.

Mersault's murder of Zagreus contains at least three different themes. The first is a debate about moral values which Camus inherits from Gide. If indeed happiness is man's only goal and if collective values do not exist, why should Mersault not kill Zagreus and take his money? Playing a Gidean game, Camus reverses conventional ideas about the relative value of money and human life. But Zagreus acquiesces in his own death, which is a kind of suicide. He has lived by the code of *L'Envers* and *Noces*; he has ignored ambition and love in order to concentrate on the ecstasy of life. Now the moment of death, which he has been anticipating for years, has arrived. So he sits motionless and he does not look at Mersault because the look is the mark of division; instead he 'contemplates the inhuman beauty of the April morning'. He is a part of that morning and he is merged with it when he dies. The ritualistic precision with which Mersault fires the bullets indicates the sacrament of suicide which is taking place.

But the sacrament contains murder too. Zagreus' money is only a pretext for Mersault; any other pretext would have been as good. In his passion to live Mersault simply sweeps Zagreus away. Since he is already confronting his own death, Mersault sees no wrong in becoming the agent of Zagreus' death. The question of morality is never posed because suicide and murder are mere transitions. Anyway Zagreus is a cripple so he cannot participate in the universal ballet except by dying.

This is a less complex and less ambiguous crime than the murder of the Arab in *L'Etranger*. It is a part of the harmonious universe which is depicted in lyrical passages like the one which opens the novel: 'It was a beautiful April morning, sparkling and icy, the sun was dazzling but cold and everything was a pure, frozen blue. Near the villa, amidst the pines which dotted the hillside, a pure light coursed along the tree trunks. The road was empty. It went a bit uphill. Mersault was carrying a case and, in the glory of the dawning world, he strode along, his footsteps crackling on the cold road and the handle of his suitcase creaking steadily.'[6]

This is a newborn universe from which politics, history and man himself are absent. Geographical details are meaninglessly precise: the road goes a bit uphill but how much and from where? As in *L'Envers* objects are parts of a greater whole. Mersault too is part of this whole, although none of his thoughts or emotions is depicted and he is presented in the same way as the road or the hill. Yet both of these and the world itself are personified. Meanwhile the novel is narrated from the viewpoint of the April morning.

The goal of Mersault's apprenticeship is to reconcile his individual awareness with the newborn universe. Camus returns to the theme of the mother and explains that Mersault's mother had taught him abnegation. They were poor, they rarely spoke and he did not weep at her funeral; yet there was 'a secret happiness in this simplicity'. The emptiness of their life was an initiation into indifference. Now Mersault lives alone in his mother's bedroom and lies awake intoxicated by the scent of the orange flowers outside.

Like a monk he learns to deny himself and to rid himself of his personality. He deliberately takes on habits because, although habit can be a diversion which prevents man from facing his condition, it can also be, if freely accepted, a step towards death. For life itself is moving in circles. Camus stresses this by using repetition in his writing. In *La Mort Heureuse* he offers the Prague episode from *L'Envers*, *L'Etranger* contains the story of *Le Malentendu* while *Le Premier Homme*, Camus' last book, completes the circle by drawing on scenes from *L'Envers*. Meanwhile habit and repetition turn Mersault's life into a kind of game. Camus has no sense of law: existence is sanctioned by nothing except itself. Yet it can possess an order which will be both arbitrary and harmonious like the rules of soccer. So Mersault plays the games of office and café which are a further initiation into indifference, as are the hours that he spends sitting on his balcony contemplating and belonging to the Algiers streets.

Mersault is moving towards the extinction of his awareness. His friend, Emmanuel, tells horrified, fascinated stories of the Marne massacre but Mersault is just bored by them. They neither frighten nor tempt him because he lives hourly with death. His reward for contemplating the body's weakness is the revelation of the body's grace. In an intriguing scene Camus juxtaposes a docker bleeding from a wound with Mersault who is joyfully running along the harbour. Here once again are the two sides of Camus' vision. Remembering his days as a forward in the schoolyard he depicts running as a ballet where the body responds to the thrust from the ground beneath. Mersault is also a student of feminine beauty. Women do not exist as individual beings nor as love-objects; they are part of a greater harmony: 'Lucienne displayed and guaranteed a secret rhythm which bound her to the earth and reshaped the world around her movements.' The sharp, impersonal desire which Mersault feels for her is akin to his enjoyment of the sea or the sun.

The journey to Prague and the casual comradeship of the 'House-in-front-of-the-world' are merely further stages in the initiation and Mersault uses them to prepare for his death. He is familiar with the death wish for he notes, while swimming, that it would be easy to sink to the bottom. But Camus depicts a higher form of suicide where Mersault strives to confront his death as Zagreus had done. Mersault does not hide from his illness or delude himself with hope or give way to fear. While hating it, he consents to a death which was already present in his own indifference and in the Algerian mountains. So the closing lines of the novel depict his extinction as a part of the finite yet pantheistic universe: 'A stone among stones, he returned, in the joy of his heart, to the truth of the unmoving worlds.'

The dilemma of *L'Envers* seems resolved. Mersault has forced his consciousness to face its own dissolution. No longer is it separate and individual; it is now merged into what it used not to be. Death is happy and man is at one with the desert stones. Yet Mersault hates his death, which brings back the contradiction of *L'Envers*. Moreover Camus was not convinced by his novel and did not publish it. His reasons were complex: the book was too autobiographical and the depiction of Mersault's jealousy was too close to the jealousy which Camus had felt for Simone. Secondly Camus was not good at plots and characters so the 'Bildungsroman' did not really suit him. *La Mort Heureuse* has little movement, the minor characters do not live and the various settings are too much alike. Most of all the language is monotonous and inflated. One tires of passages like this one:

'In the silence populated by the silky sounds of the heavens, the night lay like milk on the world. Mersault walked on the cliff, filled with the night's grave meditation. Just below the sea whistled softly. It was full of moon and velvet, supple and soft like a wild beast.'[7]

Once more this is not a matter of weak writing. Camus is trying to achieve the impossible: to personify the universe while killing it. The litany of adjectives masks the vagueness of the experience. In order to depict Mersault from the viewpoint of consent Camus would have had to elaborate on the harmony of the opening passage and given free rein to his religious sense. Yet he cannot do so because the universe is also cold and alien to man. A minor character called Bernard injects into the novel a word of caution: sunbathing and contemplation are not enough; the goal of oneness may be just another desert mirage. The weak writing proves that Bernard is right. Camus has fallen into the trap that awaited Algerian writers: windy rhetoric. He would now cut off his religious longings and his inflated style, like a surgeon who amputates his own limbs.

The next three works all attack the concept of totality. The oneness depicted in *La Mort Heureuse* is burst asunder into its two components. Consciousness cannot be reconciled with death although moments of consent may occur and may become the touchstone of other values. But the religious impulse is criticized as a fruitless nostalgia, while death is reinstated in its stark horror. The sacraments of murder and suicide are exposed to scrutiny. More important, Camus' language changes so that *L'Etranger* is as concise as *La Mort Heureuse* was wordy. *Caligula*, *Le Mythe de Sisyphe* and *L'Etranger* also offer a more critical vision of the Algerian heritage: Camus approaches the mystery of the midday sun with caution and irony.

Not that these three books are the same. Camus was justly irritated when Sartre used *Le Mythe de Sisyphe* to interpret *L'Etranger*. To write about the alien universe in a book of ideas was different from depicting it in a novel. As pieces of writing these works have separate as well as overlapping origins. *Caligula* grows out of the Equipe theatre, *Sisyphe* out of the kind of philosophical essay which Camus discussed with Grenier and *L'Etranger* out of a reaction against the earlier, more sentimental prose. So each work will be discussed separately although they revolve around the same problem: how can man live without oneness when his whole nature craves it? How can man live in the absence of God?

The simplest of these works is *Caligula*, a play about the young, half-demented Roman emperor who butchered his courtiers and appointed his horse as consul. At the outset of the play Camus' Caligula is shocked by the death of his sister, Drusilla, with whom he has been having an incestuous love affair. He sets out to revenge her death in an orgy of killing and dissipation that lasts until he is assassinated by the patricians he has tormented.

Caligula belongs to the Equipe's last and best period. Camus wrote the first draft while he was putting on *Playboy* in early '39 and he wanted to be as bitter and as disenchanted as Synge. The switches of tone – Caligula's soliloquies are juxtaposed with the farce of the patricians' discomfort – are reminiscent of *Playboy* and are supposed to disconcert the audience. Although classical, *Caligula* has an Algerian brutality and the emperor is a thorough barbarian. Camus probably grew interested in Caligula while he listened to Jacques Heurgon's lectures on the Augustine Age. He intended to play the part of the emperor himself and to cast Jeanne Sicard as Caligula's mistress Caesonia. *Caligula* contains two plays within the play which would have suited the *Equipe* and it was to be performed with the simple, stylized scenery which Louis Miquel built so well.

Camus had absorbed the lessons of the Théâtre du Travail. *Caligula* has scant political content and the emperor's antagonists are the gods rather than the patricians. This is 'philosophical' theatre, if one wishes to use that misleading term. All the philosophy in the world could not help Caligula but, since his actions are presented not as a piece of bizarre psychology but as an example of the human condition, then the play might be called 'philosophical'. It contains the weaknesses which were potential in the Equipe and which will ruin Camus' post-war plays. In the theatre more than in his prose he lapsed into rhetoric. Determined to depict the few heroic moments when a man confronts his fate Camus forgot to make his characters human and complex. The motives and actions of *Caligula* are often ridiculous: one patrician, Cherea, slaughters the man he admires while another, Scipion, is reconciled with his father's murderer. The speeches often grow abstract and repetitive. Yet the character of Caligula – logical and passionate, humorous and cruel – is fascinating while the farcical scenes help create the 'upside-down' world.

Why then does Caligula kill? The short answer is that he has read *La Mort Heureuse* and that he too is seeking the mystical state of oneness. Drusilla's death has plunged him into a dualistic universe where he is confronted by otherness; unable to bear it he gives way to nostalgia. Scipion and he hold a conversation which is reminiscent of *La Mort Heureuse*. They lyricize about the Roman countryside and the harmony between earth and man. Once more the tree gives place to the line and the road to the darkness. Once more the silence of the evening is a moment outside of time. But Caligula is not satisfied because he knows that Mersault's quest to reconcile himself with death is impossible. Caligula demands a more traditional kind of oneness: immortality. Whereas Mersault was content with the earth, Caligula keeps saying that he wants the moon.

144

One must peel away the motives he offers for his crimes. He claims that he wishes to liberate the Romans who are trapped by habit and privilege; they must confront the otherness of the universe in order to overcome it. But Caligula converts no one and does not really care. He has a more personal goal which he spells out with excellent cartesian logic. Drusilla's death has demonstrated that man is at the mercy of the gods; ergo his only significant acts are those which assume the gods' prerogatives, namely, suicide and murder. As in *La Mort Heureuse* there is a link between violence and totality. Caligula has a death wish: he feels a kinship with his victims and he courts assassination. Conversely he kills in order to achieve the immortality which the gods have, until now, kept for themselves. When he poses to his courtiers as Venus he takes on a 'stupid, incomprehensible countenance' and becomes what the adolescent Camus had called 'a God of whom we can ask nothing'. Caligula wants to escape from the divided human condition and attain 'the unlimited joy of the unpunished murderer'.

Camus was now rejecting the strain of violence that ran through his earlier books. Indeed much of what he would write after *Caligula* may be read as a warning against man's lust for bloodshed. He links the need to kill with the striving for immortality. Suicide is an escape from the fear of death and murder is the quest for a scapegoat.

Caligula cannot bear the pain that each day brings: 'My skin hurts me, my chest and limbs too ... I have only to move my tongue and everything turns black and people become loathsome to me.' This is the anguish of man's mortal condition and *Caligula*'s special place in Camus's early writing is to express it. *Sisyphe* finds reasons to be happy while *L'Etranger* depicts mortality as an absence; in *Caligula* it is presented as a mind trapped in a confrontation with what it is not. Since the emperor cannot stand this he is overwhelmed by hatred of others and of himself. Yet murder offers no solution because the murderer's supposedly unlimited joy is as finite as everything else. When he has killed one person Caligula, like all other terrorists, has no choice but to kill someone else. Whatever he does, he remains an object of hatred to himself.

This is shown by the mirror motif which continues the theme of the glance. *Caligula* is framed by the two mirrors which are broken at the end of Acts 1 and 4. The first time he breaks the mirror Caligula leaves only his own image, foreshadowing the murder of the patricians. The second time he destroys the whole mirror and dies himself. He can no longer stand the sight of himself: 'It's always you I meet, you are always there opposite me and I hate you.'

Caligula is caught up in a confusion about guilt and innocence. Camus had a need for innocence and expresses it through the ritual of sea-bathing which he depicts as a second baptism. Like most theologians he links innocence with oneness and guilt with division. Yet the pursuit of absolute purity can lead men to crime because such innocence is outside the human condition. Camus knew this even if he continued throughout his life to feel a nostalgia for innocence. Caligula, however, cannot bear the burden of guilt. Everyone, he says, is guilty because there are no judges who could declare that men are innocent. Restated, this means that all men are guilty because they are going to die. Camus is standing orthodox catholic doctrine on its head. The punishment meted out for original sin was loss of immortality; here mortality creates the awareness of evil. Refusing to admit that he is partially guilty and partially innocent and that he can live even if Drusilla is dead, Caligula sets out to recover the lost innocence of Eden.

Only during the last act does he begin to confront his condition. When his assassins draw close he is afraid, which is human if not heroic. 'I am still alive,' he cries as the blows rain down. For the first time he is asserting his soiled, dualistic existence.

Le Mythe de Sisyphe is a philosophical essay which explores this dualism. Camus now turns to another figure from the ancient world: Sisyphus who was condemned by the gods to spend eternity pushing a rock up a hill and watching it roll back down when it reached the top. Whereas the Mersault of *La Mort Heureuse* wanted to become a stone, Camus' Sisyphus attains an identity by asserting that he is not a stone and that he is not at one with the universe.

This constitutes what Camus called the state of the absurd. Superficially *Sisyphe* is a book about suicide but in reality Camus has already banished the temptation of suicide by deciding not to publish *La Mort Heureuse* which was an apology for suicide. *Sisyphe* is a book which tells man that he can go on living because he has had the courage to give up the quest for primeval innocence and to confront his condition. He is a man because he is aware of the contradiction between his need for oneness and the finite world. This is a source of anguish but also of values. As man faces the alien universe he gains lucidity and courage which are the seeds of what Camus calls revolt.

The simplest definition of the absurd would be a rephrasing of Descartes' proposition 'I think, therefore I am'. Camus might have stated that 'I am another to myself, therefore I am'. The absurd is not a state to be overcome because it represents a victory over the previous state of suicidal mysticism. Yet it remains a religious vision because man does not forget his need for God and become a pragmatist who is content to give a shape to his earthly existence. Camus' originality lay in his attempt to preserve man's religious sense although it could not be satisfied and to make him live in the absence of God. This would seem ridiculous to Sartre and to many of Camus' readers. But Camus simply could not give up the images of eternity which he had depicted in *L'Envers* and in *La Mort Heureuse*. In *L'Etranger* Meursault says that the longing for oneness is no more important than the desire to swim faster or to be better-looking. But in *Sisyphe* this longing is man's essential characteristic.

There is a contradiction here and Camus did not help the cause of clarity by choosing to present *Sisyphe*'s arguments in a philosophical form. His real model was the *NRF* essay which Grenier had deployed in *L'Esprit de l'Orthodoxie*. This was a blend of philosophy, literary criticism and personal reflections; it allowed the author to be intuitive and to suggest rather than to prove. But Camus, trained as a philosopher and attracted to as well as repelled by cartesian logic, sets out his thought as a chain of reasoning. Poirier could have forecast that Camus would do this badly and that he would resort to the artist's weapons of rhetoric and lyricism. *Sisyphe* is best read as an imaginative work.

Camus begins very seriously: 'We must ask ourselves what the ascertainable content of this proposition might be,' he says. Then he switches and announces that he is 'going back to everyday language'. His anecdotes are vivid because the absurd is not something he has discovered in a philosophy text book but a part of his experience. He treasures the examples that he finds on the Algiers streets: a man in a phone-booth gesticulating but sealed off is the best demonstration of dualism. By contrast the philosophical pages of *Sisyphe* are

147

simplistic. Camus invokes the traditional arguments for scepticism but ignores the arguments against it. Although he discusses many philosophers he has absorbed none of them. He uses second-hand sources and works of vulgarization. Realizing the shortcomings of the popular cartesianism that was instilled by the French education system, he rejects all other philosophies along with it. The real meaning of *Sisyphe* is expressed in lyrical passages which depict the absurd as an adventure: 'Shall we then accept the heart-rending, marvellous gamble of the absurd? Let us make a first attempt to do so, let us face the full consequences. Man's body, his nobility, his tenderness, creation and action will recover their place in this absurd world. He will rediscover the wine of the absurd and the bread of indifference, which will nourish his greatness.'[8]

Of the multitude of authors whom Camus discusses one will single out only two: Husserl and Malraux. Camus' analysis of Husserl's phenomenology helps us realize what is instinctive and special about his vision of the absurd, while his remarks on Malraux enable us to place the absurd in the context of French writing.

Camus uses Husserl, the German philosopher who was studied a good deal in 1930's France, to destroy the comfortable cartesian universe: 'to think is no longer to unify, to explain appearances in the light of some great principle'. This is only partially correct because, while Husserl did not feel that the universe was a closed totality, he did feel that there was some unity and that man could know it. If he did not, like Descartes, believe in the idea of a chair, he did believe that all chairs contain something invariable which can be ascertained by description. One of his disciples spent an entire semester describing a letter-box to a group of students. The letter-box was not situated in a realm outside man's intelligence; man could know it, however slowly and imperfectly.

Camus exaggerates Husserl's scepticism because he is himself sceptical and because he wants to show that the world is dualistic. In *La Peste* there is a passage which repeats this view of Husserl: Rieux notes that, while he can know Tarrou's gestures, he can know nothing of the man. But according to Husserl consciousness does engage in a difficult dialogue with the outside world. There is not the sense of irremediable

148

otherness which is present in *La Peste*. Camus is making Husserl more pessimistic than he really was.

Having over-emphasized Husserl's dualism, Camus then accuses him of resolving it falsely. According to Husserl, says Camus, there are in the universe extra-temporal essences which man can know by intuition. This is not correct because Husserl did not make such a harsh distinction between reason and intuition and did not situate the 'essences' outside of time. But since Camus can perceive knowledge only as a leap of faith, he attributes such a leap to Husserl and then rebukes him for it. The personal slant in Camus' criticism is clear: he himself will not resolve the dualism which is the starting-point of the absurd.

The criticism which he makes of Dostoevsky, Kierkegaard and the other writers he discusses is that they undertake similar leaps of faith. Camus is really refuting his own earlier books; Husserl and Dostoevsky are accused of pursuing the quest of *La Mort Heureuse* which Camus has now given up. He has discovered that the state of the absurd is not merely an anguish or an amputation; it is also a matter of nobility and creativity.

The values he perceives in it grow clear when he discusses Malraux. The novel he analyses is *Les Conquérants* (1928) but since this was a trial run for *La Condition Humaine* (1933) he might have considered the two together. Political commitment, argues Camus, is only the instrument which the conqueror uses to give shape to his life. This is certainly correct because Bolshevik man is the peg on which Malraux drapes his own ideal. His heroes like Garine or Kyo choose to side with the working class in order to fight for their own dignity. Dignity is not primarily a political value because the revolutionary has no illusions about the intrinsic value of the working class and even wonders whether there will be any place for him in post-revolutionary society. Dignity is a metaphysical value because the conqueror is able in the political struggle to overcome the anguish which the absurd universe inspires in him and which threatens to destroy his identity. Like Camus, Malraux felt the absurd as the conflict between man's desire for meaning and the shapelessness of his condition. Dignity is the way to transcend that condition: Sisyphus attains it when he affirms his superiority over the rock.

149

To Camus dignity was a value that he felt instinctively and that he linked with his Spanish heritage. Like Malraux he derives other values from it. Both writers talk much of virility. Neither has succeeded in creating women characters who are memorable and both exalt male fraternity. The brotherhood among the revolutionaries was the value which Camus most admired in *La Condition Humaine*. The Bolshevik Katow gives the cyanide that could save him from torture to two comrades who are lying in prison beside him; they die easily and he goes out like a martyr to be burned alive.

Yet there were great differences between Malraux and his young admirer. In analysing the conquerors Camus leaves out their essential characteristic: their hope that they will be transformed as they face their death. The terrorist Tchen turns his assassinations into religious rituals and then seeks out the special ritual of suicide. In deciding to throw himself under the dictator's car along with his bomb he is hoping for a flash of eternity, a moment that will reshape his entire life. This is the hope that drives Katow to give up his cyanide. Malraux loved gambling because it propelled man into a confrontation with destiny which could destroy or remake him; Camus was a more prudent gambler who no longer believed in such transformations. Sisyphe expects no miracles; he merely carries out his task with stoical pride.

What separated him from Malraux was Camus' sense that the absurd could in itself be a source of values. To Camus the terrorist Tchen was, like Caligula, a sterile figure whose religious quest was a vicious illusion. Man should abandon not pursue suicide; ordinary life offered possibilities. So the absurd was not an unbearable anguish and the flash of eternity was an impossible miracle. Conversely man could be happy in his divided condition. These differences explain why Malraux flirted with the Communist Party for longer than Camus did and why he turned to De Gaulle whom Camus admired much less. Communism and Gaullism offered revealed truths and miracles; Camus believed in neither but he did believe in a more modest brand of dignity. It is not surprising that, when Camus and Malraux met during and after the war, they never became friends.

A comparison with two other writers who mention *Le Mythe de Sisyphe* demonstrates Camus' peculiar optimism. In *Molloy*

Samuel Beckett writes sarcastically that 'certain commentators' depict a happy Sisyphus.[9] This seems silly to Beckett whose narrators are incapable of happiness because they are corroded by the meaninglessness of things. In *Féerie pour une Autre Fois* Céline discusses *Sisyphe* although he certainly had not read it. In his case, he remarks, the rock keeps falling back on his head. He too is saying that the absurd is painful and that it cannot be a source of values. Perhaps it might be conjured away with humour and ballet but it cannot be confronted heroically. Such criticisms do not alter one's opinion of Camus' writing but they emphasize that the absurd is more than a matter of anguish.

Indeed *Sisyphe* sets out the new code of moral, political and aesthetic revolt. Camus reveals his deep moral sense when he affirms that, although man cannot know himself, he is capable of behaving morally. His starting-point should be the liberation that comes from the absurd. If transcendentalism is abandoned, man can turn to this life with greater zest. This is the energy which Camus attributes to Don Juan, to the actor and to the conqueror. The actor – one remembers the style of acting in the Equipe – tries desperately to become Prometheus or the Playboy because he can be it for only a few hours. Don Juan is not looking for God in the arms of women; because he knows that there is no God he loves as many women as he can. Camus, the primitive, stresses the need to cast off restraint and the young people who read *Sisyphe* in the 1940's welcomed in it the call to live and to trust only one's direct experience.

Yet Camus' thought is nuanced. Don Juan is not a passionate lover, the actor juxtaposes his energy with the awareness that he is playing a part, while the conqueror knows he can win no political victories. All three are conscious of limits. To Camus limits are not restrictions for they sharpen the intensity of experience just as the rules of soccer heighten the skill of the players. Moreover other values emerge from the free acceptance of limits. Don Juan demonstrates courage and lucidity, perhaps the most traditional of French moral values. Refusing to believe in the false mystique of love he seduces his last woman and waits to die, aware that he is old and ridiculous. The actor shows lucidity when he emphasizes the edge of nothingness that is present in all his roles.

Clearly this is a masculine, aristocratic morality. Don Juan is generous rather than kind, virile rather than tender, stoical

151

rather than sensitive. The absence of the traditional values of women is striking as Camus would acknowledge. The plague, he later writes, is a world without women; Rieux and Tarrou are aristocrats but nothing can fill the place of women.

Today's readers would agree and would find the call to heroism rather hollow; the most interesting part of Camus' moral thought seems now to be the flat rejection of violence. In *Sisyphe* lucidity tells that there can be no pantheistic universe and no conquest of the moon so it is useless to gun down Zagreus or to murder idle patricians. 'We cannot praise force unless it is clear-sighted,' says Camus who feels that violence is rarely clear-sighted. The sophisticate in Camus is speaking; this is the un-Algerian Camus who invokes limits to correct the violence of his fellow-Algerians. It is a historical paradox that the Red Brigade's leader, Renato Curcio, should have read *Sisyphe* and drawn from it the conclusion that life is worthless and extremism justified. *Sisyphe* was a milestone on Curcio's road to terrorism.[10] Yet the correct interpretation is that terrorism is self-indulgent and that the violence implicit in the hot midday of Algiers must be curbed.

Sisyphe's political content is thinner and mostly negative. When he writes that the conqueror can never win Camus is attacking the mystique of revolution which is another form of false oneness like religion or cartesianism. This is the theme which he will treat at greater length in *L'Homme Révolté*. Yet one wonders why Camus rejects more moderate forms of the political struggle without even discussing them. If revolutions are impossible, then why does the conqueror not work for gradual reforms? Why not join the Socialists instead of the Bolsheviks? But Camus remains the young man who had castigated Fouchet. Reformism cannot change the human condition. Just as there is no psychological diversity so there are no differences between high and low inflation rates. Only failed revolutions suit Sisyphe who is more of an absolutist than he seems. Yet this undermines the value of Camus' critique of violence because violence is a political as well as an ethical problem. If it is to be abandoned, then other paths to social change must be indicated. This contradiction will plague Camus' post-war writing.

At first sight it seems astonishing that the crusading journalist of *Alger-Républicain* should write such an unpolitical book as *Sisyphe*. Then one remembers the silence which surrounded his best articles. The condemned prisoners on the galley-ship are metaphysical as well as social victims and anyway there is nothing the journalist can do to help them.

Sisyphe does contain a more convincing aesthetic argument which begins with the ideas thrown out by Caligula. The emperor was an artist who described his murders as poetry and theatre. Conversely he disliked writers who explained and consoled; valid literature was to show an awareness of death. In *Sisyphe* Camus explains that art is an act of willpower which allows the artist to reshape the universe. But it is also incomplete because the universe contains no totality. Camus makes a rather facile distinction between philosophy which deals with the spirit world and literature which deals only with the concrete. Then he goes deeper when he argues that art must not explain and that it must criticize the order it creates. It may offer a deliberately incomplete narrative, as Camus will do in *L'Etranger*. Or it may depict an 'upside-down' world like the Equipe.

Camus is hovering between two views, the one traditional and the other new. He calls for a new brand of classicism and demands that art be concise and lucid. Elsewhere he writes that French classicism is the model for modern writers and that he would give all Hemingway for a hundred pages of the seventeenth-century novel *La Princesse de Clèves*. This reveals the conservative strand in his thinking and reminds us of his liking for classical tragedy. Camus was suspicious of avant-gardes and distrusted showy stylistic innovation. During the Second World War he would invoke French cultural traditions as a weapon to be used against the Nazis.

Yet the concept of a new classicism is not exciting because modern writing cannot, except in the most general way, resemble the seventeenth century. Camus is more innovative when he stresses that the work must contain its own refutation. Lucidity becomes a destructive force which undermines the artist's imaginative conquest. So the work will 'say less'. Camus' three novels – *L'Etranger*, *La Peste* and *La Chute* – are all attempts to tell a story while leaving out an essential part of it. This section of *Sisyphe* continues the article on *La Nausée* where Camus criticizes Sartre for believing too much in writing. Here Camus even wonders whether absurd art is possible at all.

He is revealing perhaps that fear of writer's impotence that always lurked in the depths of his mind. He concludes that art is possible but that it will be short, dry and ironic – like *L'Etranger*.

Despite the talk of irony, limits and stoicism *Sisyphe* has a lyrical conclusion. Not only is Sisyphe happy but his act of defiance has transformed all things: 'in the universe, which suddenly reverts to its silence, the thousand, wondrous voices of the earth are heard'. This is the experience of reconciliation which had been the theme of *L'Envers* and of *La Mort Heureuse* and which *Sisyphe* has supposedly rejected. The undercurrent of lyricism which is felt in the book and which swells up here is a sign that Camus still dreams of oneness. The effort which Sisyphe has made to overcome his futile task is akin to the upsurge of vitality which Camus had felt at Vicenza. Now he tells us that this upsurge must always be unsatisfied. Yet it still constitutes the core of man's being. *Sisyphe*'s values are not really relative or pragmatic because they spring from man's need for the absolute.

One should not explain away the contradiction in Camus' thinking. Having denied God, he now hints that the universe might after all be shaped in His image. He cannot bring himself to give up a religious urge which springs from his sense that the world is beautiful. The delight he took in the Algerian countryside was so intense that, deny it as he might, he felt it must possess some greater significance. Without the universal ballet courage and lucidity were impossible. So Camus revelled in man's religious sense even as he repeated that it must be amputated. The language of *Sisyphe* goes deeper than the philosophy: Camus struggles against the temptation of lyricism but he does not overcome it.

This lyricism, while it may seem facile today, was another reason for *Sisyphe*'s popularity in the '40's. It hinted that in casting off restraint man was not after all destroying traditional moral values or going beyond God. Generosity, hope and even the dream of innocence made their way back into the world by a subterranean route. *Sisyphe*'s rhetorical ending might be contradictory and vague but that did not matter. It won for Camus far more readers than his philosophy could win and it established him as a prophet of hope. The reader of today may, however, feel that the victory of hope over anguish is too easily won and that *Sisyphe* is not one of Camus' best books.

L'Etranger contains similar contradictions but its best pages present the absurd as a tragic absence or amputation. The novel is so well-known that it scarcely needs to be summarized. Meursault buries his mother, goes to the beach, meets a girl Marie and becomes friendly with a thug Raymond. Next come the most puzzling pages in all Camus' writing. Raymond has quarrelled with an Arab who follows him to the beach. In the blinding midday heat Meursault walks on the beach, meets the Arab and shoots him. Then comes the second half of the book where Meursault is tried for his crime and condemned to death by a court which seems meaningless to him.

In the opening pages Meursault has none of the qualities that Camus associates with the absurd; he is neither brave nor generous. Surrounded by a universe he cannot penetrate he displays the indifference which Camus depicts so well. As a narrator Meursault tells a story that he cannot understand. So the point of view from which the novel is written reveals the frustration of humans trapped in an incomplete universe.

L'Etranger is a reaction against *La Mort Heureuse*. Having tried to write a long novel with several shifts of place and a group of characters, Camus decided to leave out such things and to 'say less'. This enabled him to succeed where he himself, Roblès, De Fréminville and others had failed and to write an outstanding Algerian novel. The emptiness which hovers around the edges of *L'Action* lies at the centre of *L'Etranger*. Other Algerian writers had felt it but only Camus makes it into his main subject. By the various techniques of free, indirect speech, the avoidance of the simple past and the like, he succeeded in writing from the viewpoint of this emptiness instead of merely writing about it. After three generations French Algeria gave birth to its great novel.

The so-called 'Americanness' of *L'Etranger* is a false trail. Camus stated afterwards that he had used Hemingway's techniques in order to portray a character who is 'ostensibly without awareness'.[11] But Camus was always willing to admit that he had submitted to influences and he often exaggerated their importance; it was part of his desire to be honest and nice. Only a few passages of *L'Etranger* are written in the manner of

The Sun Also Rises. As Meursault stands on his balcony he surveys the street; he limits himself to visual observation and does not reconstruct what he sees. Even this owes less to Hemingway than to Camus' evolution. He had always noted the details of Algerian popular life. Previously he had lapsed into sentimentality but he had schooled himself to write more objectively.

Anyway, most of *L'Etranger* is written in very different language, as the first oft-quoted sentences show: 'Mama died today. Or perhaps yesterday, I don't know. I received a telegram from the home: "Mother passed away. Funeral tomorrow. Yours truly". That doesn't mean anything. Perhaps it was yesterday.'[12] Society's reaction to the death is formal but uncaring; Meursault does not care either but he does think. He probes the telegram to discover when his mother died. For the director of the home the event is finished but for Meursault it is an unsolved riddle which nags at him. This is quite different from *The Sun Also Rises* where the narrator notes but does not puzzle over what happens. Meursault's special trait is that he does not understand but that he keeps trying. His narrative is punctuated by 'I think' and 'I believe'. At the funeral he wonders about the old people and, when he is in prison, he tries to make sense of the rules. His aim is to understand but he never can.

Other technical innovations widen the gulf between what is happening and what Meursault thinks is happening. Expressions of time are deliberately vague because Meursault does not perceive a sequence in what happens. Yet because he searches for such a sequence the book is littered with 'soons' and 'not long afterwards'. Similarly Camus does not use the simple past – 'I did' – which is the usual tense of the French novel. The simple past depicts a succession of events and implies that they have a coherence which the narrator can perceive. Camus uses the perfect tense – 'I have done' which links the experience more directly to the narrator but does not organize it.

The sense of otherness is strengthened by the use of free indirect speech:

'He stated that he wanted to discuss with me a plan which was still very vague. He only wanted my opinion on the subject. He intended to set up an office in Paris which would do business directly with the big companies and he wanted to know if I would like to work in it. I would be able to live in Paris.'[13]

The last three sentences follow from the initial 'he stated' but they are a long way away from it. Camus had used this technique in *L'Envers* in order to allow his working-class characters to speak for themselves. Here he goes further and presents fresh points of view without identifying them. The boss' views stand in the text like a block of experience which is not Meursault's but appears to belong to no one else. The 'he' contrasts with Meursault's 'I' and Meursault is not able to dominate it.[14]

One remembers the comment 'ostensibly without awareness'. Meursault does possess an awareness but it never impinges on events or emotions. So he oscillates between total comprehension and total scepticism. In prison he agrees that the rules are reasonable and a guard compliments him: 'You understand, you do.' More often he is sceptical. When Marie asks him whether he loves her, he answers like a philosopher: 'I replied that that didn't mean anything but that I thought I did not.' He is not certain of his own feelings and anyway the interesting problem is whether Marie's question can be asked at all. A neighbour, Salamano, has a dog which he torments to the outrage of the other people in the building. Only Meursault asks whether Salamano really dislikes the dog and he concludes that 'truthfully no one can tell'. Meursault looks forward to Beckett's narrators who keep telling us they understand nothing and have nothing to tell us.

In Beckett's novels the world has started to crumble and only a ruined cartesian consciousness remains. Meursault, however, is surrounded by sensations like the salt of the sea or the smells of the docks. He even has feelings: he dislikes policemen and brothels. But he dismisses such feelings as foreign bodies which do not constitute a character or a personality.

Although he feels indifference he does not cultivate it as the Mersault of *La Mort Heureuse* did. To Mersault sunbathing and swimming were stepping-stones towards consent, whereas in *L'Etranger* they are fragments of experience to be enjoyed but discarded. Only in the second, less original half of the book are there hints that Meursault's ability to enjoy swimming and confront monotony is a source of values and even a sign of reconciliation. But the first half of *L'Etranger* is a story told by a narrator whose lucid mind fails to make sense of what is happening.

The novel changes when Meursault shoots the Arab and opens up a pandora's box of problems. The first difficulty with these pages is that they do not fit because their language is different. Camus reverts to the solar lyricism of *La Mort Heureuse*: the sun shines with 'opaque intoxication' and its rays are 'swordblades of light'. The point of view shifts too for when Meursault exclaims 'I understood that I had destroyed the harmony of the day,' he is showing a comprehension that he has never shown before. This is a different and second Meursault who knows more than he did and yet does not fully understand what is happening. So this episode has no coherent point of view. Of course the murder is in part an artifice which allows Camus to move to the second half of the novel where he depicts yet another Meursault who is persecuted by society. But it is more than an artifice because it continues and contrasts with the murder of *La Mort Heureuse* and it is an oblique comment on European-Arab relations in Algeria. It is an integral if ambiguous part not only of *L'Etranger* but of Camus' early writing.

Why does the second Meursault kill and why does he kill an Arab? The answer to the first question must be sought in the theme of the 'look' and in the relationship between oneness and violence. This moment is a variant on the moments in *L'Envers* and *La Mort Heureuse* where man ceases to be a separate individual and becomes part of the universe. Once more space and time dissolve: 'the sound of the waves was ever lazier and more even than at midday. It was the same sun, the same light on the same sand which stretched way out.' Then Meursault is blinded. Until now he has stared with incomprehension at Algiers; now he is caught up in 'an ocean of boiling metal' and he re-enters the mystical world of *La Mort Heureuse*.

In short Meursault is going to die. His death is a sacrament where he is to be sacrificed to the sun. In this stylized setting the river appears as a refuge defended by the Arab. If Meursault is to reach the coolness and avoid dying, then he has to dispatch the Arab. The sacrament changes shape: from victim Meursault becomes executioner. By killing the Arab he is able to live for the Arab is dying in his place. Meursault cannot face his death, as his namesake had done in *La Mort Heureuse*. He is not willing to return to the earth and become a stone among stones. So the Arab is to be his scapegoat.

Although he half-explains this the second Meursault does not really understand what is happening. What does he mean when he exclaims that he has destroyed the harmony of the day? This is different from *La Mort Heureuse* where the murder is in harmony with the universe. Camus now demonstrates that murder is not a shortcut to mysticism; like Caligula, Meursault recognizes that killing is no solution. Yet this admission of guilt is vague because until now there has been in *L'Etranger* no harmony to destroy. So the comment does not elucidate the murder which is not depicted from one clear point of view.

Why then the Arab? Like other French-Algerian writers Camus depicts Arabs as models of silence and contemplation. In *L'Envers* the narrator's reflections on the infinite are triggered off by an Arab café: 'the owner of the café seems to be looking at my empty glass . . . I hear him breathing very loudly and his eyes shine in the semi-darkness'. He never speaks and never moves; his look is absorbed into the glass and the darkness. Much more than the narrator, the Arab contemplates the universe and is at one with it. In *L'Etranger* the Arab is not merely defending the stream. Part of his body is exposed to the sun and he can tolerate its rays. He is not threatened by death like that second-rate sun-worshipper Meursault. Similarly both he and Meursault are creatures of indifference but the Arab is more indifferent. So he is brother and rival, a more authentic Meursault. This would not have bothered the first Meursault who lived with the incomplete and the inauthentic. But it is a threat to the second and midday Meursault, the seeker of eternity.

Other French-Algerian writers had shown that Arab-European relations contained this germ of violence. In *L'Action* Roblès perceives a threat in the Arab's contemplative gaze. Yet when violence erupts it is committed by the European against the Arab. The strike-leader, Astore, sends the Arab, Hadj, to his death. When Hadj tries to kill a European he fails; the Europeans make no such mistake. Camus too shows that, while the Arab threatens the European, he quickly becomes a victim.

The incoherence in the point of view and the ambiguities of this episode must reflect Camus' own hesitation. In his

Alger-Républicain articles he laid bare European injustice but then he stopped. In his imaginative works he went further and *L'Etranger* depicts the kinship, rivalry and bloodlust between Europeans and Arabs. Camus felt and dreaded this violence, just as he dreaded the violence of another world war. He knew that the French-Algerian's reckless passion for life spurred him on to acts of bloodshed which had to be directed against his rival and victim, the Arab. The darker side of Camus' imagination did not believe that Mediterranean medleys and Keynesian economics could prevent this. Sooner or later the jealous European would strike down the Arab. Camus felt this but, since the only genuine solution was independence which meant the death of the European, there was nothing he could do. Like Meursault, Camus felt that he was willing this violence and he blamed himself for it. Yet he could only depict European violence in this ambiguous way, stranding it between the two halves of *L'Etranger*.

On its own it may stand as a parable about French-Algeria. The theme of authenticity has a general validity. Usurpers in this land, the Europeans had to become its legitimate owners. So they faced the deserts and the droughts. Yet they remained less authentic than the Arab who became an object of fascination and jealousy. The distance between Louis Bertrand's hatred and Robert Randau's admiration was smaller than it seemed. There came a moment when the French-Algerian realized that he lived in a few isolated cities surrounded by desert and Arabs. Then the jealousy of the Arab became intolerable, just as the sun becomes intolerable to the sun-worshipper Meursault.

Camus shows further ambiguities when he tries to link the crime with the rest of the book. The differences between the Meursault who buries his mother and the midday Meursault are great enough to vindicate the former and to confirm the change that had taken place in Camus' thought since *La Mort Heureuse*. The Meursault of the opening pages could not have committed this crime; it is not a part of his divided universe. What of the second half of the book? Conor Cruise O'Brien points out that the trial is unrealistic. Meursault would never have been condemned for the murder of an Arab and his case would have been dismissed as legitimate self-defence.[15] Yet this is not a proof that Camus ignored the question of French-Algeria's guilt. Such realism would have been unwarranted in a novel as stylized as *L'Etranger*. Moreover Algerian justice is depicted as arbitrary and Meursault's trial reminds one of El Okbi's. Accused of killing an Arab, Meursault is tried for killing his mother; accused of murder, El Okbi was tried for being an Arab spokesman. Either way action against Arabs is ignored while action on their behalf is punished. French-Algerian justice is a vicious fantasy.

But Camus' depiction of it is complicated by the theme which dominates the second half of the book: Meursault's persecution by society. As Meursault begins to assert the values of his absurd life so he grows more and more innocent of the murder of the Arab. A third Meursault emerges who has read *Sisyphe* and who begins to show courage and lucidity as society threatens to destroy him. The murder of the Arab fades away as the question of whether Meursault murdered his mother grows in importance. That Camus should jumble together the mother and the Arab is a pointer to the stand he would take during the Algerian War. But, whatever the Freudian subtleties of this substitution, the problem of Meursault's precise responsibility for the Arab's death is smoothed aside.

It is ridiculous to conclude that, when he depicts this murder, Camus is showing the reaction of the pied-noir who hates Arabs. But this episode does not deal with the European-Arab problem in a way that is aesthetically convincing and it is not a good piece of fiction. In the second Meursault's half-admission of guilt and in the fantasy of the trial Camus comes close to declaring that the warnings against violence which he was issuing in *Sisyphe* were not specific enough and that the form of bloodshed he dreaded the most was colonial violence exercised against the Arab. But one must agree with Conor Cruise O'Brien that this episode contains weaknesses and that Camus never comes to grips with colonial violence. He was too much of a pied-noir to consider himself a colonizer.

The third Meursault who undergoes the trial is less interesting than the first Meursault. Up to the murder Meursault has tried to make up stories about his life; afterwards other people make them up for him. A new and false consciousness is introduced: the look and the rhetoric of society. It reaches a climax in the speeches of the two lawyers, one of them painting Meursault as a monster, the other as a dutiful son. The defence lawyer uses the 'I' form which robs Meursault of any personal existence.

The more original theme of the opening pages remains present because, although Meursault resents the imposition of other consciousnesses, he admits that his own is useless. Frustrated at being left out of the trial he wants to make a speech. Then he gives up: 'When I thought about, it, I had nothing to say.' As before, Meursault thinks but he does not understand; he does not know why he killed the Arab or put his mother in a home. Yet his indifference is gradually turning into a value and the focus of the book is shifting.

In a preface written in 1955 for the American edition of *L'Etranger* Camus stated that Meursault was a man who died for truth, persecuted by an unjust society.[16] This is an over-simplification which ignores the first half of the novel. But Camus did try to insinuate into the second half the rudimentary values that he discussed in *Sisyphe*.

Meursault trusts only his own experience and dismisses philosophy and tradition. This leads him to a battle with the prison chaplain where he rejects heaven and hell, just as Camus had rejected pheonomenology. Meursault changes here. He makes the categorical statement that value judgements are unimportant; previously he would have been too sceptical to affirm this. He begins to construct an identity around his scepticism. He shows the courage which *Sisyphe* had recommended; he trusts only his direct sensuous experience of the sea and of Marie.

L'Etranger ends joyfully. Meursault hopes that the crowds will shout their hatred at him as he is led out to execution because this will reassert the difference between them and him. He is dying without pseudo-idealisms, other people's judgements or false consolations. He even knows the experience of oneness: 'I woke up with the stars on my face . . . the wondrous peace of that slumbering summer came flooding over me.' This is the ecstasy which concludes *Sisyphe*; the world is dualistic and yet somewhere there is consent. The first Meursault knew that he was guilty – of his mother's death, of the inconvenience he caused his boss, of everything. 'One is always a bit at fault,' he says. Man is mortal and hence flawed. But the Meursault of the closing pages is innocent and he goes to the guillotine reconciled with the universe.

The primitive pantheistic upsurge remains the greatest theme of Camus' early writing. It is checked in the last three books; Camus warns against it and struggles against it. But it drives him on and it continues to break out as lyricism. It is, despite its contradictions, the reason why his early writing could be read in the '40's as a message of hope. For there are in these books two different Camus. The first was a tragic writer, determined to show not merely how men can live without God – most men manage this rather easily – but how a religious man can live in the absence of God. The second Camus discovered even in this absence a more elusive presence: the presence in the human condition of courage and a capacity for joy. It is this second Camus who would become the moral conscience of his generation.

But not all Camus' readers were looking for moral lessons or for an exaltation of earthly life. *L'Etranger* was read in the prison camps of Nazi Germany and many readers were struck by its pessimism. One of them describes it as a view from the other side of the moon.[17] The primitive Camus called on men to die as well as to live more directly. The student of Augustine depicted a world flawed by some original sin and the '40's had every reason to believe in original sin. For such readers Meursault, the frustrated cartesian, was more interesting than Meursault, the imprisoned innocent. Before he dies Meursault gathers together the memories of his room and tries without success to rebuild them into a 'summa' of his existence. This passage offers neither lyricism nor morality but it reveals Camus' ability to 'say less'.

By the time *L'Etranger* was published Camus had left Algeria and would never return there to live. His life would change dramatically at the Liberation and his work would change too. But Algeria remained present, as a lost dream of innocence and as an insoluble and tragic problem. Just as he never went beyond God, so Camus never went beyond Algeria. However much he changed, he remained an unrepentant pied-noir.

6

A Writer at War

Camus had a personal reason for not wanting to leave Algeria in 1940: he was engaged to be married. He had met Francine Faure in the summer of '37 when she came from Oran to stay at the House-in-front-of-the-World. She was fair-haired and pretty and she had large, beautiful eyes; this appealed to Camus – Simone Hié had also had fine eyes. He made a point of seeking out Francine and he talked to her about the theatre. Francine was impressed. The House-in-front-of-the-World both overawed and delighted her because its floating population of students and artists was a change from her strict family in Oran.

One year younger than Camus, she came from a family that was as authentically Algerian as his. One of her great-grandparents had been a Berber Jew who had lived in Algeria before the Conquest. Her grandfather and her father had run a construction business in Oran but her father was killed in the First World War. Although this created a bond between her and Camus their upbringings had been very different. Madame Faure was plunged into poverty by her husband's death and had to take a job at the post office. But she had impeccably middle-class ideas and she tried to instil them into her daughter.

Francine learned that she must be educated, accomplished and charming and, when Camus met her, she was all three. She was studying mathematics at a Paris 'lycée' and hoped to go on to the university. She played the piano and talked well about music. She had the kind of prettiness that was universally recognized and she was accustomed to being admired. She was also high-spirited and somewhat daring. Camus was not at all like the correct young men who courted her in Oran and on whom her mother smiled benignly. He was poor, he had no regular job and he was almost a communist. Yet he was also the uncrowned king of the House-in-front-of-the-World and his many talents dazzled her. He was good-looking and Francine had the pied-noir's appreciation of good looks.

When she returned to Paris they wrote to each other. Camus carried on this relationship simultaneously with several others. It was now that he met Blanche Balain and he was still close to Christiane Galindo. Although such diversity suited Camus' temperament, he knew that he would not be able to treat Francine like a casual conquest. A well brought-up young lady, she would have to be wooed.

Camus understood this and to the amazement of his male friends he transformed himself into a polite suitor. When Francine came back to Algiers in the summer of '38 the two carried on a correct courtship. Poncet remembers seeing them walk together in a park. Francine was wearing a light summer dress with a large hat, while Camus had a tie; they were arm-in-arm, very much the young couple. Camus' sudden need for ties amused his friends. If he had been something of a dandy in his schooldays he had long since given up the pursuit of elegance. Now he came around to Bénisti's house and asked to borrow a clean shirt and a tie.

By now Francine had given up the idea of studying at a French university. Her health had suffered from the strain of doing advanced mathematics and she returned home to Oran.[1] This might have been a warning signal to Camus. Although she possessed a touch of daring, Francine was a delicate girl who was still dominated by her family. As well as her mother she had two strong-minded sisters who made most of her decisions for her. Francine was accustomed to being led rather than to leading. Yet her attachment to family and convention did not displease Camus. Despite or because of his disastrous first marriage he was preparing to marry again. He was looking for the stability and the gentleness that a wife would offer. He and Francine were well-matched. She was a conventional girl who was willing to take a risk while he was an outsider who strove to be normal.

During 1938–39 Francine came to Algiers frequently and, whenever he could escape from *Alger-Républicain*, Camus went to Oran. He brought Francine into the Equipe group and tried to find a part for her in one of his productions. Meanwhile she found a job as a teacher in an elementary school and she lived at home. But her mother and sisters were less than delighted with her suitor. Madame Faure had hoped that her pretty daughter would marry well and was disappointed with Camus. She disliked *Alger-Républicain* and was appalled by Camus' political views. The thought of having a penniless communist as her son-in-law caused her great distress.

Camus did not help matters when he came to Oran. Although he exerted his charm in the Faure household he was irritated by Madame Faure's pretensions. She kept asking about his mother and referred to her as 'Madame Camus'. 'There is no "Madame Camus",' he snapped in reply; the term 'Madame' was reserved for the middle-classes.

Francine battled against her family and persuaded them to accept Camus. He and she talked about marriage and he began the legal proceedings to obtain a divorce from Simone Hié who was preparing to marry Léon Cottenceau. In February 1940 the divorce was granted although it would not take effect until the autumn. Just when Camus was free to marry, *Alger-Républicain* collapsed, confirming Madame Faure's worst suspicions about her son-in-law.

Francine and Camus made their plans. Camus would have to go to France but Francine would join him as soon as they could legally marry. Camus kept saying that they must not allow the war to interfere with their lives and Francine was comforted by his determination. Moreover her very intelligent sisters agreed that this suitor might not, after all, be unsuitable. There was no formal engagement but Camus was to write regularly and to send for Francine as soon as he could.

Their parting made Camus feel all the more depressed when he set out for Paris. He had two assets: a job of sorts and a friend, Pia. But he was leaving behind Francine, the Equipe group and the Algerian spring. Paris offered him winter and loneliness. When he reported to *Paris-Soir* he discovered that his reputation as a crusading journalist had preceded him. 'No politics here,' said the man who interviewed him. 'Naturally,' answered Camus. His work, like Pia's, consisted of setting the pages, a craft which he had learned at *Alger-Républicain*.

Both he and Pia despised *Paris-Soir*. Owned by businessmen Jean Prouvost who would enter the Vichy government, it was known as *Pourri-Soir*. It avoided serious discussion of politics but such opinions as it had were conservative. Crimes, divorces and film-stars took up its other pages. It exemplified the commerical press which *Alger-Républicain* had castigated. Camus particularly disliked the human-interest stories; their gushing sentimentality was the antithesis of his stoicism. He came to loathe the editor, Pierre Lazareff.

There was no question of writing for *Pourri-Soir*. Camus devoted his spare moments to his own writing. In May he finished *L'Etranger* and set about finishing *Sisyphe*. As the phoney war dragged on he wrote doggedly. He had not changed his view of the war but, having lost *Alger-Républicain*, he could no longer combat it.

Since he had little money, he moved from one cheap hotel to another. At *Paris-Soir* he made friends with the printers who shared his contempt for the paper but he still felt terribly alone in Paris. He liked Les Halles in the early morning: the burly lorry-drivers who started the day with a glass of red wine reminded him of the Algiers dockers. More often Paris was anonymous and dead. One cold, wet day he climbed the Montmartre hill: Paris 'stretched out in the rain like a mist; it was a shapeless grey swelling of earth.'[2] Camus suffered from the lack of colour: the trees were black and pigeons merged into the murky sky. A woman in his hotel committed suicide. Desperately lonely, she used to hang around the owner and invite herself for meals. One day she jumped out of the window.

Her death shook Camus who felt that Paris life was a test of will-power: 'it is hard and terrible, a torture that leaves you hovering on the brink of madness'.[3] Against Paris' indifference he asserted his own. Survival was in itself an act of courage. Yet Bénisti who visited him found Camus overwhelmed by misery. He asked eagerly about Poncet and the others and described himself as an exile. One day he met a Spaniard who had fought against Franco. The Spaniard spoke no French, had no money and was bewildered by the Paris bustle. Camus felt a kinship with him.

The phoney war ended with the German onslaught and the flight from Paris. This changed Camus' view. No longer were the French almost as guilty as the Nazis. Hitler now became the incarnation of that cruel absurdity which Camus had felt months before on the Algiers streets. Yet he could not combat the Nazis. He was cast adrift on the ocean of total war, one of millions of displaced persons.

Pourri-Soir had done a deal with the new prime minister Laval. It would settle in Clermont-Ferrand, Laval's hometown, and would rent his printing-press. With superb disregard for politics, Laval had made the same offer to the socialist *Le Populaire* and to the *Action Française*; money came before ideology. On June 10 Camus set out with the rest of the *Paris-Soir* staff for Clermont. The roads were blocked with retreating soldiers and with civilians streaming out of Paris. The car overheated and threatened to go on fire, so Camus went rushing to the trunk to save the manuscript of *L'Etranger*. Once more he whiled away the boring hours talking to the printers. One of them had known ex-communist Victor Serge and Camus asked eager questions about him.

Clermont made Camus regret Paris. Laval's building was too small even for the skeleton staff and it was hard to find a place to live. They crowded into hotels, sharing bedrooms, bathrooms and hot plates. Camus queued for milk and took his turn at cooking. The armistice plunged him into agitation. Fascism, triumphant all over Europe, had won in France now; the Vichy government was a coalition of his enemies. Camus was sure that he would soon be arrested. He wanted to return to Algeria, to get as far as he could from the Germans.[4] He kept noticing Clermont's lunatic asylum and wondered whether one of its inmates had escaped: in his own building he was kept awake at night by a madman yelling.

Gloom was a spur to comradeship and Camus could forget his fears when he caroused with the printers. One summer's day they climbed a mountain near Clermont: 'We stayed at the top a long time, playing like a bunch of children. Then we had a glorious country meal in the village inn. Camus brought the evening to life: he went from clowning to sadness.'[5] When he acted, Camus felt like a human being and was released from the threat that hung over him.

In October 1940 *Paris-Soir* moved to Lyons, where most of the old Paris papers had taken refuge. Once more Camus had to look for a cheap hotel, once more work conditions were cramped. Camus cheered the printers up with a stream of jokes and obscene songs. One of them was sung often – 'She was born on the Feast of the Dead – which was pretty sad/She was seduced by the Trinity – which was really bad.'[6] By now Pia had turned up. He had been mobilized when the Germans advanced but his unit had then been forgotten in a wood outside Paris. This confirmed his view of the French army and his prophecies of defeat. Now he rejoined *Paris-Soir*.

The mood in Lyons was mixed. The town was Vichyite and in November Camus watched while crowds applauded Pétain. Yet, since Lyons was in the free zone, it was flooded with refugees from the North, especially from Alsace-Lorraine. There were curfews and food-shortages but there was rebellion too. Lyon was 'for the unoccupied zone a capital of misery and hope: the misery of the refugees, the displaced persons and the persecuted but the hope of the Resistance.'[7]

Camus was still bent on survival. He had finished the first part of *Sisyphe* and had started to rewrite the second. This was his own aesthetic act of resistance. Whenever he could, he escaped from the city into the countryside. In a village he met an old lady whose son had been wounded at the Marne; she had gone to fetch him so that he could die at home. Now she asked Camus whether this new war was really over. The only way he could combat the sense of having no control over his existence was to write down such meetings in his note-book.

Through all his moves he had been sending letters to Francine. The war, he kept telling her, must not be allowed to prevent their marriage. On a freezing December day she arrived at Lyons, exhausted with the boat and train journey. The hotel had no heating and the wind came whistling down the twin rivers that run through Lyons. On December 3 she and Camus were married in a civil ceremony at the town hall. Pia was a witness and the only other guests were the printers. 'It was such a simple way to get married,' one of them recalls, 'just three or four printers in the wedding party . . . when we came out of the town hall we went for a drink in a café.'[8]

Francine and Camus had planned to remain at Lyons but almost at once he lost his job. *Paris-Soir* was publishing a smaller edition and needed fewer workers. As a recent recruit Camus was one of the first to be laid off. He and Francine decided to go back to Oran where she could work and where they could live in part of her mother's house. Material needs dictated this course. And while Camus was not eager for Madame Faure's company he was pleased to return to Algeria.

Oran, where he spent the next year and a half, both cheered and depressed him. The flood of young girls on the beach in the spring of '41 demonstrated that beauty could survive amidst war. Camus gorged himself on the scents and colours of the Mediterranean. On an outing to Mers-el-Kebir he relished the white almond trees, the smell of pastis on the streets and the sea 'like a sheet of blue metal.' Yet he rediscovered the emptiness of Algeria, accentuated by Oran's provincialism. Just as Vicenza was not really different from Prague, so Oran could be as inhuman as Paris. The tables of its cafés were 'coated with dirt and scattered with bits of dead flies.' The girls were sexy but made no pretence of love or even affection. Camus was, however, convinced that Algeria taught the lessons of courage and measure so he rejoiced in Oran's brainlessness. He noted that the Virgin Marys in the antique shops had lascivious smiles. There was nothing spiritual about Oran; it was 'the Chicago of our absurd Europe'.[9]

What depressed Camus most was his own situation. Their flat had a bed, a piano and little other furniture. It was as bare as his bachelor hotel rooms had been. Francine found a teaching job and he managed to get part-time work at two schools. The Vichy laws against Jews compelled Oran Jews to enter private schools or to set up their own classes. Camus taught at two such institutions. A pleasant chore was coaching the boys at soccer and a photo remains of him surrounded by his young team. But Camus felt that he was merely surviving, which was not enough. His ambition was thwarted, he could get no better job and the political situation remained bleak. The former *Alger-Républicain* sports correspondent, Paul Balazard, met him now and felt that he looked shabby and depressed. 'I am just about hanging on,' Camus told him.[10]

Madame Faure admired Pétain, which did not improve relations with her son-in-law. Whenever he could, Camus escaped to Algiers to be with his old friends. An Italian visitor describes them: 'They spent all their time together. In the days they went swimming or walking in the hills and in the evening they listened to records or danced. They hated Pétain and cheered on Britain.'[11] As he had done with the printers and as he would do with Sartre and Simone de Beauvoir, Camus found in this group a focus of defiance. If the war was pervasively dehumanizing, the group composed an island where man could be honest and happy. Dancing was a form of revolt.

Camus could see no political way to combat the Nazis. He

listened to the BBC, he mentioned resistance but he did nothing. Charles Poncet had access to shipping information and tried to pass it on; Camus encouraged him but he himself belonged to no group, either in Algiers or Oran.[12] There was little resistance in Algeria until the Anglo-American landings and anyway Camus could not see what to do. His pessimistic vision enabled him to grasp the corrosive impact of Fascism but not how it might be defeated. The Nazis were holding in Europe, while Vichy had a firm grip on France and Algeria. The only resistance he could offer was in his own life and, obliquely, in his writing. Two pieces he wrote for *Tunisie Française* hint at his feelings. He mocks the Vichy theme of repentance – France has not lost the war because of the Third Republic's corruption – but he admits that Germany's strength is great. The sword might not be mightier than the pen but the tank probably is. Against it Camus pits the values of *Sisyphe*: 'tough pride and calm frugality'.[13] Yet he offers no hope of victory.

His writing was a way to bear witness. By depicting an inhuman world he was asserting man's place in it. After finishing *Sisyphe* in February 1941 he began at once on the next cycle of books. Camus did not rely on surges of inspiration. He drew up detached, longterm plans for work and then he executed them. His books draw on a few, personal images but they are hammered into shape during hours and years of effort. The best cure for lack of inspiration, Camus told a younger writer, was three hours a day at one's desk.[14] The second cycle had been plotted before the first was completed. Once more there would be a novel, *La Peste*, a play, *Le Malentendu*, and a philosophical essay, *L'Homme Révolté*, but the focus would be different. The first cycle was to depict inhumanity while the second would assert man's freedom against it.

One might doubt this interpretation. Contrary to what is often said, the second cycle of Camus' writing is scarcely more hopeful than the first. The upsurge of hope is more convincingly present in *Noces* than in *La Peste*. But the origins of the second cycle are found in this Oran period. Although *L'Homme Révolté* reads like a book about the Cold War it was started under the Occupation. By the time *L'Etranger* was published in July '42 Camus was already thinking about *La Peste*. In July '41 there was an outbreak of typhoid in Algeria and Roblès told Camus about the sanitation and isolation measures which the government was taking. Camus listened carefully and used Roblès' information in *La Peste*.

Meanwhile his tuberculosis returned. Francine saw him coughing and tried to prevent him from walking and swimming. As ever, Camus refused and continued his trips to Mers-el-Kebir. By mid-1942 he was very ill and, when he insisted to his friends that they should not surrender to Vichy, his eyes had fever in them. He admitted that he needed a change of climate and Francine found a solution. She had a cousin who ran a boarding-house in Le Panelier, a village in the Massif Central, close to Saint-Etienne and not far from Lyons. Camus could live there cheaply and the mountain air would help him. He managed to obtain a travel permit from the authorities and set off in August. Francine accompanied him but she would have to come back to Oran when her school re-opened. Camus could stay on until his health improved.

At Le Panelier he rediscovered the alien mountain countryside which he had known in Savoy five years before. At dawn the pine trees massed on the hillside like an army of barbarians waiting to attack the village. Later came the seasonal changes, more subtle and more banal than in Algeria. Autumn was windy and then the snow fell, destroying sensation and colour. Only in the early morning were there sounds as the icicles melted and the drops of water pattered against the windows. Once more Camus was in exile: 'thinking of Algeria is like looking at a child's face. And yet I know everything is not pure.'[15] The El Okbi trial and the Auribeau labourers were part of Algeria but Camus still missed it. Francine returned to Oran and he stayed on alone. Lonely, he despatched a letter to Blanche Balain, to whom he had not written since the outbreak of war. In Le Panelier he knew no one except Francine's cousin. He worked in his room, stopping to bicycle into Saint-Etienne, where he was treated for his illness, or to visit Pia in Lyons.

In Oran Francine was anxious. Rumours abounded that some spectacular military action was imminent. She sent a message telling Camus to return at once. Camus phoned Pia and asked him to buy a ticket. Pia did so but it was too late. The Allies invaded North Africa, the Germans occupied the free zone and Algeria was cut off from France. 'Caught like rats,' notes Camus.[16]

He had suffered during his life from many misfortunes but the Allied invasion was a disguised blessing. Had he gone back

172

to Algeria, he would never have entered the Resistance network *Combat*, which would be, after the success of *L'Etranger*, the second reason for his Liberation fame. He would not have become friendly with Sartre and he would not have met Maria Casarès. At the time, however, the invasion came as a tremendous blow. He was trapped in the alien mountains and cut off from his wife, his mother and his friends. He searched for ways to communicate with them via neutral countries but it was difficult. Once more he had no job and no money.

Having nowhere else to go, he stayed at Le Panelier. His illness dragged on, which depressed him even more. He was almost thirty and felt he was growing old. Old age terrified Camus, who treasured his good looks and his athlete's stride. His illness brought back his sense of death and he addresses his lung rhetorically: 'Must I listen as you rot slowly away?'[17] He drew on his old ability to battle but found few allies. In particular he loathed the smallish industrial town of Saint-Etienne: 'Saint-Etienne in the early-morning fog; the sirens summon men to work amidst a jumble of towers, factories and huge chimneys, from which waste pours out into the darkened sky.'[18] This was working-class life at its worst: monotonous, passive and untouched by Mediterranean grace. If hell existed, it would be like these interminable grey streets. After his visits to the doctor, Camus went to a café where he drank lemonade sweetened with saccharin and gazed out at the lifeless pavements.

His illness, exile and depression gave him an insight into occupied France. One day he took the little train into Saint-Etienne and watched the other passengers. Their faces were racked by winters of privation and even their suitcases looked exhausted. You could tell the date by the number of people smoking: cigarette rations ran out by the middle of the month. Camus was able to perceive the war from the viewpoint not of Vichy's rhetoric-loving politicians nor of frontline soldiers but of civilians, who were caught up in a conflict without knowing how or why. The war entered their life and corroded it: they were not fighting nor were they persecuted; they were just crippled. Camus notes a woman with a wounded husband who takes in washing so that she can buy him meat and a worker who is hungry but has no money for a blackmarket restaurant.

As he would in *La Peste*, Camus caught the totality of modern war. It was not limited to armies and battlegrounds; it involved everyone in every moment of his life. Its impact was random – why had a man from Belcourt with a wife in Oran been stranded in Saint-Etienne? Camus grasped the powerlessness of the civilian population. Two years earlier he had noted in his meticulous way the remark of a conscript who had been made to swallow chalk-solution so that he could be x-rayed: 'Before I used to shit black, now I shit white, that's the war.'[19] The man was trying, pitifully, to explain. To the barbarian Camus the loss of beauty was terrible. Cold and clothes-rationing transformed women into shapeless bundles. But the loss of understanding was even worse.

It is ironic that *La Peste*, one of the great Second World War novels, was partially written in the Massif Central, where there was no fighting, by a man who had never seen tanks rolling. In 1943 Camus felt the war as an absence: of love, beauty, theatre and dance. Like so many other Frenchmen, he was neither a hero nor a villain, neither a collaborator nor a resistant. Like them, he was not primarily concerned with good and evil; he wanted to get home to his wife or he wanted to eat better or he wanted a friendly conversation. Unlike the others, he felt these privations as a heightened form of a universal absurdity.

Camus missed his wife. In his *Carnets* he talks of chastity, but he did not wish to cultivate it. Blanche Balain had answered his August letter and he kept pressing her for a meeting. He told her how lonely he was at Le Panelier and how he missed Algeria. Eventually she agreed to meet him, first on the neutral ground of Valence and then at Saint-Etienne. She found him changed by the hardships of the Occupation.[20] He was delighted to see her and insisted that they go out to eat in the blackmarket restaurants of Saint-Etienne. *L'Etranger* was selling so he had some money which he spent eagerly. He drank pernod, exclaiming that tomorrow they might all be dead. He had, she felt, become a more anguished man than the self-confident Camus of the Equipe rehearsals.

His fear and dislike of the Germans were apparent. Saint-Etienne was full of German soldiers and Camus clenched his teeth as they went past. He was still afraid that because of his anti-Fascist past he was on some list for imprisonment. Blanche had heard rumours about the deportation of Jews and about concentration camps. 'They are true,' said Camus, 'there's no avoiding it. We must struggle.' She felt his strength of character once again and he in turn was revived by her admiration. He pressed her to keep visiting him or to move to Lyons. Sensibly enough she refused and they did not meet again for several years.

Camus' determination to struggle did not lead him to enter the Resistance, although he had ample opportunity to do so. In the Oran of '41 there had been no anti-Vichy group but in the spring of '43 the Resistance was flourishing all around him. It was present in Le Panelier itself. At nearby Chambon-sur-Lignon an efficient organization smuggled Jews out of France, while Saint-Etienne had a *Combat* network. As an outsider in Le Panelier Camus might have been unable to make contact with the resistants but this does not explain why he did not enter *Combat*.[21] In 1942 Pia gave up journalism and joined the Resistance, for which he was well-suited. His love of mystery, his recklessness and the perfectionism he brought to everything he undertook made Pia a valuable recruit. Soon he became the deputy to Marcel Peck, the head of *Combat* at Lyons. When Camus came on his periodic visits he and Pia talked, if guardedly, about the Resistance, while Pia introduced him to other recruits like the poet Francis Ponge. Why then did Camus not join *Combat*?

The reason lies in his old indifference. Certainly he was anti-Nazi and certainly he wished to struggle. But he did not feel that he was the man to blow up trains or even to organize liaison groups. He still felt that he was an exile, although this is not an adequate explanation. There were many exiles in the Resistance: some of *Combat*'s founders were university professors who had fled from Alsace-Lorraine. But Camus was inwardly an exile, oppressed by the feeling that the war was outside his control. When he rallied, he did so as an individual and as an artist.

His pied-noir friends would pour scorn on the judgement that Camus was not a man of action. Yet he had not really ignored Grenier's comment that most action was agitation. His religious sense tended to confirm it. Moreover he was weary of unsuccessful action. He had sold the PCA newspaper and rallied his acquaintances behind its policies; the experience had scarred him. He was becoming more and more a writer: a man whose chief and often sole passion lies in setting words on

175

paper. The Occupation strengthened his conviction that the only way he could oppose the world's cruel irrationality was to write. Art was itself a moral and political act, which drew on the individual Camus' ascetic struggle and which bore witness of it to others. Indifference and bearing witness are the key themes of Camus' war-years. He steeled himself to stare back at the German soldiers in Saint-Etienne and he asserted his values against the Nazis.

Two other factors in Camus' life help explain why he stood aside from *Combat* throughout the winter of '42 and the summer of '43. The first was his health. It may be no coincidence that Camus joined the PCA in a period of relatively good health and left it when he had a relapse. Now his illness weighed on him, paralysing him with a sense of futility. The second was his caution. Pia was like a gambler who feels the rules of the game are so ridiculous that he has nothing to lose. Clandestinity, meetings on railway stations and hours of tense solitude were things which Pia relished. Camus, however, did not wish to throw himself into a project, the outlines of which he could only dimly perceive. Once more he was a prudent gambler.

He told Ponge that he felt he could do nothing to help the Resistance. Indeed how could there by any Resistance in Saint-Etienne? Its gloomy, grey streets were tailor-made for Fascism.[22] This is ironic since there was in Saint-Etienne a *Combat* network linked with Pia's Lyons network. The remark indicates Camus' inner exile. On August 15, 1943 he received a visit from Louis Miquel. Miquel arrived by train and Camus bicycled to Saint-Etienne to meet him. It was freezing cold and the two pieds-noirs shivered. Miquel found Camus depressed and lonely, bewildered by the Massif Central and its taciturn inhabitants.

So the Camus who joined the Resistance as soon as it began is a legend, constructed after the war. Camus joined the Resistance either in late 1943 or in January 1944 – witnesses give two different dates – some six months before the Allied landings in Normandy. The contemporary reader sees no reason to blame him for this. The Resistance was smaller than is often thought. In 1943 *Combat* had no more than 75,000 men, while another organization, *Franc-Tireur*, had only 25,000. Camus made the best contribution he could through his writing; he published the first part of the *Lettres à un Ami Allemand* in '43. More surprising is the way he allowed the legend to grow after the war. At least two people who spread it derived or could have derived their information from him.[23]

Not that he was so presumptuous as to claim that he had been a Resistance leader. Yet many people who knew him after the war are surprised to discover now that he joined the Resistance so late. At least two of his Algerian friends thought he had organized a group at Oran and one of them believed he returned to France to join *Combat*.[24] Even the unkind Simone de Beauvoir never doubted that Camus was an important member of *Combat* when she and Sartre met him. Yet this was not so. Camus' deviously angelic nature led him astray after the war. To have been an important resistant suited his role as moral conscience, apostle of courage and fraternity. He allowed his participation in the Resistance to be retrospectively exaggerated just as he allowed his participation in the PCA to be minimized. Had he entered the Resistance in '41 he would have lived the war differently. He might not have felt so much of an exile, which means he might not have written *La Peste*.

The *Lettres à un Ami Allemand* are richer than the *Tunisie Française* pieces of 1941. Camus is certain now that the Allies will win the war. The old doubts linger: heroism is a trivial thing, writes Camus, happiness is more difficult and the war has destroyed happiness. But the values of pride and frugality are depicted as French and as part of a French moral vision. Against the Nazi reliance on force, Camus pits the French theme of intelligence. Behind this antithesis lies his old dilemma about absolutes. Feeling that history made no sense, the Nazis took a leap of faith and embraced the thousand-year Reich. They made the same mistake as the Communists or Saint Augustine. Camus' attack on them looks back to *Sisyphe* and forward to *L'Homme Révolté*; it is another chapter in his dialogue with his own religious temperament. He extols intelligence because it is a relative value – scrupulous and cautious.

Already *Sisyphe* had shown the part of tradition in Camus' thought. The classicism of which he had spoken is re-expounded here. French culture contains its own measure; the Resistance is fighting for clarity. Elsewhere Camus affirms that French writing is 'a new classicism which bears witness to the two values which are most under fire today: intelligence and France.'[25] Such remarks are characteristic of Resistance thinking. To resist the Nazis it drew on France's cultural heritage. 'It's for Racine that our comrades are derailing German troop trains,' said Camus to a friend. 'It's with Racine too,' the friend replied.[26] Works which demonstrated the peculiar richness of French culture were weapons against the Germans. Barrault's production of Claudel's *Le Soulier de Satin* was a special triumph in the difficult Paris of '43. This was not the first time that French intellectuals used their tradition as an armoury. During the 1914 war Jacques Rivière, who went from a prison camp to become editor of the *NRF*, had explained the difference between German Faustianism and French classicism. Now Camus, the *NRF*'s newest recruit, was showing that he belonged. Of course it was facile to juxtapose Faust and Racine but this was war-time writing.

Equally characteristic of Resistance thought was the utopian strain in the *Lettres*. Once more Camus was hesitating about the relativity of his values. He makes a sober comment about the distinction between 'energy and violence, force and cruelty';[27] this was the lesson he had tried to teach French Algerians. But the certainty of triumph leads him to exalt the Resistance's idealism. 'We are going to come out of the war with our hands clean,' he exclaims.[28] This was sheer nonsense because the Resistance's hands were not clean. It killed German soldiers knowing that reprisals would be taken against French civilians and it executed both collaborators and some who had not collaborated. There can be no absolute purity in war. Yet many like Camus took a Manichean view of the struggle; they had to, because the odds were against them.

By now Camus was emerging from his Le Panelier solitude and making frequent trips to Paris, to which he moved in the autumn of 1943. When he was stranded by the North African landings, Gallimard had come to his rescue. As well as receiving money for *L'Etranger*, he was paid as a publisher's reader. This was standard practice at Gallimard which employed many writers usually at low salaries. Camus went on the payroll in '42 and remained on it until his death.

When France was occupied the German authorities wanted to restart both the Gallimard publishing house and the *NRF*. Gaston Gallimard felt he had two choices: either he could withdraw and let the Germans install their favourites or he could remain in charge. The price was that the review would have to take a pro-German line. Gaston Gallimard's solution was a masterly piece of *NRF* strategy. Although he did not much like Gide, Gallimard had learned from him that the exclusion which clearcut choice entailed was an unwelcome amputation; to avoid it, Gide kept all his options open, advancing simultaneously down several different paths. Now Gallimard did the same. Drieu la Rochelle, an almost convinced Fascist, took over the review; Gallimard ran the publishing house separately and looked around for anti-German writers. The only hinge between the two was Jean Paulhan, who helped Drieu choose the texts for the *NRF* while writing in Resistance periodicals. Paulhan was another apostle of subtlety.

The strategy worked well. Protected by Drieu's ardent collaboration, the publishing house kept publishing. Only Drieu compromised himself as, driven by his suicidal nature, he flaunted his Nazi sympathies long after the Allies had gained the upper hand. At the Liberation the review was banned but the infinitely more lucrative publishing house continued to publish. It had genuine anti-Fascist credentials: Sartre, Malraux, Mauriac and Camus were all Gallimard writers. Had accusations been made against Gaston Gallimard he could convincingly have refuted them. By its subtlety the *NRF* outwitted Nazis and purgers alike.

Gaston Gallimard had been looking for good writers with a left-wing slant and Camus suited the part. Delighted to escape from Le Panelier and eager for comradeship, he considered the publishing house a 'temple of joy'.[29] He arrived 'thin in a worn overcoat,' showing his usual blend of warmth and distance. His glance was 'direct, penetrating, immensely attractive and yet amused, malicious, full of an irony which seemed careless but could be disconcerting too.'[30] Camus was wary. He remembered the grim months he had spent in Paris three years before and he was consorting for the first time with a group of French writers. To them he still seemed the archetypal pied-noir. When he dressed up, he put on a bright suit and a red tie. He talked in his Algerian accent about soccer and swimming. Then in the middle of a conversation, he would break off and lose himself in space, like Ivan in *Brothers Karamazov*. No one was surprised to discover that he loved the theatre. 'He would stand on a Saint-Germain street corner wearing his trenchcoat turned up against the rain . . . as if he were playing the part of Camus in an unfinished film.'[31]

He quickly made friends with Gaston Gallimard's nephew, Michel. Michel Gallimard was 'red-haired, with grey-blue eyes, thin, highly-strung, rather small, astonishingly honest with himself and with others'.[32] His frankness and enthusiasm appealed to Camus who was sympathetic to his melancholy. Michel, too, had had tuberculosis. He had been married to an Englishwoman who had been killed in an accident. He himself had encountered danger for he had served in the French airforce and helped combat the far superior German planes. Camus found Michel more natural than the other people he met now and he may have been glad that Michel, who worked in the publishing house, did not himself write. Moreover Michel had money, which was a rare commodity among Camus' acquaintances. He invited his friends to restaurants and then back to his spacious flat in the rue de l'Université, where they drank and laughed. Often they stayed after the curfew imposed by the German authorities and had to sleep on sofas or on the floor. The informality of such evenings relaxed Camus: once more he had found a group.

Another friend who had to sleep on the floor was Father R.-L. Bruckberger, Dominican monk, resistant and cinema enthusiast. Camus had long been drawn to monasticism, now he had found his monk. Bruckberger, who was of a mixed Austrian and Auvergnat family, was a militant priest, proud of his white habit which he flaunted in publishing houses and elegant restaurants. He had been a friend of Bernanos and the two had much in common: they were battlers, aggressively male, uncompromisingly catholic but scornful of bishops. When the war broke out, Bruckberger was delighted: 'I love war,' he admits. He served with an élite corps led by Joseph Darnand, future chief of the Vichy militia. Then their paths separated for Bruckberger met *Combat* leader, Claude Bourdet, and entered the Resistance. He was also taken up by Gaston Gallimard, who wondered whether this integral yet rebellious Catholicism might not become a motif in post-war writing.

Bruckberger liked Camus, who looked like a boxer and in whom he saw his own violence. Camus disliked priests who were tepid or who made concessions to modernity. It is no

180

coincidence that his favourite monk has turned into a staunch opponent of Vatican II. Priests, Camus felt, should wear their cloth proudly and quote Aquinas rather than Freud. He relished Bruckberger's maleness and was pleased to discover that Bruckberger liked to watch girls. Indeed Bruckberger's friendship with actress Marie Bell, who had just been acclaimed in *Le Soulier de Satin*, scandalized the church authorities.

Camus plagued Bruckberger with questions. One day he came bursting into the Gallimard offices and asked him to explain evil: how could he justify the massacre of the innocents? Another day he infuriated him by insisting that Catholics had an easy life. If anything went wrong, they had only to remember that it would be put right in eternity. To Camus' eager interrogation, Bruckberger opposed a rock-like certainty. Camus' litany of questions could never be resolved except by an act of faith: life was a gift from God and could not in itself make sense. This was precisely what Camus wanted to hear. Bruckberger was not bridging the gulf between God and man because to Camus the act of faith was impossible. God remained remote and nothing could be asked of Him. Yet Camus could enjoy, vicariously, the confidence which Bruckberger radiated.

In September '43 the two went to Bruckberger's monastery Saint-Maximin. Situated in the South of France, it offered an austere gothic cloister and a row of cedar trees. It pleased Camus as much as Fiesole had done. He relished the tranquillity and charmed the monks by reading them *Le Malentendu*, which he was just finishing. 'There was a good deal of the monk in Camus himself,' says Bruckberger.[33] The old meditation on Marx and Augustine was still going on. Francis Ponge, who was then a Communist, was surprised at Camus' visit to Saint-Maximin. In his reply Camus stated that, while he was no believer, he admired the religious urge which sent men into monasteries. Catholicism and Communism were absolute forms of belief which tempted him even as he rejected them. The reply displeased Ponge, who wrote back that there was nothing absolute about Communism. But Camus continued to satisfy, via Bruckberger, his own longing for oneness and their conversations leave a mark on *La Peste*. Camus has given a one-line portrait of his friend: 'an energetic, disputatious Dominican who loathes Christian Democrats and dreams of a Nietzschean christianity.'[34]

In this exciting autumn of '43 Camus had his first real conversation with Malraux*.[35] They may have been introduced by Pascal Pia in 1940. Certainly Malraux had been one of the readers for *L'Etranger* and had recommended it. But it was only now, on one of Malraux' supposedly clandestine visits to Paris, that they talked. They walked for hours along the Seine and often Malraux was the listener, a rare role for him. He seemed eager to hear what the younger Camus had to say about the war. The two agreed there must be personal commitment; a man must impose his own law on the chaos around him. But they went no further and their conversation did not lead to a friendship. Malraux went back to his resistance fighters, his role as a hero and his increasing sympathy for De Gaulle.

Camus had made another friend with whom he would be more closely linked but with whom he may have had no more in common: Sartre. Along with Claudel's *Le Soulier de Satin*, *Les Mouches* was a theatrical triumph in 1943 because Oreste's rebellion against Jupiter was a clarion-call to the Resistance. At the first performance Camus introduced himself to Sartre to thank him for an article which Sartre had written on *L'Etranger*. A second meeting in the café Flore began shyly but then the two discovered that they shared an admiration for Francis Ponge and a love of the theatre. Hearing that Camus had directed plays in Algiers, Sartre asked him to take charge of *Huis Clos* which he had just written. Camus should play the part of Garcin and direct the production. Camus agreed and even started rehearsals before the scheme collapsed.

Simone de Beauvoir describes Camus when she first met him: 'He had a hearty appetite for fame and success ... now and again he showed a touch of unscrupulous ambition but he didn't

*There was a third person present at this conversation: Jacques Poirier, Malraux' 'English officer'. Jean Lacouture and other biographers repeat that Malraux was brought into the Resistance by an English agent. In reality Poirier was and remains entirely French. Parachuted into France from London, he claimed he was English because he wished to avoid the political squabbles which plagued the Resistance. No one else spoke English so he was not found out. He gives an intriguing picture of Malraux, the resistant: Malraux talked his way into their network, pressed for wildly implausible missions, fired at tanks with a pistol and on his 'clandestine' visits to Paris walked into restaurants where everyone knew and acclaimed him. He was superbly egotistical and his indifference to physical danger both delighted and appalled his comrades.[35]

seem to take himself seriously . . . his mixture of casualness and enthusiasm made him really charming.'*[36] When Picasso wanted to put on his surrealist play *Le Désir Attrapé par la Queue* Camus acted as stage-manager. Brandishing a cane which he periodically banged on the ground, he guided the actors who included Sartre. Picasso took his play seriously but Camus did not, although he enjoyed the celebration that followed. During another even more drunken evening Sartre, locked up in a cupboard, directed an imaginary orchestra, while Camus played military marches with saucepans.

The Camus-Sartre relationship is misunderstood if one imagines either that there was a long period of friendship before the furious break or that the two men had much in common. The period of real friendship ran only from '43 to '45. The intellectual ties went back to *La Nausée* and *L'Etranger* but did not continue afterwards. The two writers were linked by the popular press and branded as 'existentialists', which infuriated Camus. *Sisyphe* had stated that there could be no metaphysical system; existentialism was a philosophy, a statement about the entire universe and hence an affirmation of man's ability to understand it. Moreover Camus disagreed with the primacy awarded to existence. Already he wondered whether lucidity and courage might not be values that predated the state of 'being-in-the-world'. As for character, Camus and Sartre were very different men.

Camus was not specially drawn to Sartre; Michel Gallimard and Bruckberger were more congenial company. Camus liked men who drank, swore and admired women, who declaimed their opinions or else said nothing. Pia's flamboyant scepticism or Bruckberger's crusader-swagger were pieces of theatre which he relished. He enjoyed Sartre's energy and liked to drink with him. Sartre was in an outgoing phase and evenings spent carousing with young actresses in the Flore appealed to Camus. But Sartre's energy also took the form of immense intellectual

*Simone de Beauvoir's memoirs are, of course, a dubious source for Camus because by the time she wrote them she cordially detested him. She and Camus never had much in common. Yet, if one remembers her prejudice, her comments are interesting. The real problem with her memoirs is not prejudice but the retrospectively marxist viewpoint from which they are written and which superimposes on her experience and her period a framework which they did not possess at the time.

curiosity: he was determined to penetrate and explain. Such burrowing either bored Camus or else troubled him. He did not want the private core of his being subjected to exhaustive analysis. Sartre explained Genet so completely that he almost destroyed him. Camus was right to be wary.

Sartre felt a stronger attraction. He had always been curious about people and he and Simone de Beauvoir spent hours analysing their friends. Camus fascinated them because he was working-class. From his adolescence Sartre, the sheltered middle-class child, was drawn to the working classes. Their politics did not at first interest him; he liked them because they were solid and real. His own childhood, he felt, had lacked substance and his family was riddled with pretence and pretension. Now Camus brought the cockiness, the wit and the sudden silences of the Algiers streets. His Equipe friends had considered him aristocratic and cool but to Sartre he was thoroughly Algerian. His schoolmates from Bab-el-Oued thought he was an intellectual but to Sartre he seemed a tough guy.[37] Sartre admired him because he was good-looking, because he could dance and because he could seduce. Camus' mimicry sent Sartre into gales of laughter.

The intellectual parallels and contrasts cannot be understood without a brief look at Sartre's past. From his family's pretension Sartre drew a disgust for what was false. However, he was quite different from the NRF writers of the previous generation – Rivière or Gide – who had stressed the authenticity of individual experience. Sartre rejected the validity of inner life and was convinced that consciousness was empty. Beyond it lay external reality which fascinated but eluded it. A chasm yawned between the thinking but empty mind and the solid but impenetrable reality.

In the early 30's the young Sartre went no further. Another admirer of Synge, he used to compare himself with the Playboy who treats the external world as a game. Things had a life of their own, which cartesian man ignored and which bourgeois society reduced to function. Sartre liked surrealism because it played with objects: a Dali watch was a shape and a monster as well as a machine for telling time. In the Marx brothers films Sartre discovered his own sense that the external world was organized differently from men's minds. In his happy moments Sartre could enjoy both poles of his dialectic: the mind had an exhilarating irresponsibility like the Playboy, while the world was rich and diverse. But Sartre's vision was deeply pessimistic: the mind was trapped in its own emptiness while the world was a mass of dying matter.

This is the viewpoint from which *Le Mur* and *La Nausée* were written. Terrified at its isolation, the mind runs screaming into madness or violence. A heroine insists on making love with her lunatic husband, a hero goes out into Montparnasse with a revolver. Roquentin discovers that objects are elusive and hostile; the chestnut-tree rots aggressively before him. The solution of *La Nausée* lies in literature itself, which imposes a necessity upon the random universe. But, as Camus had pointed out, if consciousness was empty, language could not be trusted. In *Huis Clos* the stories which the characters make up about their lives remain mere stories. Sartre's concept of literature was changing and he would lay greater emphasis on the reader.

Meanwhile he had looked for another solution in phenomenology, which he interpreted differently from Camus. He too used Husserl against Descartes and he too admired the manifold richness of the phenomenological world: 'Husserl has restored to things their horror and their charm. He has re-created the world of artists and prophets: frightening, hostile, dangerous, with moments of grace and love.'[38] But Husserl's bid to understand the universe was not, as Camus had claimed, a leap of faith. Phenomenology offered explanations that did not rely on causality or idealism but that embraced the particular. Husserl was right and Camus was wrong: the universe could be known, if partially and imperfectly.

Sartre's passion to discover the external world received fresh impetus in 1940. As a soldier and a prisoner, he was caught up in the chaos of the defeat. He liked the working-class men with whom he served and he encouraged them to resist in the Stalag. On his return to France he developed the concept of situation. Man could not avoid external reality – social, political and economic. It shaped him and he should not resent this. Isolated, his awareness had no validity and his freedom was as illusory as Oreste's at the start of *Les Mouches*. But he need not accept the constraint or the chaos of his situation. Instead he should assert his awareness through an act of revolt: Oreste becomes Clytemnestra's son and then slaughters her. Literature too is caught up with situation because it is written by a particular writer for a particular reader, each marked by his social environment. It is no longer supposed to create a dubious necessity but it will provoke the reader.

The concept of situation and the twist Sartre would give it after the Liberation were to separate him from Camus. Sartre could welcome social restraints as a relief from Roquentin's isolation. Camus had lived amidst such restraints and had sought to escape them. Moreover his religious temperament told him that man's condition was a frustrated dialogue with God and that it could not be transformed by social action. The more daring Sartre was willing to gamble on the Heideggerian sense of 'bursting-out-in-the-world'; Camus distrusted such extremism.

Yet in 1943 Sartre could see in Camus a kindred spirit. The essays of *Situation 1*, which include the study of *L'Etranger*, are fascinating because Sartre is spying out the contours of his age. Written in lively, dramatic language, this book both interprets the 40's and draws the period together around Sartre's own thought. The philosophy of the age is phenomenology, the poet is Ponge, while Camus, not Mauriac, is the new novelist. Mauriac imposes on his writing a global viewpoint which Sartre dismisses as false; the novelist can offer only the partial understanding which his limited awareness allows him. The world will appear as a chaotic mixture of subjective insights and external objects. Conrad and Faulkner are examples of the new novel but the most recent example is Camus. *L'Etranger* is 'not a book that explains' but one that sets man 'opposite the world'.[39] Meursault is present by a consciousness that does not penetrate Algiers which is depicted for itself. Not surprisingly, Sartre considers the first half of *L'Etranger* better than the second.

The place which Camus was starting to occupy in French writing is further revealed by the triangular relationship which he and Sartre shared with Ponge. After publishing his *Douze petits écrits* in 1926 Ponge remained silent until 1942, when he published his second book of poems. During these years he meditated on language which seemed to him an arbitrary invention. It turned the world into personifications and fantasies, creatures of the human imagination. Might there not, Ponge wondered, be a way to circumscribe objects more precisely? As the title indicates, *Le Parti Pris des Choses* reconstructs the world without the causality which ordinary language presupposes. *La Bougie* depicts a candle which does not exist to give light for reading but has a form of its own and is a being among such other beings as moths and plants. This delighted Sartre, who rediscovered in *Le Parti Pris* Roquentin's dilemma.

To earn a living Ponge worked as an insurance salesman and on newspapers. He knew Pia, who was well able to appreciate his meditation on language and who got him a job in the Lyons paper, *Le Progrès*. Ponge met Camus and read *Sisyphe*, which intrigued him because he saw in it an echo of his own scepticism. Yet he felt that Camus was haunted by a religious nostalgia, which prevented him from exploring the possibilities he had opened up. One returns yet again to the debate about absolutes. 'There are relatively successful forms of expression,' writes Ponge.[40] Accepting the limits on man's understanding, Sisyphe should attain concrete if partial results in his attempt to learn about the world. Fresh forms of writing like humour, description and even logical discourse would become possible again.

Ponge helps us realize that Camus' work was appreciated in the '40's not merely for its social and moral content and not merely as a lyrical upsurge. The stylistic innovations of *L'Etranger* were admired because they dethroned traditional narrators and philosophers. Camus was becoming famous, along with Sartre and Ponge, as a writer who gave glimpses of a godless, manless universe. But whereas Ponge saw linguistic possibilities in man's limited condition and whereas Sartre would soon seek to transform it by a synthesis of self and situation, Camus clung fast to his absent God.

By now he and Sartre were both active in the Resistance. Sartre, who had tried to form a network after his return from Germany, was working with the Communist-dominated National Committee of Writers, while Camus now entered *Combat*. By the end of '43 men were flooding into the Resistance in anticipation of an Allied victory. But Camus' entry was consistent with his previous reluctance. He joined in order to accomplish a specific task for which his writing talent fitted him.

The date he joined *Combat* is subject to dispute. One witness remembers that he came to the newspaper meetings as early as autumn '43. Claudie Bourdet and Pia insist that his first contact was not until January '44.[41] He was brought in, Bourdet recalls, to organize a literary magazine, the *Revue Noire*, which was to be the banner of *Combat*'s cultural policy. But the *Revue Noire* collapsed so Camus moved into the *Combat* newspaper itself. The two accounts are not incompatible. By autumn '43 the *Combat* leadership had moved to Paris, having no reason to remain in Lyons after the German invasion of the South. Pia, who had done well as Peck's deputy, received wider responsibilities. He became editor of the paper but he also undertook such tasks as distributing funds and arranging contacts with London. The other *Combat* militants admired him without fathoming him. Everyone had his Pia story. There was much ambition in the Resistance and much talk of how jobs would be allocated at the Liberation. Pia asked only that retirement age be fixed at forty-two because he was already forty-one. His popularity brought recruits to the newspaper and Camus probably did attend meetings with him in the autumn of 1943. Certainly it was Pia who introduced Camus to Claude Bourdet in January 1944.

By this time *Combat* was well-established, both as a network and as a paper. It had been started as early as '41 by Henri Frenay, an ex-soldier, and by the intellectual Bourdet. It then spun its web across Northern and Southern France and was responsible for armed attacks, sabotage, information-gathering and propaganda. Its main propaganda weapon was the newspaper which printed 10,000 copies in '42 but as many as 100,000 by '44. When it was started it merely replaced the cyclostyled leaflets which the *Combat* militants had been handing out. It gave information about the war and rallied hope of a German defeat. Its secretary, Jacqueline Bernard, put the articles together and organized the distribution. Gradually *Combat* developed a coherent viewpoint.

It had a moral slant that would suit Camus: 'we want to ensure that a victory of the spirit will follow the defeat on the battlefield'.[42] Politically *Combat* was left-wing and a regular chronicle attacked the Vichy government's labour policy. *Combat* called for a 'renewal of republican mystique; not the rotten republicanism of the last twenty years but a real mystique'.[43] All this was deliberately vague because *Combat* wanted to attract the largest possible number of sympathizers.

So the paper supported De Gaulle while grumbling about his supposedly reactionary views and it welcomed the Communist entry into the Algiers government although it disliked the PC's attempt to infiltrate all the Resistance organizations.[44]

Combat's language grew more rhetorical as the Allied armies advanced. It promised purges, exhorted workers to join the maquis and prophesied utopias. Pia's entry in mid-1943 provoked a welcome note of satire. *Combat* began making jokes about Petain's huge salary. But this was a rare frivolity and by 1944 the paper was running huge, declamatory headlines about the final battle.

Camus did little to shape the clandestine *Combat*. The moral appeal, the left-wing stance and the rhetoric were present already. He and Pia brought greater professionalism which was valuable as the paper expanded its circulation. Pia had less and less time as his liaison duties compelled him to travel across France. When Claude Bourdet was arrested in the spring of '44 many *Combat* leaders wanted Pia to replace him on the National Council of the Resistance. Pia refused, offering no explanation. Yet he now began to leave the running of the paper to Camus, Jacqueline Bernard and the others.

She remembers meetings on the rue d'Aboukir where a janitor kept watch while they planned the lay-out of the paper. As a practical journalist Camus had hundreds of suggestions. He wrote only a few articles but he brought recruits from Gallimard and he inspired the others by his laughing enthusiasm. Most people in *Combat* knew Camus as Beauchard which was his clandestine name. Jacqueline Bernard knew that he was the author of *L'Etranger*. Camus began to confide in her and to tell her how lonely he was. His mother did not even know if he was still alive and he had no way of reassuring her. He missed his wife and their separation could last indefinitely. He had had no news of her for over a year. Such a separation was bound to damage their marriage.

Yet the confusion of Paris in '44, the spice of danger and the need for game-playing suited Camus. He acted out his various roles – *Combat* journalist, Gallimard reader, Flore carouser – as well as Bogart could have done. He enjoyed the contact which *Combat* offered with working-class people. One boy who sold the paper was called Pierrot; he was a street-urchin who stuck political posters on walls by night and who found blackmarket tyres for Camus' bicycle. Camus loved to talk to him, swapping Algiers for Parisian slang.

By now Camus was living in Gide's flat on the rue Vaneau. Gide had gone to North Africa and had been cut off by the Allied invasion. He found his way to Algiers where he lived in Jacques Heurgon's house and made the acquaintance of Fouchet, Edmond Charlot and Camus' other friends. As if to show his gratitude he allowed Camus to take over part of his flat. There was a bed-sitting room where Gide's young friend, Marc Allégret, had lived. Camus moved in and used the flat for meetings of the *Combat* group. At one such meeting the paper's sub-title 'From resistance to revolution' was coined.

Camus' life had changed along with the war. If the sense of exile remained he was no longer the doubting, isolated Camus of '42. He had many friends and he was growing famous. His books were helping to shape the period which, consequently, looked to him for guidance. Already plans were being made for the post-war *Combat* which he and Pia were to run. Yet all these things may have been less important than the love which he now felt for Maria Casarès.

In January '43 he had seen her act in Synge's *Deirdre of the Sorrows* – another example of the 'Irish connection' – but he did not get to know her until later.[45] She first saw him at the performance of *Le Désir Attrapé par la Queue*, to which a friend brought her so that she could meet her compatriot Picasso. Casarès spoke only a word to Picasso and remembers nothing about his play. She was at a loss all evening since she had never heard of Sartre, knew little about surrealism and even less about existentialism and had read neither *L'Etranger* nor *Sisyphe*. She did, however, remember Camus who read the stage directions with 'calculated monotony' and seemed to play the role of a destiny who was rather weary of being a destiny.[46] She assumed that he was an actor and wondered whether he could play Don Juan.

Casarès was twenty-one years old and her life had been pure theatre. Her father was Santiago Casarès Quiroga, Spanish republican and head of the Galicia autonomists. In 1930 he had been arrested and thrown into jail at Jaca. Each morning he expected to be taken out and shot but he was instead transferred to a Madrid prison where his wife used to pass his young daughter through the bars to embrace him. Maria-Victoria remembered this early glance at death and took a closer look in 1936 when the Spanish Civil War started and she worked, aged fourteen, in a hospital. As the wounded soldiers wailed and joked, she noticed that the man closest to death was the king of the ward. Camus could have told her why.

Her father was prime minister in 1936 and rather than arm the Madrid workers, which was technically an unconstitutional act, he resigned. He sent his family to France for safety, followed them when the war was lost and spent the next war exiled in England. He contracted tuberculosis which created a bond between him and Camus and he did not see his daughter until 1945 when she had become famous. There was in him a loneliness which she never fathomed and which heightened her awareness of death.

That awareness spurred her, as it did Camus, to live. She was haunted by her childhood in Celtic Galicia: 'that damp, dark-green land with its quickly-changing skies and its drizzling rain that cast a melancholic mask over the forests'.[47] Although it was quite different from Algeria, it had its ocean and its peasants who walked with the dignity of Camus' grandmother. In France Casarès rediscovered Galicia in Brittany. She walked around the rocks near the Pointe du Raz and looked out at her ocean. But, instead of plunging into the 'Breton disease', she determined to rediscover the intensity of her childhood. Doubly exiled like her father, she turned to the theatre.

As a child she was spoiled, proud and independent. She had the peasant's dislike for towns and she was afraid of crowds. Even when she became famous, she was nervous at parties and could scarcely hold a glass without trembling. In the early '30's she went to school in Madrid with the children of government ministers who overawed her. She was 'paralysingly timid' and, when she spoke, the others made fun of her Galician accent. This made her all the more resolute and she insisted on reciting. Striving to prove herself she broke into a frenzy, overacted and fell ill.

In France she learned to act as she learned French. When she first took the Conservatoire examination, the examiners told her to go home and improve her French. She studied French writers and came to love rich language – Racine's tirades or Claudel's lyricism. Even as Camus was guiding the Equipe to an intense style of acting where the actor emerged from silence to live for a few concentrated hours, Casarès was discovering these new lives in Paris. She passed the Conservatoire examinations and worked hard. She and her mother lived on the rue de Vaugirard; it was a tiny flat and they had little furniture although light streamed in from their balcony. There was no word from her father and she lived in fear of the Nazis who periodically rounded up Spanish republicans.

The role of Deirdre was offered to her by Marcel Herrand, whose Mathurins theatre was an oasis in the cultural desert of the Occupation. Herrand, who is best known outside France because he took the role of the murderer, Lacenaire, in the film *Les Enfants du Paradis*, was a remote figure. An ironic and pessimistic man, he loved to discover talent and understood both Casarès' mixture of extreme youth and experience and her acting power.

Maria, too, played in *Les Enfants du Paradis* where she took the part of Baptiste-Barrault's wife. Nathalie is a thankless role for she is overshadowed by Arletty-Garance whom Baptiste loves. Yet Casarès brings to Nathalie a concentrated passion which makes the part memorable and complements Arletty's remote charm.

Such emotion became her trademark in the theatre. She was not the traditional tragic actress, regal and prone to grandiose gestures. She was slight and the parts she played seemed to overwhelm her. But this added to the electricity she discharged. A few years later, as Gina Sanseverina in the film *La Chartreuse de Parme*, she would be playful and subtle but in 1944 she 'always seemed as if she were going to break, to tear herself apart'.[48] Her style suited the moment because emotion was welling in a Paris that waited to be liberated. Casarès was like the actresses of 1830 who played in boulevard melodramas while the barricades went up around them. Along with Gérard Philipe she would become a Liberation star and another voice of the period.

Her admirers repeat even today that Casarès wept real tears on the stage and went into a trance. She herself laughs about the trances: she was merely terrified, she says. Stories circulated: that she fell on the floor during one rehearsal and bit a producer in the ankle, that her acting was the sexual sublimation of an 'ardent virgin', that she was a disciple of the Spanish mystic,

Saint Theresa of Avila. Herrand knew better and admired her professionalism. She burrowed her way into each role, seeking first to understand it. Then, as she possessed it, she allowed it to take possession of her.

Whereas the cinema dispersed, the theatre concentrated; freed of the camera the actress could create herself. Yet Casarès felt that beyond all conquest lay abandonment of self. When she played Deirdre, she was surprised at how the role turned out. She realized that she could not control but could only gamble. Sometimes she and the spectators would share a new existence, sometimes she would fall into a horrible emptiness, harbinger of death.

This emptiness was all too familiar to Camus, who met Casarès via Marcel Herrand. Herrand had read *L'Etranger* and he encouraged Camus to bring *Le Malentendu* to the Mathurins. When he arrived for the reading, Casarès recognized in him the weary destiny of *Le Désir*. It was 'that same proud, unaffected look, that same nonchalant indifference'. In particular she recognized 'the mixture of vulnerability and strength that comes from exile'.[49] Camus was nervous and Casarès stared at him – she was the Don Juan now. He read the first act boldly and then there was a break. When they resumed, Camus was even more nervous and began coughing. Casarès kept staring at him until he faltered and Herrand intervened.

In March '44 rehearsals began for *Le Malentendu* and by now Camus and Casarès were in love. She had been admired by film director Georges Clouzot and protected by Herrand but this was her first love. Aged twenty-one she flung herself into it as if into the theatre. Since she was acting in Camus' play the two things went together. Love was like a role: a leap into the unknown, a gamble of all or nothing. Camus was equally moved, more moved perhaps than he had been since he fell in love with Simone Hié. He was no longer cold, no longer a seducer and no longer merely tender. With Casarès he almost forgot his indifference.

Usually they met at Gide's studio. Sometimes they went to La Mère Catherine in Montmartre where they knew an old violinist and a hard-drinking Russian pianist who played for them the Piaf song *La Vie en Rose*. Other times they went to Spanish concerts. Under the pretext of recitations the Spanish republicans gathered to defy the Occupation and Franco.

Casarès recited Lorca while the proud Camus looked on. They discovered that they both liked to dance so they found cheap nightclubs where she 'danced away her exuberance'. Camus danced with equal enthusiasm but more measure. He teased her about her exuberance: 'if you were chewing the cud in a field, you'd do it with passion'.

Occasionally there was danger. One day the police stopped a crowd of people near the rue Réaumur. The men were searched, the women asked to show identity cards. Camus pushed into her hand a bundle of *Combat* paper. Fearing that the police would change their minds and start searching the women, Casarès swallowed it. She knew Camus was in *Combat* but he told her little about it. She herself continued to live in fear as friends – Jews or communists – were deported. Yet the war was also their ally for Camus had told her he was married; at the Liberation Francine would rejoin him and their love would be over.

The months preceding the Liberation were dangerous and unreal. Camus brought Casarès to the parties he attended and Simone de Beauvoir remembers her 'wearing a Rochas dress with purple and mauve stripes; her black hair was drawn straight back; a slightly loud laugh showed her white teeth; she was very beautiful.'[50] On the night of the Allied landings they drank too much brandy and water. They returned to Gide's flat on a bicycle, Casarès sitting on the handlebars. 'Perhaps the bicycle is drunk,' she kept saying as it swung from side to side.

In long conversations Camus confided in her. Reluctantly he told her of his tuberculosis, of the lethargy into which it plunged him and of his 'evil indifference'. They talked of death and he insisted that, if he died, she must forget him and live to the full. At lighter moments they quarrelled about Celts and Latins, rain and sunshine. They agreed about their Spanish heritage but argued whether the windswept Galician sea could equal the Algiers bay. Each claimed to be more barbarian than the other. Casarès saw the best side of Camus: his quest for some truth which included social and political justice but did not stop there. Despite her loyalty to the republican refugees who flocked to the Rue de Vaugirard, Casarès had no political views. Although Camus instructed her, she felt that his brand of truth was both unpolitical and unattainable. He seemed to feel, as she did, that it lay in his childhood and that he was groping through his exile to recover it. It was also aesthetic: a form, perhaps a circle, that he was trying to trace.

As well as seeing the best in Camus Casarès brought out the best in him. She was no love-object but a strong woman who shared her vitality with Camus and sometimes battled with him. She resisted the passion she felt and struggled against 'a love that placed me at the centre of life but left me completely vulnerable'.[51] She could not forget that this love was stolen from time, that it was a fragment of innocence thrown up by the war. To protect herself she raged against Camus who laughingly called her 'War and Peace' and tried to calm her. Yet his own calm was purely outward because he lived in a state of 'armed alert', ready at any moment to erupt into love or anger. He could not bear their future separation any better than she could. He said they must emigrate to Mexico to be together. One long drunken evening he confided to Marcel Herrand that they would leave as soon as the war ended.

In June *Le Malentendu* was performed. The role of Martha, hard and worn, did not seem to suit Casarès who studied it even more carefully than usual. On the first night Camus borrowed a bicycle which broke down on the way. The critics from the collaborationist newspapers flocked to the theatre for one of their last premières; soon they would be retreating with the German armies. Casarès was superb: 'she showed the frenzy of a murderess and of a judge; she was an implacable servant of an evil god'.[52] All evening she had to battle with the audience for the play was a flop. Sartre and De Beauvoir were not surprised: they had disliked *Le Malentendu* when Camus had read it to them. Camus and Casarès were bitterly disappointed despite her triumph. Once more masking his feelings, Camus hinted that he had been too pessimistic for the audience. But the truth was simpler: the play was cold and even Herrand and Casarès could not bring it to life.

Camus, Sartre and the others were continuing their parties. One evening they gathered at the home of theatre director Charles Dullin, Camus accompanied by Casarès. Everyone drank a lot and Dullin's mistress went to bed drunk before re-appearing to dance a complex paso doble with Camus. Drinking was a relief from the danger of the Occupation and from the torturing hope of freedom. They feared that the 'tomorrows full of song', which the Resistance kept promising, would not be realized. The curfews were turning Paris into a prison camp and the Nazis might never leave. Not trusting the future Camus lived in the present.

The comradeship which the anti-Nazi writers felt for one another was never stronger than in these last weeks. They clustered together to listen to the BBC, aware that they were still outlaws. They drank because alcohol liberated their imaginations and kept the Nazi patrols from the door. Never had Camus acted so much; he was Ivan, Bogart, the Playboy, all his favourite roles. His actor's sense of unreality was heightened by the contrast between the parties and the streets outside. Such gaiety could not be recreated because the tension which underlay it would be banished at the Liberation. Camus and Sartre were closer now than they would ever be again. Their parties were 'happenings', less celebrations of victory than victorious acts of defiance.

Camus' dilemma was all the sharper because the Liberation would separate him from Casarès. In July Jacqueline Bernard was arrested and the *Combat* members scurried for shelter. From the countryside Camus made a desperate appeal to Maria who was supposed to join him but did not. Once more he pressed her to go to Mexico with him. But she refused, alleging that she could not leave her family. The real reasons on both sides were, one feels, very different. If they went to Mexico she would be unable to act and he would be a linguistic exile. Did he seriously think of abandoning the Paris he was about to conquer? It was so unnecessary. If Camus really wished to live with Maria he could do so in Paris by divorcing or separating from Francine. It would be unkind but the war knew many such cases. Although Maria Casarès would reject this explanation, Camus must have been reluctant to take the step of asking her to live with him. Perhaps the commitment he would be making was too great. It would infringe on that edge of distance and freedom that he sought to preserve.

On her side it was still all or nothing and, since she could not have all, she chose nothing. She was too proud to be the mistress of a married man. Camus seemed almost frightened of their affair: 'so much love, so many demands, so much pride. It's clear that it can't do us any good,' he wrote, adding defiantly: 'no one will ever love you as I love you.'[53] Yet he was too prudent a gambler to bid for the all. Although he revelled in her emotions he may have distrusted them too. Were her acting and his writing reconcilable? Perhaps both of them felt dimly that they were not. But Camus could not believe that their love would end with the war and could not accept that it must. It was Casarès who had to make the break and she did it when she refused his plea to flee to Mexico. Although they saw each other briefly at the Liberation, her decision to leave him was made.

The last weeks had a feverish quality. Louis Miquel took Camus to a little restaurant called the Saint-Benoît which Le Corbusier had frequented; they talked about architecture while the sirens wailed outside. Paris seemed unreal. The Nazi administration had collapsed and the Resistance had not yet taken over. On August 12 Sartre and his cohorts gathered as so often in the Flore, where they drank ersatz gin and talked in whispers. Paris had no underground, no electricity and no food. There were rumours that the Germans intended to destroy the city as they withdrew. The tormented but meticulous Camus was preparing to bring *Combat* above ground. In a few days he would no longer be a writer at war.

7

The Trials of Combat

'We are going to run a reasonable newspaper,' said Pia, 'but, since the world is absurd, we shall fail.' The first number of the non-clandestine *Combat* appeared on August 21, 1944, two days after the start of the Paris insurrection. It contained a minute-by-minute account of the fighting and a fiery editorial by Camus. Paris, he declared, was to be liberated not by the Allies nor even by De Gaulle but by the Parisians themselves. Outside the barricades were up and the resistants were exchanging shots with the departing Germans. Newsboys sold the first number on streets where bullets were flying. They returned to the *Combat* offices and poured the money into waste-paper baskets. This is how the printers were paid at the end of the week.

In the days that followed *Combat* urged people to set up ever more barricades, told them where they could buy bread or milk and welcomed De Gaulle. Sartre arrived at the rue Réaumur office to find that 'the door was guarded by boys with machine guns. From top to bottom of the building chaos and gaiety reigned. Camus was exultant.'[1] As she walked back to the Left Bank Simone de Beauvoir saw SS troops withdrawing. Canons resounded, resistants passed on bicycles and women wondered aloud whether the Germans would now bomb Paris. On August 26 De Gaulle marched up the Champs-Elysées and went to Notre Dame where shots were fired in the roof. In *Combat* Camus called on the Parisians to fight Fascism and to make sure they had their meat coupons.

The best pieces in these early numbers were written by Sartre. Camus sent him out to report from the streets. He depicted a blind accordionist playing *Traviata* in the middle of a shoot-out, a carload of resistants who looked like gangsters in a film about Chicago and a woman who stood buying food while the Germans sprayed the street with machine-gun bullets. 'You can't stop eating just because there's a war on,' she told Sartre.

These articles catch the crazy, unreal side of the Liberation while Camus' more solemn editorials contain the hope of rebirth. First the Germans must be driven out and then French society must be transformed. 'We want to create at once a popular, working-class democracy,' writes Camus.[2] The key words in these editorials are 'honour', 'energy' and 'purity'. The old, doubting Camus who had condemned the war and who had shared the ambiguities of the Occupation has vanished. The *Combat* editorialist is giving free rein to his lyrical optimism.

The organization of *Combat* had been worked out during the meetings in Gide's flat. Afraid that the Allies would start their own newspapers, Pia acted quickly. He had the others file a legal document which established the group as owners of the new paper. This gave them 'a semblance of legality' and broke with pre-war practice. No longer would newspapers have owners who used them to serve their business or political ambitions. *Combat* belonged to the journalists who could write what they pleased. Next Pia hunted out a printing-press. Along with two other Resistance papers *Combat* took over a building in the rue Réaumur that had belonged to a collaborationist paper. Somehow Pia managed to find a supply of paper.

The group of journalists was expanded. Georges Altschuler and Marcel Gimond were professionals whom Pia had known when he was with *Paris-Soir*. Camus brought in Albert Ollivier who had worked at Gallimard before the war. Ollivier had then worked for the Vichy radio where he wrote touching broadcasts about Pétain's youth and read Malraux in the evenings. He quickly abandoned Vichy and moved into *Combat*. A student of revolutions, Ollivier never believed in the hopes of the Liberation. He had a cold strain in him which Camus disliked but his concept of journalism was close to Camus': newspapers should be 'bearers of spiritual discomfort'. Ollivier helped set *Combat*'s ascetic tone and one of his earliest editorials was entitled 'New Duties'.[3]

Pia himself quickly settled into his *Alger-Républicain* habits. He would arrive at rue Réaumur around two o'clock in the afternoon, bringing a thermos of coffee and sandwiches prepared by his wife. He read through the news agency reports and then held a meeting with the others. He stayed in the office until midnight and reread every line of the paper. He corrected the language and in particular the use of the subjunctive.

Like *Alger-Républicain*, *Combat* explained where it obtained its information and analysed its sources. It shunned sensational stories about crime and sex and tried, unsuccessfully, to moderate its rhetoric. It began a review of the press to which Pia attached great importance. *Combat* rebuked its fellow-papers for their jingoism; it complained that they were denouncing the Germans as a race instead of analysing Fascism. Such rebukes displeased the other newspapers which complained that *Combat* was much too self-righteous.

Pia had many talents but book-keeping was not one of them. *Combat* could not always keep its money in waste-paper baskets so Jean Bloch-Michel was made its accountant. Bloch-Michel, who had been captured and tortured in the Resistance, came from a family that had been socialist since the turn of the century. He became friendly with Camus who made fun of this socialist heritage. As with Fouchet, Camus teased Bloch-Michel about the socialists' lazy reliance on progress. When Pia asked him to become *Combat*'s accountant Bloch-Michel replied that he knew nothing about book-keeping. 'Fine,' said Pia, 'all accountants cheat their papers, you won't be able to.' This was a characteristic comment but Bloch-Michel neglected *Combat*'s finances, which proved a grave handicap.

Camus kept recruiting new journalists. Pierre Kaufman, who wrote mostly about foreign affairs, was interested in psychiatry and used to ask Camus what he thought about psycho-analysis. This disconcerted Camus who refused to reply. Sartre provided several more recruits. Jacques Bost had been his student and was the model for Boris in *L'Age de Raison*. Camus sent him to be a frontline reporter in Eastern France, which pleased Bost because it gave him the right to eat in special American restaurants that offered such delicacies as tinned ham. Albert Palle was another of Sartre's students. He was sitting in the Flore with Simone de Beauvoir when Camus arrived. 'You must take Palle into *Combat*,' said De Beauvoir. 'What has he written?' asked Camus. 'Nothing,' replied Simone de Beauvoir, 'but he has lots of talent.' 'We can't take everyone who has talent,' said Camus but he did take Palle.[4] He sent him to Deauville to do a piece on the big hotels where rich people lived lavishly and ignored rationing. Palle's articles infuriated the people in the hotels but they amused Pia.

Simone de Beauvoir felt that opening *Combat* was like opening her morning post. Another recruit from the Flore was the future film director Alexandre Astruc who used to go nightclubbing with Sartre and usually passed out more quickly. Astruc was working at another paper but Camus had him transferred – like a soccer player, he said. It was a shrewd move because Astruc wrote some of the best articles in the early *Combat*. Sent to cover the collaborators' trials, he made fun of the vagaries of Liberation justice and his satire of courtroom formality reminds one of *L'Etranger*.

Astruc liked *Combat* because it rejected 'the conformism of victory' and had an 'anarchist strain'. This was injected by Pia who loved to make fun of ministers or to publish two conflicting articles on the same subject. He was probably pleased to discover that military censorship still existed: *Combat*'s articles on the war appeared with blanks as *Alger-Républicain* had done. Pia refused, however, all non-military censorship. When De Gaulle would not allow Roosevelt to go to Algiers, the government tried to stop *Combat* from printing the story but Pia was adamant. Nor was he corrupted by the social temptations of his new position. Invited to meet foreign dignitaries, he invariably declined. Meanwhile Camus contributed to *Combat*'s irreverence by his Suetonius articles. Exchanging the moralist's for the satrist's mask, he complained that higher taxes on the cinema meant empty seats and wondered whether the government was raising rail prices because it preferred to run the trains empty.*

Such irreverence was one reason for *Combat*'s success. After years of Petain's paternalistic speeches, after years of intellectual impoverishment more debilitating than food-rationing, people were ready for heresy. *Combat* was read by the same intellectual public as listened to Boris Vian's jazz and read Genet's novels. Astruc stressed that young people were looking for adventure. American detective stories, hard to obtain under the Nazis, were now the rage. Anything American, from New Orleans jazz to army surplus jeans, was welcomed as exotic and

---

*Regrettably these Suetonius articles have not been included in the Pléiade volumes. In Astruc's opinion they are Camus' best pieces.

liberating. Faulkner, Dos Passos and Hemingway, who had all been read in the '30's, were rediscovered. Film directors like William Wyler and Orson Welles were preferred to better French directors like Carné and Clouzot. Along with Americanism went the popular version of existentialism that made Sartre and Camus famous. Since life made no sense each man must give meaning to his individual existence. Saint-Germain, which was already becoming a tourist attraction, was full of despair and non-conformity.

This was only one part of the Liberation atmosphere. The young journalists of *Combat* knew, too, that they were lucky. Vichy's demise left a vacuum in politics, publishing, the theatre and the press. Ambitious men could rise faster than ever before and many who occupy top posts today began their climb at the Liberation. Pia was the exception in refusing to be successful. Publishing houses opened to the young writers who had been pro-Resistance. Camus had an influential position at Gallimard, his editorials set the tone in Saint-Germain and *L'Etranger* was discussed in numerous articles.

His ambition was softened by the comradeship which persisted among men who had banded together to survive the Occupation. So many had been killed or deported that the survivors felt a special closeness. The memory of the days when they were without jobs, money or papers persisted, while distinctions of class and background mattered less. Sartre talked about his 'family' of friends and Camus treated the *Combat* journalists like brothers.

Yet there was an unreality about the Liberation. The Paris insurrection was a conscious replay of the 1830, 1848 and 1870 uprisings and the barricades were erected on the very same streets. Chroniclers who look back on this time depict it as an interlude between the end of the Occupation and the start of the Cold War. Claude Roy talks about the invasion of Germany as Fabrice del Dongo talked about the battle of Waterloo: Roy keeps wondering whether he was really there.[5] Then exaltation gave way to disenchantment. As early as September Camus began to ask whether the popular, working-class democracy could ever be realized. Bénisti, who visited him in October, says that Camus was already sick of *Combat*. Camus knew that Liberation fraternity was not as real as the Algerian sun or the Belcourt streets.

The sense of unreality ran alongside the Resistance's moral

absolutism. Camus told his young recruits that his aim was to impose on politics the language of morality. The Liberation seemed to demonstrate that the Resistance had been right: bearing witness was not useless and courage could defeat force. So Camus had found his audience. The moral thinking, which he had practised as a young boy, was welcomed. The values of lucidity and toughness, which he had advocated in *Sisyphe*, were those of 1944.

'Political revolutions cannot do without moral revolutions,' insists Camus. He reveals his old distrust of power: the Resistance is not a new social force that will dominate but a new élite that will revitalize. Camus is still an aristocrat and he is still willing to jump from the individual to the universal. He defends the purges by invoking justice against charity; later he will condemn all political trials. Neither time does he examine the kind of justice meted out at the Liberation or the kind of crimes committed by the collaborators.

To Camus, Liberation man was a new Prometheus or Sisyphus who was engaged in a metaphysical revolt. Camus repeats the need for limits: journalists should have 'a sense of the relative', the innovations of 1944 are a 'very limited experiment'. As in the '30's measure is pitted against the cries for revolution. 'We do not believe in definitive revolutions,' writes Camus, 'every human endeavour is relative.' Ponge might have applauded. But Camus could also write that 'intransigence has become the greatest of duties'. This was the old dilemma of the PCA and of *Sisyphe* and it now led Camus to write sheer nonsense about 'relative utopias'.

The faults which were present in his *Alger-Républicain* articles grow because the genre of the editorial, which leaves out factual detail, flattered Camus' weaknesses and because the exaltation of the Liberation turned them into seeming strengths. His Manichean vision is expressed in sonorous antitheses – 'the harsh, marvellous task of our age'. He is prone to rhetorical excesses – 'if we fail, humanity will return to the depths of the night' – and to the abuse of superlatives – 'the most pitiless and the most resolute justice'. In the best *Alger-Républicain* articles there was understatement; the journalist had said all he could but he knew there was more. In *Combat* Camus fills the void of his scepticism with inflated language.

Although these editorials were well-received in 1944 there

was an undertone of criticism. Altschuler notes that Camus' moralizing irritated some readers and that others, like Pia, did not take it seriously. Some felt it was ridiculous for Camus to denounce the press for devoting space to the Saint-Germain night-spots when he frequented these same night-spots. When the former *Paris-Soir* editor, Pierre Lazareff, returned from the United States, Camus refused to shake hands with him. No one at *Combat* had any use for Lazareff but many felt that Camus was being silly. Of course it is wrong to judge Camus' editorials by his life when the weakness lay in the writing itself. Today these articles are almost unreadable, not because their topicality has faded but because Camus' moral impulse made him simplistic and dogmatic. This is moralizing rather than moral thinking.

Although he grumbled to Bénisti, Camus enjoyed the first months at *Combat*. He arrived in the afternoon and discussed his editorial with the others. Then he wrote quickly in his illegible handwriting and dictated his final draft. He tried to make his editorial as simple as possible – one idea, two examples, three columns. He often stayed at *Combat* until late at night and helped Pia set up the paper. He enjoyed talking to the printers who flattered his sense of being working-class. Eager to show them that he understood their craft, he was all too generous when he negotiated with them about work-rates and holidays.

In October Francine arrived from Algeria. At once the autumn turned cold and they discovered that Gide's flat was badly-heated. Camus used to swing on Marc Allégret's trapeze and people who walked in thought he was mad. Francine bundled up in overcoats and rugs. Food was scarce and she had to spend much time scheming to obtain butter and coffee. At *Combat* Camus was paid the wages of a skilled worker and he was on leave from his *NRF* post. The war had prevented Gallimard from printing larger editions of *L'Etranger* so Camus did not have much money – he was famous but not wealthy.

This did not trouble Francine who was accustomed to living cheaply but she worried that her husband was spending too much time at *Combat* and one day she went to rue Réaumur to tell the others that they ought to send him home in the evenings. Camus' circle of friends liked Francine – Simone de Beauvoir describes her as 'blond, fresh and very pretty'.[6] Francine enjoyed Sartre's curiosity and his flood of jokes and she felt at ease with him.

Francine and Camus had resumed their marriage and she soon became pregnant. Camus was both pleased to be married and inwardly tormented. Since the Liberation he had seen nothing of Maria Casarès. When her mother died, he sent her a letter which left her in no doubt that he still loved her. She did not, however, reply. One day she saw him walking near the Seine but he did not see her and she did not approach him. Another evening they sat in the same row in the theatre and he kept looking at her: 'it was a violent stare of defiance that broke all the rules of politeness'.[7] She appeared in a play with Gérard Philipe where, according to one spectator, 'they almost made love on the stage'.[8] Camus was furiously jealous and he never forgave Gérard Philipe.

He would have liked to resume his affair with Maria but she stuck by her decision. If it was all or nothing, she would choose nothing. In his diary Camus offers glimpses of what he was feeling:

'You can't build on love . . . it's a flight, a torment, a moment of ecstasy or an abrupt fall.'

'Love can only be made to last by reasons that are extraneous to it, moral reasons for example.'

'My heart is growing old. To love and to see nothing remain of it!'[9]

Simone de Beauvoir remembers one evening when Camus treated her to a long discourse on love. 'It can burn or last,' he said, 'but it can't do both.'[10] With Francine he found affection and stability but he missed Maria's more passionate nature. For her part Francine was content to be married and she wanted Camus to behave like a husband.

Camus tried but marriage did not prevent him from taking advantage of the opportunities offered to him in Saint-Germain. However engrossed he was in a conversation, he would break off the moment a girl walked down the street. When he went to New York he could not understand why the men did not eye the women as they did in Paris. In Paris many thought his habits were Algerian but his pied-noir friends thought he was exceptional. Camus needed to seduce. He could be cold about it: at one party he never spoke to a girl with whom he had just made love; at another he described in detail to a rival when and how he had slept with the girl they admired. At *Combat* he boasted of his seductions to the other men but he also confided in them how guilty he felt at deceiving his wife. Neither time, they thought, was he completely sincere. He would ask for advice to which he invariably paid no attention.

Contemporary readers are not troubled by the gulf between Camus' moralizing and his life but it bothered him. Yet he could not stop womanizing because he needed the excitement of fresh seductions. Since he was still in love with Maria Casarès he had to console himself with other women but he then felt guilty about Francine for whom he genuinely cared. These mutually contradictory, equally intense desires made his existence complicated, which depressed him still more. He fell into lethargic indifference, only to be restored to life by the next pretty girl he encountered. Clearly tuberculosis aggravated these cycles.

On New Year's eve he and Francine spent the evening carousing with Sartre and Simone de Beauvoir. Sartre drank heavily and happily but Simone de Beauvoir felt that the evening lacked the tense, concentrated joy of their Occupation parties. Sartre relished Camus' wit and he has recently described their relationship at this time:

'Camus didn't know then that he was a great writer. He was very funny and we used to have a good time together. His language was pretty colourful and so was mine. We used to tell a lot of dirty stories and his wife and Simone de Beauvoir would pretend to be shocked ... He was like an Algerian street-urchin, a little ruffian, really funny.'[11]

Camus could not always play the street-urchin for Sartre and in his other incarnations he annoyed him. Simone de Beauvoir felt that there were two Camus: the hard-drinking friend who was 'cynical, funny and very coarse' and the intellectual 'who clammed up once the discussion grew serious, became stiff and haughty and replied to objections with resounding periods, high-flown sentiments and self-indulgent anger'.[12] Both Camus betrayed the vulnerability present since his childhood. When challenged he withdrew into his boxer's stance; charm and arrogance were ways to seduce or rebuff the challenger. Nor did

Camus conceal his sentimental strain for he was prone, especially when drinking, to lament about his life.

Certainly he was enjoying his new-found fame. He went out drinking with the *Combat* journalists in the cafés near Les Halles. If there were women present he would dance, aware that he danced well and that the others were watching him. He liked to hold court in Saint-Germain, to tell stories and set the whole café laughing. Even men considered him good-looking: 'he was like Bogart but more exuberant,' said one.[13] The compliment he treasured the most came from a young boy who had helped to distribute the clandestine *Combat*. When he learned that Beauchard was Albert Camus, the author of *L'Etranger*, he was amazed. 'That's wonderful', he said and Camus beamed. Such praise was worth more than Sartre's article.

Sartre was not jealous of Camus' fame which did not surpass his own. But he felt that Camus had begun to believe in the character of Albert Camus – distinguished writer, *Combat* editorialist and man of all talents. Sartre could have tolerated Camus' occasional conceit but he could not long put up with the rhetoric about honesty and goodness.

The cooling of the friendship overlapped with growing intellectual differences. Sartre was preparing to launch his magazine *Les Temps Modernes* which was to replace the *NRF*. Since it had appeared during the Occupation, the *NRF* was now banned so the Gallimard writers intended to band together in *Les TM*. Camus was to be on the committee, as were Malraux and Paulhan. But Camus soon edged away, reluctant to take on further responsibility and suspicious of Sartre.

When Sartre's introduction to the first number appeared, Camus realized that he had been right. Sartre had written with his usual nervous aggressivity. Whereas the *NRF* had been a web of contradictions, Sartre's magazine was to be dogmatic. Moreover Sartre was expounding a view of literature which Camus could not share. Literature was to depict man's situation and to spur the reader to change it. Sartre affirmed more strongly than ever that man could emerge from his metaphysical emptiness only by immersing himself in political and social reality. Such action would lead him to know and to liberate himself; the political act of rebellion was the only possible form of metaphysical revolt. So the artist must depict man in his social condition. Discarding such empty values as 'posterity' and 'universality' he must speak to and of the French reader of 1945. His writing would be good if it disturbed the reader and forced him to look differently at his condition.

Camus expressed his disagreement with Sartre in public and he argued with him in his diary.[14] He refused to believe that metaphysics was a matter of politics or that literature should become a direct vehicle of social protest. Not that Camus had a clear sense of the relationship between metaphysics and politics or between the critical self-awareness that marked modern writing and the act of political revolt. He would mull over these problems during the long years he spent writing *L'Homme Révolté*. But he felt instinctively that Sartre was ascribing too much importance to politics, just as Sartre felt that Camus was foolish to pursue universal moral values. This difference explains why the two men were taking opposing political stands: Sartre was much more pro-communist than Camus.

In January '45 Camus fell ill. He had been working too hard and he came down with a fresh bout of tuberculosis. Although he soon recovered, the illness brought back his sense of death. He told a friend that he was sure he would soon die but that he hoped to have ten more years; that was what he needed to complete his work. By March he was back at *Combat* and he took part in a debate organized by a Catholic group. He delivered a characteristic piece called *In Defence of Intelligence* which reasserted traditional French moral and intellectual values. The argument against intelligence was made by *Témoignage Chrétien* leader, André Mandouze. They would clash again during the Algerian War.

In April Camus went back to Algeria for the first time in three years. During his absence the country had continued to fester. The Arab population was still increasing and Arabs were still flooding into the towns. 1945 was yet another 'exceptional' year of famine. De Gaulle's government had made promises to the Arabs but, when it moved to Paris, the French Algerians regained control. The Arabs responded with violence; they rioted across the country and killed a handful of Europeans at Sétif. Planes were used to machine-gun the insurgents and as many as forty-five thousand Arabs may have been killed. The *Echo* commented happily that 'the policeman's hour has come.'[15]

Camus was welcomed by his mother, who could not grasp

how her son had suddenly become famous, and by his uncle Etienne. He borrowed a car from Poncet and set out on a trip that took him nearly a thousand miles across Algeria. He kept saying how much he had missed the desert and how cold the Parisians were. In the articles which he wrote for *Combat* on his return he condemned the repression at Sétif but he did not discuss the discrepancy between the violence of the insurgents and the violence employed against them. He showed a reserved sympathy for Arab spokesman Ferhat Abbas who was now calling for limited independence. Camus was slightly more timid than Abbas who would be too timid for young Arabs.

In Algiers Camus paid a call on Gide who was still living at Jacques Heurgon's house. When Camus phoned him Gide had discovered in Heurgon's library a copy of *Noces* of which he deigned to approve. Then Camus came in person and charmed him: 'it was a perfect visit ... no embarrassment, no misunderstanding, a simple, genuine cordiality'.[16] Throughout his life Gide had sought the new, the promising and the heretical. Now he put out his sensitive antennae towards Camus and tried to feel his way into the culture of the Liberation.

When he returned to Paris in May he and Camus saw much of each other. They listened to the proclamation of victory in Marc Allégret's studio. Gide told Francine to play the piano as much as she liked, it would not disturb him; after that Francine never dared to play again. When her cat strayed Gide would bring it back, appearing at the door with a bemused expression and the cat wrapped around his neck. To Francine he seemed a figure from the past with his berets, his shawls and his use of the imperfect subjunctive. There was no real kinship, either personal or intellectual, between Gide and Camus. The combination of unconventional morality and ritualistic ceremony which reigned in Gide's household bewildered and rather shocked Camus. He would have died to defend homosexuals' rights but he did not much like them.

A few weeks after his return Gide invited Malraux to dinner with the Camus but this was another acquaintanceship which did not blossom into a friendship. Malraux had already visited *Combat* and a photo shows him looking haggard and smoking the inevitable cigarette while Pia and Camus stand by in shirt-sleeves. But in mid-1945 Malraux had set out on his Gaullist adventure and he distrusted in Camus the left-wing intellectual. Left-wingers, Malraux felt, simply wanted to stage a spectacle of barricades and red flags; they were romantic, puerile and outmoded. Camus and Malraux saw each other occasionally after the dinner at Gide's and Camus was shocked to hear Malraux declare that too much attention was paid to the working-class; that sounded strange from the author of *La Condition Humaine*.[17] Camus was not tempted by Gaullism and he watched from afar as Malraux drew closer to De Gaulle.

By now Camus' Algerian friends had come streaming into Paris. Jeanne Sicard and Marguerite Dobrenn found jobs in the civil service and in politics; they came frequently to see Francine who was delighted to talk about Oran. Robert Namia, who had been in the Italian campaign, turned up with parcels of food and stayed a few days in Gide's flat. Camus and Robert Jaussaud were reconciled: the dispute of September '39 had been settled when the Nazis entered Paris. After publishing Resistance writing in liberated Algiers Jean Charlot came to start a publishing house in Paris. With him came Claude de Fréminville whom Camus kept encouraging to write but who eventually gave up.

De Fréminville felt that Camus had changed. Because of his success he was always on show while his success itself separated him from them. They were all still travelling on the same train, Frémin said, but Camus was going first-class. Charlot would have liked Camus to resume publishing with him but Camus would not give up Gallimard. Yet he was always willing to help his friends. Men with North African accents turned up at Gallimard or at *Combat* and he would put them up or help them get jobs. He would also go carousing with them and he enjoyed these occasions more than his outings with Sartre. When he was hurt by political or literary attacks he retreated to his 'Algiers mafia'.

Gide's return to Paris meant that Camus had to look for somewhere to live. For the summer of '45 he managed with Michel Gallimard's help to find a villa east of Paris near Vincennes.[18] Francine was expecting her baby in September and Camus was hard at work on *La Peste*. As he toiled away his usual self-doubts assailed him. It was four years since he had finished *L'Etranger* and he had still not completed a second novel. The success of *L'Etranger* weighed on him and he was sure he would not be able to equal it. He took time off from his novel to go into *Combat* and to help with the rehearsals of *Caligula* which was to be performed in the autumn.

On September 5 Francine gave birth to twins: a boy who was called Jean and a girl named Catherine after Camus' mother. The delivery was easy and Camus was delighted. He went around the *Combat* office boasting of his potency and asking the others whether they thought it was wonderful or ridiculous to have twins. Camus was very much the Mediterranean father. He was eager to play with his children but diapers and milk-bottles were mysteries to him. He reminded everyone that the twins were one quarter Spanish and he used to sing Spanish lullabies to them.

On September 26 *Caligula* was performed with sets by Louis Miquel, costumes by Marie Vitton and Francine's cousin Paul Oettly as producer. Simone de Beauvoir, who disliked the play, felt that Gérard Philipe's performance as emperor redeemed it. Acting with panache the young Philipe was able to catch Caligula's many moods. In general the critics were luke-warm and Ollivier wrote an embarrassed article which did not improve his dealings with Camus.[19]

During the winter of '45 the Camus family moved twice: first to a house right on the other side of Paris and then to Michel Gallimard's flat on the Left Bank. Camus wanted to find an appartment on the Left Bank but for the moment there was nothing. It was not so easy for a father of twins to move as it had been for a bachelor and Francine found the combination of moving, babies and winter very taxing. Camus intrigued to get coal and one day a truckload was delivered by mistake to the *Combat* office. Michel Gallimard used his family's influence to get extra milk and baby-food, while friends kept Camus supplied with the coffee he loved.

He had now gone back to Gallimard and had begun to work regularly as an editor. He had his own office in the huge labyrinth of the Gallimard building on the rue Sébastien-Bottin and he was one of the privileged few whose office had a terrace. Camus was inordinately proud of the terrace and visitors were taken out to see it even on the coldest winter days. He also had his own collection, *L'Espoir*, and his special place in the web of the *NRF* – he represented the new writing of the Liberation.

Although he was now going only occasionally to *Combat* Camus was always rushed. Gallimard, the paper and *La Peste* took up a great deal of time; friends and carousing took most of what remained. After working at Gallimard Camus liked to go out and sit in cafés. He would drink and watch the girls walk past until inevitably some of his many friends came to join him. Francine, left at home with the babies, began to complain. Meanwhile the honeymoon of the Liberation had faded and *Combat* was having difficulty maintaining a coherent left-wing position. It supported De Gaulle's government and was wary of the Anglo-Saxons, while it was generous to the Soviet Union and to the French Communist Party. Camus sums up *Combat*'s ideal of unity: 'General de Gaulle, the parties of the Resistance and the Communists set the seal during the struggle on a fraternity that they will not abandon.'[20] But Camus' doubts about De Gaulle and the Communists grew quickly.

He had been invited to join the committee of a Communist magazine, *Lettres Françaises*; he contributed one article and then withdrew. He explained to Pierre Kaufman what *Combat*'s attitude to the Communists must be: we are not going to indulge in anti-communism but, when we disagree with them, we shall say so. In its review of the press *Combat* rebuked *L'Humanité* for claiming to be infallible and presenting only one side of a debate.

The Communists were quick to reply because they feared that *Combat* would prove a dangerous rival. Although the Communists were trying to appear open-minded they hoped to establish a cultural hegemony over the new society that was emerging from the Liberation. This meant eliminating other poles of attraction, even or especially when they were friendly. Sartre was surprised that the PC attacked him precisely when his thought was growing more marxist; that may, however, have been the reason. *Combat* was a rival because it was left-wing but libertarian. Its irreverence contrasted with the PC's dogmatism, while Camus' moralizing made the Communists seem ruthless. Soon they began denouncing *Combat* as a 'Fascist paper'.

Combat was scarcely kinder to De Gaulle. It applauded the expropriation of the Renault car works and the first nationalizations but it kept calling on the government to block prices and reform the currency. Camus began criticizing De Gaulle's grandiose ambitions in foreign affairs. During the dispute with England over Syria Camus warned that France no longer had the strength to conduct a far-flung foreign policy. His sense of limits contrasted with De Gaulle's sense of grandeur which formed an easy target for *Combat*'s irreverence.

Camus wanted to offer a left-wing alternative to De Gaulle and the Communists but he could not. Georges Altschuler was pro-socialist and *Combat* felt closer to the Socialists than to any other party. But Camus continued to feel that the Socialists were not daring enough. He would have liked to offer Scandinavian social-democracy as an ideal but Sweden had clearly not accomplished the political and moral renovation which he advocated in his editorials. So Camus hesitated and he told Bloch-Michel that, if there were a party of people who did not know what they thought, he would join it.

He had succeeded in making the cultural page of *Combat* really interesting. To cover painting he brought in Jean Grenier who applauded the artists who had been out of favour under the Nazis – Picasso, Kandinsky and Dubuffet. Abstract art appealed to Grenier's sense of a world that lay beyond reality. Camus still distrusted abstraction and one day he went around the office looking for someone who would write about representational art – there were no volunteers. To cover the theatre he brought from Gallimard Jacques Lemarchand who explained the new, so-called 'philosophical' plays of the Liberation. Camus also launched a campaign to rehabilitate Nietzsche, insisting that he not be dismissed as a pre-Nazi agitator. This cultural page was as much read as the editorials.

In April '45 *Combat*'s task was made even more difficult when Pierre Mendès France resigned from the government. Mendès left because he wanted a rigorous reform of the currency which would tax the black market fortunes and reduce inflation. He had had the support of *Combat* which considered him the most honest and the most ascetic politician of the non-Communist left. Now *Combat* published two editorials which criticized De Gaulle for letting Mendès go. Mendès was one of the very few politicians whom the sceptical Camus admired. He would support Mendès again during the Algerian War.

Camus' feeling that he did not know what he thought was strengthened by the trials of the collaborators which took place throughout '44 and '45. The Communists were loudest in their demand for justice but *Combat* had initially agreed. In November '44 Camus had applauded the creation of the special tribunals and had declared that he 'was willing to destroy a living part of the country's body in order to save its soul'.

François Mauriac was pleasantly shocked by Camus' readiness to destroy. On the front page of the *Figaro* he began an argument which aroused controversy in Paris and boosted the sales of both papers. Mauriac teased Camus: 'The Inquisition too burned people's bodies in order to save their souls.' Camus was really too much of a zealot – 'there are traces of suppressed Christianity in the young masters of *Combat*'. With malicious kindness Mauriac delivered a sermon about charity.[21]

It is an inadequate explanation to say that Mauriac was jealous of Camus' abrupt rise to fame. This is possible, but there were deeper reasons for the controversy. Mauriac's resistance credentials were impeccable – better than Camus'. But he turned against the Resistance because he was a heretic of the old *NRF*. He distrusted the culture of the Liberation which Camus seemed to exemplify; it was unsubtle, over-committed and Manichean. Mauriac protested that France could not be divided into the good and the evil. Evil was not a simple matter and it could not be eradicated, as Camus implied, because it was caught up with self-deception and habit. 'Our blood is full of sickly germs of which we are not even aware,' writes Mauriac. His battle with Camus pitted Mauriac's vision of an all-corroding evil against Camus' dream of innocence. Mauriac sums it up when he mocks 'the purity which some people dream of introducing into that most impure thing politics'.

Behind the controversy lay a curious complicity. The Camus of the Prague visit and the article on the prison-ship was all too ready to agree with Mauriac. He demonstrated this as early as January 1945 when the Fascist Robert Brasillach was condemned to death. Brasillach posed the dilemma of the trials in its clearest form. His claim to sympathy was that he had remained in France when most collaborators had retreated with the Wehrmacht. He had genuinely believed in Fascism and had not, like so many others, been guided by greed. He had, however, written for the virulently pro-Nazi *Je Suis Partout* and had named resistants who had been arrested by the Germans. At his trial he was condemned to death but a petition was circulated asking De Gaulle to spare him. At first Camus refused to sign but then he agonized. His dislike of the death-penalty returned and he hated being in the role of a judge. Eventually he signed the petition which De Gaulle rejected.

As '45 wore on Camus agreed more and more with Mauriac. The trials of Pétain and Laval disgusted him: everything was done to save Pétain whereas Laval was hastily executed. In '46 Camus openly admitted that Mauriac had been right. Later, when Céline wanted to return to France, Camus was willing to sign petitions for him and to declare that 'political justice disgusts me'.[22] He had given up his dream of renovation which now seemed an unattainable mirage. The most men could do was to avoid bloodshed which meant giving up the purge.

The best piece which Camus wrote for *Combat* in '45 was an attack on the Hiroshima bombing. The Liberation moralist and the pre-1939 pacifist joined forces to denounce this 'organized murder'. Many French observers broke into a chorus of triumph at the success of the atomic bomb. Camus was a rare voice of dissent.

In March '46 Camus set out for the United States, invited by the French cultural services to lecture.[23] He had always felt that travel was an ascetic experience; now he whiled away the boat journey listening for curious anecdotes. He liked a story told by one passenger of an American who had his leg amputated in Mexico and who brought it home in a box. At New York harbour he had the troubles with the Immigration Service which are familiar to all foreigners who visit the US. He was fêted and he gave his lecture at Columbia University. The abundance of New York amazed him: huge meals, bustling crowds and drugstores. Yet he disliked America. He complains that it lacked any sense of the tragic, which is a hoary old myth that he had picked up from other European travellers. New York's anonymity overwhelmed him: he had first experienced the monotony of modern life when he had worked in the Algiers town hall, but this was infinitely worse. He notes with fascinated horror a man whose job consisted of counting the cars that came through the Holland Tunnel. He felt that the skyscrapers were huge tombstones that towered over the rainy skies.

Not that he was abandoned in the United States. He was kept busy with trips: one was to Vassar College where he looked at the girls with a connoisseur's eye; another was to Quebec and the Saint-Lawrence. For a brief moment he recaptured the sense of nature which he loved in Algeria: 'the air, light and water are fused in infinite depths'. Back in New York he found an attractive young woman, Patricia Blake, to be his companion. They went dancing together for Camus enjoyed the dingy dance-halls of mid-town Manhattan. He also liked Chinatown and the Bowery where the street-life reminded him of Algiers. He relished its ugliness, noting in his diary a nightclub full of decrepit old hags. Its very sordidness made it seem human.

Such moments gave way to fresh loneliness and Camus was afflicted with a bout of indifference. Gloom overwhelmed him and he looked desperately for companions who would liberate him from the tedium of his hotel bedroom. The US and Camus never really met: he had strayed too far from the Mediterranean.

His Columbia lecture proposed themes which he had stated often and which were turning into platitudes. However they were so popular that they became the platitudes of the age and the raw material from which the bowdlerized Camus, moral conscience of his generation, was forged. Camus accused himself of embracing a nihilism that had led to violence – although in reality he had never been nihilistic. 'We are all responsible for Hitler,' he told his audience which shivered with delighted guilt.[24] Then he asserted the importance of revolt which was man's refusal to accept this violence. Once more the audience was pleased because revolt seemed a simple, happy matter.

Yet it was also imprecise because he did not list the forms which revolt should take. Camus suggested abolishing the death-penalty but he laid more emphasis on relegating politics to its 'rightful place which is a secondary one'. This was part of his disagreement with Sartre but it was a purely negative definition of revolt. One cannot help feeling that Camus' popularity rocketed because the values he advanced were so vague and so traditional that anyone could subscribe to them and because, having conjured up the spectre of despair, he quickly banished it with the fragile wand of revolt.

He returned to France in June and went off to the countryside with Francine, the babies and *La Peste*. In September he made a brief visit to the South of France which delighted him: 'immense silence . . . solemn countryside that is austere despite its beauty'.[25] This is the kind of language he had used to describe Algeria and Provence was becoming his substitute for Algeria.

Autumn brought Paris and another move. The Camus were to live on the rue Séguier in a flat owned by the Gallimard family. The location was ideal but Francine was disappointed with the flat itself. It had high ceilings and was impossible to heat. The wind came whistling through the cracks and one evening it was so loud that it drowned out the dinner conversation. The floor-space was as cramped as the ceilings were high and Camus had to work at a desk in the little drawing-room. The babies took most of what space there was and, when Camus describes this flat in his short-story *Jonas*, he depicts himself working on a platform which he has erected up in the ceiling. He had to shop for pieces of furniture, the quest for wood and coal started all over again and the babies were more of a handful for Francine as they started to crawl and to walk.

Camus now finished *La Peste* which left him a little free time. He spent several evenings with Sartre and with a new acquaintance, Arthur Koestler. Koestler intrigued Camus because he was an ex-communist who had had a longer and more painful experience of the party. Their conversations confirmed Camus' view that the party destroyed its militants by subjecting them to a new form of inquisition. It was infallible so the militant felt guilty if he disagreed with his party; yet the party changed its line so often that the militant had to give up his personal integrity. This plunged him into further guilt and increased his devotion to the party.

In October Camus spent an evening with Koestler, Malraux and Sartre and each of the four talked about his favourite topic while the others paid no attention.[26] Camus reiterated the theme of his Columbia lecture and suggested that they should re-affirm the simple moral values that lay beyond nihilism. Malraux declared that the working-class was no longer histor-ically significant, while Sartre repeated that he could not take a stand that was solely anti-Russian because he would be betraying the working-class. This irritated Koestler who kept saying that Communism was bound to betray its followers.

Camus was closer to Koestler than to Sartre but clashes of personalities overlapped with political opinions. A friend had

217

once told Koestler that he had an inferiority complex as big as a cathedral but in the '40's it turned into a superiority complex. Koestler spent hard-drinking evenings anathematizing communists and prophesying a war between Russia and the United States. Anti-communism had become his raison d'être; he wanted no rivals and saw appeasers under every stone.

During another autumn evening he, Camus and Sartre, having mixed vodka with champagne, turned to politics. Koestler issued diatribes against Stalin and then denounced Camus and Sartre as pro-Moscovites. This seems like a scene from *Darkness at Noon*. Camus was not usually attacked as pro-communist, Sartre was rarely accused of emulating Camus. But Koestler, intoxicated by the success of his novel and relishing his new-found role as prophet of the Cold War, wanted to be the sole bulwark against Stalin.

Camus could not understand why a writer he admired should be so disagreeable but he continued to support Koestler. A dispute was going on between Koestler and Maurice Merleau-Ponty. In *The Yogi and the Commissar* Koestler distinguished between action to change man's situation and action to change man himself. This had been the theme of Huxley's *Ends and Means* – so many of these debates merely repeat in a more acrimonious form themes from the 1930's – and it interested Camus because it was the same argument as he was having with Sartre. Koestler sides with the yogi and repeats Camus' view that there is a segment of human experience which lies beyond social and political reality and with which man can engage directly. This led Koestler to attack Communism for reducing everything to economics. In his reply Merleau-Ponty, who was then one of Sartre's closest collaborators, rebuked Koestler with encouraging passivity and supporting capitalism.

This infuriated Camus who saw in Merleau-Ponty's argument an example of the Communists' inquisitorial tactics: anyone who attacked the party was automatically a tool of capitalism. Camus arrived at a party where Sartre, De Beauvoir, Merleau-Ponty and others were listening to Boris Vian's jazz. He was not mellowed by the music and he launched into Merleau-Ponty. Sartre supported his henchman which annoyed Camus even more. Muttering about 'Left Bank revolutionaries', he stalked out of the room. Sartre went after him but Camus refused to be mollified. For the next several months he and Sartre were not on speaking-terms.

In early December Camus, as if looking for different allies, gave a lecture at the Dominican monastery in Paris. His friend Bruckberger accompanied him and the hall was full. Camus was 'clearly tired and ill but he spoke very movingly'.[27] He seemed to make no concessions. He attacked the church for not speaking out against Hitler; it might justify its inaction by reaffirming its belief in divine providence but an unbeliever could not agree. He himself could not believe in such a providence because the evil in the world contradicted it. Camus compared himself with the young Augustine. Evil tormented him and he could not understand why the Church seemed to explain it away.

A confused discussion followed and one priest appalled Camus by telling him that death was not the embodiment of evil; it was merely one more aspect of the human condition. Most of the Dominicans were more sympathetic because they detected in Camus that need to believe which was, in their eyes although not in his, the starting-point of faith. Camus left the hall feeling that an iron curtain separated him from these men who were so sure of their beliefs.

Camus was in a paradoxical position. Although he was so famous he was already becoming an isolated figure in the intellectual world. He half-liked Catholics but could not emulate them, the nascent Cold War had separated him from Sartre, while the right, whether Gaullist like Malraux or non-Gaullist, was alien to him.

In January '47 Camus went to the mountains of Briançon. His tuberculosis had flared up yet again, worsened by the damp chill of Paris. He hated being ill and his mood was gloomy; he whiled away the time reading Orwell's *Burmese Days* and wishing he was on the Mediterranean. 'The evening spreading slowly over these cold mountains is enough to chill your heart', he laments.[28]

Not long after he returned to Paris a deputation from *Combat* came to see him. Camus had scarcely set foot in the *Combat* office since his return from the United States but he knew of its troubles.[29] The previous November Jacqueline Bernard had asked for his help and he had given her a series of articles called

Ni victimes ni bourreaux. These reflect the change that had taken place in his thinking during the last two years. Having given up the hope of social transformation he went back to the problem of violence which had haunted him in the '30's. The purge, the atom bomb and the widening split between Russia and the United States revived his fear that mid-twentieth-century man was prone to murder. *Ni victimes* calls for a world government and a campaign against all wars. This makes scant political sense because world government is just as much a utopia as moral renovation. But the articles were widely-read because French intellectuals were looking for a third way between Russia and America.

Despite the boost it received from *Ni victimes*, *Combat* drifted deeper into political and financial trouble. At its peak it sold over two hundred thousand copies but it soon declined. By the end of 1946 Pia had had enough. He was tired of the ten hour days and the financial worries. He did not want the responsibility of a large paper with one hundred and fifty workers. He was not made to be a successful editor. Better, he felt, to find an owner and to work for him as news-editor. Better still, perhaps, to give up. Pia had never believed that the press could be reformed and *Combat*'s demise would prove this.

Pia was also growing tired of Camus. When Jacqueline Bernard brought him the *Ni victimes* articles she was surprised to discover that Pia was annoyed. Camus was always ready, Pia felt, to play the role of the saviour. He deigned to intervene from on high and rescue the paper. But he was not prepared to work full-time and in the long periods which elapsed between his occasional, grandiose gestures he was content to see Pia struggle. There was some truth in this: Camus did not want to be a journalist before all else and he was growing weary of politics. As one contributor put it, 'Camus was the star but Pia did the work.'

Both Pia and Camus could see, too, that *Combat* had not resolved its political dilemma. Its quarrel with the Communists had grown sharper and its friendship with the Socialists no warmer. If the Socialists had offered convincing policies *Combat*'s task might have been easier, but the non-Communist left was in disarray. This destroyed *Combat*'s balance and its anti-communism became its main trait. Ollivier declared in his editorials that 'the Communist Party was neither democratic nor left-wing' and that 'it was a Russian party'. Ollivier himself was moving towards Gaullism. Throughout 1946 he castigated the parties for their bickering as De Gaulle was doing. Meanwhile Raymond Aron began writing more frequently and expounding the themes for which he has since become famous: financial austerity required a firm government and capital investment a liberal economy. Anti-communism, Gaullism and liberal economics, *Combat* had certainly swung to the right even if Camus disliked this.

In February 1947 the financial situation grew desperate as sales dropped below one hundred thousand. There were three alternatives: Pia's suggestion that the paper commit suicide, help from the Gaullists and sale to an owner. One possible buyer visited the *Combat* office but he was appalled at the chaos and withdrew his offer. The Gaullist solution was anathema to Camus while Pia's solution would have put the *Combat* printers out of work.

The approach of the Cold War hastened *Combat*'s confused drift to the right. Aron and Ollivier, who were sharing the editorials, multiplied their attacks on the Communists: they were tools of Russia and they were blocking Marshall Aid. Aron doubted De Gaulle whereas Ollivier championed him. This had become the main debate of the paper which had long since ceased, in Simone de Beauvoir's eyes, to be left-wing. The tone had changed too: Astruc had gone and Camus' Suetonius articles were no more; *Combat* was no longer irreverent. The political disputes overlapped with personal dislikes: Aron considered Pia and Camus to be foolishly romantic, no one liked Ollivier, while Pia did not conceal his dislike for Camus, who would have liked to stand aside from the quarrels but could not.

To complicate matters further Pia had been converted to Gaullism. Perhaps he was influenced by his good friend Malraux. Certainly he disliked the Communists and was bored with the left-wing orthodoxy of the Liberation. Driven by his reckless nihilism Pia sought in Gaullism fresh adventures.

On February 14 the printers went on strike and the furious Pia walked out. He gave no hint of if and when he would return. Then he sent a brief telegram: 'Do not count on me.' When they read this the group were furious and a deputation was sent to Camus.

On March 17 Camus resumed his editorials and denied that

Combat was to be sold to a financier. He took up the theme of personal freedom and attacked censorship on the radio. He resumed his moralizing and called on the French to put aside their hatred of the Germans. But Camus was making only a token effort. He could not and did not seriously try to resolve *Combat*'s problems. On April 22 he wrote an editorial in which he re-asserted the paper's independent stance and refused to decide for or against De Gaulle. But it was too late. Ollivier wanted to reply, declaring that he had become a Gaullist, while Aron wrote a sharp piece attacking De Gaulle. More important, Camus' return brought no increase in sales.

In May a solution was found that allowed the group to break up without selling out to the Gaullists and without sacrificing the printers' jobs. Claude Bourdet would take over *Combat* and continue it as a left-wing paper. Altschuler and Gimond, both professional journalists and worried about their future, received a block of shares and stayed, as did Jacqueline Bernard. Camus, Pia, Ollivier and Bloch-Michel all left.

On June 3 the arrangements were completed and Camus wrote for the first number of *Combat* to be published under the new regime. He paid tribute to Bourdet but he was clearly saying farewell – 'our departure frees us from all further obligations'. This annoyed Bourdet who wanted to stress *Combat*'s continuity – 'neither the political stance nor the tone of the paper will be changed'. Bourdet felt that Camus was being arrogant and did not want him to succeed. If Camus could not run a left-wing paper, then no one should.★

Pia broke completely with Camus who was deeply hurt. In May '47 Camus had dinner with a young *Combat* contributor near the Montagne Sainte-Geneviève. Afterwards they paced the street while Camus repeated that he owed everything to Pia, that he could not understand why Pia, the anarchist, should become a Gaullist and that he especially could not understand why Pia had taken such a dislike to him.[30]

After 1947 the two men went separate ways. Camus continued to send Pia his books but he received no reply. Indeed Pia rarely missed a chance to ridicule Camus, mocking both *L'Homme Révolté* and the award of the Nobel Prize. In

★'Camus' *Combat* couldn't last,' says Astruc, 'it was too much fun. If it had lasted it would have turned into boredom and lies.' Bourdet's *Combat* was less 'fun' than Camus' but it offered a more coherent left-wing position.

1949 Pia was involved in yet another Rimbaud 'discovery'. This time Breton detected the fraud and it was exposed. Was Pia deceiving or deceived? A fresh mystery was added to the others. Pia's Gaullist period did not last long and, when De Gaulle came back to power in 1958, Pia, guided by his old loathing for governments, tried to persuade Malraux not to become a minister. During the Algerian War Pia supported the Algérie Française movement. Camus was amazed but Pia had not really changed: since international opinion had cast the pieds-noirs as the villains, he would defend them.

Today Pia talks about Camus objectively but without friendship. Other *Combat* journalists attribute his break with Camus to jealousy. Certainly it has been Pia's misfortune to be overshadowed first by Malraux and then by Camus. But his decision to break with Camus cannot be explained by jealousy; it was a part of his refusal of success and his determination to go his own way. The loss of this friendship was perhaps the most important of the many blows that struck the seemingly so triumphant post-war Camus. Pia's humour would have been an invaluable asset in the grim years of the Cold War. Camus had lost his father-figure.

Yet the demise of *Combat* coincided with the period of his greatest success as a novelist. When he left the paper he gave a couscous dinner to a group of friends and then took them back to the rue Séguier flat. On the dining-room table were the newly-printed copies of *La Peste*.

8

Of Plagues, Cold Wars, Tedium, Revolts and Quarrels

La Peste seems such a traditional novel. A plague strikes the North African town of Oran. First the rats come above ground to die and then the people fall ill and cannot be cured. The authorities are helpless and the population despairs. A group of men band together to combat the plague: Rieux, the doctor who can limit the plague's ravages but can no longer heal, the mysterious Tarrou, who has crusaded against the death-penalty, the journalist Rambert, who at first tries to escape but then realizes he must stay, Paneloux, the Jesuit for whom the plague is a trial of his faith, and Grand, the minor civil servant who spends his evenings writing the first sentence of a novel. The group sets up special hospitals and vaccinates people until the plague disappears as suddenly as it has come. Paneloux and Tarrou have died while Rieux is left to tell the story.

Camus stressed that *La Peste* was to be a more positive book than *L'Etranger*. Rieux and his friends demonstrate the moral values of courage and fraternity which do not defeat the plague but which bear witness against it. *La Peste* was read as a parable about the Occupation and Rieux' band was perceived as a group of resistants who are fighting against the overwhelming power of the Nazis. Yet one doubts whether these more positive values represent Camus' main achievement. The outstanding feature of *La Peste* is the way this seemingly simple tale is told and the way in which the narrative technique breaks with traditional novel-writing.

A quotation from Daniel Defoe stands at the head of the book but Defoe's narrators are omniscient; they tell their tales like men who are sure they dominate the world. *La Peste*, however, is recounted by a narrator who flaunts the limits of his understanding. Camus is continuing down the path he had traced in *L'Etranger*. Meursault had tried to understand his life and to communicate its meaning to us. He did not succeed but at least there was an 'I' in the novel. In *La Peste* the story-teller remains anonymous. Not until the end does he identify himself as Rieux; for most of the novel he is a disembodied voice. He too tries to interpret what is happening but the plague defies his attempt to understand and hence dominate it. The opening lines set the tone: 'The strange events which make up the subject of this chronicle, took place in 194–, in Oran. They were untoward and somewhat out of the ordinary, at least in most people's opinion. At first sight Oran is in point of fact an ordinary town, nothing more than a French prefecture on the Algerian coast.'[1]

The precision of time and place is banished by phrases like 'in most people's opinion'. These simple facts are not necessarily true; they depend for their veracity on other unnamed narrators. Nothing is real, Camus is telling us, unless it can be stated by a human intelligence; yet the narrator's intelligence enables him only to speculate without affirming. As if trained in cartesian logic he draws general conclusions from the specific traits of Oran. But his 'therefores' are soon entangled with 'buts', while his long paragraphs are composed of statements, developments and contradictions.

Whereas Meursault had relied on his own impressions, this narrator is a dutiful historian who parades his documents and witnesses. But this is a subterfuge because he does not trust them: 'he proposes to use them as he thinks fit and to cite them whenever he pleases. He also proposes ...' The only real witness is a narrator who does not finish his sentences and about whom the reader knows nothing.

The inadequacy of the narration cannot be stated until it has been resolved. Then Camus writes of the bond between Rieux and his mother: 'a love is never strong enough to find its own expression so he and his mother would always love each other in silence'. Writing should be a confession; instead it circles around its subject. Free indirect speech – the hallmark of *L'Etranger* – recurs in *La Peste* because it weakens the emotional veracity of the confession. In important moments such as Rambert's decision to stay in Oran, Camus allows his characters to speak directly. Rambert states that he will join with the others to fight against the plague; this is an affirmation of human courage. But such moments are rare because the narration must remain remote.

The theme of story-telling lies at the heart of *La Peste* which abounds in discussions of language and in narrators. First come the official story-tellers like the town government and the newspapers. The government hides reality behind bureaucratic jargon while newspapers console; they keep forecasting that the plague will soon end. Men in authority make bold, ridiculous pronouncements: 'There are no rats in the building,' says the janitor while the rats die all around him. By contrast the theatre offers what Camus might have called 'upside-down' insights. A play is put on and the actor who takes the part of Orpheus is stricken by plague as he descends into hell.

Each of the main characters – Rambert, Paneloux, Grand and Tarrou as well as Rieux – acts as a story-teller and each is a part of the greater anonymous narration. Rambert poses an intriguing problem. A professional journalist, he is the man who should write about the plague. Yet he does not because Camus feels that journalism is a particularly inadequate form of language.

Paneloux, who is an expert on Saint Augustine, delivers two sermons. The first affirms that the plague is a punishment sent by God and that the people of Oran must repent and do penance. This is a traditional piece of rhetoric and Camus uses another story-teller to mock it: Tarrou says that he is waiting for silence to replace bombast. The second sermon affirms that the plague is not sent by God; it is part of an evil which is present in the universe and which the Christian must confront. This sermon is filtered through the scepticism of Rieux who is sitting in the church. He notes that it is heretical but that its very doubts contain some truth. Paneloux' language is more restrained than in his first sermon, while Rieux' language is even more tentative. The second sermon contains some truth because it depicts evil as a painful riddle.

The difficulty which these story-tellers encounter when they start to tell their tales is personified in the figure of Grand. His one-line novel is both an expression of Camus' fear that he will be unable to write and an illustration of the uncertainty of language. Grand puzzles over such words as 'promise' and 'right'; they have a life of their own and they do not convey what he thinks they should. Grand is a frustrated cartesian who would like to make general statements, but when he makes them, they come out as platitudes. 'Never put off until tomorrow,' says Grand. Even then he has to qualify his remark by adding 'as people say where I come from'.

Grand has another aim which is to express fully what he feels. He has been married to a woman called Jeanne whom he still loves. So he wants to write her a love-letter that will make her realize what she means to him. Once more writing should be a confession but Grand cannot find the words to express his love so he sets about his novel instead. One might see in this a parable about absurd art. Language cannot seize human experience directly or totally; it must offer partial insights by 'saying less'. Grand's inability to go beyond the first sentence is a parody of the anonymous narrator's inability to explain the plague.

Tarrou's diary is the best example of 'saying less' and it contains some of the finest writing in *La Peste*. 'Tarrou's chronicle seems to stem,' says the anonymous narrator, 'from a quest for insignificance ... he sets out to be the historian of things which have no history.' Camus had thought of composing an anthology of insignificance but Tarrou's journal is a substitute for it. Convinced that the world does not make sense, Tarrou describes objects and conversations detached from their context and indicating only the absence of coherence. This seems like Meursault but it is not. Meursault hoped to understand Algiers, whereas Tarrou knows there is nothing to understand in Oran. He asks questions to which he does not expect answers and he spends a page describing the bronze lions on the main square. Irony and brevity are the keys to his art which must surely have appealed to Francis Ponge.

Yet there is a trap in Tarrou's lucidity. Since he knows everything he could become an omniscient narrator, which would contradict everything he knows. In order to preserve the incomplete nature of Tarrou's art Camus presents it via his anonymous narrator who does not understand Tarrou's aim and puzzles over his sentences. He wonders why Tarrou describes the bronze lions; they have no historical or allegorical quality and are just ridiculous objects. Such incomprehension prevents Tarrou's cult of insignificance from becoming an explanation of the world.

As *La Peste* goes on, a tension arises within the narration. In yet another discussion about language the medical authorities shrink from using the term 'plague'. 'It doesn't matter whether you call it plague or growth fever,' argues Rieux, 'what matters is that you prevent it from killing half of Oran.' Language cannot be used propositionally but it can be a weapon. It can combat the plague even if it cannot explain it. So the anonymous narrator turns out, unsurprisingly, to be the plague's chief enemy, Dr. Rieux. If stated at the outset this would have robbed the novel of its remote character; Rieux had to remain anonymous in order to depict the plague as an entity outside man's understanding. But he now states that he has 'deliberately sided with the victims' and that he is 'speaking for everyone.'

The gradual change in the point of view is accompanied by a change in the themes. Camus spells out the values which enable men to battle against their condition. The key theme is indifference which is Rieux' special trait. In order to make his rounds and to isolate the people who are infected he has to repress the pity and sympathy which he feels for them. The doctor-patient relationship turns into inadequacy and hatred; the patients hate Rieux because he cannot cure them. But he must ignore this hatred and get on with his work. He feels that he is growing less and less human and that he is as 'abstract' as the plague.

Camus is, characteristically, showing how a destructive force may be creative. The indifference which Rieux feels is a kind of courage which is shared by the men around him. The common bond of courage creates the second value of fraternity. Camus' moral thinking has never been more austere and heroic. Rieux, Tarrou and the others are an aristocracy who sacrifice their personal happiness in order to fight the plague.

The flaw in this moral thinking was pointed out by Sartre and by Roland Barthes.[2] Camus had asserted the need to act but he had not treated the more difficult problems of which action one chooses, how one is changed by it and what influence it will have. Although the plague was non-human, it was supposed to be an image of the Occupation. But the Occupation was far from non-human and it involved agonizing choices. Tarrou illustrates this weakness when he links his stand against the plague with his rejection of violence. Sharing Camus' views on the death-penalty and on left-wing tyranny, Tarrou affirms that he will not kill. So he can combat the plague but he could have combatted the Germans only if one assumes, as Camus did in '43, that the Resistance had its hands clean. Even if one sets aside the problem of the parallels with the Occupation the flaw in *La Peste* remains. Any political or social action would sully the purity in which Tarrou – like Camus – believes.

So the aristocrats of *La Peste* are frozen in their heroic posture. They defy the plague rather as Sisyphus defied his rock and their values are religious rather than practical. This is less a union of men who have very different characters and backgrounds than a communion of indifferent saints whose asceticism has dissolved all character. Tarrou, who broods ironically on sanctity, is writing yet another chapter in Camus' dialogue with his own religious temperament.

Yet these men are not saints, as Camus' Dominican friend, Bruckberger, pointed out.[3] Examining Paneloux' death Bruckberger writes that the Jesuit confronts an absent God in static silence; he does not rail against Him, love Him or live with Him. Grace, love and prayer are all absent from *La Peste*. Bruckberger's criticism complements Barthes': neither the religious notion of grace nor the human virtue of practicality is present in Camus' moral thinking.

The present-day reader may take yet a different view and he may feel that Rieux and Tarrou are exaggeratedly heroic. Indeed Camus' moral thinking is at its best when it depicts the inadequacy of heroism. The dying Tarrou is not content with courage so he turns to Rieux' mother in an appeal for love. Rieux himself is desperately lonely when he walks through liberated Oran at the end of the novel. He and Tarrou are the most masculine of men – tough, ascetic and proud. Yet *La Peste* echoes with the absence of what have traditionally been the values of women: tenderness and warmth. This is far more convincing than the philosophically dubious, uselessly saintly heroism.

The need to present these moral values brings about the gradual change in the narration. At the outset Rieux is a character like Tarrou or Grand and he knows no more than they. Then he begins to show a greater understanding of his friends and of himself. He traces the growth of his indifference and he watches Rambert's hesitations. Meanwhile the anonymous narrator strikes a lyrical note in this description of Oran:

'The streets were deserted and the wind sighed out its ceaseless, lonely lament. A smell of seaweed and salt mounted from the raging, invisible sea. The deserted city, white with dust, saturated with briny odours, re-echoes with the cries of the wind and moans like an island of misfortune.'

This is a visionary's insight and it reminds us of the moments of oneness in *L'Envers et l'Endroit*.

As the novel goes on the two tendencies – Rieux' awareness and the anonymous narrator's lyricism – increase until they fuse into the discovery that Rieux is the narrator. This makes the novel more conventional because Rieux almost becomes a traditional, omniscient story-teller. Camus tries to prevent this by reverting to the earlier, fragmentary manner but even Tarrou's diary has changed. From being whimsical and insignificant it has become a treatise about insignificance. Camus is grappling with a real problem: there is a thin line between depicting men who show courage in the face of the unknowable and affirming that the world is unknowable so men must show courage. Once one tilts towards the second position then omniscient narrators and traditional novels re-enter by the back door. Camus' language grows more rhetorical and his antitheses – 'man's poor and awesome love' – grow heavier.

Yet the incomplete quality of the narration persists to the end. The last entries in Tarrou's journal are puzzling reflections on Rieux' mother and they open a new and mysterious theme of Tarrou's mother. The closing pages of the novel are written in the same remote style as the opening pages. There are celebrations, reunions and dancing; they take place according to some new order which is as undefinable as the old.

Despite the presence within the narration of a moralist, *La Peste* does not really make the world more human or more penetrable than *L'Etranger* did. Anonymity and amputation remain the watchwords of Camus' art. He tried to offer a viewpoint which would be positive because collective but the pages where it dominates are conventional, whereas the remote narrator who puzzles over Grand and Tarrou is a superb and thoroughly modern achievement. However, most of Camus' contemporaries did not interpret *La Peste* in this way. Camus, the tragic writer who depicted an alien universe, gave way to Camus, the apostle of brotherhood. This view of his writing, which he himself fostered, helped to shape his life over the next years.

La Peste sold one hundred thousand copies immediately and was translated into many languages. Gallimard is jealous with its financial secrets but *La Peste* was one of the best-sellers of the post-war period and it turned Camus into an affluent if not wealthy man. He was delighted and slightly embarrassed by his success: 'my book is selling like a sob-story for young girls', he said. He was deluged with fan-letters and requests for interviews. A friend who visited him at Gallimard found him replying to a young man who had written to say he was about to commit suicide; it was Camus' tenth suicide of the week. Newspapers carried photos of him, trenchcoated and in his Bogart pose. He could no longer go to a café without being recognized. He began to talk about 'the sadness of success'[4] and to feel that he was trapped in the role of 'a great writer' who was also 'a moral conscience'.

The underside of Camus' life belied his success. It would be easy to argue that his post-war career was a series of failures: the collapse of *Combat*, the break with Pia, the quarrel with Sartre, the Algerian War and a growing writer's impotence. More important, Camus felt his life as a failure or as an amputation. His diaries show that he was haunted by death. Now he wants to die lucidly and to live out his last moments; now he wants to die suddenly without realizing what is happening. A friend commits suicide which reminds Camus that he has often contemplated suicide. Indifference is a kind of death from which he escapes into love but the loss of self in love is just another kind of death. This stream of remarks forms an inner monologue that Camus conducted with himself.

Until 1940 Camus' existence may be seen as a struggle against well-defined adversaries like poverty. This gave it a shape of which he was aware. Then too Algeria was a healthy presence. Swimming with Jaussaud or chatting in Charlot's bookshop, Camus felt a carefree happiness. Now his existence was a struggle against more devious adversaries like the Cold War.

To defeat them he had to write his next book, *L'Homme Révolté*. He began before finishing *La Peste* to gather documentation and he read innumerable tomes of philosophy. *L'Homme Révolté* was to be a study of Hegel, Marx, Nietzsche, the surrealists and many other prophets of revolt. A philosophical essay, it was to expound the moral and political values that lay beyond nihilism. Its secondary purpose was to criticize the false concept of revolution that was then being expounded by the Communists and by *Les Temps Modernes*. Camus would show that violence could not be justified in the name of a future utopia. All the political battles which he carried out over the years between 1947 and 1951 were mere skirmishes that prepared for *L'Homme Révolté*.

These were years when Camus' life was dominated by politics. He hated this, talked of burying himself in the countryside and lamented that the healthy, instinctive side of his character was being destroyed. Moreover nothing was more drearily repetitious than the Cold War. Again and again Camus talked about the need to find a third way between Russia and the United States; again and again his antagonists branded him as a conservative. Although such arguments irritated him, his very vulnerability made him continue. He must, he felt, speak for his family and show how men could be liberated. He must offer his readers reasons to live in order to discover them for himself.

His life settled into an outward shape. Each day he worked at home on his book, went to Gallimard, lunched with friends. The year was divided up by travel. He explored Provence; he was invited on official trips which he loathed but occasionally accepted; his tuberculosis obliged him to retreat to the mountains, to Le Panelier or to the Alps. In the winter he made his sacrosanct visit to Algeria and his mother, while in the summer he packed Francine and the twins off to Provence where he later joined them. It was a restless life but its diversity barely masked the obsession with death and with his new book.

In the summer of 1947 he took Francine and the children to Le Panelier. For once the Massif Central delighted him: 'Wonderful day. Sparkling, gentle light around and above the big beech trees. It seems as if the branches themselves have secreted it. Clusters of leaves tremble in the golden blue.'[5] Camus worked as well as rested. He read books about the Russian anarchists whom he compared and contrasted with the Communists. This material would be used both in *L'Homme Révolté* and in the play *Les Justes*. However Camus turned away from *Les Justes* because Jean-Louis Barrault, who admired *La Peste*, asked him to write a play about the plague. This would be *L'Etat de Siège*.

In August Camus made a long-planned trip to Brittany. Jean Grenier had introduced him to Louis Guilloux who came from Saint-Brieuc and whose novels about working-class life Camus admired. Guilloux took Grenier and Camus along the Brittany coast and around Saint-Brieuc where Camus visited his father's grave. The others left him alone in the cemetery and he said not a single word when they rejoined him. Brittany disappointed Camus who complained that it rained too much and that the Celts wallowed in their misery. Their graveyards were ostentatiously perched on top of hills as if glorifying death. Camus told Guilloux that he would take him to see the bare Arab graveyards in Algeria.[6]

When Guilloux came from Saint-Brieuc to Paris he used to visit Camus at Gallimard and he was taken out to see the terrace. By now Camus had a very intelligent secretary, Suzanne Agnely, a tuberculosis patient whom he had befriended. One of her tasks was to head off the innumerable people who came to ask Camus for money, for his signature on a petition or for help with an unpublishable manuscript. She had lists of people who could see him whenever they wished and lists of people who had to make an appointment. Answers to letters fell into several categories: tuberculosis patients received one letter, potential suicides another, unpopular political causes a third. Young women on one list were ushered straight in, those on another list were told Camus was away. Many moved quickly from the first list to the second.

Not everyone at Gallimard admired Camus. He never got on well with Jean Paulhan who disconcerted him as he did so many younger men. Paulhan loved to tease and his humour was more subtle than Camus'. He also distrusted Camus and, as with Mauriac, jealousy does not explain why. Paulhan was most interested in language and in contemporary poetry. He had encouraged Ponge and had opened the *NRF* to the surrealists. Camus knew little about modern poetry and one day he horrified Paulhan by telling him that he preferred long, traditional poems that said something. This confirmed Paulhan's suspicion that Camus was too crude, too political and too old-fashioned a writer.[7] Like Mauriac, Paulhan disliked what he perceived as the Liberation establishment and he preferred technical innovation to committed writing.

But Camus had his circle of friends at Gallimard: Jean Grenier, his ex-*Combat* colleague Jacques Lemarchand, Michel Gallimard and others. With them he was relaxed and did not protect himself behind his mask of coldness. When besieged in Gallimard Camus became a moralist who pronounced in rhetorical monologues. But, when Michel Gallimard came in, the two would joke and go off to long lunches, dragging with them the gourmet Bruckberger who also had an office at Gallimard. Camus hated his role as an influential editor. Power held no charms for him for he took himself tragically but not seriously. He made decisions about books quickly and he hated to reject a manuscript. He was happiest sitting on his terrace with Michel Gallimard, telling obscene jokes and laughing about his reputation as a moralist. 'I'm not really an old bore,' he used to say.

Camus fostered the kind of writing he liked in his *Espoir* collection. He did routine publishing and even handled contracts and money but he devoted much time to spying out books for *Espoir*. It is a characteristic title, although the collection grew in a random way. Friendly with Sartre, Camus published Sartre's protégés – Bost, or Violette Leduc. Leduc's book was called *L'Asphyxie* which provoked jokes in Gallimard about the collection's title. Camus published works by other friends like Jean Daniel and works that interested him personally like the unorthodox catholic writing of Simone Weil.

The book which best renders the spirit of the collection was Emile Simon's *Une Métaphysique Tragique* (1951). It depicts philosophy as a personal quest and argues that men should be less concerned with understanding life than with living it. Reason is inadequate so man is stranded in the absurd. His task is to revolt against it while rejecting such utopias as marxism or catholicism. *Une Métaphysique Tragique* is bowdlerized Camus and the *Espoir* series was a collective version of *L'Homme Révolté*. It was not commercially successful so Gallimard abandoned it in 1955.

In September '47 Camus drew closer to another Gallimard writer, René Char. Char invited him to his home at l'Isle-sur-Sorgue, a village in the Provence hills south and east of Avignon. Camus slept in a 'large bedroom that opens onto the autumn ... the wind blows the dead leaves from the plane trees in beneath the curtains which are decorated with embroidered ferns'.[8] He and Char went tramping over the bare Provence mountains where the rocks reminded Camus how much he loved bare contours and where the smell of rosemary carried him back to Algeria. The shrubs were emaciated, hawks hovered overhead and the streams ran clean and swift. This was the tough Mediterranean countryside which Camus liked. A photo shows him standing next to the huge Char; both men look bronzed and tired after their hike.

It is no coincidence that Camus became friendly with Char shortly after his break with Pia: Char became something of a father-figure to him. Camus began to send him his manuscripts and to seek his advice in his polemics. An old surrealist, Char had broken with Aragon and despised the Communists. He had also broken with Breton who had fled to the United States during the war. Char had remained in France and become a Resistance leader. His combination of political scepticism and personal courage appealed to Camus who loved to tell an anecdote about Char's resistance years: when De Gaulle summoned Char to Algiers his band of maquisards lit fires all across the Vaucluse mountains to speed him on.

Camus recognized in Char another primitive. Char's poetry, writes Camus, is about 'the mysteries of nature, running water and light'.[9] Camus used to quote a line where Char describes the springy grass of Provence as 'kind to madmen and unkind to executioners'.[10] During this September stay Char encouraged Camus to explore Provence and to think about buying or renting an old house.

The autumn brought politics and polemics that made Camus long for Provence. His quarrel with Sartre had been patched up and the two were once more on speaking terms. But the intellectual dispute remained. Sartre disliked *La Peste* because the personification of evil as a plague allowed Camus to omit the problem of situation. This made good and evil very simple matters, which permitted Camus to moralize and explained *La Peste*'s suspiciously large audience. For his part Camus had not forgiven Merleau-Ponty. In his diary he notes that, while Merleau-Ponty dismissed the quest for moral values by insisting that they could not be separated from their political context, he also managed to prove that Stalin was always right.

This is an unfair comment but it indicates the gulf which now separated Camus from *Les Temps Modernes*.

Yet he and Sartre went back to their hard-drinking evenings, one of which brought a second quarrel with Koestler. At a Russian nightclub and after much vodka, Koestler began declaring that friendship was impossible without political agreement. He then proved his point by throwing a glass at Sartre's head. The nightclub owner accompanied his famous guests to the door where Koestler threatened Sartre again. Camus, scarcely less drunk than the others, intervened, whereupon Koestler punched him in the face. The furious Camus set on him and had to be dragged off by Sartre. The group broke up and Camus insisted on driving Sartre home, which terrified Simone de Beauvoir. Camus was weeping alcoholic tears of rage and he never forgave Koestler. Even with political agreement friendship with Koestler was impossible. After this evening Camus tried to cut down his drinking; he continued to enjoy wine but he drank less hard liquor.

In November he stumbled into a polemic that dragged on for a year. When he re-published his *Ni Victimes ni Bourreaux* articles in Jean Daniel's magazine *Caliban* he was attacked by D'Astier de la Vigerie. Ex-Resistance leader D'Astier, who was now a fellow-traveller, discovered in *Ni victimes* the flaw which Sartre had detected in *La Peste*. 'You shun politics and take refuge in morality,' said D'Astier. He made the usual gibe about lay saints and called Camus 'an unconscious accomplice of capitalism'. The weary Camus hit back in the next number of *Caliban* and he too repeated himself. *Ni victimes* was designed to combat war which was the supreme evil; D'Astier was risking war by his extremist doctrines – a code word for communism.[11]

D'Astier resorted to the pages of the Communist paper, *Action*, which had already been thundering against Camus. As if determined to prove that the violent, pamphleteer-style writing associated with the far-right could come from the left as well, *Action* regularly denounced Camus as a 'jackal' of the ruling-classes. Competing in banality, D'Astier now vilified him as a Pontius Pilate.

If D'Astier was more virulent Camus was the more skilful polemicist. His best weapon was the lofty stance which he adopted in his second reply. D'Astier has missed the point but Camus will not insult him by dwelling on his stupidity; instead he will point out the real issues. Such condescension infuriated D'Astier and won sympathy for the injured Camus; honour was to Camus a strategy as well as a virtue. Camus also showed his dislike of middle-class, left-wing intellectuals: 'I abhor men who talk more than they act.' This was another good polemical weapon: draping himself in the garb of a Belcourt proletarian Camus issued rebukes to the pampered revolutionary, D'Astier. In his private conversations Camus went much further, denouncing D'Astier as a 'red marquis' and complaining about 'the female left'.

After publishing *Ni victimes* in November Camus escaped to Algeria. For the first time he went by plane which terrified him. The Mediterranean, however, worked its usual miracle: 'glorious morning on the Algiers port. The sea-blue landscape comes flooding through the windows and spreads into every corner of the bedroom.'[12] Yet Camus noticed that his dealings with his friends like Poncet and De Maisonseul had changed. 'You can never go back', he concludes. De Maisonseul felt that there was something false about Camus' nostalgia for Algeria. When Camus kept saying that he would like to come back there to live, De Maisonseul cut him off. Camus' place was in Paris – in his Gallimard office and his Left Bank flat; talk of returning to Algeria was nonsense.

The first months of 1948 brought a trip to Switzerland, a second visit to Algeria and a brief stay in England. The Switzerland trip was unhappy because Camus was visiting Michel Gallimard who was convalescing from tuberculosis. Camus relived both the disgust which the illness provoked in him and the weary fatigue of fighting each day against it. He tried to cheer Michel up but grew depressed himself. Algeria was a welcome diversion especially since Camus was accompanied by Louis Guilloux whom he was repaying for the Brittany trip. Camus took Guilloux to Tipasa and tried, unsuccessfully, to convince him that the Mediterranean peoples lived closer to nature than the Celts. Guilloux' outstanding memory of the trip is his meeting with Camus' mother. 'She had the nobility of a queen,' he recalls. She and Camus scarcely spoke to each other but their silence contained an understanding which Guilloux could feel in the room.

Camus came to England in May, invited by the French cultural services and accompanied by Francine. Like the

United States, England evoked no real enthusiasm in him. He enjoyed the green of London as so many other French travellers had done before him. 'A city of gardens where the birds wake me up in the mornings,' he calls it.[13] He was dutifully impressed by the quiet of Oxford and he liked Edinburgh because the port was full of Chinese and Malayans.

Back in France he had a momentous encounter on June 6. Precisely four years after they had returned to Gide's flat on the drunken bicycle, Camus and Maria Casarès met on the Boulevard Saint-Germain. Casarès describes it:

'A wavering, a momentary hesitation left us standing silently in the street which seemed suddenly empty and quiet.
"Where are you going?" he asked in slightly hoarse voice.
"To the theatre," I stammered. "And you?"
"To Gide's".
And since then we have never been separated.'[14]

Casarès had lived through four hectic years. She had left the Mathurins theatre although she was still friendly with Marcel Herrand. Her mother had died and her father had returned from England with tuberculosis. The rue de Vaugirard flat was still a centre for refugees who were realizing that they might never be able to return to Spain. Casarès had been on the verge of marrying an actor, Jean Servais, who had attacked her and threatened to kill himself. In '47 she went to Rome where *La Chartreuse de Parme* was filmed and where she had the affair with Gérard Philipe, who was playing Fabrice del Dongo. *La Peste* was published during the filming and Philipe presented her with a copy.

In June '48 Camus did not suggest that they flee to Mexico. He insisted that 'between the all and the nothing there was . . . the 75% possible'.[15] This was not a compromise but a gamble; they would struggle amidst her acting and his writing to love each other. Their love was an important part of that truth or form that they were seeking but it could not be all. At the Liberation Maria had been unwilling to accept such a rule but she did so now. She had been living what she felt to be 'an empty dispersed life' and she hoped that Camus would pull it together 'like a hard, compact stone'.*[16] She could see, as Simone Hié

---

*In reading Maria Casarès' memoirs written twenty years after Camus' death one is struck by the Camusian language she uses.

had seen, the strength that lay behind Camus' nonchalant charm. But Maria had a strength of her own which explains why Camus was as much in love with her as he had been at the Liberation.

From this meeting onward Maria was the dominant female presence in Camus' life. They met at the rue de Vaugirard where the presence of her father imposed a formality which Camus was careful to respect. Sometimes they went out to Spanish restaurants where there were little dance-floors and where they were sure they would not meet other writers or actors. They had a favourite Martinique restaurant called 'La Canne à Sucre'. Most of all the theatre drew them together and Maria starred in *L'Etat de Siège* and in *Les Justes*; they agreed that their theatre work should be both thoroughly professional and a part of their love.

Yet this was no easy affair. Casarès found the 75% rule hard to keep and she raged at Camus as she had done before. Camus' anger was cold; he once stood at his office door and trembled with silent fury as Maria walked out. This was the love that burned, the love of two exiles. Maria struggled to accept the demands that Camus' work and his marriage made on his time. Camus had the better part for along with his passion for Maria he had a wife and a string of casual seductions.

So he went off that summer to Provence where he had rented a house near that of René Char. Francine complained about the house because it had little shade and was isolated; she was abandoned there with the children who kept crawling out towards a nearby canal and had to be hauled back before they drowned.[17] Camus, who loved to take the twins in his arms and play with them, was little help in looking after them. He spent much time upstairs writing *L'Etat de Siège* and brooding on the contradictions of his life. His diary shows the undercurrent of guilt which never left him:

'You have to encounter love before you encounter morality. Otherwise you are torn apart.'
'To love somebody is to kill everybody else.'
'Because I know my own weakness I have tried my best to be a moral man. Morality destroys.'[18]

Otherwise this was a happy period because Camus felt his way into the Provence countryside. It offered him the moments of oneness which he had known in his youth and which he could never recapture in Paris. Char strengthened him in his belief that the world was beautiful and that nature nourished man, whereas politics and philosophy destroyed him. Camus' diary contains flights of lyricism: 'Night on the tops of the Vaucluse mountains. The milky way flows down into the nests of light in the valley. Everything is blended. There are villages in the sky and constellations of stars in the mountains.'[19]

September brought Paris and politics. Stung by D'Astier's taunts, Camus felt that he had to give concrete form to his plea for world peace. This led him to participate in one of the most curious capers of the Cold War – the Gary Davis affair.

Davis was an American who gave up his passport, declared himself a world-citizen and appealed to the United Nations. This was a lure and trap for Camus: Davis was placing himself outside both blocs and he was appealing for world government as Camus had done; yet Davis himself was as flimsy as the campaign which sprang up around him. Sartre laughed at him but Camus was obliged to take him seriously. So when Davis began his sit-in at the Palais de Chaillot, which was the temporary headquarters of the UN, Camus lent his name to the cause.

In November he gave a talk in a café near the Palais de Chaillot and explained how the courageous Davis was resisting the drift towards a third world war. This was vintage Camus: the belief in individual effort and the praise for a man who was working outside established political parties. Privately Camus was sceptical of Davis and he told a friend that Davis combined Sancho Panza's thickheadedness with his master's illusions.[20] By December Camus could see that the Davis affair was a Parisian storm-in-a-teacup and that he himself was behaving like the left-wing intellectuals he so despised. He quickly abandoned the world-citizen.

On December 13 Camus offered a helping hand to Sartre by speaking at a peace rally organized by the Rassemblement Démocratique Révolutionnaire. Sartre had helped found the RDR because he, too, wanted to give concrete shape to his political vision. Put crudely, Sartre was neutralist and pro-USSR while Camus was neutralist and pro-Western but such a simplification does justice to neither man's position. Camus wanted to turn Western platitudes about freedom into a philosophy of revolt, while Sartre wanted to inject life into the moribund marxism of the Soviet Union.

He and Camus were maintaining a rather formal friendship and they skirted dangerous topics. Privately Camus felt that Sartre was cheating when he affirmed that the Russian revolution was a genuine if flawed revolution and that it should not be judged by standards which were drawn from the capitalist culture of the West. Honesty and lucidity were, Camus felt, excellent yardsticks by which to measure the USSR. Camus thought that Sartre was naive about communists because he had no political experience and had not even voted during the '30's, whereas Camus and his friends – Char and Guilloux – had long been active in left-wing movements.

During this same autumn of '48 Camus found a better outlet for his political energies when he helped form the Groupe de Liaison Internationale. The syndicalist paper, *Révolution Prolétarienne*, launched an appeal on behalf of victims of political discrimination. The socialist trade union, Force Ouvrière, responded, as did individual intellectuals. Camus threw himself into the GLI partly because of his old sympathy for unionists and partly because it intended to act rather than talk. *Combat* friends like Bloch-Michel volunteered, while Robert Jaussaud represented the Algerian Mafia.

The GLI was supposed to be 'a kind of pre-Amnesty International'.[21] During meetings at the office of FO unionist Roger Lapeyre it organized visas, flats and jobs for refugees. Jaussaud, a civil servant, could obtain passports; Camus was always willing to take as his personal secretary people who knew no French. He was also generous with his time and money and he allowed the GLI to use his name in its petitions. The scattered community of refugees was a new version of the Equipe; they were exiles like Maria Casarès and himself.

The GLI's second task, which eventually undid it, was to disseminate information about political oppression. Its bulletins contain a piece by Orwell, a study of displaced persons and exposés of the Russian camps. The first number of the bulletin, published in March 1949, outlines its position: 'Man's reasons to live are especially threatened by Stalinist ideology . . . they are also threatened, albeit less, by the American worship of technology.'[22] This slant was in harmony both with Camus' previous statements and with the group's majority. Syndicalists and socialists could mask the gulf which separated them by denouncing communists. Force Ouvrière had just split off from the Communist trade union, the CGT, while *Révolution Prolétarienne*, which jealously guarded the heritage of revolutionary syndicalism, loathed the Soviet Union.

Soon quarrels broke out. Lapeyre argued with the syndicalists and both quarrelled with a Russian anarchist called Lazarevitch. He wanted the GLI to re-examine the last forty years and to define its political creed; he called for auto-critiques and rehabilitations. This annoyed Camus who began to look bored during the meetings and tried to guide the discussion back to jobs and visas.

In October '48 Camus had an aesthetic disappointment that hurt him more than the political bickering. *L'Etat de Siège* was the fruit of his collaboration with Jean-Louis Barrault who had asked him to write the play. Moreover Barrault was looking for his playwright. He had worked with Claudel but Claudel was old and he had narrowly missed Sartre. Now Camus answered a need.[23] The rehearsals took place in an euphoric atmosphere enlivened by Camus who was delighted to be working with Maria Casarès. She was to play Victoria and Barrault was her admirer Diego, while Pierre Brasseur, another veteran of *Les Enfants du Paradis*, and Madeleine Renaud helped complete a very good cast. Camus and Barrault worked well together and Camus helped with the details of the production.

Yet when the play opened on October 27 it was a disastrous flop. 'What a disappointment,' said a not unfriendly critic, 'what a catastrophe.'[24] Barrault said that the plague was half-metaphysical and half-political which confused the spectator. Others blamed Barrault himself and admirers of Maria Casarès felt that he had played the love-scenes badly and destroyed her performance. She was bitterly disappointed while Camus, who was too massively self-critical to see the flaws in his work, was depressed for months. He hid in his Gallimard office and refused to discuss the play. But dogged as ever, he spent the winter working on his next play, *Les Justes*, and on *L'Homme Révolté* which was growing ever longer and was draining his energy.

In June 1949 Camus set off on a cultural mission to Latin America. He was not looking forward to it, for journeys always provoked in him the dread of separation and the lurking fear that he would die all alone and far from anyone who cared about him. He accompanied Francine and the twins to their rented house in l'Isle-sur-Sorgue and he was unusually effusive when he kissed Jean and Catherine goodbye. Robert Jaussaud, who drove him to the boat, noted that Camus grew more agitated with every mile. When they arrived he rushed through his goodbyes, ran up the gangway and shut himself in his cabin.

The sea-voyage bored him and his thoughts turned once more to suicide – he could well understand why men did away with themselves. He disliked the first-class passengers and went to the third-class bar where emigrants sang and played the accordeon. There were no pretty girls on board. Camus spent hours gazing at the sea which tormented him. It contained that mystery which underlay all existence and which he wanted to express in his writing. But would he ever be able to say what he must say? The fear of writer's impotence came over him and he remembered that *L'Homme Révolté* was far from finished.[25]

At Rio his gloom persisted. Since this was an official mission he was surrounded by diplomats, pretentious poets and upper-class women. When he did manage to isolate one likely young lady, she began reciting her poetry at him. One of the many lunches so infuriated him that he almost got up and left. Instead he tried to steer the conversation to soccer or boxing and he asked to be taken to a dance-hall where poor blacks went.

His ironic humour is shown in the anecdote he notes in his diary. A man was killed in a street accident at Rio so passers-by threw a cloth over the corpse and guided the cars around it. A Brazilian model prison had one drawback: the prisoners kept committing suicide. There was a profession in Rio called the death-helpers; they aided people to die by kneeling on their chests and stuffing hands in their mouths.

Gradually Brazil became a country in Camus' imaginary world. It is 'a land without men' and a 'land of indifference'. He journeyed into the interior which appalled him because it was so much wilder than Algeria. The pilgrimage of Jesus de Iguape, with its blend of catholic and pagan rituals, seemed to him to demonstrate how much the Brazilians needed a God in the huge emptiness of their jungles.

From Brazil Camus went to Argentina where he stayed with Drieu la Rochelle's friend Vittoria Occampo. From there he flew on to Chile but he could not escape from politics. A rise in

243

the Santiago busfares had provoked riots and the army had taken over the town. Camus was supposed to lecture at the university but another hall had to be found. Finally he was allowed to return to Argentina and then to Rio.

By now he was exhausted, lonely and full of self-pity. He was taken to visit a lunatic asylum where the doctor seemed to him as mad as the patients. To his horror Camus discovered that the doctor would be flying to Paris on the same flight as he. He was still afraid of flying and mad doctors made it worse. He could feel his tuberculosis taking possession of him and he grew irritable and restless.

In late August he returned to France, collected Francine and headed for Le Panelier, hoping that the mountain air would revitalize him. In the autumn came the rehearsals for *Les Justes* and more illness. In his diary he strikes an exceptionally gloomy note: 'After believing for so long that I was getting better I should be crushed by the return of this illness. And I am crushed. But coming as it does after an interminable series of misfortunes it almost makes me laugh ... Madness can be a liberation.'[26] The draughts of the rue Séguier flat and the noise of the children made him feel worse than ever so he fled to Michel Gallimard's flat. Michel, who had married one of Camus' old girlfriends, was a fellow-patient and his flat was quieter.

On December 4 a pale-faced, weary Camus was present at the first night of *Les Justes* which was a triumph. Camus had lived for years with the 1905 Russian anarchists and now he made them live for the audience. But the play's success owed most to Maria Casarès' performance as Dora. 'Thinner than ever in her tight, severe black dress, she was ready to kill or die without a trace of weakness and yet she was burning with compassion.'[27] As in *Le Malentendu* Casarès proved the ideal actress for Camus. Her special ability to convey tense emotion suited a playwright who had come to rely on simple dramatic techniques and on general rather than individual psychology. Simone de Beauvoir thought *Les Justes* was 'academic' but transformed by the production. A kinder critic agreed: the characters were wooden but lyricism came flooding across the stage.[28] Retrospectively *Les Justes* seems no better a play than *Le Malentendu* and *L'Etat de Siège* but it was Camus' first and only success on the Paris stage.

Camus could not shake off his illness in Paris and his doctors told him that he must go to the South. L'Isle-sur-Sorgue was too cold in the winter so he decided on Cabris, a village in the mountains near the perfume-capital of Grasse. Cabris had been a favourite haunt of Gide whose daughter, Catherine, owned a house there and was willing to lend it to Camus. He set off wearily, dragging with him the unfinished manuscript of *L'Homme Révolté*.

Provence welcomed him: 'the mistral has given the sky a clean, new skin, as brilliantly blue as the sea. The songs of the birds explode with jubilant power.'[29] The sounds and scents of the Mediterranean returned with the spring and Camus was kept awake by concerts of toads – now harmonious, now raucous. Yet his illness responded slowly to treatment and the antibiotics he was taking made him lethargic. Some days his tuberculosis took possession of him and turned him into a plaything; other days he was liberated by one of the fits of madness he had mentioned. He felt that he was getting old and he worried that he was losing his memory. If he could not remember, he would be unable to write. He planned to note down everything in his diary and he questioned the doctors about the drugs they were giving him. One of them, streptomycin, is now known to have unpleasant side-effects; it can cause disturbance of sight and hearing.

Camus was reading Graham Greene's *The Heart of the Matter* which the French catholic magazines had compared with *La Peste*. Scobie's dilemma is not unlike Tarrou's: neither can bear the burden of the evil he is causing. Camus notes in his diary some of Greene's gloomier reflections – that life is too long and that love is doomed to failure. He may also have seen in Scobie, the man caught between two women, something of himself.

On February 17, 1950 he received a phone call from Maria Casarès: her father had died. Camus, who had liked the gracious Casarès, was sad and he felt guilty that he could not be with Maria at this moment. But convention and his illness forbade it. She dropped out of *Les Justes* for three days and then returned.

In August Camus and Maria escaped to a farm in the Vosges mountains while Francine and the children were in Provence.[30] Camus' tuberculosis was dragging on, while the outbreak of the Korean War strengthened his fear that the world was heading for destruction. He notes that the Vosges churches were the colour of dried blood; centuries of warfare were enshrined in the red stone. Yet Maria cheered him up and took him for long walks in the pine forests. It rained so they resumed their old arguments about the Algerian sun and the Galician mist. As they returned from their walks they would see the farmer and his wife coming home from the fields and leading their oxen. Camus found nicknames for the farmer – he loved to rename people – and in the evenings he and Maria went dancing in the nearby village of Petit Valter. These were 'genuine mountain festivals' and there was no one to recognize the Parisian celebrities.

When he returned to Paris Camus had the thankless task of dissolving the GLI. It was short of money and bedevilled by ideological disputes. Lazarevitch had depressed many into retirement and, although Camus hoped briefly to restart the organization with new members and new money, he decided that it was better to give up. At the last meeting, which was held in October, he stated that the GLI had helped a certain number of refugees and could do no more. He looked more weary than ever and he was secretly hoping that he would finish *L'Homme Révolté* and that he could then withdraw from politics.

Although he never knew it, Camus and the GLI had just had a narrow escape. In June the GLI had been invited to send a delegate to a seemingly innocuous Berlin congress for cultural freedom. In reality this was the conference of the three Ks – Korea, Koestler, Kultur – and it was a landmark in the Cold War. It was financed with American money which turned out, retrospectively, to be CIA money. The GLI did send a delegate to the congress but Camus himself did not go. He never, knowingly, had any dealings with the CIA although he occasionally wrote in *Preuves* which was, like *Encounter*, financed by the congress for cultural freedom.[31]

As if to continue their 'pas de deux' Sartre had abandoned the Rassemblement Démocratique Révolutionnaire before Camus dissolved the GLI. The RDR contained its own anti-communists and they were looking to the United States for financial help. This appalled Sartre who wanted the RDR to be the ally of the Communists, sharing their revolutionary mission but correcting their authoritarianism. The fledgling party broke up in a welter of confusion and the PCF, which was pursuing its strategy of attacking rivals, did nothing to help the pro-communist group. Like Camus Sartre was constantly attacked by the PC. When he put on *Les Mains Sales*, where the character of Hoederer seemed to Camus a ridiculously idealized portrayal of the communist militant, the PC chose to vilify him. But Camus and Sartre drew different conclusions from these battles. Sartre drew closer to the Communists because the failure of the RDR had convinced him that they alone could prevent the reconstruction of Europe along capitalist lines. Camus grew ever more critical of the Communists and of Sartre and was preparing to refute them in *L'Homme Révolté*.

During the autumn of 1950 Camus took time off from his work and looked for a new flat.[32] Francine was heartily sick of the rue Séguier and Camus managed to find a larger flat in the rue Madame where the *NRF* had been housed before 1914. It was convenient because he could walk to his Gallimard office and it was in the heart of the Left Bank neighbourhood which he both liked and loathed. The rue Madame was solidly middle-class but Camus did not care. He was satisfied that Francine liked it and that the twins, who had just passed their fifth birthday, had more space.

Francine was delighted with the flat but less delighted with her husband. His affair with Maria Casarès was public knowledge and he had less and less taste for domesticity. Friends who visited Paris were given the phone numbers of various young women in whose flats Camus could be reached. Often he fled to a little hotel near the Palais Royal where he could work and seduce in peace. Francine had to phone Gallimard to find out where he was and the more often she phoned the more Camus tried to escape her.

After moving to the rue Madame Camus had once more to leave the damp cold of Paris and return to Cabris to convalesce. Even the South failed to cheer him this winter. He had come to hate Grasse with its flashy opulence and its perfume-buying tourists. He was tired, *L'Homme Révolté* was still unfinished and his private life seemed to be approaching a crisis. Both Francine and Maria Casarès were demanding in their different ways. 'What madness draws men to enter the terrible house of passion,' he had noted, rather melodramatically, after a scene with Maria.[33] In the solitude of Cabris he felt guilty about her. She was an eternal migrant and he was not helping her find a home. He talked to her about the need for courage and work but then he abandoned her. Francine asked him for domestic stability and he was not giving it to her. Polemics with his wife pleased Camus no more than polemics with D'Astier; marital squabbles were as repetitious as political bickering.

When left by himself in Cabris he grew lonely and he summoned an old confidante Blanche Balain who was still living in Nice. He poured out his troubles but, although she was sympathetic, she knew him too well to believe he was quite sincere. He would neither ask Francine for a divorce nor be faithful to her; he simply hoped that the problem would go away.[34]

The only solution Camus could see was to finish *L'Homme Révolté*. In February 1951 he wrote to Char: 'for a month I have been buried in undisturbed work. Total solitude and the urge to finish. I am spending ten hours a day at my desk.'[35] On March 7 he notes in his diary: 'The draft of *L'Homme Révolté* is done. With this book the first two cycles of my work are completed. I am 37 years old. Shall I now be able to create freely?'[36] The exhausting labour of his philosophical 'summa' was over and he made plans for essays and lyrical sketches. Yet his relief was premature because he spent the next months putting the finishing touches to *L'Homme Révolté* and he was not done with them until early July. He felt none of the exaltation he had hoped for. He was emotionally drained and he felt suspended in mid-air. He went off to Le Panelier with Francine and corrected the proofs while the rain poured down over the mountains.[37]

L'Homme Révolté, which was published in October 1951, is an enormous treatise that analyses the various prophets of literary and historical revolt – Sade, Baudelaire, Rimbaud, Lautréamont, Breton, Saint-Just, Nietzsche, Hegel, Marx, the Russian anarchists, the French Communists and Sartre. From his criticism of these thinkers Camus draws his own vision of revolt. He was, so he felt, speaking for his family and offering answers, however tentative, to the Cold War. The trouble was that others did not share this view. *L'Homme Révolté* was to turn against him, accentuate his loneliness and force him into the roles of lay saint and right-winger which he detested. This book, over which Camus agonized as he had never before agonized, is not merely his worst book but one that did him great harm.

Today its one merit seems obvious. It is a long rhetorical lament on the religious conception of politics which flourished from the '30's to the '50's. There is nothing new about its message for it is yet another chapter in the 'God-that-failed' saga. Yet it is an important banality because so many intellectuals viewed left-wing politics as a drama about heaven and hell in which the revolution is to banish original sin. Camus reiterates that there can be no such revolution and he strikes a personal note when he warns against violence.

'Politics is not a religion, if it becomes one then it becomes an inquisition,' he writes. He catalogues the various forms which political violence may take. This is the Camus whose father was killed in 1914, who had seen French Algerian bloodlust, who had been a pacifist in 1940 and who had written the murder chapter of *L'Etranger*. He is reinforced by a Camus who has given up the Liberation dream of renovation, who has been disgusted by the purge of the collaborators and who had denounced stalinism.

L'Homme Révolté's first weakness lies in its form. In *Sisyphe* Camus had hesitated between the essay and the treatise but had tilted towards the essay; here he tilts towards the treatise. Ever the good student he had read Hegel and Marx – albeit only in extracts – and had devoured commentaries on them. He had pored over historians and he had gone back to old favourites like Chestov and Nietzsche. Such erudition is too much and yet not enough. Camus attempts a literary and philosophical 'summa' in order to show how Western culture since the French Revolution inspires men to murder. But the gaps in his reading are apparent and the reading itself blurs his intuitive understanding. André Breton quarrelled with his interpretation of Lautréamont, Sartre told him he knew nothing about Hegel and even friends disputed what he said about Bakunin.*

Moreover Camus distorts or neglects the thinkers he discusses. He admits that he treats only one, superficial aspect of Baudelaire, while he condenses the surrealists into a few pages. If he were writing an essay it would not matter that he ignores the historical mechanisms of revolution. But he cannot write a treatise about the Terror without examining not merely

*Pascal Pia did not miss the chance to tear apart what Camus wrote about Rimbaud.

the psychology it encouraged but the social group it brought to power.

The style demonstrates another kind of false inflation. Camus gives free rein to the Mediterranean, rhetorical urge which underlies his other books. This passage is characteristic:

'What place is there in Sade's universe for pleasure, for the glorious joy of consenting, sharing bodies? He offers only an impossible quest to escape from despair and it finishes, of course, in despair. It is a flight from servitude to servitude, from prison to prison. If nature alone is true and if desire and destruction are the only natural forces, then man must rush headlong from destruction to destruction – indeed the human realm itself will be insufficient to slake his thirst for blood – until he reaches universal annihilation.'[38]

Such apocalyptic language reveals the images of bloodshed which haunted Camus. *L'Homme Révolté* is full of prisons: Sade's castle, the Nazi concentration camps and fortress Russia show Camus' abiding fear that he is trapped in an alien universe.

Camus' language is powerful but it is also monotonously highflown. Centuries of writing and politics are reduced to the same few metaphors and the same rhetorical questions. Seemingly concise sentences, riddled with antitheses, reveal bare generalizations:

'Nothing can discourage the passion for divinity which lurks in the hearts of men.'
'All modern revolutions end by strengthening the state.'
'All revolutionaries end up as tyrants or heretics.'
'Artists can create but they cannot kill.'
'In the sound and the fury of history each consciousness desires, in order to be, the death of all others.'

Camus rebukes Saint-Just because his 'cascade of dogmatic affirmations' constitutes a 'guillotine' style. But *L'Homme Révolté* is full of dogmatic affirmations which belie its call for measure. In *Sisyphe* Camus spaced out the purple passages and dosed his statements with irony. Now he repeats the mistake of his *Combat* editorials and his vision of destruction turns into flabby, facile sentences. The 'God-that-failed' theme can inspire good writing. In *Darkness at Noon* Koestler's hatred of communism acts as a lucid intelligence that enables him to lay bare the party's secrets. But much of Camus' art is caught up with concision and the lamentations of *L'Homme Révolté* do not suit him. The murder scene of *L'Etranger* is, despite its ambiguity, a better warning against violence than this long harangue.

Rhetoric draws attention to *L'Homme Révolté*'s second weakness: that Camus' concept of revolt goes no further than it did in *Sisyphe*. Man is still balanced on a tightrope between his sense of the sacred and his awareness that he must die and revolt is still a demand for unity which the world cannot answer. It is a negative trait, a creature of division and a stoical contemplation. It cannot construct values which would dissolve the scepticism that is one of its components. Its chief characteristic is that it refuses the leap of faith which revolution represents.

Although Camus is trying to offer values and although he needed to believe that his work was growing more positive, revolt means only that man must defy the absurd as Sisyphus defied his rock. While spending hundreds of pages attacking marxism Camus offers few alternative forms of protest. This robs his book of diversity and turns it into ever more of a lament. It also exposed him to the attacks of *Les Temps Modernes*.

Since his real concern is not with Saint-Just but with the Communists and Sartre one may single out what he says about them. He condemns Hegel for deifying reason and inserting it into history. This is an oversimplification because Camus depicts the hegelian concept of reason as a kind of fate whereas Hegel felt that, although the historical order was not created by man, man was not a pawn and could free himself by working within that order. But Camus cannot perceive any fruitful interaction between self and the universe except for the religious moments of oneness and the defiance of *Sisyphe*. Sartre is closer to Hegel in welcoming the notion that man can realize himself through others, although Sartre too is dualistic. Camus, however, sees in Hegel's reason only a machine for crushing the individual. Once he has established this he denounces Marx for claiming that the mechanism of reason is the class struggle. Then he takes the last and most important step: he attacks the French Communists for declaring that the individual must bow to the iron rules of the class struggle as the party interprets them.

251

Camus' best comments are in asides which show his intuitive vision. He dislikes industrialization rather than capitalism and he prefers the artisans and workshops of Belcourt to the conveyor-belts of huge factories. Like Orwell, he feels that historical necessity is simply a mask for totalitarianism. Private relationships deteriorate under dictatorships; loyalty and love are destroyed by the rage to conform and betray. Camus shows how language is distorted and how left-wing jargon becomes newspeak. He repeats Koestler's theme that in communist societies today's judges are tomorrow's victims; whenever the party changes its line it makes sacrificial offerings to the god of historical necessity.

Camus' analysis of terrorism remains valid today. There are, he argues, two political paths that hegelians might follow. The first is opportunistic acquiescence because history is moving towards pre-ordained, rational goals; the second is the attempt to anticipate history by actions which are justified because they serve those goals. The second option led to nineteenth-century Russian terrorism.[39] Confronting a backward society the terrorists decided that reason could be advanced only with guns and bombs. Had he lived Camus might have analysed contemporary European terrorism in the same way. Both Italian and German terrorists are looking for a historical shortcut; disappointed with the 1968 disturbances they wish to hasten a revolution that is politically unrealizable. The religious zeal which Camus ascribes to the Russian terrorists and to Communists inspires the Red Brigades.

When he turns to Sartre Camus affirms that the errors of existentialism spring from its limitless pessimism: 'in existentialist philosophy there is a tendency to depict an actionless, reactionless anguish where the man of anguish never transcends the anguish which is his highest achievement'. Sartre should, Camus feels, explain the moral philosophy that will turn the panic-stricken exhilaration of anguish into a code of revolt. This is a common criticism of Sartre, although Sartre has never responded to it. Morality was an object of suspicion to him; it was part of the pseudo-idealism which contaminated his childhood. Better to act on the outside world and change it, he felt, than to worry about how one should behave within its confines. So Sartre leaped straight from metaphysics into politics. This, Camus feels, was his error. In order to escape from the anguish of his condition into political action Sartre was ready to abandon traditional moral values and to accept the Communist mythology of historical determinism.

Sartre might have retorted that his concept of commitment contains its own restraints. But Camus wants to contrast it with his own concept of revolt. So he discusses the forms which political revolt – for *L'Homme Révolté* is really a book about politics – might take. He lists three such forms – aristocratic fraternity, revolutionary syndicalism and social democracy.

The first is exemplified by Simone Weil who interested Camus because she went to work in a factory and lived the proletarian condition instead of talking about its transformation. She is depicted in *L'Homme Révolté* in rather the same way as Rieux and Tarrou are depicted in *La Peste*. This is an aristocratic code of behaviour which could not easily be turned into mass action but which might become the code of a group like the GLI.

The best recruits for such a group are the revolutionary syndicalists 'who trust in the freedom and spontaneity of the working class'. Camus praises Bakunin, the Spanish anarchists and the magazine *Révolution Prolétarienne*. His admiration is partly negative: these men are anti-stalinist. Yet in writing about them he shows that tinge of anarchism and that relish for working-class life which are the most attractive features of his thought. He foreshadows the resurgence of anarcho-syndicalism after '68 and he would probably have admired the present-day union, the CFDT. Yet he cannot pretend that *Révolution Prolétarienne* is more than a voice in the wilderness.

The third option is reformist, labour party-style politics. But Camus remained Fouchet's critic and the divided *Combat* editorialist. Once more he mentions Swedish social democracy without elaborating on it. This should be Camus' political viewpoint because it corresponds to his belief in relative values. In the last section of *L'Homme Révolté* he pits the absolutism of North Europe with the sense of limits which supposedly characterizes the Mediterranean. But if this is so, then surely social democracy with its belief that society may gradually be improved is the correct political code. Camus' refusal to embrace it shows his absolutist belief that the tragic universe cannot be reformed.

This is why *L'Homme Révolté* does not mark a milestone in

French thought. Its most able defenders claim that it substituted a relative for an absolutist viewpoint: Camus understood that the age of barricades was over and was indicating more sober options.[40] Yet if his analysis of these options is so thin it is because revolt was not a relative value. As Raymond Aron pointed out, Camus' thought contained a good dose of the religious fervour which he castigated.[41] The syndicalists, for example, do believe that the human condition can be transformed. Camus did not believe this but he never explains how his concept of measure can be fruitful. It remains an amputation and an absence – an absence of revolution.

Most reviewers of *L'Homme Révolté* were favourable. Marcel Arland, a voice of the old *NRF*, liked the theme of revolt and could see that the critique of extremism was in the *NRF* tradition. Raymond Aron paid Camus a poisoned compliment, declaring that he was less foolishly romantic than Sartre. The Communists were predictably virulent and *Action* journalist, Pierre Hervé, wrote a diatribe which infuriated Camus, who was also engaged in a polemic with the few remaining surrealists.

André Breton had attacked Camus' interpretation of Lautréamont's poetry. By ignoring its liberating power and stressing its nihilism Camus was 'siding with the worst conservatism'.[42] Breton was no better pleased with Camus' remarks about him and he seized the chance to start a quarrel which suited him well. Surrealism seemed old-fashioned after '44 so Breton was trying to revive it by issuing the fiery denunciations which had served him so well in the '20's. Camus, the leader of the Liberation generation, was an inviting target.

Camus declared that he would not indulge in 'vain polemics' and then he repeated that Breton had betrayed himself by joining the PC. Camus was egged on by René Char who was continuing his own feud with Breton; Breton countered when a group of would-be surrealists published an attack on *L'Homme Révolté* to which Camus would not condescend to reply.

A genuine debate was buried beneath this game-playing and *Le Soleil Noir* presented a different view of man from *L'Homme Révolté*. 'At the centre of the most brilliant midday the night is lurking,' write the surrealists.[43] Man was a creature of darkness. If he destroyed while seeking to escape from his servitude, then so be it. Camus simply disagreed. Man was indeed a creature of darkness but he could and must control himself. The surrealists were intrigued by the night of the subconscious and wanted to unleash what was hidden in man. Camus, however, felt that what was hidden was the impulse to kill. Once he was unleashed man would turn into a murderer; this was the danger that lurked behind Breton's 'arrogant innocence'.

The surrealists counted for little in Paris but *Les Temps Modernes* counted for a great deal. Since *L'Homme Révolté* had criticized existentialism Sartre's reply was eagerly awaited. Around the time *L'Homme Révolté* was finished there was a revival of the friendship between Camus and Sartre because Maria Casarès acted in Sartre's play *Le Diable et le Bon Dieu*. Camus came to collect her after rehearsals and stayed to chat with Sartre. On the opening night the group went out to dinner and for a moment the old cordiality was restored.

Yet Camus and Sartre were intellectually further apart than they had ever been. Naturally Camus disliked *Le Deuxième Sexe* which 'ridiculed French males'.[44] De Beauvoir felt that his reaction proved her right and that he did not wish women to define themselves instead of being defined by men. This was less important than the political arguments between Camus and Sartre. Camus was more and more irritated by Sartre's cult of the working-class which seemed to him an inverted snobbery. 'The proletariat should not become a mystique', argued Camus.[45] His Belcourt background taught him that workers could be prejudiced and mistaken; their oppressed condition did not make their political judgement infallible.

Sartre was in no mood to tolerate such rebukes because his own temper was rising. In the Cold War propaganda he saw the triumph of his enemies. The despised French middle-classes were using their old weapon of illusory ideals in order to batter down the workers. Rhetoric about the Free World was enabling them to hold onto their privileges. Camus' talk about third ways, world peace, limited revolt and the evils of revolution seemed nonsense to Sartre. Whatever his reasons might be, Camus was helping the conservative cause. Like Camus, Sartre was approaching breaking-point and the humour he had shown in '44 was a distant memory.

Months went by before *Les Temps Modernes* replied to

Camus. Sartre had asked for a volunteer to review *L'Homme Révolté* and Francis Jeanson had stepped forward. 'He promised to be tactful,' says Simone de Beauvoir, 'and then he got carried away.'[46] This was predictable because Jeanson, although well-liked by everyone who knew him, was intellectually uncompromising. He had already published two articles on Camus.[47] In the first, which is sub-titled *Le mensonge de l'absurde*, he argued that, if the human mind could erect the absurd into a concept, then it could create other concepts; Camus was wrong in stopping at Sisyphus' contemplation of his rock. Jeanson criticized *La Peste* because the narrator views the plague from the outside and is not a part of the evil he depicts. In general Jeanson's view of Camus' writing was like Sartre's: Camus deified the absurd and refused to combat it; he had a religious not a political vision.

Les TM had itself given up any pretence of compromise or tact. In the May 1952 number, which contained Jeanson's long-awaited article on *L'Homme Révolté*, there was a review of Marcel Aymé's *La Tête des Autres*. While praising him for satirizing judges, *Les TM* condemned him for suggesting they were irrevocably stupid; this left no space for protest and reform.

Jeanson followed the same line. He talks about Hegel but neither he nor Sartre really cared about the philosophical dispute. He criticizes Camus' style because its flowing sentences are a mark of acquiescence rather than protest. His main criticism, however, is that by personifying revolt and revolution and turning them into deities of good and evil, Camus is detaching himself from the flux of existence. If he entered it in a dialectic of revolt and situation he would be able to change it. More simply, Jeanson is saying that *L'Homme Révolté* contains many dire warnings against rebellion but no vision of revolt. Its practical conclusion is 'that nothing can be done and that the only wisdom is to observe the status quo.'[48]

The irritated Camus made a characteristic reply. As if Jeanson did not exist, he addressed his article to Sartre and then, as if remembering Jeanson, he dismissed him as 'unworthy'. This lofty tone infuriated Jeanson and seemed to corroborate his criticism: Camus was perched on the top of Mount Sinai. Camus claimed that he was replying in order to defend not himself but human freedom. This did not, however, prevent him from demonstrating his skill as a polemicist. He branded the entire *TM* team as bourgeois intellectuals and shame-faced stalinists who were not willing to discuss the Russian camps.

The controversy could not have occurred at a worse moment. In May 1952 General Ridgway arrived in Paris to become commander-in-chief of NATO. When the PC organized demonstrations against him the government replied with a red scare strategy and arrested the Communist deputy-leader Jacques Duclos. The charges against him were preposterous but hysteria was mounting. On June 4 the PC launched a protest strike which flopped – to the resounding glee of *Le Figaro* and the right.

To Sartre this glee was the ultimate humiliation and he exploded with anger. In July he published the first part of *Les Communistes et la Paix* and in August he replied to Camus. He saw a link between *L'Homme Révolté* and Ridgway's victory. Like a pen-wielding NATO Camus was one-sidedly attacking the Communists and was advising the French working-class to submit rather than rebel. Of course Camus took a different view. Refusing to link the French working-class with Russia he considered the June 4 strike a Communist trick.

The tone of Sartre's reply to Camus was more important than the content: it was a furious, injurious onslaught. Sartre issued many such excommunications and Raymond Aron would receive one in May 1968. At these moments Sartre's aggressivity overwhelmed him and he turned into a virulent pamphleteer. Not for nothing had he admired Céline. His anger showed him the chinks not in Camus' argument, which he dismisses in a few paragraphs, but in his character. Camus is 'a mixture of brooding arrogance and vulnerability'. He is not a Belcourt proletarian but a prosperous intellectual. 'Tell me, Camus', asks Sartre, 'what is the mystery that prevents people from discussing your books without robbing mankind of its reasons to live?'[49] With such hammer-blows Sartre shattered the statue of the lay saint.

In *Les Communistes* Sartre elaborated on the political dispute. Violence is an integral part of the class struggle and working-class rebellion is a healthy response to the daily oppression of capitalism. 'When he is submissive the worker is turning his back on his own humanity; when he revolts he is refusing the inhuman,' writes Sartre.[50] Refusing to admit that June 4 proved the working class was no longer revolutionary, Sartre insisted on the need to act. The correct political choice was to undertake revolutionary action that would revive working-class militancy. The PC had led the way on June 4.

One can agree with Sartre's critique of Camus without accepting this analysis. *Les Communistes* must be one of Sartre's poorest books because it denies his own concept of situation and because the concepts of 'party' and 'class' are so simplistic. The working class, Sartre says, is itself only itself when it rebels. The PC is the party of the working class even when it is most blindly stalinist. But surely the working class remains itself when it compromises as well as when it rebels and surely no party can arrogate to itself the legitimacy of being the party of the working class. Sartre was committing precisely the error of which Camus had accused him in *L'Homme Révolté*. He was making a leap of faith and he was forgetting his own dictum about working within history. The concept of situation implies a struggle between the individual's freedom and the constraints of external reality. Working-class docility is one such constraint and it cannot be banished with a wave of the dialectical wand.

The present-day observer may feel that the Sartre-Camus battle ended in a draw but Sartre's article was a terrible blow to Camus. Although British and American intellectuals sided with him against Sartre, Parisian intellectuals did not. While they did not necessarily agree with Sartre's political analysis, they felt he was a better thinker than Camus. Moreover the verbal violence of Sartre's article was devastating. If he had not refuted *L'Homme Révolté* he had certainly buried it.

Camus called together some friends at Gallimard and put on a brave face. Sartre, he said, was a tool of the Communists and his article was just propaganda.[51] But Camus knew that Sartre had made a laughing-stock of him. Robert Jaussaud's wife, who visited him in his office, saw that he had been cut to the quick. His dislike of things Parisian reached a crescendo and he felt sadly inferior to Sartre. He oscillated between tearful anger and gloom. With Jaussaud he played at being tough: 'Thank you for what you say about this polemic (Jaussaud had advised him to go swimming and forget about Sartre) which is continuing although without me. I never know what to say when people attack me personally. I feel incapable of replying. What am I to do? Our Algerian method of dealing with such matters would be considered quite inappropriate here. And anyway with these pansies . . .'[52]

Surrounded by his Algerian Mafia Camus could take refuge in masculinity and feigned indifference. Elsewhere his resentment broke through. For the rest of his life he preserved an enemies list of communists, existentialists and intellectuals, while his writing is full of indirect gibes against Sartre. Far from liberating him, *L'Homme Révolté* confirmed the pattern of depression and isolation which marked his life.

9

Camus the Dramatist

The crisis of *L'Homme Révolté* overlapped with a crisis in Camus' work as a playwright. Despite the success of *Les Justes* (1949) he had written no new plays in the past three years. This might have been explained as a temporary writing block caused by the strain of *L'Homme Révolté* but after he finished his long essay Camus wrote no plays of his own during the last eight years of his life. His theatre had, after the promising start of *Caligula*, run into a dead-end. *Le Malentendu* (1944), *L'Etat de Siège* (1948) and *Les Justes* are superficially very different plays but they all contain the same weakness. They are suicidal cries of defiance where the characters are wooden and death itself is monotonous. To understand why this is so one must first recap and glance at the Equipe, *Caligula* and the Liberation theatre.

The Equipe had hesitated: was modern drama to follow traditional tragedy or was it to depict a more arbitrary 'upside-down' world? Camus was not sure. He did know that the theatre must not merely be political, that it must tend towards the 'philosophical', that its scenery must be stylized and that its actors should be free to create their own roles. The theatre was different from the novel. Because it was a joint creation of writer, director, actor and spectator it could dare to confront death. *L'Etranger* and *La Peste* could be no more than fragments of an unknown whole but *Prometheus in Chains* had spoken directly about man's condition. The problem was how to depict the drama of man's rebellion against his fate. The meaninglessness of the world could be whimsical and farcical as well as grim and painful.

In *Caligula* Camus was still hesitating. The emperor commits hubris by seeking to change the order that governs the world but death is arbitrary as well as inevitable so the play is full of movement. Farce succeeds murder, while the character of

Caligula swings from one extreme to another. But during the 1940's Camus began to concentrate on what he calls the 'paroxysm': the moment when the tragic hero realizes his condition.[1] This led Camus back to traditional tragedy and in *Le Malentendu* he tried to write a modern version of such tragedy.

Presented just before and just after the Liberation, *Le Malentendu* and *Caligula* were interpreted as examples of the new theatre. Once more Camus had anticipated his generation's taste. Just as he disliked the pomp of Algiers opera, so young Frenchmen resented the slick drawing-room comedies of the '30's. Before 1939 people went to the theatre, to borrow Artaud's phrase, as they went to the brothel. Now the theatre was to be high-brow rather than clever, demanding rather than frivolous. Like Camus, the Liberation generation had no fear of 'philosophy'. *Combat* critic, Jacques Lemarchand, defended the theatre of ideas; if presented boldly, ideas could make exciting drama.

For the theatre was not to become a cold, intellectual exercise. Camus wanted to jolt the spectator and Antonin Artaud, the eccentric poet, playwright and producer who had worked with Barrault, declared that the audience must be submerged in a cathartic delirium of destruction. Camus thought that Artaud's views were too extreme but he intended *Le Malentendu* to be brutal.* The style of acting in which Maria Casarès excelled emphasized Camus' concept of paroxysm.

Le Malentendu depicts a son, Jan, who returns to his home in central Europe after years of absence. Without revealing his identity he stays as a paying guest in the hotel which his mother and his sister, Martha, run. His wife, Maria, tries to dissuade him but Jan insists that he wants to observe his mother and sister before he reveals who he is and offers them a new life in the Mediterranean country where he now lives. But Martha and her mother kill and rob their guests in order to obtain the wealth that will allow them to escape from their dreary home. They kill Jan before they realize his identity. The mother commits

*In January 1947 Camus attended the lecture at the Vieux-Colombier theatre where Artaud talked about electric-shock treatment and the mental hospitals where he had spent several years. Camus was stunned but he considered Artaud's life more appalling than interesting. Maria Casarès' father had greater sympathy for Artaud and used to discuss him with Camus.

suicide and Martha makes a speech of defiance before she too kills herself.

The themes are vintage Camus. Like Caligula, Martha hopes for the 'unlimited joy of the unpunished assassin'. The money for which she murders is a pretext; she and her mother kill because their lives are unbearable. Killing is a short step from suicide: 'I must give him the sleep that I would like for myself,' says the mother as she prepares to dispatch her son. For *Le Malentendu* is another chapter in Camus' indirect dialogue with his mother. Jan wishes to be reconciled with his mother but he does not tell her who he is because he wants more than a tepid mother-son relationship. If he remains a 'stranger', it is because he hopes to dissolve that strangeness in a greater oneness. Indeed he achieves this when she joins him in his grave.

The death-wish that dominates *Le Malentendu* is expressed in a debate about language which also reveals the obstacle that Camus the dramatist faced. Many spectators complained that the play was artificial because Jan could so easily have revealed his identity and prevented the violence. 'All I have to do is find the words,' he says. 'Just talk simply,' says his wife but Jan, like the Grand of *La Peste*, knows it is no easy matter. He wants to find 'the words that will settle everything'. He is not content with luke-warm expressions of affection or with qualified statements. His mother offers him such fragments: 'In a way I am disappointed that you have decided to leave,' she tells him, 'but then I say to myself: after all there is no reason why I should consider it so important.'[2] The disappointed Jan presses her for absolute declarations. When she calls him 'my son' he is delighted, only to relapse into despondency when she tells him 'it's just a way of speaking'.

Jan has recourse to the language of prayer but when he calls on God the only response comes from a silent, old servant who is helping to destroy him by hiding the passport which would have told his mother who he really is. So prayer is worthless and the valid language of the play is contained in two pieces of rhetoric: the mother's monologue of Act 1, scene 7, which is a meditation on suicide, and Martha's defiant justification of her murder in Act 3, scene 3.

In these two seemingly opposite but in fact complementary speeches lies the problem which faced the dramatist Camus: the 'paroxysm' is reduced to a murderous-suicidal cry of rebellion.

In traditional tragedy some order is present behind the gods' cruelty; the Greek heroes puzzle over it and, although it may be terrible, it is also rich. In Camus' plays death is merely a horrible banality. Conversely, death is too pervasive to allow man the margin of freedom which he enjoyed in the 'upside-down' world, so movement and farce are banished. The characters do not evolve or look deeply into themselves. *Le Malentendu* does not brutalize the spectator because it remains a cold work, an allegory where the old servant represents the absent god and where the characters indulge in a monotonous lament about their condition.

The reason why the play failed is not that Camus was a novelist who had strayed into the theatre and did not grasp its special art. Camus was a man of the theatre to his fingertips. Yet this mobile artist, who loved masks and mime, allowed himself to be trapped in a sterile attempt to find a language that could confront a meaningless death.

When Maria prays at the end the old servant utters his only word: a categorical 'no'. One cannot help comparing him with Beckett's God who simply remains absent. This allows the tramps, Lucky and Pozzo, to talk; they lament, wax eloquent and joke. The best post-war dramatists have drawn on the silence which haunted Camus. Their plays take place in the relative rather than in the absolute, in what Beckett calls 'the last but one'. Lucky and Pozzo speak without caring whether they are telling the truth. Camus, however, was obsessed with the 'no' and with the rebel's 'yes' which is another 'no'. *Le Malentendu* could not evolve because these two poles were really one.

Camus' concept of the theatre contains traits which foreshadow Beckett and Ionesco. He stressed that there can be no 'characters' because psychology is secondary to the metaphysical. This might have allowed figures like Lucky and Pozzo who are unpredictable because empty. But in *Le Malentendu* he offered only fragments of static rhetoric which revealed the weakness of the Liberation theatre. Man's tragic condition remains an idea and is not brought to life. Clearly this could not satisfy Camus who set to work on a very different play, *L'Etat de Siège*.

Barrault, who asked him to write it, had worked with Claudel and had been influenced by Artaud who had analysed the links between the plague and the theatre. One can imagine how Artaud would have written *L'Etat de Siège*: enormous puppets, monsters and frenzied crowds. But Camus did not believe that a deluge of cruelty could be liberating and he felt that drama was impossible unless human courage and solidarity were depicted. Moreover his concept of death posed a further difficulty. Since he did not believe in Artaud's 'life-in-death', it would have been difficult for him to spin the web of dark lyricism that would make the plague a deity. In *La Peste* it had been an absence but here it would be portrayed directly. Claudel, so different from Artaud, could have waxed lyrical about the plague because it would have possessed a divine order, however remote and however tangled with evil.

Camus could not do this and in *L'Etat de Siège* the plague is a tyrant who overthrows the cowardly governor of a Spanish town and imposes his rule of death. Diego, a doctor, rebels, aided by Victoria who loves him. But he can overthrow the plague only by offering his life. He does so, liberates the town and leaves Victoria alone.

Camus tried 'to mix together all the forms of dramatic expression from the lyrical monologue to collective drama'.[3] *Le Malentendu* had been too much like traditional tragedy; *L'Etat de Siège* would draw on another strand in the Equipe and the Travail. It would emulate the crowds, battles, strange lighting and political messages of *Révolte dans les Asturies*. Camus drew too on the Spanish theatre of the golden age. He set his play in medieval Cadiz and jumbled theology with farce.

The first act of *L'Etat de Siège* is excellent drama. A comet sets a tone of mystery and the crowds that throng the streets continue it with their questions. Once more silence and words are an explicit theme: the plague gags the people until the chorus fights back with 'a long stifled cry . . . that speaks to us of the sea beneath the midday sun'. Movement is also explicit. The town governor is 'the king of stasis', while the people flee towards the sea. This is a kind of theatre which suited Camus.

Yet as soon as the struggle between the people and the plague develops in Act 2, movement is destroyed and the play turns into an allegory. Only the plague's language is convincing: he uses an Orwellian newspeak, turning 'to concentrate' into 'concentration camp'. Elsewhere he is lifeless, neither god nor devil. Barrault's remark that *L'Etat de Siège* failed because the spectators did not know whether the plague was metaphysical or political is only partially true. The plague is both. He is too literal an allegory of the Occupation – he talks of total war and of killing hostages – and he is too remote. Camus tried to make him live by turning him into a bureaucrat. Remembering the hours he spent filling out forms in the Algiers town hall, he satirizes the plague's methodical abstractions.

But the plague remains as wooden as his opponent Diego, who is not enough of a doctor or a lover to be interesting as a human being and who incarnates a very bland brand of goodness. By Act 3 the play's movement has turned into a mechanical tug of war between Diego and the plague and the suspense of Act 1 has died. The two phantoms of good and evil resemble each other and, despite Diego's victory, *L'Etat de Siège* is a theatrical triumph for the plagues of silence and stasis. Appropriately, Diego has to die so that his rebellion can be complete. Like Martha and the Kaliayev of *Les Justes*, he can flaunt his contempt for death only by offering to die. In a burst of weak rhetoric the chorus calls him 'a solitary singer pleading beneath a silent sky for an impossible reunion'.

After an Artaud-like endeavour and a good first act, after starting a play so different from *Le Malentendu*, Camus returned to his old dead-end. He had opened up possibilities which other dramatists could develop; crowds, choruses and the concept of the theatre as a festival were fruitful innovations. But Camus was not to expand on them.

Les Justes marked a return to traditional tragedy: five acts, a remote historical setting – although less remote to the Liberation audience – unity of action, noble language. Missing is the great virtue of the French classical theatre: psychological analysis. When he discussed the play Camus repeated that he was interested in the universal and not in the particular but this should not exclude psychology. Racine's characters are embodiments of jealousy and love but they are fascinating because they display the extravagant contradictions of these passions. Camus' characters offer the shell, not the emotion itself. He had fallen into a false classicism as he occasionally did in his essays. *Les Justes* moves, drama-less, to its conclusion which is about to be repeated since the play will begin again as

Dora follows Kaliayev. In Camus' novels the monotony of death is a merit because it is wrapped in mystery; in his theatre he is too explicit.

Les Justes depicts the Russian terrorists of 1905. Kaliayev is a moral man and he is in love with Dora but his task is to kill the grand duke. Another revolutionary, Stepan, rejoices in the need for violence but Kaliayev loathes it. Yet he murders the grand duke and goes to his execution rejecting the consolation of prayer. Left alone like Victoria, Dora plans to throw the next bomb.

Camus did try to do something new: to write a love scene. The dialogue between Dora and Kaliayev in Act 3 was one reason for the play's success. It elaborates on a theme that had been sketched in both *Le Malentendu* and in *L'Etat de Siège*. In the first play Jan's wife tries to prevent him from remaining at the hotel but, when she offers him love instead of his strange quest, he refuses. Woman's love, however beautiful, must be transcended by heroic man. In *L'Etat de Siège* Victoria's love spurs Diego to combat the plague while deserting her.

This view of love came naturally to Camus, obsessed with indifference, drawn to but distrusting women. It overlaps with his Don Juanism, his masculine code of morality and his unfinished dialogue with his mother. It is implicit in *La Peste* where Rieux sets aside his wife before combatting the plague. But until now woman's love had been too easily vanquished by heroism. In *Les Justes* Dora and Kaliayev oscillate between tenderness and devotion to the revolution so the scene is human and complex. Not that Camus' view has changed: 'We are the just,' says Dora, 'there is a warmth that is forbidden to us.' But her regret is hauntingly convincing and she is Camus' best woman character.

Dora brings a moment of movement to *Les Justes* but it soon vanishes. The ostensible drama comes from the clash between Kaliayev, the moral revolutionary, and Stepan, who believes only in efficacity. But the sympathy which Stepan comes to feel for Kaliayev reveals their common bond. Stepan's real motive for killing is to forget the humiliating experience when he was whipped and when his companion Vera committed suicide in protest. Like Martha, Stepan kills because his life is unbearable. As for Kaliayev, he is determined to commit suicide. He states that he must sacrifice his life in order to justify his terrorism: 'To die for one's idea is the only way to be worthy of it.' In reality he is tempted by suicide which puts man on death's side and liberates him from fear of death: 'Between the act of assassination and the scaffold . . . there is an eternity.' Unlike his creator, Kaliayev rejects the temptation of normalcy. A fellow-prisoner offers him commonsense, a policeman offers him his life and the grand duchess offers him heaven. But Kaliayev has his own heaven: it is that nostalgia for Algerian innocence which lurked behind *La Peste*. Camus was up against the problem he had faced in *La Mort Heureuse*. He could not make his vision of harmony credible without exploring its religious possibilities. So Kaliayev's terrorism remains the expression of a death-wish which all the terrorists feel and which robs them of any human complexity.

By now Camus' theatre had reached a third dead-end. Man's fight against his condition, the motor of these 'philosophical' dramas, had ended in silence. Abstract phantoms had battered their heads against prison-walls until they died. In 1949 Camus gave up his attempt to write modern tragedies.[4]

Kaliayev would have liked to be an actor but Camus does not allow him the actor's zany freedom. Yet Camus himself needed that freedom all the more after the failure of his theatre and the polemics of *L'Homme Révolté*. So he began to direct, to adapt and to work more closely with actors. Other men's texts helped him to break out of his prison. He turned to artists who had succeeded in writing tragedy – Calderón – or who had written plays full of movement – Lopa de Vega. He hoped that his adaptations would lead him around his dead-end and enable him to resume writing plays. But in the meantime he sought in them a new form of creation and he exchanged the writer's for the director's mask.[5]

10

1952–1958: A Pied-Noir at Bay

In the summer of 1952 Camus, still reeling from Sartre's onslaught, started to look for a theatre where he could direct, adapt and work with actors. Maria Casarès' mentor, Marcel Herrand, had been asked to organize a summer theatre festival at Angers and he suggested that Camus help him. In a letter to a friend in the autumn Camus wrote of the possibility of becoming director of a Paris theatre, the Récamier.[1] Nothing came of this but he continued his search.

He could not avoid politics that autumn and he made two interventions. In the first he defended a sailor, Henri Martin, who had distributed propaganda leaflets denouncing the Indo-China war. Camus protested that the five-year prison sentence imposed on Martin was too severe. Camus was not at his ease in this argument because Martin was a communist and had the backing of Sartre. 'I have no illusions about the communists' enthusiasm for democracy,' Camus writes, adding, 'joining with the *Temps Modernes* group to defend freedom means compromising the very values of freedom.'[2] On November 30 Camus spoke at a mass meeting in the Salle Wagram in protest against Spain's admission to UNESCO. This was an easier task and the crowd applauded as Camus reiterated his lifelong opposition to Franco and praised the Spanish republicans as 'popular, libertarian leftwingers'.[3]

Abandoning politics, Camus at last found time to write about the Provence countryside. He and René Char met a photographer who accompanied them on their walks in the hills around L'Isle-sur-Sorgue; Camus wrote short notes to accompany the photographs and Char added an introduction. Relieved at finishing *L'Homme Révolté* Camus gave free rein to his lyrical impulse. He restricts himself to depicting objects but he personifies and deifies them. The trees defy the harsh god of the mistral wind and the ribs of rock in the mountains are like prehistoric monsters. Camus' concision allows the objects to stand as images of a half-revealed mystery:

'From the trunks of old willow trees spring garlands of fresh branches. It is the first garden of the world. And each dawn brings the first man.'
'The plane tree springs with all its smooth muscles towards the distant sky. Like a snow leopard.'
'The stream has turned the old wheels of the forgotten mill into a knot of dark cords which traps the sunlight.'[4]

The wheel is yet another example of the circle which Camus can never quite retrace and the objects of nature dissolve into a dance before he can grasp them. Yet there is a oneness in the Provence countryside and Camus is reconciled with it: 'Man surrenders his pride and learns how to die in the harmony of the evening.'

These little prose poems contain some of Camus' best writing and he composed them when he was beginning a new and troubled period of his artist's life. He laid plans for a third cycle of work: a novel, a play that would be a variant on the Faust and Don Juan themes and a philosophical essay on love. But the strain of *L'Homme Révolté* had been too great and Camus shrank from ambitious projects. Instead he planned a series of short stories to be called *L'Exil et le Royaume*. One of them was to demonstrate that he could write about working-class people: this would be *Les Muets*. Another would turn into *Jonas* which would show how an artist is destroyed by fame and flattery. These stories were to be experiments that would allow Camus to write more easily. However he encountered great difficulty when he began work on them and his fear of writer's sterility grew stronger.

In December 1952 he paid his winter visit to Algiers and his mother. He then drove deep into the interior to the oasis of Laghouat.[5] The desert, which he had not visited for years, delighted him and he tried to see it as if for the first time. Another of his stories, *La Femme adultère*, describes a woman from Algiers who is fascinated by the wind, the changing shapes and the purity of the desert. Camus' writing experiments were taking him back to the images that had dominated his youth.

He returned to France and reluctantly settled down to his

routine: work at home, lunch with friends and Gallimard. The polemics of *L'Homme Révolté* had made him feel that he was trapped between flatterers who took up his time and jealous rivals who seized every chance to ridicule him. In February he poured out his gloom: 'Some mornings I am so tired of all the hassle, so discouraged when I think of the work that awaits me, so sick of the madness of the world which leaps out at me whenever I open a newspaper that the only thing I want to do is to sit down and wait for night to fall.'[6]

He broke out of his gloom as the 1953 Angers festival drew closer. He had adapted two plays for it: Pierre de Larivey's *Les Esprits* and Calderón's *La Dévotion à la Croix*. The first was a direct link to the Equipe because Camus had done his adaptation in 1940 and had hoped to produce it in Algiers. *Les Esprits* is a sixteenth-century play which Larivey himself adapted or translated from the Italian. It is a tale of resourceful valets, avaricious fathers and complicated loves. Camus felt that it was a piece of pure theatre and in his adaptation he emphasized the crowd scenes and the bawdiness. He suggested that the actors mime and that they wear masks. To remind the spectators that this was the illusory reality of the theatre, Camus lengthened the prologue and the ending where the actors speak directly to the audience.

Calderón appealed to him because he was a writer of the Spanish golden age who drew on the 'autos sacramentales' – the medieval mystery plays. *La Dévotion* depicts a heroine, Julia, who loves the man who has killed her brother, who enters a convent and then leaves it and who finally dies as a martyr. The theme of confession runs through the play and it had a special interest for Camus who would write a confession of his own in *La Chute*. 'Let everyone in the universe know that I am Julia, Julia the criminal, the worst and most evil of women,' cries the heroine at the moment of her death.[7]

Camus also hoped that *La Dévotion* would offer the diverse moods which make up the tragic experience. If he had failed to convey this diversity in *Le Malentendu* he could now try again via Calderón. He emphasizes the different roles that Julia plays: she is a nun, a woman in love and a repentant sinner. Maria Casarès was both the ideal actress to play Julia and an assistant in the adaptation. Camus did not know enough Spanish to translate Calderón on his own so he relied on previous translations and had Maria Casarès check every line of his version.

The work had been completed when Marcel Herrand died of cancer a few weeks before the festival opened in June. Camus took over as director and brought to the rehearsals his old enthusiasm. He was still faithful to Jacques Copeau's dictum that a play was a total work: the joint endeavour of writer, director, actor and spectator. But of the four Camus preferred the actor. His adaptation of Calderón 'aims at providing a text which can be acted, which is written for actors . . . which tries to bring the spectacle to life and to recreate its movement'.[8] As a director Camus was reluctant to cut the actors' parts and he encouraged them to invent. In the Angers rehearsals he drew closer to his actors and tried to participate in their creation. It was a marvel, he declared, 'to hear an actor speak in the very voice you have heard in silent solitude'.[9]

At such moments Camus broke out of his inner prison and made contact with others. Many of his acquaintances laughed when he talked about 'the team' of actors: professional, Parisian actors could not recreate the fraternity of the Equipe. Yet Maria Casarès felt that the Angers rehearsals were like a holiday for Camus. He enjoyed the company of actors far more than the company of writers and politicians. Actors needed to be admired and loved so they understood that he did too. Photographs show Camus at the centre of an animated group or else watching intently as Maria Casarès rehearsed her part in an incongruous trouser suit. The two plays were performed outdoors in the courtyard of a medieval castle with turrets and a drawbridge. The audiences were large and appreciative and Maria Casarès was especially applauded.

This was no more than a joyous interlude for Camus because that same summer Francine fell ill.[10] There were physical symptoms which the doctors found hard to diagnose but she suffered from a nervous breakdown. Camus went off with her and the twins to the French Alps but Francine did not get better, while Camus grew irritated because his writing block would not go away. He tried to be an attentive husband and to help with the twins but it seems obvious that the principal cause of Francine's illness was their unsatisfactory marriage. Since Camus was less than ever willing to break with Maria Casarès or to be faithful to Francine, his very sincere gestures of affection did not help. Francine needed a full-time husband and father of her children.

Her illness strengthened Camus' feelings of guilt but it also made him wary. The psychological breakdown reminded him of Simone Hié's drug-taking. If he had not been able to help her when he was young and vigorous, there was scant chance he could help Francine now. Yet he still did not ask her to divorce him. His instinct was not to make sharp decisions but to battle on. When he eventually finished *L'Exil et le Royaume* he dedicated it to Francine and *Jonas* is an attempt to interpret their marriage. Camus explains that the role of a famous writer is incompatible with the role of a devoted husband. Flatterers, critics and socialites devour Jonas and leave him no energy to look after his family. Yet even in this fictional form Camus scarcely hints at the real dilemma of his marriage: the difficulty of reconciling artistic creation itself with the emotional and sexual ties of marriage.

The demands of his wife and children were draining him, Camus sometimes felt, of that primitive energy which inspired his books. Conversely his seductions offered him flashes of feminine beauty which encouraged him. The links between sexuality and creation are too complex to permit facile generalizations but it is surely no coincidence that Camus now began to keep a more explicit diary in which he described and analysed his seductions. It was as if he were trying to harness his sexual energy to the task of creation. Baudelaire once wrote: 'the more man cultivates the arts, the fewer erections he gets.'[11] Camus was trying to prove him wrong.

He was also concerned about his children who were now nearly eight years old. He got along well with his daughter and he boasted to his friends that she was vibrant and feminine and would grow up into a fine young woman. Jean gave him more trouble because Camus had to keep him in order; the role of an authoritarian father did not suit Camus. He preferred to spoil his children and, aware of his own silent childhood, he was very affectionate with them. He tried to spend time with them at least on week-ends and in the summers when he dragged them off on walks in the Provence hills. He followed their progress in school and boasted to Suzanne Agnely that Jean was very intelligent. But he also worried that he was not offering his children a stable family life. They too suffered from the demands his writing made on him and they might be suffering, he feared, from the failure of their parents' marriage. Camus told Suzanne Agnely that he dreaded the moment when Jean and Catherine would have the insight to understand the family situation.

Meanwhile his relationship with Maria Casarès was changing. She explains: 'When the first period of passion was over Camus and I were bound by a friendship as pure and as hard as stone.' The moralist Camus repeats this in different words: 'We lived wonderful hours in '44 . . . but they were sullied for a long time and even after we came back together by our pride.'[12] They had now learned to give up exclusive possession and to live by the 75% rule. Camus was both the more erring and the more jealous but he needed Maria as his existence grew ever more difficult.

1954 brought no improvement in Camus' life. He started to adapt Dostoevsky's *The Possessed* for the theatre but it was difficult to envisage this sprawling novel with its tribe of characters as a play. Camus began to wonder whether his adaptations were helping him. He persisted in telling his friends that adapting was a form of personal creation. Few agreed and he himself had doubts. His stories were progressing with painful slowness and in June he told a friend that 'my *Possessed* has come to a halt along with everything else I am writing'.[13]

In July he had a fresh outburst of depression. He had written nothing for six months. The careful planning which had enabled him to write his books was no longer sufficient. Camus felt that he was growing old. He was now forty and older than his father had been when he was killed. Camus wondered how much longer he had to live and whether old age was preferable to an early death.[14]

Camus longed to escape – to Algeria, to Greece, anywhere far from his writing desk. In the autumn of '54 he did make two short journeys. The first was to Holland where he submitted to receptions and speeches. He found time to tramp around the Hague in the rain and to pay a quick visit to Amsterdam where he took a boat ride around the canals. When he returned he had little to say to his friends about Holland but the Amsterdam canals imprinted themselves on his writer's imagination as a modern version of Dante's inferno. In *La Chute* they form a hell in the centre of which the narrator, Jean-Baptiste Clamence, delivers his monologue. The second journey was to Italy where Camus spoke in several different cities and visited the Greek temples at Paestum.[15] This visit, about which Camus talked freely and which revived his love of pre-socratic Greece, has left no trace in his writing.

When he set out for Italy in November he did not realize that he had received another terrible blow. On November 1 the Algerian rebellion had begun. Ferhat Abbas seemed timid to young Arabs and even Messali had less appeal. A group of Messali's young followers determined to act. They dared to think what was to French Algerians the unthinkable: the 1830 conquest was not permanent, Arab revolts had not ended in the nineteenth century and the Aurès mountains were fertile ground for freedom-fighters. This was the nucleus of the FLN (Front de Libération Nationale), the new fact in Algeria which Camus would have to face.

Camus could claim, correctly, that he had foreseen this danger and that he had spent twenty years exhorting French Algerians to make reforms before it was too late. But when the too late arrived he was slow to react. He thought this rebellion was another local outburst of violence and he worried about the repression it would provoke. He had no idea that he was confronted with a war of independence.

Earlier in the year he had published his third book of Algerian essays, *L'Eté*, written over a period of years. The writing is different from *L'Envers et l'Endroit* or *Noces* because Camus is looking back at the Algiers bay. Now he writes like a fluent essayist, now he lapses into a rather silly classicism. The best writing is in *Le Minotaure* where he uses the deliberately incomplete narrative which he had used in Tarrou's diary; the people of Oran are presented by a narrator who does not explain them.

The lyrical upsurge is still present and the dream of oneness inspires *Retour à Tipasa*. There can be no return, Camus knows, to the harmony which he felt as a youth when he swam near the Roman ruins. Yet Tipasa retains a joy which can still refresh the forty-year-old writer. Division comes from outside: from Europe and Hitler. Or rather Camus remains as ambiguous as in the murder scene of *L'Etranger*. The desert cacti are 'cruelly' as well as 'gloriously' innocent, while force and violence sit among the Algerian gods. Violence is part of the ballet and, if it erupts, it will destroy the harmony.

Yet as long as it can be checked by fraternity, measure and concise language Algeria can remain a fountainhead of innocence and creativity. The god of the wind is an artist: 'bearing only grains of sand this tough sculptor corrodes the contours and reshapes them. In the solitude of the desert he builds strange monuments to invisible pharaohs.'[16] Camus' own art must participate in this divine creation.

It is ironic that *L'Eté* was published in the very year of the rebellion. The FLN were about to shatter the ballet. *L'Eté* in turn foreshadows Camus' reaction: how could he give up *his* Algeria which was the most vital part of him and the source of his art?

In February 1955 he went to Algeria. After spending a few days with his mother he visited Orléansville which had just been ravaged by an earthquake and which Jean de Maisonseul was helping rebuild. As always Camus told Poncet how delighted he was to be in Algeria and how cold the Parisians were. The RUA gave a dinner for Camus who talked about the soccer matches he saw on Sundays in Paris. He was flattered by the number of old acquaintances who came to shake his hand and he kept telling them that he still felt a part of the RUA. Yet his old soccer-playing colleague, Paul Balazard, felt that Camus was an outsider who was happy to return for one evening. Preparing already to leave Algeria, Balazard felt that Camus understood nothing of the war which had not then touched Algiers.[17]

On returning to Paris Camus began work on an adaptation of Dino Buzzati's *Un Cas Intéressant*, a satire about businessmen and bureaucrats. Camus agreed to adapt it because the theme appealed to him and because he liked farce. He shortened Buzzati's scenes and heightened the parody of medical and business jargon. The adaptation was completed in two weeks and it confirmed Camus' feeling that he could write farces of his own. Buzzati, an Italian writer who was flattered at collaborating with Camus, came to Paris for the opening on March 12. He was surprised to discover that the author of *La Peste* looked more like a garage mechanic than a writer and that at the party following the première Camus shunned literary conversation and danced all evening.[18]

The summer brought fresh journeys. Camus went to Greece where he lectured on the theatre and then in July he and Maria Casarès slipped away to Italy. They drove slowly down the Adriatic coast which was 'littered with petrol stations, cafés, sports fields, camp grounds, open-air dance floors and outdoor cinemas where the white screen towered into the blue sky'.[19] This crowded anonymity suited them and they danced for hours in the evenings. One night they passed an outdoor cinema and saw Gary Cooper's cowboy hat with a full moon behind it. Then they turned inland and drove through the mountains around Siena. Camus talked about Piero della Francesca and as well as seeking out his paintings he kept saying that the Tuscany farmers whom they met looked like figures by Piero.

In September Camus met William Faulkner at a Gallimard reception. Camus felt that Faulkner had succeeded in writing modern tragedies whereas he himself had failed. He therefore wanted to adapt *Requiem for a Nun*, a half-novel and half-play which revolves around a long confession. The details had been arranged and Camus was ready to start work when Faulkner came to France on a visit. But the meeting at Gallimard produced no friendship and not even a real conversation. Camus had to wait a long time before he could shake hands with Faulkner and in the meantime he was mobbed by admirers. This was the kind of occasion he hated and by the time he met Faulkner he was too confused to say anything. Faulkner, who once admitted that he always felt like a 'treed coon' at parties, was equally taciturn and the two men turned away and did not meet again.

Meanwhile Camus realized that the Algerian rebellion was fast becoming a war. In November 1954 the Mendès government had sent troop reinforcements but had appointed as governor Jacques Soustelle who was considered pro-Arab. Soustelle imposed emergency rule and set about defeating the rebels by military action and by raising Arab living standards. Both policies failed. The FLN extended its grip on the countryside and the cycle of terrorism and repression which Camus so dreaded set in.

Camus had a shock when an Arab neighbour of his mother was stabbed. Alarmed, his mother and uncle came fleeing to France. They disliked it and soon returned to Algiers but the seed of fear for his mother was sown in Camus' mind. He discussed the war at length with his friends. Jeanne Sicard was working for René Pleven; perhaps the centrist politician Pleven could launch a campaign of reconciliation. But Pleven did nothing, confirming Camus' opinion of politicians. In Algiers Roblès was trying to bring together Europeans sympathetic to the Arab cause. He wanted Camus to help but, when he heard there were communists involved, Camus backed away.

By mid-1955 the conciliatory Mendès had been defeated in parliament, while the hatred between the French Algerians and the Arabs was growing more overt. At long last Algeria was to erupt. Many of the actors in the tragedy would be Camus' old acquaintances. Amar Ouzegane reappeared in different garb, Cheikh El Okbi had a small role, the PCA would at last resolve its contradictions and the Equipe would be reformed. In France Sartre, Jeanson and Claude Bourdet would support the rebels, while André Mandouze was busy in Algiers. Camus could not stand aside and in the autumn of 1955 he planned a double-pronged intervention: a campaign in Algiers on behalf of the European 'liberals' and a series of articles in *L'Express*.

In October *L'Express* changed from a weekly to a daily paper and announced that it would have as collaborators Mendès, Mauriac and Camus. Camus had already contributed articles on Algeria but he was now to write regular, twice-weekly editorials. For a brief moment he even considered becoming editor but then thought better of it. In his eyes *L'Express* should be the new *Combat* and, when he had written his editorials, he read them to the other journalists as he had done at the Liberation.

Mauriac was supposed to attract catholics, Camus lay left-wingers. As everyone at *L'Express* realized, the two men still disliked each other. Other acquaintances resurfaced: Jean Grenier wrote about painting and Alexandre Astruc about the cinema. Jean Daniel was a political correspondent and the old activist Robert Namia set the pages. Francis Jeanson denounced them as wishy-washy liberals and Pierre Hervé, who now broke with the PC, published his confessions in their columns. A photograph shows Camus in a *Combat*-like pose surrounded by the printers. To celebrate the opening there was a huge party thronged with celebrities who irritated Camus so much that he hid in his office and locked the door. *L'Express* had the backing of Jean-Louis Barrault, Madeleine Renaud and – for some unknown reason – Gina Lollobrigida.

Like *Combat, L'Express* could claim that its supporters were not wealthy and that it was owned by the team of journalists. Yet its principal owner, Jean-Jacques Servan-Schreiber, was quite unlike Pascal Pia. Practical and ambitious, Servan-Schreiber had precise goals for *L'Express*. An election was coming up and Mendès must win it. The policy of a negotiated peace in Algeria was part of Mendès' campaign and Camus' role was to popularize it. He was to play the part of the committed intellectual which he had always accepted, reluctantly, to play. *L'Express* criticized writers of the old *NRF* because they ignored social problems and it published Sartre's thoughts on the need for a working-class theatre.

Ever since *Combat* had supported Mendès during his 1945 resignation, Camus had partially exempted him from his distrust of politicians. Mendès called, in a Camusian manner, for a politics based on honesty; party intrigues must no longer dominate and there must be moral and political leadership. Mendès offered revival of the non-communist left and he was himself anti-communist which appealed to Camus. He summed up his attitude towards Mendès in a letter to Poncet who had encouraged him to enter *L'Express*: 'I don't think Mendès by himself will be able to settle everything. I see his limits and then too I'm not the man for parties or elections. But I also see (or think) there is a chance he will help to rebuild the nation economically and perhaps even morally.'[20] Much of Camus is in these sentences: the moral concern, the sense of limits and the scepticism.

Mendès condemned the drift towards war in Algeria and he promised negotiations and genuinely free elections. This was an issue he hoped to use against the centrist government which seemed to have no Algerian policy and against the right which was demanding that the FLN be crushed. Mendès did not envisage independence. 'Partnership' and 'reconciliation' are the words that recur in his speeches.

Just as Mendès was bolder than other non-communist politicians so Camus was slightly ahead of enlightened public opinion. In his articles he called for a cease-fire to be followed by negotiations which would lead to elections. This was a repetition of his 1930's and his 1945 stand. Reforms were to take place in a French context and a French presence was assumed – 'the French and the Arabs are condemned to live or to die together.'[21] In the '30's Camus had been lightyears ahead of French opinion; now Mendès' supporters had caught up with him. Of course Sartre and Jeanson were much more daring in recognizing the FLN as the legitimate spokesman of the Algerian people. Jeanson formed a network to help the FLN; Sartre sided with the rebels as a part of his private war with the French upper-classes.

Camus repeated his old lesson about primitive vitality: 'Algeria is dying, poisoned by hatred and injustice. She can only save herself if she submerges her hatred in an outburst of creative energy.' He also revealed his old ambiguity: with whom was the French government to negotiate? Camus did not make it clear because he would not come to grips with the FLN who were denying the inevitability of a French presence.

Other forces tugged at Camus. As Louis Germain's pupil, he could not believe that France was a racist country; it conflicted with the moral patriotism he had exalted during the Resistance. Then too he deeply distrusted Nasser. His articles are littered with phrases like 'other imperialisms', 'foreign schemings', 'pan-islamic dreams' and 'the mirage of an Arab empire'. Almost like Louis Bertrand, Camus, who had never followed Jean Grenier's advice to examine Eastern thought, spun fantasies of vast Arab intrigues. The next step was to link Cairo with Moscow and to argue that the FLN was being duped by pan-islamists and communists. Then Camus found a place in his conspiracy for Franco whom he accused of masquerading as an FLN supporter. Even the Americans were part of the anti-French plot. Camus called on young Arabs not to become 'soldiers of Nasser backed by Stalin's tanks or soldiers of Franco, prophet of Islam and the dollar'.[22] Nasser-phobia was rampant in Western Europe but it is hard not to see in these cobwebs of conspiracy the lurking fear of the French Algerian.

Camus reiterated the theme of *L'Homme Révolté*: violence was always harmful. Terrorism and repression simply reinforced each other and the only way to break the cycle was to open negotiations. That the French Algerians were colonizers whose very existence depended on exploitation and that the Arabs had been won over by the hard men of the FLN were truths which Camus could not believe. In late 1955 there was a difference between his editorials and the reports which Jean Daniel was sending from Algeria. 'Like them or dislike them,' writes Daniel, 'the FLN are heroes and martyrs for young Arabs.' Daniel took a grim view of the pieds-noirs: 'there is hatred, fear and distrust here; the violence has vastly increased racism.'[23] Although Daniel espoused the Camus-Mendès concept of reconciliation his articles cast doubt on it.

Camus plunged ahead and prepared for his visit to Algeria which was to reinforce the effort that his friends were making. In what he calls 'a new performance of the Equipe theatre',[24] Poncet, Miquel and the others were holding meetings with a group of Arabs. The meetings began as discussions on how to foster arabic drama but they soon passed to politics. Among the Arab members were Amar Ouzegane, who had been expelled from the PCA several years before, and a relative of his, Mohammed Lebjaoui.

Ouzegane and Lebjaoui were members of the FLN. Poncet, who had known Ouzegane since the '30's, suspected this but none of the Europeans knew that Ouzegane was in close touch with the FLN leadership. To the FLN the 'Friends of the Arab theatre' were a chance not to be missed. Privately Ouzegane was appalled at the Europeans' ignorance of things Arab but he guided the discussions around to the subjects of cease-fire and civilian truce. The notion of a civilian truce suited Camus who was following the meetings from Paris; it was a practical cause which would reverse the drift towards war. How the FLN viewed it is less clear. Ouzegane and Lebjaoui both claim the FLN took it seriously.[25] They did not believe it would work but, if it did, the FLN would gain political status as a responsible group capable of imposing a truce. If it did not work, then the European community would be split. The government's bad faith would be exposed and Camus' liberals would draw closer to the FLN.

One might be sceptical about the first part of this explanation because the FLN could not afford to stop using terror against civilians. Since they could not match the French army on the battlefield, terror was their main weapon. Even as they were discussing the truce with Camus' friends the FLN launched the slogan: 'Carry the war to the Europeans.' Such contradictions did not trouble the FLN which pursued both policies simultaneously and stressed whichever was the more convenient. If they could win Camus over or exploit his international fame, they would do so.

Camus and the Equipe were only one card in the FLN's pack. André Mandouze, the Témoignage Chrétien leader and expert on Saint Augustine, was now a professor at Algiers university. He had formed a group which supported independence and published FLN texts in a magazine called *Conscience Maghrébine*. To Mandouze's group the FLN had been more blunt: 'If there are arms to be borne, European, you must bear them with us.' Mandouze agreed. He himself took no part in the fighting but a doctor friend of his tended the FLN wounded.[26]

It was the issue of *La Peste* over again. A man cannot keep his hands clean, says Mandouze. He knew his were covered with blood but Algeria was no country for innocence. Mandouze wonders whether Camus' resolute moral purity might be linked with his agnosticism. Since there is no God to forgive, man must not sin. Mandouze's criticism complements Sartre's attack on *La Peste* but neither made any impression on Camus who reiterated that he would have no truck with terrorists. When he came to Algiers he refused to meet Mandouze who was, in his eyes, encouraging violence. But Camus could not escape the risk that he might be unable to act at all because he would not dirty his hands.

The two strands in Camus' strategy were supposed to interweave in January 1956. First there were elections which Mendès would win. He would implement 'a courageous revision of our North African policy'. Jean Daniel, who may have been more sceptical than he pretended, had just discovered in Algeria 'a most spectacular event – the birth of a powerful liberal movement'.[27] Camus' January visit would launch the appeal for a civilian truce which would be a catalyst for Mendès' bid to restore peace.

But the first strand unravelled when the election results became clear. Mendès' coalition, the Front Républicain, won 32% of the vote and was the largest group in the new parliament. But Mendès' party, the radicals, won only 12% so that the socialists with 15% were the largest body within the coalition. Their leader Guy Mollet was the natural choice for prime minister.

This disappointed Camus who was also appalled that the PC

had won 25% of the vote and the right-wing rabble-rouser, Pierre Poujade, 13%. 'Seven million Frenchmen have voted . . . for the death of freedom,' said Camus bitterly.[28] He was moved to another of his many meditations on decadence. His belief in a Char-like revival of lyricism and in a politics of revolt had waned and his *Express* articles are full of dire warnings:

'Death, as we all well know, lies in wait for our country.'
'The democracy of the mid-century is weak and corrupt.'
'Our élites have capitulated.'

Some of this was true. Louis Miquel claims that Camus foresaw already not merely the long Algerian war but the expulsion of the pieds-noirs. His fear that his Algeria was being destroyed gave him a Cassandra-like insight.

On January 18 he arrived in Algiers. The slaughter had not been checked by the elections and the previous week-end had seen ninety deaths. Meetings of the Poncet-Ouzegane group were scheduled to organize the public manifestation of Sunday, January 22, but at the first meeting Camus received another shock. An Arab schoolteacher berated him for not supporting the FLN and for seeking utopian solutions. Camus oscillated between despair and defiance, bewildered by this transformed Algiers. 'It's all over,' he said one minute; 'What do they want us to do – kiss their arses?' he asked the next. He grumbled that his friends had dragged him into a den of terrorists. 'I wonder what I'm doing here,' he lamented.[29]

The FLN supporters were equally unimpressed by Camus. He was 'far from understanding the real situation' and he was 'unsure what to propose'.[30] Nonetheless, they persisted in their attempt to gain at least a propaganda victory. At a second meeting Ouzegane and Lebjaoui hinted broadly that they could speak for the FLN and that they could guarantee the truce. According to Lebjaoui this delighted Camus who told him he could guarantee French acceptance. One wonders whether Camus was really so enthusiastic at consorting with the FLN but certainly he was being forced to recognize that he had little choice of interlocutors. When he arrived in Algiers he had talked of third forces, he had contacted Ferhat Abbas and he had arranged to meet Cheikh El Okbi. The reunions had shown him how strong was the FLN grip on the Arab population. His vagueness about Algeria was disappearing.

The next and even more brutal lesson came when he encountered the European population. At Algiers university Mandouze had to be guarded by his students; Camus fared scarcely better. The French government, which was or was not being honest, warned him that attempts would be made to kidnap him and advised him to cancel the public meeting. Poncet invited him to sleep at his house. Camus refused, resorting to male bravado: 'I'll get my Belcourt lads to protect me.' By now he knew that both Belcourt and Bab-el-Oued were bastions of right-wing European opinion. French Algerians had resorted to the virulent extremism which Camus had seen during the Popular Front and which was the colony's natural political temper. It was Rozis' posthumous victory over *Alger-Républicain.*

Reforms and truces, the Mediterranean medley and the French Algerian sense of measure seemed far distant when the meeting took place. It was held at the Cercle du Progrès, a hall built by the ulemas in the '30's and well-known to Camus. The fact that it had been chosen by the FLN was another sign of how Algeria had changed. Lebjaoui told Camus that, since the Cercle was near the Casbah, the FLN could guarantee security. Its militants were scattered through the hall while hundreds more ringed the building. The entrance tickets were changed at the last moment because of rumours that many had fallen into the hands of provocateurs.

These precautions proved necessary because thousands of pieds-noirs, led by a café-owner called Ortiz, turned out in a counter-demonstration. Ortiz was in part the kind of French Algerian Camus describes: unthinking, sport-loving, passionately attached to the Algerian soil; he was also devoid of measure, incapable of silence and rabidly racist. These qualities had made him a spokesman for the populist right and he now led the crowd in chants of 'Camus to the gallows' and 'Mendès must be shot'. Never had the weakness of the Equipe liberals been as apparent or the distance between Camus' Algeria and the real Algeria as great. Knowing that the Front Républicain had won the elections and fearing that the new prime minister – whether Mendès or Mollet – might make concessions to the Arabs, the French Algerians were demonstrating their resentment. Their onslaught on Camus foreshadowed the greeting they would offer Mollet two weeks later.

Inside the hall Camus was white. Making his usual effort of self-control he fought off his nervousness and took his place at the head table. He had not wanted to be the only speaker – 'I am not the law and the prophets, this is a joint action'[31] – but he was doomed to be the star. With him sat Roblès and De Maisonseul as well as protestant and catholic priests. There was a chair for Ferhat Abbas who arrived late and was thankfully embraced by Camus. The shouts of 'Camus to the gallows' could be heard in the hall but the security was impeccable. At least one of the FLN's goals was already realized. As Ouzegane puts it, 'Albert realized that a hidden force of enormous strength was standing behind the committee that had organized the meeting.'[32]

Camus was not a good public speaker and today he was worse than usual. White-faced and clenching his sheaf of papers he read, too rapidly to be heard. He repeated what he had said so often. He had 'lived the Algerian tragedy like a personal tragedy'. He had 'more doubts than certainties to express' but he was certain that nothing could come of violence. The civilian truce was self-evidently good and might be a step towards a broader compromise. Outside the shouts of 'Camus to the gallows' grew louder and inside the hall the listeners grew more tense. The nervous Camus stumbled through his last lines, sat down and told Roblès, who was acting as chairman, to wind up the meeting. There were a few short speeches and then the spectators filed out. The booing from Ortiz' men reached crescendo but the police and the FLN held firm and there was no fighting.

In retrospect it is hard to have any illusions about Camus' venture. The Cercle du Progrès was a frail bark of tolerance adrift on a sea of fury. It was manned not by Camus and the Equipe but by the FLN, which was about to realize a second goal and to demonstrate that the French authorities would not back a civilian truce.

Next day, January 23, Camus met Jacques Soustelle to discuss how a truce might be implemented. Soustelle was cordial but the governmental crisis in France made it impossible to take decisions. Camus returned to Paris and put on a brave front. An *Express* article entitled 'A step forward' described the Algiers meeting but not what was to happen next. On February 2 Camus published a glorious piece on Mozart: 'the true creator . . . excludes nothing and embraces all that is human.' It is another thinly-disguised plea for Algeria to overcome her divisions by asserting her primitive force. Camus reaffirms that the artist must 'accept his age and not sulk in his tent' yet his genius resides in his 'indestructible independence'.[33] This is a hint that Camus will not compromise with violence and may indeed return to his tent.

On February 6, when Prime Minister Mollet visited Algeria, the pieds-noirs welcomed him with well-rehearsed cries of 'Mollet to the gallows' and with showers of rotten tomatoes. He had named the liberal Catroux as governor-general but the pieds-noirs wanted to retain the ex-liberal Soustelle whom they had tamed. They forced Mollet to back down and, instead of Catroux, he named an old socialist friend, Robert Lacoste. This was precisely the kind of governmental weakness which Mendès and Camus had deplored. *L'Express* broke up. Servan-Schreiber saw that the battle was lost and the paper went back to being a weekly. Mauriac, who had been conducting another of his teasing, vitriolic controversies with right-wing catholics, broke with the Front Républicain.

Camus was the first to go and his Mozart piece turned out to be an adieu. As with *Combat*, he was half- and ashamedly-relieved. He could concentrate on *L'Exil et le Royaume* and on his Faulkner production. In any case the fragile bark of the truce had been sunk by Mollet. He received the truce committee led by Jean de Maisonseul but Mollet interrupted him as he began to speak. How much money did they have? How much European support? Mollet's questions were legitimate enough because the committee represented little except itself. Ouzegane and the other FLN-ites looked on with interest. Clearly the European liberals had no influence on the French government. No real split in France or Algeria could be accomplished. More propaganda gains might be made but 'carry the war to the Europeans' must remain the FLN strategy.

After this two-minute meeting Mollet refused to speak to the committee and Robert Lacoste, intent on winning back French Algerian opinion, threatened to silence them. Perhaps by coincidence De Maisonseul was arrested in May. Returning from Morocco, he carried a letter which he was supposed to deliver to an FLN sympathizer. He accepted the commission with the casual self-confidence of an aristocrat and then forgot to execute it. The letter was in his home when the police arrived, found it and arrested him. He was thrown into jail, as if to demonstrate that all liberals were traitors.

A set of decisions was being made about the Algerian War. In April 1956 Ferhat Abbas realized that third forces were doomed and fled to Cairo where the FLN later made him their official if powerless leader. The PCA, still a miniature of Algerian problems, entered the last phase of its tormented history. Banned in '55 for conducting its own maquis, it was partially rebuilt and went over to the FLN. The nationalists made the communists pay a high price for their decades of hesitation. PCA militants were to join FLN bands as individuals, the party was to have no contact with them and they were not to recruit. The PCA resolved the dilemma through which Camus had lived in '37 but it virtually ceased to exist.

Mollet's surrender to the French Algerians worsened the war. In April the Foreign Legion massacred hundreds of Arabs at Tebessa. In September the French forced a Moroccan plane to land in Algiers in flagrant violation of international law. It contained FLN leader Ahmed Ben Bella who was clapped into jail. At the same moment the battle of Algiers began. The paratroopers were victorious but at the cost of exacerbating Arab hatred. The FLN grew stronger and the desperate Guy Mollet, seeing that the war could not be won within Algeria, tried to win it from without by overthrowing Nasser. The Suez expedition of October '56 was, as far as France was concerned, an integral part of the Algerian War. In Tunis the FLN set up a national council, forerunner of a government in exile.

The non-communist left was fulfilling Camus' opinion of it but he himself had little to propose. When De Maisonseul was arrested, he wrote an angry letter to *Le Monde* calling for his release.[34] Yet he did not know why De Maisonseul had been imprisoned and, when Poncet explained what had happened, Camus was shocked. 'What imprudence,' he exclaimed. He was furious that De Maisonseul had had dealings with the FLN. Had he known this, Camus might not have written his letter to *Le Monde*.

Camus' position was complex. When he left *L'Express* he told Jean Daniel that he had decided to stop writing about Algeria. 'If we have no influence on either group,' he stated, 'we will have – for a while – to remain silent.'[35] This was the logical conclusion for the author of *L'Homme Révolté* to draw from the failure of the civilian truce. It brought on him the equally logical criticism that, by not speaking out, he was failing in his role as committed writer and prolonging the bloodshed he abhorred; Simone de Beauvoir spells this out with malicious glee. Yet Camus' decision was not a matter of logic.

The FLN had not achieved all it hoped with Camus. Mohammed Lebjaoui felt that Camus was sympathetic towards them. Sent to France to organize the French section of the guerrilla movement, Lebjaoui met Camus who dragged him off to his favourite couscous restaurant, the Hoggar. According to Lebjaoui, Camus embraced him when they parted and added, 'I live on the rue Madame, my home is yours.' Poncet and most of Camus' friends doubt this tale of fraternity. Either Camus still did not grasp that Lebjaoui was a high-ranking FLN-ite who was in France to spread terror or else he never made the offer.

Like Poncet, Miquel and the rest of the Equipe group, Camus realized that the FLN had orchestrated his performance but, contrary to what Ouzegane and Lebjaoui claim, he resented it. 'They made use of us,' says Poncet. 'They fooled us good and proper,' said Camus.[36] One part of his dilemma over the next years was that, although he believed – or usually had to believe – that the FLN was the only interlocutor, he refused to accept this. It was a matter of honesty, virility and blood; his whole identity was at stake.

At the moment he left *L'Express* he gave an interview to a group of Arab students. He ushered them courteously into his office and told them that, if they wished, they could sit on the carpet . . . They explained to him the grievances of the Arab population and he sympathized. He explained to them that he could not support any kind of violence. They in turn explained that the status quo involved a daily violence against Arabs; Camus replied that this violence should be corrected by reforms. Tempers rose. Camus used 'we' for French Algerians and 'you' for Arabs, which irritated them. Then he grew angry too: 'If the violence continues, duty – even for a man like me – will be to go back to one's community.'[37] He had already explained to Jean Daniel what he meant: 'Our community is made up of the non-Moslems of Algeria.'[38]

This was the other part of his dilemma. He might have been happier if he had rejoined his community as it really was. At least that would have cut through his ambiguity. But it would have meant betraying not merely *L'Homme Révolté* but his own personal Algeria. Yet *his* Algeria demanded that he consider himself a French Algerian. It was an impossible position.

Camus' real mood as he left *L'Express* was one of despair. 'I have come back from Algeria pretty despondent,' he wrote. 'What is happening confirms what I had thought. It is a personal tragedy for me.'[39] His gloom gave him new insights. He told his friends that, if allowed free rein, the pieds-noirs and the army would destroy democracy in France and impose their rule. The revolt of May 1958 when Algiers defied Paris proved that he was partially right. He was obsessed with the death of France and he continued to study Poujadism with fascinated horror.

Preoccupied with his Algeria, he grew angry with those who did not share his views. Sartre and Jeanson were beyond the pale: frivolous accomplices in murder. When Claude Bourdet and the *Le Monde* team began taking a pro-FLN line Camus dismissed them as armchair terrorists. Even Jean Daniel ceased to be a friend. 'I foresaw that one day or another we would disagree,' said Daniel.[40] He came to believe that only independence could end the violence and that he must support the FLN. This led to an estrangement with Camus who excommunicated erring friends. When a member of his truce committee, Maurice Perrin, began to show sympathy for the FLN Camus disowned him.

As in 1940 Camus was deaf to the charge that, by refusing to fight Hitler or the French paratroopers he was condoning their legal terrorism. That men must not succumb to the false determinism of history seemed to him as valid an argument as ever. But he discovered to his horror that the only people who agreed with him were right-wingers. Although the pieds-noirs considered him a traitor, right-wing French newspapers began praising him for his responsible moderation. 'I am becoming the favourite writer of *Le Figaro*,' he complained.

At this difficult moment he finished *La Chute*. He drafted the final version in February 1956 and the book was published in May. Unlike all the other books he had written, *La Chute* was not the result of years of planning. It began as one of the exile stories and it grew rapidly into a short novel. Camus rewrote it in the months when he was making his bid to halt the Algerian War. This demonstrates how his writer's impotence was caught up with Algeria. During the period when he hoped to save his Algeria he was able to write. Before and afterwards, when the cause was lost, he fell back into sterility. His self-imposed task as a writer was to recreate his sacred kingdom. But the war was destroying it and his attempt to save it with written and spoken words had failed. As the slaughter dragged on, Camus the artist simply ceased to be.

La Chute itself shows traces both of artistic sterility and of Camus' gloomy mood. By aesthetic alchemy he turned sterility into a virtue: Clamence has nothing to say – which allows him to say whatever he pleases and hence to talk endlessly. All Camus' writing is a 'pas de deux' with sterility; it is the secret that lies behind Meursault's 'I think' and behind La Peste's nilcient narrator. Clamence's volubility is a new variant. Camus' growing pessimism is demonstrated by the absence of the positive moral values which he had tried to offer in La Peste. Clamence offers duplicity within duplicity; Rieux' courage means nothing to him. This disconcerted many of Camus's readers who expected a message of hope. La Chute, which today seems one of Camus' best books, received a mixed reception. Simone de Beauvoir identified Clamence with Camus and interpreted the novel as a piece of self-criticism but this is silly. Clamence is one of Camus' many selves, a creation of the mid-1950's Camus.

Camus at last decided that he would do something about his marriage. Francine's health had improved and they had agreed that he should move out of the rue Madame and take a flat of his own.[41] He found one in the rue de Chanaleilles which was close to Gallimard and just around the corner from the rue Vaneau where Gide had lived. René Char lived in the same building whenever he was in Paris. Camus' two-room flat was small and his pied-noir friends said it reminded them of the hotel rooms he had taken in Algiers. The floor was strewn with books and there was little furniture except for a bed and a writing desk. Camus did not break completely with Francine and there was no legal separation. He returned to the rue Madame to visit the twins.

In the summer of '56 he escaped from the Algerian War into the theatre. He had finished his adaptation of Faulkner's Requiem for a Nun and he began to rehearse it. He had prowled the Paris theatres looking for actors. This was a quest he enjoyed and he spent much time in the little Left Bank theatres which he called 'pisspots'. Maria Casarès, who often accompanied him, could sit through a play without remembering a word but Camus never forgot a line or a gesture. Now he discovered a second outstanding actress. To play the difficult role of the tormented Temple Drake he settled on Catherine Sellers. Despite her surname, which was acquired during a brief marriage with an Englishman, Catherine came from a pied-noir family. She was the kind of actress Camus liked: powerful, excellent in tragic roles, a theatre not a cinema performer. She was flattered by Camus' invitation to play Temple and she worked well with him. The relationship of actress and director turned into a friendship which lasted intermittently for a few years.

Camus seemed born again during the rehearsals. He had shortened and simplified Faulkner's lines and he concentrated on Temple's confession. In Act 2, after Temple's black maidservant, Nancy, has been condemned to death for killing Temple's baby, the supposedly respectable Temple reveals that she had been a prostitute, that she had relished it, that she had planned to leave her husband and that Nancy had killed the baby in order to save it from misery and in order to prevent Temple's flight. Camus worked hard to render what he calls Faulkner's 'spiral of words':[42] the subordinate clauses, asides and sudden breaks which convey Temple's journey into her past. Camus and Catherine spent hours rehearsing it until she learned to express the way that Temple comes, tortuously and painfully, to realize the truth about her life.

Requiem opened on September 20 in the Mathurins theatre and it was an enormous success. It ran for two years and was highly praised by the critics. Catherine Sellers' performance was superb and her confession was much discussed. Faulkner intended it to have religious value. Temple's suffering is expiatory and Nancy redeems her by going to her death. Journalists teased Camus about this new flirtation with religion but he had not changed and *Requiem*'s conclusion did not appeal to him because it was a kind of salvation. No Nancy appears in *La Chute* at the end of Clamence's confession. In adapting *Requiem* Camus tried to make its reconciliation less divine and more human by strengthening the role of Temple's husband. Because Gowan demonstrates his fury at his wife's confession, the moment when he returns to embrace her has greater meaning. Their relationship is more important in Camus' adaptation than in Faulkner's original.

Spurred by his success Camus managed to complete the stories of *L'Exil et le Royaume* which were published in March 1957. They were coolly received and critics called them a minor work by a great writer. Camus, who had taken so long to finish them, found it almost impossible to start another book. His move to the rue de Chanaleilles had not worked. Once more he turned to the theatre and adapted Lopa de Vega's *Le Chevalier d'Olmedo*. Maria Casarès helped him with the medieval Spanish and made suggestions about the production.

Le Chevalier with its love stories, its comic valets, its jealous rivals and its complicated plot was performed at Angers on June 21. Camus praises Lopa de Vega because 'he nearly always sacrifices psychology for movement'.[43] This was pure theatre and Camus' adaptation emphasizes the switches of place and the comedy. But *Le Chevalier* received only a polite reception and few spectators shared Camus' view that the theatre of the Spanish Golden Age was a model for the twentieth century. *Caligula* was also performed at Angers but the actor who played the emperor was no Gerard Philipe and both Camus and his public were disappointed with the production.

Algeria dogged Camus and silence was no solution. When he had directed *Requiem* he had found an Arab actress to play the black maidservant Nancy. This spurred questions about the parallels between Southern Blacks and Algerian Arabs. Did Camus feel that the Arabs had the redemptive role which Faulkner ascribed to blacks? Camus refused to be drawn but when he published *Réflexions sur la Guillotine* in June 1957 the question of Algeria was raised again. If Camus devoted a long essay to challenging the death penalty, why did he not speak out on the slaughter in Algeria? Simone de Beauvoir reiterated that Camus was willing to protest only as long as his cause remained abstract. Camus could dismiss this but he was tormented by reports of the torture which the French army was practising in Algeria. The battle of Algiers was won with water-treatment and electric shocks and Jean Daniel wrote about the monotony of cruelty.

Camus was trapped between terrorists and torturers. He went off to the South of France with Maria Casarès and toured the towns where the medieval heretics, the Albigensians, had been persecuted by the church. Maria remembers Cordes 'with its high towers and the canopies over the beds'.[44] Camus returned to Paris facing the autumn, his Gallimard job which he had come to loathe and his continued inability to write.

It was now of all moments that he received the Nobel Prize. An official from the Swedish embassy called on him at Gallimard. Nothing was definite but the academy wished to know whether, if he were awarded the prize, he would accept. Tactfully the official inquired whether Camus would behave himself: would he agree to bring his wife and make a speech? Camus said yes but did not take the matter seriously. He told Suzanne Agnely about the visit and then forgot about it.

On October 16 the announcement was made. It was heard on the radio and relayed to Gallimard. Camus went white when he was told. He was astounded at the tidal wave of publicity that washed over him. Reporters flocked to the rue Madame. From Algiers came photographs of his mother in her tiny kitchen. Newspapers dug out anecdotes from the Resistance and quotations from *La Peste*. Suzanne Agnely worked overtime answering the hundreds of letters that poured in daily – two months later they were still running at seventy a day. Camus could not go to a café without being asked for his autograph. He hid in Michel Gallimard's flat and photographs show him turning away, as if to flee.

Yet he never considered refusing. The Nobel academicians had considered other French writers, two of whom were later crowned. Sartre dismissed the prize as a sack of potatoes and Beckett ignored it. Camus was perhaps more ambitious and he was certainly more cautious and more determined to be normal. Nobel prizes were an honour to be accepted; they might be inconvenient but it would be bizarre to refuse them. Camus had his own way of accepting. Another writer who might have been considered for the prize was André Malraux. One can imagine what Malraux would have made of it. His trip to Stockholm would have been another Long March, his speech to the academy a second appeal of June 18. Camus was less whole-hearted in his acceptance and his brand of theatre was more subdued. He went through the rituals of the Nobel Prize while laughing about them. He acted out his prizewinner's role with a dash of Bogart and the Playboy.

He had to rent a dinner-jacket. Invited to the Swedish embassy, he insisted that André Belamich, who was now translating Lorca for Gallimard, accompany him. Belamich had to rent a dinner-jacket too and Camus kept saying how ridiculous it was for men who had been to school in Bab-el-Oued to dress formally. He had told Francine that she was to travel with him. She set about buying long dresses and found out how one greeted ambassadors and princes.

Camus' humour faded as he saw the trap into which he had fallen. His numerous Parisian enemies realized what an easy target they had. Communist Pierre Daix repeated the *Action* cliché that Saint Camus was being awarded the prize because he was a bulwark for capitalism. This Camus could ignore but he was troubled by the frequent comments that he was too young and that Malraux would have been a better choice. Malraux would have been Camus' choice but the Swedish academy did not wish to crown a writer so closely identified with Gaullism. This irritated Malraux who did not hide his low opinion of Camus. Pascal Pia expressed his even lower opinion and this troubled Camus still more.

The Nobel academy had not helped by declaring that Camus had been selected because his work was 'deeply serious' and stressed 'action and nobility'; it demonstrated 'authentic moral commitment'. Once more the prison doors closed on Camus, moral conscience of his generation. Even worse were the innuendos. The Nobel Prize usually confirms the success of an artist whose work is complete. It fell like a tombstone on Camus who was wondering whether he would ever be able to write another book. Now he would have to write something worthy of a Nobel prize-winner. His artistic sterility was no secret in Saint-Germain where remarks about writers whose work was complete had a malicious ring.

The Nobel Prize was turning into a calvary for Camus and the worst torture was to be Algeria. The contrast between the Swedish academy's rhetoric and his refusal to condemn the French army was painful. 'Are you going to say anything about Algeria?' Jaussaud asked him. 'I wouldn't know what to say,' Camus replied. On December 7 he set off for Stockholm with his rented dinner-jacket and his retinue of courtiers. Photographers show him seated opposite Francine in the compartment. This was another painful twist because every

Left Bank gossip knew that their marriage had been reconstructed for the occasion. Michel Gallimard and his wife came along, which was natural. His American publishers also came but Maria Casarès was conspicuously absent. To the click of world-wide cameras the cavalcade headed north.[45]

By now Camus was nervously exhausted although he survived the dinners and congratulations, the pomp and the circumstance. The king of Sweden presented him with his award and Camus made a formal reply. He made further speeches in Stockholm and Uppsala but they were no more original. 'Beauty has never enslaved anyone,' he declared, calling for the artist to remain free of politics. Yet art must also demonstrate human solidarity, said Camus who was still wrestling with the problem of committed writing. Cassandra-Camus made an appearance and condemned 'a world threatened by collapse where grand inquisitors may well succeed in building their kingdoms on death'.[46]

For Camus himself the hour of the inquisitor had already struck. During a Stockholm press conference an Arab student spoke up. He denounced Camus as an agent of French repression no different from the paratroopers. When Camus tried to reply the youth shouted him down. Camus was furious but he kept his self-control. He insisted on replying and concluded with sentences that were flashed around the world:

'I have always condemned the use of terror. I must also condemn a terror which is practised blindly on the Algiers streets and which may any day strike down my mother or my family. I believe in justice but I will defend my mother before justice.'[47]

In context the sentence about justice and mother means: 'I condemn all terrorism, even yours, whose cause contains much justice.' At most it repeats what Camus had told the Arab students who visited him at *L'Express*: 'I cannot support the destruction of French Algeria because I am a French Algerian.' It certainly does not mean: 'I will fight on the side of the French against the FLN, although their cause is just.' Yet the reference to his mother had an emotional ring which Camus had avoided in his *L'Express* pieces. It was a cry of defiance. Camus was asserting that he was alive, that he was a pied-noir and that he had, if not a country and if not a community, then a mother. That he should introduce his mother was inevitable. More than an expression of concern for her safety, this was the last phase in a dialogue that ran through *L'Envers et l'Endroit*, *L'Etranger* and *La Peste*. His mother had remained remote from him when he was a child and he had plunged into indifference in order to reach her. At the age of seventeen he could have abandoned her but he had not. He would not now sacrifice her to please terrorists and upper-class Parisian intellectuals. His very silence on Algeria was a pale reflection of her lifelong silence. In her contemplation he had seen religious value – 'a God is present in her,' he had written. This was the stoical suffering which he was now undergoing and which seemed more precious than justice or even writing. More banally, Camus thought via myths. His introduction of his mother confirmed his sense that, if he had any identity at all, it was as a pied-noir. But he received this identity not from Ortiz or the paras but from her.

The press conference received far more publicity than the rest of the Nobel trip. The FLN, which still hoped to win Camus over or at least to neutralize him, had its Swedish student branch write him a letter of apology. This received much less publicity and the justice/mother placard was hung around Camus' neck. On his return from Sweden he fell into a nervous depression more severe than any he had known. He was so agitated that he could not sleep, much less write, and he could no longer shelter behind his indifference. He began to suffer from claustrophobia and had to rush out of cafés and trams. His tuberculosis flared up again and he had to take heavy doses of drugs. He oscillated between fever and lethargy, visited several doctors and dreamed of escaping to blue sea and calm. After *L'Homme Révolté* and the truce fiasco the Nobel Prize was the third blow which sent him reeling into sterility and despair.

By now he could hardly bear to open the newspaper and read the tales of horror from Algeria. Yet, appalling as it was, the war could and did grow worse. In February '58 the French airforce bombed the Tunisian village of Sakhiet which it considered an FLN base. By now the Mollet government had been defeated and the Fourth Republic was in the throes of a parliamentary crisis. The army and the pieds-noirs felt that the war could not be won without stronger leadership in Paris. Rumours of a right-wing coup grew, as did the rumours that De Gaulle would return.

Camus was feeling completely trapped. The winding streets of the Left Bank must have seemed to him as gloomy as the concentric canals of *La Chute*. He could not escape the role of celebrity into which 'the event' of the Nobel Prize had thrust him. In the glare of publicity Camus the man, the writer struggling to write and the French Algerian tormented by the war, ceased to exist. They were replaced by Camus the celebrity – handsome, successful and endowed with all the talents – from whom only miracles were expected. Surely he could end the Algerian war and write another novel like *La Peste*. Later he tried to thrust aside the public personage of Camus the celebrity and seek new roles as theatre director or novelist who lived in the countryside of southern France. But for the moment he was trapped in the solipsistic silence from which the Clamence of *La Chute* escapes by his windy monologues.

In the meantime the dispute about Algeria invaded even the publishing house. Gallimard had a right wing which was led by Roger Nimier, a novelist and polemicist who revived the far right's cult of vitriolic satire. 'You cannot rebuild France with Sartre's shoulders and Camus' lungs' was one of his sallies. After this Camus refused to speak to Nimier in the Gallimard corridors and had to be restrained from picking a fight with him. Nimier, who despised the FLN and glorified the French army, was no ally for Camus. Yet the Gallimard left was growing steadily more convinced that there must be negotiations with the rebels. They tried to avoid talking about it in Camus' presence but the atmosphere grew tense. Even the usually unpolitical Michel Gallimard had words of sympathy for the FLN. This appalled Camus: 'You will have blood on your hands,' he warned. He did not excommunicate Michel but he felt more alone than ever.[48]

Camus was not adhering rigidly to his code of silence. In December 1957 an FLN militant, Ben Saddok, was put on trial for killing a pro-French Arab. Many intellectuals spoke on his behalf and Sartre was a star witness. Simone de Beauvoir writes happily that 'Camus had refused to appear or even to send a message'.[49] Camus had sent a message to the court but had insisted that it not be made public. His sense of belonging to the French Algerian community would not allow him to offer public solidarity to a man he considered a terrorist. He also believed that discreet appeals were more likely to sway judges than highly-publicized manifestos. The practical strain in his character emerged again.

An old friend from the days of the Young Socialists, Yves Dechezelles, was a lawyer who defended the nationalist militants. He frequently asked Camus to write on behalf of his clients. Camus was usually willing to say that there was political oppression in Algeria which helped to explain their acts of violence; this enabled Dechezelles to obtain lighter sentences. Camus even testified for Amar Ouzegane when he was captured. Despite his dislike of Mollet he had enough contacts in the socialist party to obtain clemency in several cases. When Malraux entered the government in 1958 Camus appealed to him for the lives of three FLN militants who had been condemned to death.[50]

Camus made other political interventions. Louis Lecoin, an old anarchist who was conducting a campaign for the rights of conscientious objectors, found in Camus a supporter. He was not himself a conscientious objector, Camus wrote, keeping his usual distance, but he agreed it was a legitimate cause. His old pre-1939 pacifism led him to support the magazine *Témoins*, edited by Jean-Paul Samson who had deserted during World War One and had never returned to France. Like *Révolution Prolétarienne*, to which Camus went on contributing, *Témoins* was a syndicalist group. Both magazines were suspicious of the FLN which they considered intolerant and tyrannical.

At other times Camus fell back on his sense of being a pied-noir. In January 1958 he had a chance conversation with Max-Pol Fouchet who favoured independence. 'It's easy for you to say that,' said Camus reviving their twenty-five year-old argument, 'you're a Frenchman not a French Algerian.'[51] In a piece written slightly later Camus drew a portrait of Roblès that is a defiant apology for *his* pieds-noirs: 'Roblès is doubly Algerian because in him, as in so many of us, Spanish blood and Berber energy run together.' The myth of the Mediterranean medley overlaps with the myth of the new barbaric nation – Roblès' work depicts 'poor men's honour, tragic duty, bloody passions.'[52] Camus reiterated that the French Algerians were poor people misled by the few rich colons and betrayed by the French government. The pied-noir dislike of France, which ran alongside Camus' moral patriotism, led him to rebuke the French government for not executing reforms in Algeria. Yet he could not ignore the frenzied hatred which was boiling in French Algeria and which had been directed against him two years earlier. He was a pied-noir without a community and without a country. This was the ultimate ambiguity and it could only be lived in silence.*

Camus seemed to see religious value in his silence. 'When words lead men to dispose without a trace of remorse of other men's lives,' he wrote, 'silence is not a negative attitude.'[53] It was the prerogative of the absurd Christ on his cross. In *La Chute* Camus depicts a Christ who undergoes a Passion that has no meaning and who has nothing to say after God has forsaken him. 'To speak is to separate,' Camus had written.[54] If he spoke now he would separate French Algeria from the Arabs, whereas silence was an act of love which allowed him to remain faithful to the sterile Oran mountains. If he seemed to have turned his back on the war he participated in it by his suffering. He underwent his own useless, resentful passion.

Camus had never really been a man of politics, much less a man of action. He was a writer and a frustrated man of religion. The insoluble problem of French Algeria had allowed him to write superb novels where ambiguity and absurdity are merits just as they are burdens in the realm of politics. Now he had to live with the absence of reconciliation in Algeria just as he had lived with the absence of God.

He was still not ready to give up and in March 1958 he had a private meeting with De Gaulle. Despite the doubts he had shown during the *Combat* years Camus was starting to believe that De Gaulle might be the man to cut the Gordian knot of the war. De Gaulle talked of a federal solution: partial independence with control of defence to remain in Paris. However nothing could be done, he added, as long as the political parties pursued their selfish bickering. This classical piece of Gaullism did not fall on deaf ears.[55]

In April Camus returned to Algiers to visit his mother. He shunned publicity but had a long talk with an Arab friend, Mouloud Feraoun. Feraoun describes Camus' views: 'He feels an immense pity for those who are suffering but he knows that

*Conor Cruise O'Brien says that Camus returned to his 'tribe' which is partially true but by 1958 Camus had no 'tribe'.

298

pity and love are powerless against evil.'[56] As if to prove this, Camus' stay was marked by a private tragedy. Roblès' teenage son discovered a gun hidden in the house, took it out to play and shot himself. Camus sat up all night with the demented Roblès who was waiting to tell his wife what had happened.

On May 13 Camus' prophecy was realized when the paratroopers rebelled and threatened to invade Paris. Left-wing intellectuals talked of popular fronts to which Camus was adamantly opposed; he would tolerate no alliance with the communists. When De Gaulle announced that he was ready to assume the powers of the republic, Camus hesitated. He could hardly approve a coup d'état. Nonetheless he was so disgruntled with the left that he was prepared to give De Gaulle his chance. At a luncheon Michel Gallimard and a group of writers argued. Most were for strikes, popular fronts and resistance to De Gaulle. Camus said little but he would do nothing to oppose De Gaulle's return.[57] He would not, like François Mauriac, write panegyrics about De Gaulle. But he thought this was Algeria's last chance.

Camus even felt a flicker of hope. On May 16 Arabs demonstrated for De Gaulle and mingled with Europeans. Marc Lauriol, an old acquaintance of Robert Jaussaud and a member of parliament for Algeria, had presented a detailed plan for a partially independent, partially French Algeria. This pleased Camus and he praised Lauriol, in *Actuelles 3*. Published in June '58 *Actuelles 3* was a collection of Camus' writings on Algeria from the Kabylia series, through the *Combat* pieces to the *L'Express* articles. It was supposed to break Camus' silence and to make yet another plea for reconciliation. It failed dismally: Camus had nothing new to say and he convinced no one.

Charles Poncet, who came to Paris not long after *Actuelles 3* was published, noted how far Camus was removed from Algerian realities. He had to explain to Camus, who should surely have known, that the May 16 demonstrations were organized by the army in order to create a fiction of Arab support for the army's revolt. Moreover the Lauriol plan was nonsense because the two communities were hopelessly divided. Poncet discovered that Camus had forgotten everything he had learned in January 1956 and had started all over again to look for third forces and more sympathetic Arab interlocutors. Camus quickly relapsed into despair. He listened to Poncet in total silence and then said: 'Well, it's all over I suppose.'[58]

One may add a postscript to Camus' private Algerian war by comparing his views with those of three other writers: Albert Memmi who is Jewish and Tunisian, Jules Roy, a pied-noir and Mouloud Feraoun.

Memmi's *Portrait du Colonisé* was written as an answer to Camus and Memmi's Jewishness gave him an insight which Camus did not possess. Behind the supposed fraternization of Arabs and Europeans Memmi saw the implacable relationship of power. Whether he likes it or not, Memmi feels, Camus remains a colonizer who cannot bring about a reconciliation that would contradict the exploitation of colonial society. Left-wing colonizers are living an illusion of Mediterranean medleys and Spanish-Berber brotherhood. 'No one could doubt their generosity or their impotence,' writes Memmi, 'they live under the sign of a contradiction.'[59] Casting a cold eye on Camus' evolution he adds: 'driven to the wall the left-wing colonizer simply gives up . . . he realizes that the only thing he can do is remain silent . . . there are impossible historical situations and this is one of them'. Camus would have disagreed with this but his readers may not.

Jules Roy was a proud pied-noir from Rovigo and the kind of friend Camus liked: a man of action, a warrior. In 1943 Roy volunteered for the RAF. Later he volunteered for Indo-China, disagreed with the French government's policy and retired. He had met Camus at the Liberation and had been struck by Camus' sympathy for Arabs. The friendship was complementary: if Camus admired the man of action, Roy admired the writer and thinker. Roy published novels and poems but, when the war broke out, he awaited Camus' lead: 'I had complete confidence in his judgement and I relied on him to solve the Algerian problem.'[60]

After Camus' death Roy travelled to Algeria. Among the eucalyptus trees of Camus' birthplace, Mondovi, he saw gun emplacements; French soldiers rushed out in the night to fight the FLN. The brutality of the French army appalled Roy. He saw the camps into which Arab villagers were herded and he talked to men who had been tortured. Although he might refuse to admit it, Roy's *La Guerre d'Algérie* is a refutation of Camus' silence. 'I do not possess the calm certainty which allowed you to take a universal view of things,' writes Roy, 'I do not want to be a witness, I want to fight.'

A more cruel because more telling reply to Camus comes from Mouloud Feraoun whose diary may be the best book written about the Algerian War. Feraoun was not merely Camus' friend but also an assimilated Arab and a model of European-Arab fraternity. Yet the hard men of the FLN forced Feraoun to rethink. He realized that his supposed assimilation had been a sham: 'We took pleasure in deceiving our friends, the French, and we agreed to deceive ourselves.' Feraoun understood the difficulty of liberating oneself: 'All of us have to reach down into the depths of ourselves in order to find the strength we shall need to face our new existence.' He dislikes the FLN who are brutal and dictatorial, he knows they despise him and he wonders whether there will be a place for him in the new Algeria. Feraoun has lost his old identity and has not yet found a new one, but he refuses to turn back.

As if refuting Camus, he admits that violence can be fruitful: 'Terrorism has forced many of us to abandon our lethargy and our reluctance to think.' In his village men give up drinking and gambling and show a new pride. The armed struggle awakens in them an identity which was not previously present.

Much as he admired Camus, Feraoun thought little of his *Express* articles and paid only lip service to the civilian truce. Violence was not equal on both sides because Arab violence was a response to colonial oppression. The gulf between Feraoun and Camus is revealed in a page which Feraoun wrote in February 1956:

'Camus and Roblès are wrong in speaking out because they are stopping short. It would be a thousand times better if they kept quiet. For after all this country is called Algeria and its inhabitants Algerians. Are you Algerians my friends? If so your place is alongside the men who are fighting. Tell the French that this country is not theirs, that they have seized it by force. All else is lies and bad faith. Any other language is criminal.'[61]

Feraoun's response is all the more telling because it is not merely political and because the quality of the human experience in his diary is high. Unlike Camus he lived in Algeria and not in Paris. He was constantly in danger from the FLN and from the European right which murdered him in 1962. There is something self-indulgent about Camus' prophecies of disaster and his refusal to take sides. Yet when he fell silent he did not know the comfort which is, according to Memmi, the good colonizer's cowardly reward. In mid-1958 Camus was a broken man.

11

From Algeria to Amsterdam: Camus' Last Writing

As he experimented with his short stories in the mid-1950's Camus felt that there were in him a lot of different writers who were trying to get out. There was a Louis Guilloux-like writer of the working class and there was a Joseph Conrad-like teller of mysterious tales. Diversity is not usually a feature of Camus' art which is based on concision and repetition. But in his desperate quest to find a path that would lead him around his writing block Camus tried out several different narrative techniques.

Les Muets, a story about a group of barrel-makers who go on strike, lose their struggle and return sullenly to their jobs, depicts working-class life from the inside. Camus, who used laughingly to declare that *Les Muets* was an example of social realism, begins with a description of the work-shop and uses the technical vocabulary of barrel-making. He is good at depicting working-class psychology: the way that the inarticulate worker, Yvars, conceals his anger behind a stubborn silence. Then in *La Pierre qui pousse* Camus moves from Algeria to Brazil. The hero, D'Arrast, makes a journey through the Brazilian interior and participates in a macumba ceremony. The beginning of the story reminds one of *Heart of Darkness*: D'Arrast leaves behind the city, crosses a river during the night, is bewildered by a colony of Japanese and then loses himself amidst seas and forests.

Diversity is more apparent than real in *L'Exil et le Royaume*. The macumba ceremony turns out to be a banal mishmash of dance and drugs and when D'Arrast undergoes a genuine religious experience it is thoroughly Camusian: he helps a man to carry the sacred stone in an episode that is a variant on Christ carrying his cross. Behind all these stories are the few images that run through Camus' life and work: the dream of oneness, the Arab, the violence of the Algerian War. Three stories – *La*

Femme Adultère and *L'Hôte* as well as *Les Muets* deal explicitly with Algeria which they present as an unsolvable mystery.

Janine, the heroine of *La Femme Adultère*, goes into the desert and discovers the harmony which Camus had depicted in *La Mort Heureuse*:

'In the depths of the dry, cold night thousands of stars were formed and each sparkling icicle, detached from the rest, slid imperceptibly towards the horizon. Janine could not tear herself away from contemplating these drifting fires. She revolved with them and their immobile movement slowly reunited her with her deeper self.'[1]

This experience is linked with Janine's discovery of the Arabs whom Camus depicts more fully than ever before. They contemplate Janine and her husband: 'silent, emerging from nowhere they stared at the travellers'. Like so many French Algerian writers, Camus perceives Arabs as a remote enigmatic presence. As in Louis Bertrand, this presence can become a threat: 'silent and imperturbable the Arabs finally irritated Janine.' But her hostility contains a fascination and her mystical experience of the desert is a sublimation of the sexual attraction she feels for them. The Arabs live with the country whereas she has been living against it; they are authentic whereas she is not; their bodies have the lithe grace of dancers or soccer-players.

Camus does not develop this theme and after her moment of mystical-sexual harmony Janine returns to her staid, urban life. But Camus does indicate the violence that lurks behind the European-Arab relationship. Twice the Arab is compared with the tough French soldier; they are brothers and rivals who are doomed to destroy each other. Camus is pursuing at the deeper level of fiction the quest which he made as a journalist to explain and exorcize the Arab problem. But he merely reaffirms his feeling of helplessness. In *L'Hôte* the hero, Daru, is told to take charge of an Arab prisoner who has committed a murder. He hesitates, refusing either to take the Arab to prison or to side with him. Eventually he leaves the decision to the Arab who tramps off to prison.

The schoolmaster Daru is the good colonizer who gives the Arab food, hopes he will escape, invites him to repent and is angry with him for creating such a dilemma. The murder which the Arab has committed is a rather unsatisfactory substitute for

304

the FLN's revolt. Although this Arab is a common criminal, 'his face looks anxious and rebellious'. Footsteps around the house may signal a lurking band of guerrillas who want to rescue him. Certainly there is a threat to Daru: 'You have delivered up our brother, you will pay for it' – such is the message scrawled on his blackboard. Earlier the Arab had appealed to him: 'Come with us.' The literal meaning of the phrase is that the Arab wants the kindly Daru to accompany him to the prison and help him deal with the French officials. But like the 'my son' of *Le Malentendu* the phrase is deliberately ambiguous and has another meaning: 'support the cause of Arab revolt'.[2] This Daru will not do, so he is rejected by both communities and becomes, like Camus, a pied-noir without a country.

In these stories Camus' narrative technique is traditional. He tells his tale from the limited viewpoint of a character – Janine, Dora, Yvars – who is aware of his exile. But Camus' real task in the mid-1950's was to enter the exile's kingdom, to reconstruct the world from the exile's viewpoint. He had to devise new kinds of language that would enable him to depict the resentment, the artistic sterility and the nightmare of violence which were haunting him. The remaining two stories of *L'Exil* – *Jonas* and *Le Renégat* set out to do this.

Jonas begins as a satire of the Parisian artist but the parody of polite conversation, painting criticism and architecture jargon mirrors the inadequacy of language itself. Camus is demonstrating that intellectual language talks around its supposed subject. This offers the artist a new freedom: he can enjoy the duplicity of words. He can explore them even as he repeats that they have no meaning.

The language of *Jonas* falters when Camus starts to depict his writer's impotence. He touches on his marriage, his drinking and his need to seduce. But none of this is treated well because Camus no longer talks satirically around his subject and is not yet able to write directly about it. *Jonas* does, however, offer insights into the grimmer Camus of the mid-1950's. To shelter from the army of flatterers Jonas builds a fortress in the ceiling of his flat and withdraws into it to paint. But it soon turns into a dungeon of claustrophobic silence. Unable to create and wracked by his nerves Jonas falls into madness.

The deliberately hollow language of the first part of the story acts as a counterpoint to *Le Renégat*. Whereas *Jonas* employs circumlocution the missionary-narrator screams out his story from within. He has been sent to convert an African people who have their own religion based on cruelty and slavery. They imprison and torture him but he comes to worship them and tries to defend them against the French army.

At the outset the missionary reminds us that language is not to be trusted: 'order, an order, says the tongue, at the same time as it is speaking of something else.' The narrator's tongue has been cut out, signifying that language cannot explain or dominate. Yet he speaks in a different kind of language that is a torrent of emotion. A stage-monologue, *Le Renégat* is probably the best play Camus ever wrote. If delivered by a good actor this flood of hatred and fear would overwhelm an audience. *Le Renégat* baffled Camus' admirers because it depicts the horrors which he usually concealed behind indifferent heroes and incomplete narratives.

The story may be read as yet another comment on the Algerian War. The missionary, who wants to kill those who have sent him to Africa, is expressing the hostility which the French Algerians were demonstrating towards the French. The true rulers of Africa are the chosen, evil people who have mutilated the missionary. They massacre the Europeans because they are 'lords who want to be alone . . . to rule alone'. Might they not be advocates of Algerian independence? It would be foolish to interpret too precisely a monologue whose order lies in its irrationality but that very irrationality is an image of Camus' contradictions. The missionary sides with the barbarians although or because they are evil and yet he unwittingly helps the French whom he hates.

His emotions have their own coherence: 'I dreamed of absolute power, of making humanity bend its knee,' he exclaims, revelling in sado-masochism. Camus' values of freedom and honour are transmuted into their opposites; this is *La Peste* in reverse. *Le Renégat* offers a new kind of writing which is linked with sexual impotence – Don Juan's suppressed fear. The missionary's tongue is cut out because he tried to participate in rape. Only when symbolically castrated can he pour out his nightmare:

'Never had a god so possessed or enslaved me; my whole life, my days and nights, were devoted to him . . . almost every day I witnessed that impersonal evil act (the rape of women by the high priest) . . . I listened, my face rammed into the salt and dominated by the bestial shadows cast on the wall, to that long cry . . . My throat was dry, my head and stomach were wracked by a burning, sexless desire. Day after day went by, I could hardly tell them apart, they melted into that torrid heat.'[3]

In *Le Renégat* Camus broke out of his silence and depicted the anger which *Les Muets* had repressed. One is tempted to add that it scarcely mattered that Camus, the political journalist, had written so badly about the Algerian War; *Le Renégat* shows an insight into hatred which explains how the battle of Algiers could take place. But the missionary's monologue was too frenzied to be used in a longer work so Camus wrote a very different monologue which talked around his subject as *Jonas* had done.

La Chute is told by Jean-Baptiste Clamence, a lawyer who cultivated worthy causes, a man of virtue and a seducer. Clamence has given up all these things and has fled from Paris to Amsterdam where he waits in a dockside bar until an unwary listener turns up. Then Clamence seizes him and pours out a long confession. He talks of his many faults, of the occasion in Paris where he made no attempt to help a person who was drowning and of the stolen Van Eyck painting of judges which he has in his flat. The Amsterdam canals form the last of the many prisons in Camus' writing and Holland is an anti-Algeria. It has no sunshine or deserts; it is a land of crowds, fog and gin.

It is also the country of guilt because Clamence lives 'on the site of one of the greatest crimes in history' – the Nazi massacre of the Dutch Jews. This inspires him to confess that his every act of virtue had concealed a selfish motive; his goodness was no more than self-approbation and his kindness was merely a need to be liked.

The real contrast does not lie between innocence and guilt. Camus, who was an excellent theologian, repeats that, whereas innocence is a unity, guilt is a form of division which leaves man without any core of character, makes him subservient to others and forces him to realize that he is an 'other' to himself. Clamence's aim is to undermine the coherence of human character. A janitor's wife mourns her dead husband with noisy grief and then marries a rascal a month later. Does this prove she did not love her husband or that she loved the rascal? Neither or both, replies Clamence. Man is not wholly bad – that would be too easy – and his vicious acts may be prompted by good motives.

Clamence is a pessimistic moralist in the long French tradition that goes back to La Rochefoucauld and La Bruyère. Like them, he attributes all man's actions to egoism and then dissolves egoism itself. Unlike them, he does not aim at truth, merely at fresh layers of deceit. For Clamence is playing the role of the moralist as his wordy language will show. Camus, who undercuts Clamence's wordiness by his irony, is a true moralist and *La Chute* is a better if more pessimistic piece of moral thinking than *La Peste*.

Clamence is also a false actor. The theatre is one of 'the two places in the world where I feel innocent', he says adding that the other is the soccer field. But he does not make the journey into nothingness of which Maria Casarès speaks. Instead he takes shelter in his role as lawyer for widows and orphans. Even the supposed change in his character which occurs around the middle of the novel is a piece of duplicity. As the 'others', whether within or without, give up their admiration Clamence is forced to abandon his lawyer's role. This is accompanied by a change in his language. 'I am losing the thread of my remarks,' he complains, 'I no longer possess that clarity to which my friends paid such generous tribute.'

But his language does not really change and neither does he. He takes on the new role of a penitent who confesses his past sins. The relationship he creates with his listener is different from the fraternal bond which links actor and theatre-goer as they work together to create the play. The sadistic Clamence bludgeons the listener into submissive admiration and masochistic guilt, while he himself escapes from guilt by talking about it.

The trouble is that he can never escape completely so he is always in flight. 'I was running, running, always gratified and never satisfied,' he complains. Sexual triumphs leave him with no alternative but to attempt fresh seductions. His real fear is not guilt but the silence that awaits him if he ever finishes his confession. 'I haven't finished with all this, I must go on, it's hard to go on,' he tells us.

To escape from silence Clamence continues his monologue using fresh voices. For a moment he is Christ himself, the abandoned Christ who reappears so often in Camus' books. Then he is a false prophet – 'Elias without the messiah' – who invents new prayers and calls for public confessions. Giving way to his lust for power he becomes a pope in a concentration camp. At the end of the novel he is planning still more roles. If he has kept the stolen Van Eyck painting it is because it offers him in the future the parts of criminal and defendant. Meanwhile the listener has turned into another Clamence who could run through a similar series of roles. So the book could go on for ever.

The constant behind this parade of masks is Camus' awareness that Clamence is a false moralist and actor. He shows this by making Clamence qualify and criticize what he says like a frustrated cartesian – significantly Descartes' house in Amsterdam has been turned into a lunatic asylum. Yet there is nowhere to situate Camus' awareness and no narrator other than Clamence. The viewpoint is more remote than in any of Camus' other books.[4] In *L'Etranger* Meursault had spoken about the sea and in *La Peste* Rieux made statements which he modified until they contained some partial truths; but Clamence pontificates with abandon, knowing that he is lying and that his real aim is to affirm his existence by talking. His monologue is a 'spiral of words' which re-echo without any trace of Temple Drake's reconciliation.

The opening lines set the tone:

'Might I, dear sir, offer you my services without running the risk of intruding on you? I fear that you simply do not know how to make yourself understood by the worthy gorilla who presides over the destiny of this establishment . . . Unless you authorize me to plead your case he will never guess that you desire a glass of gin.'[5]

Whereas *L'Etranger* was written in the perfect tense, *La Chute* is full of conditionals and subjunctives. As if to demonstrate that he is inventing, Clamence invites his listener to invent the character of Clamence. He declaims like an actor and throws in asides like a story-teller. His tale is organized to protect him and to seduce the listener but the real organization comes from Camus' irony which scarcely changes throughout the book.

When Clamence drapes himself in his prophet's mantle near the end Camus lets him speak in an inflated rhetoric which is a variant on the opening lines:

'Was it not sadness that lay behind Christ's every act, the incurable melancholy of the man who heard through the night the voice of Rachel wailing for her little ones and refusing to be consoled? The lament rose through the long night, Rachel was calling for her children who had been killed for him and he was alone.'[6]

Rachel is yet another of the many mothers who lurk behind Camus' writing and she appears here to confirm that the break with the mother is the origin of division although the bond with the mother may be a kind of death. But Clamence inflates and dramatizes his anecdotes because silence is nipping at his heels. The Amsterdam landscape is 'negative' but Clamence has to talk about it. So rather than admitting that the water of the bay has no colour and cannot be described, he attributes to it 'the colour of dirty washing-water'.

All of Clamence's words depict only the silence which lies at the heart of Camus' novels. The world cannot be explained because it is empty. The absence of any narrator other than Clamence is an image of that emptiness just as his self-conscious monologue is a way of writing about it. *La Chute* is the method Camus devised to depict the painful, solipsistic state of mind into which the Algerian War had plunged him. His Algeria has vanished and has been replaced by Clamence's Amsterdam. Harmony has become division and innocence has turned into duplicity. *La Chute* is, despite the lack of redemption, a piece of religious writing where Camus reaffirms man's fallen state. More important, it is a superb novel written from the viewpoint of a world without men.

12

Death, Purgatory and a Little Justice

In June 1958 Camus escaped from the Algerian war and went to Greece with Maria Casarès. She was almost the only person who did not reproach him for his refusal to take sides. Remembering their conversations of 1944 she felt that he was making the hard rather than the easy decision and that he was being true to his contradictions. The bond between them had now turned into 'a close comradeship that we strove to create anew each day . . . he filled with his presence the places where I lived . . . my little flat, the Paris streets, even the countries I visited without him'.[1] Now that they had learned to live by the 75% rule their relationship was solid and the long periods of time when they could not be together did not weaken it. Camus was 'father, brother, lover and son', she says and her last word is well-chosen because Camus needed her strength.

In Greece he cheered up and shook off the gloom that had enveloped him in the months since the Nobel Prize and his Arab inquisitor. At Rhodes they ran into an old acquaintance, Father Bruckberger, and Camus noted gleefully that the Dominican was accompanied by a woman-friend. Then he and Maria went off on a boat rented by Michel Gallimard. Camus, who liked boats as much as he disliked planes, spent hours looking at the sea and the tiny, rocky islands that rose up all around them. This was a 'sun-drenched pilgrimage' which allowed him to re-immerse himself in the Mediterranean.[2] Maria was struck by his good humour. Their boat had a cook who was English and prepared abominable food. Camus used to laugh about it and he would wait until she was not looking and then throw his over-cooked chicken into the sea. Surrounded by people who liked him he relaxed, acquired a sun-tan and dreamed of staying on the boat for ever.

Back in France he had two projects, neither of them new. He

wanted a theatre of his own in Paris and a house in Provence near René Char. After years of labour he had finished his adaptation of Dostoevsky's *Les Possédés*. Now he wanted to produce it so he tried a second time to get the Récamier theatre. He was unsuccessful and after several more abortive attempts he resigned himself to putting on the play in the Théâtre Antoine which was not really suitable because it was on the boulevard and boulevard theatres were known for light works.

Moreover it did not answer his need for a theatre where he could stage a series of productions like the ones at Angers. He kept hoping that Malraux, now minister of culture, would help him with a subsidy. But the non-dialogue between Malraux and his old admirer continued. Malraux had a low opinion of Camus' plays and thought that Camus simply used the theatre as a way to meet young actresses. He had other plans for Camus whom he hoped to use as a spokesman for De Gaulle's Algerian policy.

Camus put some of his own money into the production of *Les Possédés* but he had saved most of his Nobel Prize money – approximately £20,000 – to buy his house in Provence. Francine and the twins were spending the summer in a rented house near L'Isle-sur-Sorgue and in August Camus joined them. They scoured the countryside looking at old farm-houses and when Francine, who now had a teaching job in Paris, returned in September Camus remained in Provence and continued to look. He enjoyed driving around the mountains looking at old houses but details of prices and plumbing bored him. He heard about a house in the village of Lourmarin, visited it and decided on the spot to buy it. When Francine came down from Paris she hesitated. The house was not at all what they had been considering; it was not very pretty and it stood on a street in the middle of the village. Camus, however, wanted to settle the matter so they bought their house, paying just under £10,000.

Lourmarin stands between Avignon and Aix and is about twenty miles from L'Isle-sur-Sorgue.[3] Today it is a week-end resort where the Marseilles middle class has second homes but in 1958 it was a remote mountain village and it had special meaning for Camus. Jean Grenier had visited Lourmarin in the 1920's and it had inspired him to explore the Mediterranean. Lourmarin was a medieval village with a stone fountain and a main street that was then called rue de l'Eglise and has now been renamed rue Albert Camus. It also boasted an old castle which Camus immediately noted down as a possible out-of-doors theatre. His house looked like most of the others on the street. It had the reddish-brown tiles characteristic of the region and was built on several different levels.

The previous owner had installed a bathroom and a kitchen and Camus, who had no particular ideas about how a country house ought to look, made few changes. He took a large upstairs room as his office and set about finding a gardener. The garden had fig-trees as well as roses and it smelt of rosemary and thyme. To tend it Camus found a man after his own heart. Frank Creac'h was a Breton who had mysteriously turned up in Lourmarin during the war. He was a conscientious objector and an anarchist who remained in Lourmarin because there were no army officers and no rich people. He and Camus held long conversations about treacherous politicians and arrogant priests. Camus, who considered him a friend rather than an employee, told Suzanne Agnely that Creac'h had done what few men did: he had gone his own way, avoiding offices and cities and refusing to work for a boss.

On his return to Paris that autumn Camus began collecting bits of second-hand furniture which he sent to Lourmarin. His old *Combat* friend Jacqueline Bernard met him one day in an antique shop and teased him about this sudden interest in possessions. A rather embarrassed Camus replied that he was buying a bed for his daughter Catherine. She was now fourteen years old and appreciated pretty things.[4]

His children were one reason why Camus was buying the house. Some of his friends feel that in mid-1958 he had decided to return to Francine but there is not much evidence of this. Camus planned to go to Lourmarin on his own during the school-year when Francine was in Paris and he did not intend to spend the entire summer holiday with her. He did intend the house to be one which his children could consider a family home. The moment he dreaded was fast arriving: soon they would be old enough to understand their parents' unsuccessful marriage. Camus wanted them to feel that he was not neglecting them and that they had a home where he lived with them. Photographs show him playing with Jean in the grass at Lourmarin. He took the children with him for walks and succeeded in inspiring them with his liking for Southern France.

A second reason for buying the house was his physical and mental health. His latest relapse had convinced him that Paris was killing him. He met Claude de Fréminville who had sat up with him during that night in 1937: 'It's pretty bad,' Camus told him, 'my lungs are rotten, still the same, it's bound to get me soon.'[5] Roblès listened to similar prophecies and thought that Camus did not have long to live. However, there is no reliable evidence that his tuberculosis was about to kill him. Certainly the Paris congestion aggravated his breathing so that some days he choked painfully at his Gallimard office. Paris also deepened his gloom so that he scarcely knew whether his claustrophobia came from tuberculosis or depression. He thus decided to winter in Lourmarin where the dry air and the solitude would be a better tonic than the drugs he hated.

Occasionally he told friends that he was abandoning Paris for Lourmarin and certainly he had less and less taste for his Gallimard work. But in reality Lourmarin and Paris made up yet another contradiction. He was continuing his attempts to obtain a theatre and, if he became a theatre director, he would have to spend most of the year in Paris. Certainly he would have to remain there in the winter and he would have to deal with bureaucrats and civil servants as well as with actors. Yet for the sake of the theatre he was willing to put up with this.

In the autumn of '58 he began rehearsals of *Les Possédés*. The part of Stepan Trofimovitch was to be played by a veteran French-Algerian actor called Pierre Blanchar whom Camus liked. To tease him Blanchar used to tell him that his eyes were greenish-blue which made him look un-Algerian; Camus would immediately lapse into his pied-noir accent and he and Blanchar would mystify the other actors by talking about Bab-el-Oued or the Casbah. Blanchar was pleased with Camus' style of directing because it allowed the actors so much freedom.[6] If they wanted to change a line of dialogue or a gesture Camus permitted them to do so. He encouraged them to invent their roles themselves and to feel their way into Dostoevsky's wild characters. To help them he organized readings and plied them with notes about Dostoevsky or nineteenth-century Russia. One day he brought vodka and records of Russian folk-songs to stimulate them. Blanchar felt that Camus would have liked to act himself but was afraid of becoming a curiosity. The popular press would have liked nothing better than a Nobel prizewinner turned actor.

Camus' adaptation of *Les Possédés* gave great importance to Stavrogin's confession which Dostoevsky had cut out of the novel but which appealed to Camus. Like Clamence, Stavrogin makes a false confession which is, as the priest Tikhon tells him, an outburst of contemptuous defiance rather than an attempt to understand himself or to rid himself of evil. According to Camus Stavrogin is 'incapable of loving but he suffers because of it, he wishes to believe but he cannot'.[7] Not that he is exactly like Clamence. Falsehood and truth are interwoven in Stavrogin who does not understand himself. The distinction is more clearly made in *La Chute* where Clamence's confession is patently false. Yet Stavrogin intrigues Camus because he tried, less successfully than Temple Drake, to delve into the part of himself which most men repress.

When *Les Possédés* opened on January 30, 1959 reviewers praised it, but coldly. Most felt that Camus had not resolved the problem of complexity. Determined to retain Dostoevsky's sense of mystery he had stranded the audience in the maze of subplots. The confession scene went well and Roger Blin was excellent as Tikhon. But Catherine Sellers was merely adequate in the role of Maria Lebyadkin which was not forceful enough to suit her. Malraux reserved a box for the first night and was accompanied by future prime minister Georges Pompidou. But after a successful first week the play attracted fewer spectators than Camus had hoped and it had a fairly short run. When it closed in July its backers lost their money and Malraux, asked to help out, remained aloof.

His one gesture towards Camus had been thoroughly unwelcome. In response to the accusations of torture by the French army Malraux offered to send France's three Nobel Prize laureates – Mauriac, Roger Martin du Gard and Camus – to conduct an investigation in Algeria. This bizarre suggestion, which may have been Malraux' revenge on his successful rivals, came to nothing but in any case Camus would not have accepted. His memories of the meeting in January 1956 were too painful.

In March 1959 he made a fleeting visit to Algiers because his mother was undergoing a hernia operation. He did not even try to phone Charles Poncet, having nothing new to say to him. Yet the Algerian situation changed in '59 because De Gaulle, brought back by the paras and the colons to keep Algeria French, began to move tortuously towards independence. Determined to end a war which could not be won, De Gaulle stated that Algeria could conduct a referendum to decide her own future.

The French army and the colons, who had no illusions about what would happen when the millions of Arabs went to the polls, began to prepare their first attempt to overthrow De Gaulle. Camus agreed with the concept of a referendum yet he did not want to believe that it would lead to independence. 'What will you do if there is a referendum?' asked a friend. 'I'll go to Algeria and campaign against independence in the newspapers,' replied Camus.[8] It was an aberration but Camus never stopped hoping that some miracle could save the Belcourt of his youth. He had gloomy discussions with De Fréminville who was now a broadcaster on Europe Un. The old question of the mother continued to unite them because Frémin's mother had refused, despite all her son's entreaties, to leave Oran. Frémin himself denounced the use of torture in his broadcasts and received several threatening letters. Yet this old champion of the Arab cause was as ready as Camus to believe in miracles of reconciliation.

Camus now published an introduction to a new edition of Jean Grenier's *Les Iles*.[9] His dealings with Grenier had grown more difficult in the last years because Grenier had started to realize that he was doomed to go down in history as Camus' master and his ironic humour was turning into bitterness. This distressed Camus who had indeed allotted to Grenier the role of benevolent master and did not want to face a sarcastic fellow-writer. He began to dread Grenier's visits to Gallimard and the innuendos by which Grenier suggested that Camus' reputation was exaggerated. He would have liked to put Grenier down on Suzanne Agnely's list of people who had to ask for an appointment but he could not.

His introduction may be read both as a sincere token of admiration and as yet another vindication of *his* Algeria. It contains the obligatory gibe at Sartre: each consciousness does not, says Camus, desire the death of all others; friendships are possible, as is the disciple-master relationship which he had enjoyed with Grenier. It is hard to imagine that this gave great pleasure to Grenier who would take a subtle revenge in his book on Camus where he disassociates himself from his pupil. Camus' aim was to demonstrate that *his* Algeria was the antithesis of Sartre's Paris. It was working-class, fraternal and innocent.

The preface was one of many contacts which Camus had with his youth during 1959. A fellow-student from Algiers university brought him photographs of Tipasa; Camus was delighted and pointed out his favourite spots.[10] An even older friend with whom he had played soccer in the Bab-el-Oued schoolyard visited him in Paris and was pleasantly surprised to discover that the celebrity Camus was eager to talk about the epic struggles they had conducted during the 12-2 lunchbreak. Camus' life seemed to be moving in the circle which had always eluded him for even Simone Hié turned up again. She had now returned from Switzerland to Paris where she was living with her husband as a registered addict. She came to see Camus because she hoped to find a job. Camus suggested that she should become a reader for Gallimard and she seemed pleased. She had lost none of her intelligence and Camus was sure she would be a good, intuitive judge of novels. He promised to introduce her to Michel Gallimard and to other editors and would certainly have done so had he not been killed.

In reality, Camus' life was not really moving in a circle or in any other harmonious form. There are two different interpretations of these last years. Most people at Gallimard feel that he was isolated and bitter, that the war had broken him and that he was finished as a writer. A few people point to Lourmarin and talk of rebirth. Either way Camus' death receives a form: it is a merciful end to an existence that had become a burnt-out case or it is a tragedy that interrupted a fresh promise. But death is no such artist. Camus was indeed trying to pull out of the depression which had paralysed him in the mid-'50's. Whether or not he would have succeeded is uncertain because tuberculosis, Paris and the FLN still lay in wait for him.

He was no closer to resolving the contradictions of his private life and he continued his casual affairs as well as his relationships with Francine and Maria Casarès. Friends noted that, as he grew older, the women he pursued grew younger. One of them has left an affectionate but perceptive portrait of him.[11]

Camus appears as a fictional character: a writer who has just won the Nobel Prize. He talks much of sincerity and he admits his own proclivity towards indifference. However he tells the heroine that she intrigues him and she is flattered. There is a touch of father and daughter: he encourages her to read *Moby Dick* and to work at her own writing. Camus is depicted as an actor who knows he is acting and as a Don Juan who does not lack feeling. Both of these were easy, pleasant roles which Camus enjoyed and where women could be convinced and yet remain unconvinced.

In mid-1959 he began a new relationship with a very attractive young woman whom he met in the Flore café on the Left Bank.[12] This might have turned into a serious affair if he had lived and it encouraged him to work at *Le Premier Homme* – a novel about his youth.

In May Camus left for Lourmarin. He discovered that it had a soccer team and that the players met regularly in a café. Camus joined them, discussed tactics with them and offered to help them raise money. He would have ended up manager of that team, says a friend. Camus used to eat in the village restaurant and he greeted everyone on the street. He also autographed his books whenever anyone asked. In a few weeks he had seduced the entire village.

Yet *Le Premier Homme* made no progress. Francine and the children came to join him but, although he enjoyed this family summer in Provence, he complained to René Char that his writing block would not go away. He was acutely aware that *La Chute* had been published more than three years before and he feared it would turn out to be his last novel. He returned to Paris at the end of the summer having written little but still determined not to give up.

In November he returned alone to Lourmarin. All he had done in Paris was to continue the seemingly endless negotiations for a theatre. At long last Malraux seemed willing to help but there was still nothing definite. *Les Possédés* began a tour of the provinces and Camus wrote frequently to the actors to encourage them. At long last *Le Premier Homme* was taking shape. His new woman friend joined him in December and he read her what he had done. He was revitalized, he reminisced about his youth and he was tremendously relieved that he was

318

able to write again. He phoned Suzanne Agnely to warn her that the first draft was ready to be typed. It was about a hundred pages and after it had been typed he intended to lengthen it, fleshing out the characters and plot.

Le Premier Homme was to depict Camus' early life in Algeria, his first marriage and his growth to manhood. It was also to speak of his father and of the pioneers who had created French Algeria. Unlike *Le Renégat* or *La Chute* it was not merely to explore violence or deception but was to depict that fountainhead of innocence which constituted Camus' Algeria. How he intended to shape this and how he intended to pit it against the amputated indifference which is the reverse side of his inspiration is not clear. Never finished and never published, *Le Premier Homme* is an image of the secrecy in which Camus lived.

One day Suzanne Agnely phoned him at Lourmarin to tell him that Gérard Philipe had died suddenly. Camus' first reaction was a twinge of his old jealousy: 'What's that to me,' he shouted down the phone. Maria Casarès had heard the news while on the stage and had remembered Rome and *La Chartreuse de Parme*. Camus' jealousy quickly turned to shock: sudden death always re-awakened in him his debate about whether a man should die lingeringly or without knowing it. Years before he had brooded on the death of his fellow-North African, Marcel Cerdan, who had been killed in a plane crash while flying to fight for the world middle-weight championship in New York.

Francine and the children came to Lourmarin for Christmas and she noted that, despite his relief at being able to work again, he had outbursts of gloom. One day he found an old trunk in the attic and half-jokingly told Catherine to lie down in it so that he could see what she looked like in a coffin. When she thought about it later Francine wondered whether he had premonitions of his death but one doubts this because such gallows humour was common with him.

Michel Gallimard arrived with his wife and daughter to spend the New Year and by now Camus was in good form. He was sure he could finish *Le Premier Homme* quickly and he had a message from Paris that Malraux was at last about to offer him a theatre. Francine and the children left on January 2 and Camus was supposed to take the train back to Paris on January 5. But when

Michel Gallimard suggested that he drive back with them Camus agreed. They planned to set off on Sunday, January 3, and to take two days over the trip.[13]

Camus hated cars as much as he hated planes. Robert Jaussaud remembers driving with Camus and another friend who was at the wheel. When they stopped for petrol Camus begged Jaussaud to take over the driving, terrified that their friend would kill the three of them. Michel Gallimard loved to drive and had a Facel Vega which could go fast. Camus disliked driving with Michel and he oscillated between begging him to go slowly and feeling that to admit his fear was unmasculine. A pied-noir should grit his teeth, a Spaniard should show more pride. He would probably have preferred to take the train back to Paris but this method allowed him to spend more time with Michel and Janine and it would also get him back to Paris a day earlier. That day he allotted to his new woman friend.

Despite his fears Camus was happy as they set off. On Sunday night they stopped near Mâcon in the Burgundy country where they enjoyed an excellent dinner. Next morning they set off early and had lunch at Sens. Camus' mood had not changed and he was eager to push on to Paris. Later, an investigation at the hotel where they lunched showed that among the four of them they had drunk only one bottle of wine. Michel and Camus were both gourmets but neither drank excessively. When they set off again Camus sat in the front with Michel, while Janine and her daughter were in the back. It was a grey day, the countryside around Sens is flat, the road was slightly damp and the traffic was light.

Near the village of Villeblevin the car swerved wildly and skidded towards the kerb. It smashed into a plane tree, careered on and smashed against a second tree. Camus was killed instantly. He was thrown up against the back of the car, his neck was broken and his skull fractured. Michel was tossed out of the car and lay alive in a pool of blood. Janine and Anne were projected into the middle of a field, shocked but with only slight injuries. Camus may have known for a second that they were going to crash but he could hardly have known that he was going to die. His face was unmarked except for a long scratch across his forehead.

Police, ambulances and other motorists flocked to the spot. Michel was rushed to hospital while Camus' body was left by the road. Near him was the attaché case containing the manuscript of *Le Premier Homme*. Janine and Anne were also taken to hospital, while Camus' body was carried to the town hall of Villeblevin.

Photographs of the car and its skid marks were used to reconstruct what had happened but the cause of the accident remained unclear. A witness reported that Michel had overtaken him at a speed of 90 m.p.h. Since Michel was known to be a fast driver this seemed plausible and he was widely blamed for the accident. His friends retorted by blaming the Facel Vega which may have broken an axle. It was never decided how such a terrible crash could have occurred on a peaceful, straight stretch of road.

The Villeblevin town hall, where Camus' body was laid, had greyish walls, naked light bulbs and was decorated only with a picture of De Gaulle and a bust of Marianne. The villagers swarmed around the door, reporters began to arrive and the news went out across the wires. Evening papers appeared with huge headlines and talked about the look of horror on Camus' face.

Suzanne Agnely rushed into a meeting to tell Gaston Gallimard what had happened. She left the stunned group, phoned Francine and went around to the rue Madame. Francine was distraught but she had to pull herself together because Malraux, who for once was acting quickly, provided her with an escort to Villeblevin. Accompanied by a police car with its siren blaring Francine arrived at the town hall. Camus' personal belongings were given to her, as was the attaché case which contained, as well as the manuscript of *Le Premier Homme*, his very explicit diary. Roblès arrived at the town hall and lifted up the sheet that covered Camus in order to look at his face. The long scratch on the forehead haunted Roblès for weeks. Jean Grenier came and broke into tears, while Camus' old *Combat* friend, Bloch-Michel, began helping Francine to plan the funeral. That night the people of Villeblevin conducted the traditional watch over the corpse.

Maria Casarès had got up that Monday morning feeling upset. She noticed that her hands were trembling and did not know why. Then she set out on the day's business. She visited a friend who was in hospital and then hurried to the radio headquarters where she was supposed to record a programme.

321

But there was a strike so she had to wait for hours until she was eventually told that she must return and do the broadcast another day. When she arrived home, exhausted, two friends were waiting: 'Albert is dead,' said one of them.

Casarès describes the next few days: 'I walked up and down my bedroom with its dark curtains and black carpets . . . the windows and shutters were all closed. I felt that I was walking on a planet that had been burned to cinders . . . I prowled around it like a she-wolf that is starving or ill.'[14] She did not go out for fear of seeing the headlines or worse still the picture of Camus with his mouth open in death and his eyes glazed. After the slaughter of the Spanish Civil War and the deaths of her mother and father this was a fresh blow and a new kind of exile. Whereas she had accompanied her father to his grave she had no official role now: 'I was forbidden to go to Camus.'

Villeblevin had gained international fame and crowds of people were present as Camus' body was placed in a coffin and carried out to a hearse. The procession set off for Lourmarin while Francine went on by train. Villeblevin was suddenly deserted. One friend who arrived late saw an empty town hall with a black cloth lying on the dusty floor. There was no other sign of Camus' life or death. On the journey to Lourmarin the weather was the same as it had been the day before. It was foggy with patches of pale sunlight and the winter countryside was dull and brown.

Advised by Robert Jaussaud, Francine had decided that Camus would not have wanted a religious burial, which seems correct. When the funeral took place on Wednesday, January 6 René Char, Louis Guilloux, Jules Roy, Gaston Gallimard and other friends attended. There were cypress trees in the graveyard and a pied-noir who was there felt that Lourmarin had the bare, arid look of Algeria. A simple tombstone was placed above the grave and it remains today, inscribed only with Camus' name and the dates of his birth and death. In Algeria a Mondovi street was named rue Albert Camus and it retained the name after independence. In Orléansville, which Jean de Maisonseul had helped rebuild after the earthquake, a Centre Albert Camus was constructed and it survived until the 1980 earthquake.

The rites of death were accompanied by world-wide publicity as well as by gossip and quarrels. The reporters who had discovered Camus' mother's kitchen at the time of the Nobel Prize went back and took fresh photographs of it. Others interviewed the Lourmarin villagers hoping for human interest stories. Frank Creac'h, who had helped to lay the coffin in its grave, was disgusted and came to blows with one zealous newspaperman. Michel Gallimard, who lingered for a week before dying in hospital, was much criticized and Jules Roy, never a man of tact, accused him of 'killing France's greatest writer'. The Gallimard family reacted by throwing Roy and his books out of the publishing house. Sensation-loving magazines wrote about the return train ticket which was found in Camus' pocket; speculation about his love-affairs helped spice the articles.

Unseemly as they were, such stories were a part of this death. Camus would, one feels, have had no patience with romantics who claimed that this sudden violent tragedy which struck him down while he was still young was the best possible death for the author of *L'Etranger*. Camus had always maintained that death was ugly, banal and shapeless. His own death confirmed this.

Francine was his literary and financial heir. She kept the Lourmarin house which remained, as Camus had hoped, a family home. Pierre Blanchar and the troupe were acting in *Les Possédés* in Northern France when they heard the news of Camus' death. After a vote they decided, correctly, that he would have wanted them to continue the tour. Several letters of encouragement which he had written to them arrived after his funeral. Simone de Beauvoir fought against the shock of the Villeblevin tragedy: after all, she felt, Camus was nothing to her. But as she and Sartre talked she forgot the 'saint Camus' she loathed and remembered the drinking-companion of the Liberation. The day after the funeral Sartre published an excellent article which retracts nothing he had said in the 1952 quarrel. But this time he stressed the value of Camus' moral thinking and of *La Chute* which best reveals it.[15] When Mouloud Feraoun heard the news in Algiers it seemed to him a part of the Algerian tragedy. A few weeks later he received his first threatening letter from right-wing Europeans.

Death continued to dog Camus' family and friends. His mother and his uncle died the same year. Not long afterwards his old friend Jeanne Sicard was killed in a car crash rather like his. The bloodshed in Algeria grew worse throughout the next two years. Three weeks after Camus' death *Les Possédés* was supposed to play in Algiers; the revolt of the barricades prevented it from opening. A year later came the revolt of the generals but this too was crushed by a De Gaulle who was now moving openly towards independence.

Camus' friends wanted to erect a monument to him at Tipasa so they found a Phoenician stone among the ruins and asked Bénisti to engrave it. Bénisti had to do the work in Algiers because the Tipasa site was periodically raked by machine-gun fire. Despairing of open rebellion, the pied-noirs formed the secret army, the OAS. As De Gaulle negotiated with the FLN the OAS tried, unsuccessfully, to assassinate him. The verb 'to plastic' entered the French language when the right-wing guerrillas carried the war to Paris. Sartre's flat was bombed so he ceased to be what Camus had called an armchair terrorist. An attempt to plastic Malraux blinded a little girl. Camus' worst fears about the French Algerians were realized as the OAS rampaged in Algiers, attacking Arabs, French soldiers and informers. 'They machine gun anything and blow up anything. The newspapers scarcely bother to mention it,' cried Feraoun.[16]

Camus' friends fared badly. Charlot had restarted his bookshop in Algiers, only to see it 'plasticked' now. A member of the truce committee, Maurice Perrin, was killed. In 1962 Feraoun and a group of Arabs were taken out of a meeting; the OAS squad lined them against a wall and massacred them. Camus' father had been killed in a war just after his birth; now his friends were dying in a war that surrounded his death. Louis Miquel left Algeria, Poncet and the other liberals took precautions.

In March '62 the Evian agreements were signed by the French government and the FLN. Immediately Bab-el-Oued erupted as the European working class declared war on the French army. The streets where Camus had walked to school were blocked by tanks. The Mediterranean values of measure and limits were forgotten as French Algeria began an orgy of destruction that was more Wagnerian than Camusian and that Camus would have called suicidal.

The OAS fired on Arabs, hoping to provoke reprisals which would force the French army to intervene. But, seeing that De Gaulle was determined not to intervene, the guerrillas decided to destroy French Algeria and send the country back to 1830. Buildings in central Algiers were destroyed with fire-bombs and the university library was set ablaze. In the '30's the university had been Camus' citadel of tolerance, now it was engulfed. In Oran, where in the spring of '41 he had taken heart from watching the young girls on the beach, OAS squads went into the Arab neighbourhoods and murdered at random.

Such was the Mediterranean summer of 1962. By now the pieds-noirs were leaving. The most sensible had gone long before and had taken their money with them. Now thousands more gathered on the harbours of Algiers and Oran, where they burned what they could not carry and drove their cars into the water. They piled into boats that carried them back across the 'Latin sea' to Marseilles, while the Arabs stood by and watched. Thirty-two years before Camus and Fouchet had watched the centenary celebrations; now French Algeria was no more.

One can only speculate what Camus would have made of all this. Certainly it would have appalled him. Certainly too the bloodshed of '62 seemed to confirm everything he had written and dimly suspected about Algeria. Yet one feels that he would not have watched in silence the flight of the pieds-noirs. Rightly or wrongly, he would have spoken if not for them then at least about them. Whether he would have criticized the FLN or De Gaulle is impossible to say. But, although one cannot imagine what he would have said, one cannot imagine that he would have looked on as French Algeria and his own past were destroyed.

Camus the Algerian grew more remote as Arab names replaced French names in Algiers. His Bab-el-Oued school was renamed after Emir Abd-el-Kader, who held out against the French in 1830. As the world in which Camus grew up vanished, the world he had created seemed to fade. The primitive, instinctive Camus was lost behind the image of a saint who had betrayed. Camus was no saint and he had certainly not betrayed but his Algerian essays became relics of a dead culture and his refusal to support the FLN alienated a generation of young Frenchmen.

The Algerian war had ended. The despairing pieds-noirs became surprisingly prosperous in France but Camus was stranded in a peculiar purgatory. He was still an enormously popular writer, whose apparently easy books were read by people who had never read Sartre. Abroad and especially in the United States his reputation as a moral thinker remains enormous. Yet in France and to a lesser extent throughout Europe his writing has been neglected by intellectuals and writers. In part this reflects the cultural change which took place around the time he died. Writing as writing replaced writing as commitment; a new novel and a new theatre, both of which Camus had anticipated, held sway. Suddenly *La Peste* seemed too solemn, too simple and too rhetorical.

This change, which is perhaps the most important cultural change that has taken place in post-war France, was foreshadowed in *L'Express* during precisely the months Camus wrote for it. Even as the editor, Servan-Schreiber, used Camus and Mauriac as committed intellectuals, he published a series of book-reviews by Alain Robbe-Grillet. Robbe-Grillet expounded a new aesthetic which undermined *L'Express'* raison d'être and was quite different from anything Sartre and Camus ever wrote. Dismissing Camus' attempt to find a link between art and the working class, Robbe-Grillet wrote: 'There must surely be parallels between the crisis of writing and the crisis of our society but it is highly unlikely that the solutions to these crises will be at all the same.'[17]

In an analysis reminiscent of the Sartre-Camus-Ponge debate of the early 1940's Robbe-Grillet argued for a novel that would abandon not merely description of society but also traditional psychology. The 'strangeness of things' must become the novelist's theme; he must depict the world in its partial comprehensibility. Robbe-Grillet was drawing on *La Nausée* and on the first half of *L'Etranger*. Later Camus and Sartre – the optimistic interpretation of *La Peste* and the Sartrian concept of situation – were to be set aside.

Robbe-Grillet and other French novelists have acknowledged their debt to Camus. The most striking feature of the French novel since 1960 has been the experimentation with different narrative forms and different points of view. All this draws on Camus who demonstrated in *L'Etranger* that a novel should not be recounted by a traditional, omniscient narrator and that the tale that the novelist tells is arbitrary and incomplete. Meursault's unusual 'I' opens the gate to the new novel of Robbe-Grillet, Michel Butor, Claude Simon and so many others. Like Camus they offer us fragments of a tale.

Camus helped to teach them that characters should not be rounded, that language is only occasionally accurate and that the work of art should contain its own explicit negation. The same is true of the theatre of Ionesco or Beckett which draws on the young Camus' attempt to convey 'the strangeness of things' on the stage with abrupt switches of mood, more direct audience participation and the like.

Yet this cultural change damaged the Camus who was depicted in the 1950's as the lay saint and the moral conscience of his generation. To younger readers, who ignored both the pessimistic reading of *La Peste* and Clamence's false monologue, Camus was an 'impostor' and a 'bleating boy scout'.[18] He incarnated the most banal strain in the French heritage – clarity and measure; he lost the battle against Sartre and was a wretched philosopher; his novels, especially *La Peste*, were facile and his language was not innovative. This view was widely held in the '60's and gained ground after '68. A few dissenters pointed out that Camus was a libertarian who consorted with conscientious objectors and refugees and who would have welcomed the explosion of May '68.[19] But the May militants, who tried to repoliticize French culture after 1968, had little use for a Camus whom they considered anti-communist, anti-FLN, moderate and traditional. Their concept of committed writing was different from his and their ideal was the global political revolution of which he was suspicious. The partial repoliticization of French culture served Camus no better than the previous depoliticization had done.

The revival of interest in his work has come in the late-'70's as the reaction against this partial repoliticization has grown stronger. When the Communists and the Socialists split in September 1977 Jean Daniel, who had hardly spoken to Camus in the years before his death, began mentioning him in the *Nouvel Observateur*. Camus' rejection of left-wing utopias suddenly seemed fruitful; his suspicion of the Communists was more correct than many had thought. A case for Camus has been made by the new philosophers who attack the left-wing culture of May '68, fear that a left-wing government would inevitably be tyrannical and call on the individual to resist at any cost the excessive power of the state. They consider Camus a forerunner: 'He proved quite simply that it was possible to resist, that courage and lucidity were possible.'[20] The new philosophers praise Camus for insisting that left-wing utopias are a pretext for bloodshed and, reversing the 1960's verdict, they award him a knock-out victory over Sartre whom they dismiss as too marxist, too pro-communist and too dogmatic. By contrast Camus is extolled as the man who resisted communist pressure during the Cold War and who attacked the Russian concentration camps in language that Solzhenitzyn would repeat.

This view of Camus is part of a complex mood that is present in Italy and Germany as well as in France and that should not be dismissed; it has helped shape the culture of the late 1970's. Yet one feels that Camus' new friends are serving him no better than his old enemies. Firstly their view is at best only partially correct. Camus himself would never have agreed that he merely resisted and would have refused to be branded as a non-left-winger. More important his new friends are emphasizing *L'Homme Révolté* which still seems his worst book.

It might be more fruitful to use the distance which separates us from Camus without using him. He was no more a '50's-style Solzhenitzyn than he was a lay saint. If one demands 'justice for Camus', as a recent *Le Monde* article has done,[21] then one must first admit that he was a man sorely tried by an impossible age. As one reads the polemics with D'Astier or with Sartre one wonders how Camus could have put up with these dreary, angry controversies. Small wonder that he preferred soccer and young actresses. Surely it would have been better to go away and finish *Le Premier Homme*. Camus' life was almost the opposite of what it seemed to his contemporaries: a long, losing battle against wars and terrorists, tuberculosis and fame. French Algeria, which had offered him instincts, passions and happiness, however tangled with poverty and prejudice, almost destroyed him along with itself.

The influence of that pernicious period is described by an Italian writer who attended revivals of *Caligula* and *Les Justes*. 'They are a great bellowing about Liberty, Prison, Discipline, Order, Organization, Bombing, Party and Terror,' he writes, 'they are full of terrorists who do nothing but gossip about their ever so sensitive souls.'[22] Such pseudo-heroic rhetoric plagues Camus' plays and much of his journalism. It tinges his essays and spoils whole chapters of *La Peste*. Yet the age of Dachau also taught him that heroic declarations were not enough because man is fundamentally evil or empty. Camus knew that God, not merely the marxist god, had failed and that he must investigate His absence. Camus' art lay in the 25% that he did not give Maria Casarès and in the edge of aloofness that he maintained even with his pied-noir friends. He mirrored the empty universe through his indifference.

This gives his novels a tragic note which is the main reason for their greatness. They are exceptional, if bleak, insights into the modern condition. One might also make a plea for the three volumes of Algerian essays because they are not relics of a dead culture but the raw material of Camus' inspiration. They depict his vision in its stark simplicity – the mother, the sea and the desert. But, because he knew that the oneness Algeria offered lay outside the human state, he had in his novels to create a darker, narrower kingdom populated by false priests, mad emperors, unsuccessful doctors, frustrated story-tellers, failed comedians, prisoners and exiles. These figures, depicted with irony, ambiguity and understatement continue to haunt us twenty years after the Villeblevin accident deprived us of their creator.

Notes and References

Chapter 1

1. This fact was unearthed by Herbert Lottman, whose biography, *Albert Camus* (Doubleday, New York 1979) is a treasure-house of facts on Camus' life.
2. Interview with Madame Albert Camus.
3. Emmanuel Roblès: *L'Action* (Soubiron, Algiers 1938) p. 53.
4. *Alger-Républicain* 9.10.38.
5. Albert Camus: *Journaux de Voyage* (Gallimard 1978) p. 36.
6. Quoted by Jean Daniel in *Le Refuge et la Source* (Grasset 1977) p. 154.
7. Louis Germain's handwritten account of AC's schooldays is contained in a copy of *Carnets* vol 1 deposited at the Bibliothèque Nationale.
8. Max-Pol Fouchet: *Un Jour Je m'en Souviens* (Mercure de France 1968) p. 12 and foll. Fouchet's book is considered by most of Camus' friends to be an unreliable account of their friendship and of Camus' adolescence. However, while many dates seem wrong, the general conclusions corroborate other sources.
9. Interview with Ernest Diaz.
10. Interview with Jean de Maisonseul.
11. AC: *La Mort Heureuse* p. 176.
12. Jean Grenier: *Albert Camus* (Gallimard 1968) p. 10 and foll.
13. AC: *Préface à L'Envers et l'Endroit, Oeuvres* (Pléiade) vol. 2 p. 6. Unless otherwise stated, all references to Camus' writing are to this two volume Pléiade edition, published 1962–65 and edited by Roger Quilliot.
14. Jean Grenier, op. cit., p. 94. Grenier was one of the first to correct the 'happy' view of Camus' childhood.
15. Robert Jaussaud states that this was a very common comment.
16. *Fragment Manuscrit pour 'Entre Oui et Non', Oeuvres* vol. 2. p. 1216. One should, of course, beware of using Camus' writing as biographical evidence but this was a first draft, discarded precisely because it was autobiographical.
17. *Le Premier Camus. Cahiers AC* no. 2 (Gallimard 1973) edited by Paul Viallaneix p. 207.
18. Interview with Louis Bénisti.
19. AC: *La Mort Heureuse Cahiers AC* no. 1 p. 140.
20. M.-P. Fouchet: *Les Bals au Bord de l'Océan* in *Et d'Eau Fraîche* (Baconnier Algiers 1936) p. 20.
21. Fouchet has recounted this trip in a novel – *La reconcontre de Santa-Cruz* (Grasset 1971). But it is also authentic – Interview with M.-P. Fouchet.
22. M.-P. Fouchet: *Un Jour Je m'en Souviens* p. 16.
23. AC to Fouchet in op. cit., p. 35.
24. Interview with Louis Bénisti.
26. *Ibid.*
26. *Un Jour Je m'en Souviens* p. 21.
27. Interview with Paul Raffi.

28. The comment was made by Paul Mathieu who taught Camus French literature – see *Oeuvres* vol. 2, p. 1173.
29. Gide's influence is apparent in the fragments of early writing which are contained in *AC Cahiers* no. 2. The retrospective view which Camus himself gives in *Rencontres avec André Gide* is distorted.
30. For a portrait of Grenier seen by another teacher see Jacques Heurgon: *Jeunesse de la Méditerranée* in *La Table Ronde* février 1960 p. 16.
31. Camus is at his most angelic in the preface which he wrote to *Les Iles* (Gallimard 1959). Grenier's book on Camus is part of his attempt to fight back: he sets an edge of distance between the two of them.
32. *Les Iles* op. cit., p. 39.
33. *Ibid* p. 87.
34. Jean Grenier: *Inspirations Méditerranéennes* (Gallimard 1941) p. 140.
35. Interview with Marguerite Dobrenn.
36. Jean Grenier: *Le Vent à Médina* in *Aguedal* octobre 1937 pp. 279–282.
37. *Sud* décembre 1931 p. 1.
38. This and all the other pieces discussed here are collected in *Le Premier Camus*.
39. Paul Mathieu op. cit. For Mathieu's view of the class see his article in *Revue de la Méditerranée* vol. 19. 1959 pp. 625–630.
40. Interview with André Belamich and Madame Jean Grenier.
41. Jeanne Delais: *l'Ami de Chaque Matin* (Grasset 1969) p. 120. This book gives a vivid but unreliable account of the Camus-De Fréminville friendship.
42. Claude De Fréminville: *Adolescences* (Poitiers 1933) p. 35.
43. De Fréminville to André Belamich in Jeanne Delais op cit., p. 155.
44. Not surprisingly Poirier's view of Camus is reciprocated by Camus' friends.
45. Jacques Heurgon op. cit., p. 17.
46. As might be expected, opinions of Simone and the marriage differ widely among Camus' friends. Herbert Lottman's account is a balanced synthesis of their views. Both Simone's second husband, Léon Cottenceau, and Jean de Maisonseul feel that Simone has been denigrated and – perhaps more important – underestimated.
47. Claude de Fréminville to André Belamich in Jeanne Delais op. cit., p. 133.
48. L. Roynet in *AC chez les Chrétiens* in *La Vie intellectuelle* août 1949 p. 339. Camus' comment is found in *Alger-Républicain* 11.11.1938.

Chapter 2

1. *Mercure de France* 15.10.1927 p. 426. The author, Henri D. Davray, was no fool, indeed he was a good journalist who wrote well about England.
2. *Alger-Républicain* 2.11.1938.
3. Paul Achard: *L'Homme de Mer* (Editions de France 1931) p. 151.
4. *Revue Algérienne* février 1937 p. 7.
5. *Alger-Républicain* 14.1.1939.
6. *Alger-Républicain* 9.2.1939.

7. Michael Hodent: *Des Charognards sur un Homme* (Editions Cafre Algiers 1939) p. 253.
8. *La Lutte Sociale* 31.7.1935.
9. Daniel's memoirs *Le Temps qui Reste* (Stock 1973) are a vivid account of growing up in French Algeria.
10. *La Lutte Sociale* 31.7.1935.
11. Emmanuel Sivan: *Communism and Nationalism in Algeria, 1920–1962*. Thesis presented at the Hebrew University of Jerusalem and consulted at the Institut Maurice Thorez in Paris. This is an authoritative analysis of the PCA and I have relied heavily on it. The best general book on pre-1939 Algeria is André Nouschi: *La Naissance du Nationalisme Algérien* (Editions du Minuit 1962) to which I am equally indebted.
12. As Herbert Lottman and others have shown, these biographical notes (*Biographie* p. XXIX of *Oeuvres* vol. 1) are riddled with errors. This is intriguing because Camus himself had supplied information to Roger Quilliot. But Camus wanted both to preserve his privacy and to present his life as he saw it in the 1950's.
13. Quoted by André Nouschi op. cit., p. 85 and foll.
14. Jules Roy: *La Guerre d'Algérie* (Julliard 1961) p. 9.
15. Amar Ouzegane: *Le Meilleur Combat* (Julliard 1962) p. 136. Ouzegane's interpretation of the PCA and of Camus' role in it is fascinating but should be approached with care. Ouzegane, who moved from the PCA to the FLN, has to justify his past.
16. Hadj Haman Abdelkader: *Zohra, la Femme du Mineur* (Editions du Monde Paris 1925). This is a good description of working-class Arab life.
17. Gabriel Audisio: *L'Opéra Fabuleux* Préface de Jules Roy (Julliard 1970) p. 12.
18. *Un Jour Je m'en Souviens* p. 25.
19. G. Audisio: *Jeunesse de la Méditerranée* (Gallimard 1935) p. 92.
20. *Sud* janvier 1932 p. 5.
21. Jean Daniel: *Le Refuge et la Source* p. 104.
22. Paul Achard op. cit., p. 6.
23. Paul Achard: *Salouetches* (Gallimard 1939) p. 19.
24. *Un Jour Je m'en Souviens* p. 41.
25. Louis Bertrand: *Le Livre de la Méditerranée* (Plon 1923) p. 331.
26. Louis Bertrand: *D'Alger la Romantique à Fez le Mystérieux* (Editions des Portiques 1930) p. 25.
27. Louis Bertrand: *Devant l'Islam* (Plon 1926) p. 29 and foll. If *Pépète* is Bertrand's best book, this is his most racist.
28. *Pépète et Balthazar* (Plon 1925 edition) p. 111.
29. Isabelle Eberhardt: *Dans l'Ombre Chaude de l'Islam* (Fasquelle 1908) p. 153.
30. Amar Ouzegane op. cit., p. 300.
31. Louis Bertrand: *Devant l'Islam* p. 29.
32. Paul Achard: *l'Homme de Mer* p. 63.
33. *Le Premier Camus* p. 223.
34. Robert Randau: *Les Colons* (Albin Michel 1926) p. 94.
35. *Ibid* p. 278. Randau wrote an article on Gambetta for *A-R* 6.12.1938.
36. G. Audisio: *Jeunesse de la Méditerranée* p. 10.

37. AC: *Noces Oeuvres* vol. 2, p. 60 and foll.
38. AC: *La Culture Indigène, Oeuvres* vol. 2, p. 1321.
39. Louis Bertrand: *Devant l'Islam* p. 141.

Chapter 3

1. Camus' sources and his knowledge of Augustine have been discussed by an Augustine expert: Paul Archambault in *Recherches Augustiniennes* vol. VI 1969, pp. 195–221.
2. *Entre Plotin et Saint-Augustin* is published in *Oeuvres* vol. 2 pp. 1220–1313.
3. *Le Premier Camus* p. 270.
4. *L'Ami de Chaque Matin* p. 138.
5. Interview with Paul Raffi.
6. AC to Jean Grenier [August '35, wrongly dated '34]. Jean Grenier op. cit., p. 45. See also AC's comments quoted by Lévi-Valensi and Abbou in *Fragments* vol. 1, p. 21.
7. *Biographie Oeuvres* vol. 1, p. 19. This is another piece of inaccurate information furnished by Camus to Roger Quilliot.
8. Interview with Pierre Salama who attended the meeting.
9. *Carnets* p. 56.
10. *La Mort Heureuse* p. 118.
11. This journey is described in great detail by Herbert Lottman, who draws on Léon Bourgeois' memories.
12. Interview with Marguerite Dobrenn.
13. *L'Ami de Chaque Matin* p. 173 and foll.
14. Preface to Louis Guilloux' *La Maison du Peuple*, reprinted in *Oeuvres* vol. 2, p. 1115.
15. Interview with Charles Poncet.
16. *La Lutte Sociale* 6.2.37 and 13.2.37.
17. *Jeune Méditerranée* no. 2 mai 37. This was the organ of the Maison de Culture.
18. *Echo d'Alger* 1.5.1937.
19. See J. Lévi-Valensi: *l'Engagement culturel* in *Revue des Lettres modernes AC* no. 5 pp. 84–106.
20. *La lutte Sociale* 15.3.36.
21. *A.-R.* 14.3.39.
22. *Révolte* has been published in *Oeuvres* vol. 1, pp. 410–438.
23. *Revue Algérienne* noël 36 p. 10. The full title of the Ben Jonson play is *Epicene or The Silent Woman*.
24. Paul Raffi: *Le Gala Pushkin* in *Revue Algérienne* avril 37 p. 14.
25. Jeanne Sicard: *Eschyle et la Méditerranée* in *Jeune Méditerranée* no. 1.
26. *Lutte Sociale* 26.6.37.
27. Interview with Robert Jaussaud.
28. Interview with Robert Namia.
29. Interview with Charles Poncet.
30. Ouzegane and Charles Poncet are at present trying to reconstruct this complex episode.

31. This is Emmanuel Sivan's opinion.
32. JG: *Essai sur l'Esprit de l'Orthodoxie* (Gallimard 38) p. 35.
33. Aldous Huxley: *Ends and Means* (Chatto and Windus London 1937) p. 9.
34. *Carnets* p. 68.
35. *Ibid* p. 75.
36. *Ibid*.
37. *AC to Jacques Heurgon 10.10.37*.
38. *AC to Gabriel Audisio* 3.12.37 quoted in *Oeuvres* vol. 2 p. 1319.
39. *La Maison devant le Monde Oeuvres* vol. 2, p. 1329.
40. *La Mort Heureuse* p. 130.
41. *Ibid* p. 132.
42. *Carnets* p. 47.
43. *Rivages* décembre 38, reprinted in *Oeuvres* vol. 2, p. 1329.
44. *Copeau, Seul Maître, Oeuvres* vol. 1, p. 1699.
45. *Echo d'Alger* 5.12.37.
46. *Echo d'Alger* 2.3.38.
47. *Alger-Républicain* 16, 18, 20, 30.3.39.

Chapter 4

1. Camus' political, although not literary articles have been published by Jacqueline Lévi-Valensi and André Abbou in the two volumes of *Fragments d'un combat, Cahiers AC 3* (Gallimard 1978). This is a superb edition because Lévi-Valensi and Abbou have amassed information on the paper as well as on Algerian history. This chapter draws heavily on their research. Unless otherwise stated, all articles discussed may be found in *Fragments*.
2. Pascal Pia in *Disque Vert* vol. 1, p. 425.
3. *Les Livres de l'Enfer du Seizième Siècle à Nos Jours* (Coulet et Faure 1978). A rare article on the recluse Pia appeared in *Le Monde* 16.6.1978.
4. See André Breton: *Flagrant Délit* (J.-J. Pauvert 1964) p. 8 and foll.
5. *Disque Vert* vol. 2, p. 84.
6. Interview with Paul Balazard.
7. *Alger-Républicain* 24.10.1938.
8. *Des Charognards sur un Homme* p. 13.
9. Mohammed Lebjaoui suggests that El Okbi was guilty in *Vérités sur la Révolution Algérienne* (Gallimard 1970) p. 150 and foll. Lévi-Valensi and Abbou disagree.
10. The article on Blanche Balain's poems appeared in *A-R* 11.10.1938 and the article on Huxley in *A-R* 9.11.38.
11. The Silone piece appeared in *A-R* 23.5.39 and is reprinted in *Oeuvres* vol. 2, p. 1397.
12. The Sartre articles appeared in *A-R* 20.10.38 and 12.3.39. They are reprinted in *Oeuvres* vol. 2, p. 1417 and foll.
13. Interview with Robert Jaussaud.
14. Interview with Robert Namia.
15. Interview with Blanche Balain.
16. *Carnets* vol. 1, p. 161 and foll.
17. E. Roblès: *Jeunesse d'Albert Camus* in *NRF* mars 1960 pp. 410–421.

18. Quoted in *Oeuvres* vol. 2, p. 1387.
19. It did return but not in the same format. At the end of the war the paper fell into the hands of the PCA and became its mouthpiece, which is an ironic postscriptum to the adventure of *Alger-Républicain*.

Chapter 5

1. Claude de Fréminville: *A la Vue de la Méditerranée* (Charlot Algiers 1938) no page numbers.
2. *L'Action* op. cit., p. 56.
3. AC: *Oeuvres* vol. 2, p. 20.
4. *Ibid* p. 38.
5. *Ibid* p. 24.
6. AC: *La Mort Heureuse Cahiers AC* no. 1 (Gallimard 1971) p. 25.
7. *Ibid* p. 191.
8. AC: *Oeuvres* vol. 2, p. 137.
9. Samuel Beckett: *Molloy* (Grove Press NY 1965) p. 133.
10. See Giorgio Bocca: *Il Terrorismo Italiano* (Rizzoli Milan 1978) p. 13.
11. AC interviewed by Jeanne Delpech in *Nouvelles Littéraires* 15.11.45 reproduced in *Oeuvres* vol. 2, p. 1426.
12. AC: *Oeuvres* vol. 1, p. 1127.
13. *Ibid* p. 1155.
14. The best study of *L'Etranger*'s narrative technique is by Brian T. Fitch: *Narration et Narrative dans l'Etranger* in *Autour de L'Etranger* (Lettres modernes 1968).
15. C. C. O'Brien: *Camus* (Fontana/Collins London 1970) p. 26 and foll.
16. Reproduced in *Oeuvres* vol. 1, p. 1928.
17. Interview with Claude Roy.

Chapter 6

1. See Herbert Lottman p. 183 and foll. and p. 217.
2. *Carnets* vol. 1 p. 205.
3. *Ibid* p. 206.
4. Interview with Pierre Salama, an Algerian friend who visited Camus in Clermont.
5. *A Albert Camus, ses Amis du Livre* (Gallimard 1962) p. 19.
6. *Ibid* p. 13.
7. Renée Bédarida: *Témoignage Chrétien* (Les editions ouvrières 1977) p. 43. She is quoting Fr. Chaillet, the founder of TC.
8. *A Albert Camus* p. 23.
9. *Carnets* vol. 1 p. 188 and foll.
10. Interview with Paul Balazard.
11. Nicola Chiaromonte: *La Résistance à l'Histoire Preuves* avril 1960 pp. 17–20.
12. This is a controversial point. Pierre Galindo passed on information from the port of Oran while Robert Namia was engaged in smuggling refugees

out of Algeria. Camus may have helped both of them but there is no evidence that he founded or belonged to a coherent group. See Herbert Lottman: p. 235 and foll.

13. *Tunisie Française* 25.1.41. and 24.5.41. The second article is reprinted in *Oeuvres* vol. 2, pp. 1465–1466 and the first was incorporated into *L'Eté*.
14. Interview with Guy Dumur.
15. *Carnets* vol. 2, p. 117.
16. *Ibid* p. 53.
17. *Ibid* p. 54.
18. *Ibid* p. 39.
19. *Carnets* vol. 1, p. 169.
20. Interview with Blanche Balain.
21. This is another controversial point. Yet Herbert Lottman too finds much evidence that Camus knew of Resistance movements and no evidence that he participated in them. See Herbert Lottman p. 269 and foll.
22. Herbert Lottman p. 271.
23. Roger Quilliot, editor of the Pléiade, and J.-C. Brisville, author of *Camus* (Gallimard 1959).
24. Interview with Charles Poncet and Yves Dechezelles.
25. *Sur une Philosophie de l'Expression de Brice Parain Oeuvres* vol. 2, pp. 1671–1682.
26. R.-L. Bruckberger: *Tu Finiras sur l'Échafaud* (Flammarion 1978) p. 339.
27. *Lettres à un Ami Allemand Oeuvres* vol. 2, p. 224.
28. *Ibid* p. 223.
29. R.-L. Bruckberger: *Une Image Radieuse* in *NRF* mars 1960 p. 515.
30. Jean Blanzat: *Première Rencontre* in *NRF* mars 1960 p. 427.
31. Dominque Aury: *Deux Places Vides NRF* mars 1960 p. 449.
32. R.-L. Bruckberger: *Tu Finiras sur l'Echafaud* p. 331.
33. R.-L. Bruckberger: *Une Image Radieuse* p. 520.
34. *Oeuvres* vol. 2, p. 1476.
35. Interview with Jacques Poirier.
36. Simone de Beauvoir: *La Force de l'Age* p. 576.
37. This is a common enough phenomenon but it would plague the Camus-Sartre relationship and spill over into their political dispute. See Chapter 8.
38. J.-P. Sartre: *Situations* vol. 1. (Gallimard 1947) p. 34.
39. J.-P. Sartre: *Explication de l'Etranger Cahiers du Sud* no. 253 pp. 189–206, reprinted in *Situations* vol. 1, pp. 100–121.
40. Ponge's letter on *Sisyphe* is reprinted in Francis Ponge: *Tome Premier* (Gallimard 1965) p. 205–210. Fragments of the Camus-Ponge correspondence are scattered through the Pléiade volumes.
41. Claude Bourdet: *L'Aventure Incertaine* (Stock 1973) p. 312 and foll. Bourdet repeated this to me in an interview and Pia corroborated it but Jacqueline Bernard insists that Camus began attending *Combat* meetings in autumn 1943. See also Herbert Lottman p. 302 and foll.
42. *Combat* no. 1 décembre 1941. An almost complete set of the clandestine *Combat* may be consulted at the Bibliothèque Nationale.
43. *Combat* no. 2 février 1942 p. 1.
44. This resentment crops up even today in discussions with ex-Resistants.

Camus may have seen in the PC's infiltrations a second version of the PCA's attempt to take over the Arab nationalists.

45. Herbert Lottman p. 316.
46. Maria Casarès: *Résidente Privilégiée* (Fayard 1980) p. 225.
47. *Ibid* p. 25.
48. Claude Roy quoted by Dussane: *Maria Casarès* (Calmann-Levy 1953) p. 38.
49. Maria Casarès op. cit., p. 232.
50. Simone de Beauvoir: *La Force de l'Age* p. 596.
51. Maria Casarès op. cit., p. 232.
52. Dussane op. cit., p. 42.
53. Quoted by MC op. cit., p. 230.

Chapter 7

1. Simone de Beauvoir: *La Force de l'Age* p. 610.
2. *Combat* 28.8.44. A complete set of *Combat* may be consulted at the Bibliothèque de l'Arsenal in Paris. Most but not all Camus' articles have been republished in *Oeuvres* vol. 2. Some were published by Camus himself in *Actuelles 1 and 3* while the others were collected by Roger Quilliot.
3. Ollivier collected most of his editorials in *Fausses sorties* (La Jeune Parque 1946) p. 15.
4. Interview with Albert Palle.
5. The second volume of Roy's memoirs, *Nous*, catches this note better than any other autobiography.
6. Simone de Beauvoir: *La Force des Choses* (Gallimard 1963) p. 28.
7. Maria Casarès: op. cit., p. 249.
8. Interview with Guy Dumur.
9. AC: *Carnets* vol. 2, pp. 120, 124, 135.
10. Simone de Beauvoir: *La Force des Choses* p. 65.
11. J.-P. Sartre: *Autobiographie à 70 ans, Nouvel Observateur* 7.7.75. p. 71.
12. Simone de Beauvoir op. cit., p. 65.
13. Jean Daniel: *Le Temps qui Reste* p. 37.
14. The first number of *Les TM* was delayed and did not appear until October '45. Camus' public reply came in his *Lettre au Directeur de La Nef*, reprinted in *Oeuvres* vol. 1, p. 1746.
15. Quoted by André Nouschi op. cit., p. 143.
16. *Cahiers de la Petite Dame Cahiers André Gide* no. 6 (Gallimard 1975) p. 350. This visit took place on April 24.
17. Jean Lacouture describes one such meeting – *André Malraux* (Seuil 1973) p. 325. Herbert Lottman adds to and corrects Lacouture – op. cit., p. 404.
18. Herbert Lottman p. 360.
19. Albert Ollivier: *Caligula d'Albert Camus* in *Les TM* no. 3. décembre 1945 pp. 574–576.
20. *Combat* 30.9.44.
21. Mauriac republished some of his editorials in *Le Bâillon dénoué* (Grasset 1945) p. 94 and foll.

22. *Le Libertaire* 20.1.1950.
23. Camus has described this trip in his *Journaux de Voyage* (Gallimard 1978). Herbert Lottman gives an exceptionally detailed account and draws on Patricia Blake's reminiscences – op. cit., p. 376 and foll.
24. This lecture has been published by the *Revue des Lettres Modernes Albert Camus 5* pp. 136–176. The best account of the atmosphere during the lecture is given by Justin O'Brien – *NRF* mars 1960 pp. 559–561.
25. *Carnets* vol. 2, p. 176.
26. *Ibid* p. 185. All the Camus-Sartre-Koestler meetings are also described by Simone de Beauvoir. By the time she wrote her memoirs she had about as much affection for Koestler as for Camus so she is not always objective.
27. Julien Green: *Journal 1928–58* (Plon 1961) p. 663. See also L. Roynet: *Albert Camus chez les Chrétiens* in *La Vie Intellectuelle* avril 1949 pp. 336–351.
28. *Carnets* p. 191.
29. This account of the break-up of *Combat* is based on a series of interviews. The participants do not agree about details or motives. Bloch-Michel is hard on Pia, Bourdet is hard on Camus. The most objective of them, Jacqueline Bernard, still feels that Pia's actions were inexplicable. Albert Palle reverses Pia's comment: *Combat* failed because it was an unreasonable paper in an all too reasonable world.
30. Interview with Auguste Anglès.

Chapter 8

1. AC: *La Peste Oeuvres* vol. 1, p. 1219.
2. See AC to Roland Barthes 11.1.55 *Oeuvres* vol. 1, p. 1973.
3. R.-L. Bruckberger: *Le Cheval de Troie* no. 2 août-septembre 1947 pp. 368–376.
4. AC: *Carnets* vol. 2, p. 202.
5. *Ibid* p. 199.
6. Interview with Louis Guilloux. See also Jean Grenier op. cit., p. 95 and foll.
7. Interview with Guy Dumur.
8. *Carnets* vol. 2, p. 216.
9. AC: *René Char Oeuvres* vol. 2, p. 1164.
10. *René Char* (Seghers 1951 collection Poètes d'aujourd'hui) p. 124.
11. Emmanuel d'Astier: *Arrachez la Victime aux Bourreaux Caliban* avril 1948 pp. 12–17. AC: *Réponse à E. d'Astier Caliban* juin 1948 reprinted in *Actuelles 1 Oeuvres* vol. 2, p. 356. E. d'Astier: *Ponce-Pilate chez les Bourreaux Action* 14.7.48.
12. *Carnets* vol. 2, p. 233.
13. *Ibid* p. 245.
14. Maria Casarès op. cit., p. 325.
15. *Ibid*
16. *Ibid* p. 326.
17. Herbert Lottman op. cit., p. 446.

18. *Carnets* pp. 252–254.
19. *Ibid* p. 252.
20. Interview with Jean Bloch-Michel.
21. Interview with Robert Jaussaud.
22. Quoted by Gilbert Walusinski: *Camus et les Groupes de Liaison Internationale La Quinzaine Littéraire* 1.3.79 pp. 21–24.
23. J.-L. Barrault: *Souvenirs pour Demain* (Seuil 1972) p. 203 and foll.
24. Gabriel Marcel: *L'Heure Théâtrale* (Plon 1959) p. 161.
25. AC: *Journaux de Voyage* p. 53 and foll.
26. *Carnets* vol. 2, p. 283.
27. Dussane op. cit., p. 71.
28. Simone de Beauvoir: *La Force des Choses* p. 214 and Guy Dumur: *La Table Ronde* février 1950 pp. 152–155.
29. *Carnets* vol. 2, p. 309.
30. Maria Casarès op. cit., p. 379.
31. Gilbert Walusinski op. cit., Conor Cruise O'Brien also raises the question of Camus' ties with the Congress for cultural freedom.
32. Herbert Lottman op. cit., p. 487.
33. *Carnets* vol. 2, p. 327.
34. Interview with Blanche Balain.
35. AC to René Char 27.2.51 quoted by Roger Quilliot *Oeuvres* vol. 2, p. 1627.
36. *Carnets* vol. 2, p. 345.
37. Herbert Lottman op. cit., p. 492.
38. AC: *L'Homme Révolté Oeuvres* vol. 2, p. 454.
39. This is another oversimplification of Hegel's thought. Hegel distinguishes between two kinds of morality – 'Moralität' which is individual and 'Sittlichkeit' which pertains to the community. There is an interplay between the two and man has no right to abandon 'Moralität' in order to promote 'Sittlichkeit' with bombs.
40. See the best defence of *L'Homme Révolté* – Germaine Brée: *Camus and Sartre, Crisis and Commitment* (Delacorte Press NY 1972).
41. Raymond Aron: *L'Opium des intellectuels* (Calmann-Lévy 1955) p. 64.
42. *Arts* 12.10.51 reprinted in André Breton: *Flagrant délit* (J.-J. Pauvert 1964) pp. 127–133. For Camus' reply see *Arts* 19.10.51 reprinted in *Oeuvres* vol. 2, pp. 731–736.
43. *Le Soleil Noir* février 1952 p. 25.
44. *La Force des Choses* p. 208.
45. *Ibid* p. 250.
46. *Ibid* p. 279.
47. *La Revue Dominicaine* février 1947 pp. 104–107 and novembre 1948 pp. 223–226.
48. Francis Jeanson: *Albert Camus ou l'Âme Révoltée* in *Les TM* mai 1952 p. 2082.
49. J.-P. Sartre: *Réponse à Albert Camus TM* août 1952 p. 335.
50. J.-P. Sartre: *Les Communistes et la Paix* in *TM* juillet 1952 p. 49.
51. Sartre's stalinist period did not last long. In 1956 he broke with the Communists when the USSR invaded Hungary. Then he drew closer to them again during the Algerian War. Many Anglo-Saxon observers

exaggerate the closeness of Sartre's ties to the French Communists. The PCF itself made no such mistake.

52. AC to Robert Jaussaud 12.9.1952 Archives of M. Robert Jaussaud.

Chapter 9

1. See Roger Quilliot's notes and documents which accompany Camus' adaptations – *Oeuvres* vol. 1, p. 1892. This volume contains all Camus' plays and his adaptations as well as his writings on the theatre.
2. *Oeuvres* vol. 1, p. 157.
3. *Ibid* p. 187.
4. This analysis owes much to what is the best book on Camus' theatre – Raymond Guy-Crosier: *Les Envers d'un Échec, Étude sur le Théâtre d'Albert Camus* (Lettres Modernes 1967).
5. Interview with Guy Dumur. Guy Dumur, today literary editor of *Le Nouvel Observateur*, met Camus in 1943 at Gallimard. Since he had lived in North Africa and was himself a TB patient he became friendly with Camus whose enthusiasm for the theatre he shared. He has written sympathetically about Camus' plays and adaptations.

Chapter 10

1. AC to Jean Gillibert 28.11.52 *Revue d'Histoire du Théâtre* décembre 1960 p. 356.
2. *Défense de la Liberté Franc-Tireur* décembre 1952 *Oeuvres* vol. 2 p. 777.
3. *Création et Liberté Oeuvres* vol. 2, p. 784.
4. AC: *La Postérité du Soleil* Photographies de Henriette Grindat. Itinéraire par René Char (Edwin Engelberts, Geneva 1965) no page numbers.
5. Herbert Lottman op. cit., p. 516.
6. AC to Pierre Berger 13.2.1953 *Oeuvres* vol 1, p. 2062.
7. *Oeuvres* vol. 1, p. 597.
8. *Ibid* p. 525.
9. *Ibid* p. 1718.
10. Herbert Lottman op. cit., p. 527.
11. Charles Baudelaire: *Journaux Intimes* (Crépet et Blin 1949) p. 95.
12. Maria Casarès op. cit., p. 122 and p. 239.
13. AC to Jean Gillibert 8.6.1954 *Revue d'Histoire du Théâtre* décembre 1960 p. 358.
14. Roger Quilliot reports this conversation – *Oeuvres* vol. 1, p. 2037.
15. Herbert Lottman op. cit., p. 538 and p. 541.
16. *L'Eté Oeuvres* vol. 2, p. 1835.
17. Interview with Paul Balazard.
18. Buzzati is quoted by Roger Quilliot in *Oeuvres* vol. 1, p. 1862.
19. Maria Casarès op. cit., p. 379.
20. AC to Charles Poncet 7.12.55 quoted by Yves Courrière in *La Guerre d'Algérie* vol 2 (Fayard 1969) p. 247.
21. *L'Express* 18.10.56. Most, although not all, these articles are reprinted in

Actuelles 3(Gallimard 1958). See also *Oeuvres* vol. 2, pp. 887–1018 and pp. 1839–1885.
22. *Oeuvres* vol. 2, p. 979. It is amusing to see Camus' dislike of the US resurface.
23. *L'Express* 10.11.55 and 28.12.55.
24. AC to Charles Poncet 28.12.55 Yves Courrière op. cit., p. 260.
25. See Amar Ouzegane – *Le Meilleur Combat* (Julliard 1962) and Mohammed Lebjaoui: *Vérités sur la Révolution Algérienne* (Gallimard 1970)
26. Interview with André Mandouze.
27. *L'Express* 13.10.55 and 28.12.55.
28. *L'Express* 6.1.56.
29. The Ouzegane-Lebjaoui version of the talks conflicts with the version given by Poncet and Roblès. See also Yves Courrière p. 247 and foll. and Herbert Lottman p. 568 and foll.
30. Mohammed Lebjaoui op. cit., p. 40.
31. AC to Charles Poncet 12.1.56 Yves Courrière p. 251.
32. Amar Ouzegane op. cit. p. 235.
33. *L'Express* 2.2.56.
34. Reprinted in *Oeuvres* vol. 2, p. 1003.
35. Jean Daniel: *Le Temps qui Reste* p. 250.
36. Quoted by Yves Courrière p. 263.
37. Ahmed Taleb Ibrahimi: *De la Décolonisation à la Révolution Culturelle* (Algiers 1973 Société nationale d'édition) p. 182.
38. *Le Temps qui Reste* p. 257.
39. AC to Jean Gillibert 10.2.1956 *Revue d'Histoire du Théâtre* décembre 1960 p. 359.
40. *Le Temps qui Reste* p. 78.
41. Herbert Lottman p. 579.
42. *Oeuvres* vol. 1, p. 1868.
43. *Ibid* p. 717.
44. Maria Casarès op. cit., p. 380.
45. See Herbert Lottman p. 607 and foll. For the Swedish academy's statement see *Oeuvres* vol. 2, p. 1893.
46. Camus' statements are reprinted in *Oeuvres* vol. 2, pp. 1071–1096.
47. Quoted in *Le Monde* 13.12.56 reprinted in *Oeuvres* vol. 2, p. 1882.
48. Interview with Robert Gallimard.
49. Simone de Beauvoir: *La Force des Choses* p. 404.
50. Interview with Yves Dechezelles.
51. Interview with Max-Pol Fouchet.
52. AC: *Notre Ami Roblès* in Simoun vol. 8, p. 30.
53. Quoted by Mouloud Feraoun in *Preuves* avril 1960 p. 23.
54. In *La Postérité du Soleil*.
55. De Gaulle seems to have kept no record of this conversation. Poncet, Bloch-Michel and others report what Camus told them.
56. Mouloud Feraoun: *Journal 1955–62* (Gallimard 1962) p. 44.
57. Interview with Guy Dumur.
58. This was the last time Camus and Poncet discussed the war at any length.
59. Albert Memmi: *Portrait du Colonisé* Préface de J.-P. Sartre (J.-J. Pauvert

1966) p. 35 and foll. The first extracts of this book were published in *Les TM* avril 1957.
60. Jules Roy: *La Guerre d'Algérie* (Julliard 1960) p. 14.
61. Mouloud Feraoun op. cit., p. 76.

Chapter 11

1. *L'Exil et le Royaume Oeuvres* vol. 1, p. 1574.
2. This is another round in the heavy-weight contest between Germaine Brée and Conor Cruise O'Brien. O'Brien interprets this phrase in the second sense and draws a stern rebuke from Brée. One tends to side with O'Brien except that the phrase is deliberately ambiguous.
3. *L'Exil et le Royaume Oeuvres* vol. 1, p. 1587.
4. This was pointed out at once by Maurice Blanchot: *La Confession Dédaigneuse NRF* no. 48 décembre 1956. pp. 1050–1056.
5. *La Chute Oeuvres* vol. 1, p. 1477.
6. *Ibid* p. 1533.

Chapter 12

1. Maria Casarès op. cit., p. 388.
2. *Ibid* p. 380. Herbert Lottman op. cit., p. 630.
3. See Herbert Lottman p. 634 and foll.
4. Interview with Jacqueline Bernard.
5. Jeanne Delais op. cit., p. 308.
6. Pierre Blanchar: *Camus, Artisan du Théâtre Simoun* no. 31 pp. 58–68.
7. *Oeuvres* vol. 1, p. 1866.
8. Interview with Jean Bloch-Michel.
9. Reprinted in *Oeuvres* vol. 2, pp. 1157–1161.
10. Interview with Pierre Salama and Emmanuel Diaz.
11. Adélaide Blasquez: *Mais que l'Amour d'un Grand Dieu* (Denoël 1968) p. 52 and foll.
12. This woman refuses categorically to allow her name to be mentioned. In general the women Camus loved display a reticence which the biographer finds both regrettable and admirable.
13. See Herbert Lottman p. 661 and foll.
14. Maria Casarès op. cit., p. 392.
15. J.-P. Sartre: *Albert Camus France-Observateur* 7.1.1960 reprinted in *Situations* IV pp. 126–129.
16. Mouloud Feraoun: *Lettres à ses Amis* (Seuil 1969) p. 192.
17. *L'Express* 20.12.1955.
18. See, for example, J.-J. Brochier: *Albert Camus, Philosophe pour Classes Terminales* (Balland 1970).
19. Maurice Joyeux: *L'Anarchie et la Révolte de la Jeunesse* (Costerman 1970).
20. Claudine et Jacques Broyelle: *Le Bonheur des Pierres* (Seuil 1978) p. 49.
21. Alberto Arbasino *La Repubblica* 16.11.78 p. 13.
22. Bertrand Poirot-Delpech: *Justice pour Camus Le Monde* 5.8.77 p. 11.

Short Bibliography

Camus' writings published in America in English translation

The Stranger (Knopf, 1946)
The Plague (Knopf, 1948)
The Rebel (Knopf, 1954)
The Myth of Sisyphus and Other Essays (Knopf, 1955)
The Fall (Knopf, 1957)
Exile and the Kingdom (Knopf, 1958)
Caligula and Three Other Plays (Knopf, 1958)
The Possessed (Knopf, 1960)
Resistance, Rebellion, and Death (Knopf, 1961)
Notebooks 1935–1942 (Knopf, 1963)
Notebooks 1942–1951 (Knopf, 1965)
Lyrical and Critical Essays (Knopf, 1968)
Neither Victim Nor Executioner (World Without War, 1968)
Cahiers I: A Happy Death (Knopf, 1972)
Cahiers II: Youthful Writings (Knopf, 1976)

Camus' writing in French
Most of Camus' writing is contained in the Pléiade edition of his work:
Théâtre, Récits, Nouvelles Préface par Jean Grenier, Textes établis et annotés par Roger Quilliot (Gallimard 1962) and *Essais* Introduction par R. Quilliot, Textes établis et annotés par R. Quilliot et L. Faucon (Gallimard 1965). Not included are:
Carnets, 2 volumes (Gallimard 1962 and 1964)
Journaux de Voyage (Gallimard 1978)
Cahiers Albert Camus – La Mort Heureuse, vol. 1, 1971, *Ecrits de Jeunesse*, vol. 2, 1973 and *Fragments d'un Combat*, vol. 3 1978. The Cahiers are directed by Jean-Claude Brisville, Roger Grenier, Roger Quilliot and Paul Viallaneix and published by Gallimard.
La Postérité du Soleil Photographies de Henriette Grindat. Itinéraire par René Char (Edwin Engelberts, Geneva 1965).

Books and articles on Camus
An enormous amount has been written on Camus and the present writer makes no pretence of having read all of it. The best bibliography of criticism on Camus is: *Albert Camus* (Calepins de bibliographie Lettres Modernes Paris 1972) edited by Brian T. Fitch and Peter C. Hoy. This is continually updated by Peter C. Hoy: *Carnet Bibliographique* in *Albert Camus Revue des Lettres Modernes* nos 2–9, edited by Brian T. Fitch. The following is a short list of the books which have proved most helpful to this study:

A *Albert Camus, ses Amis du Livre* (Gallimard 1962).
Albert Camus Revue des Lettres Modernes nos 1–9, 1968–1979, edited by Brian T. Fitch.
Germaine Brée: *Camus* (Rutgers University Press 1959); *Camus and Sartre, Crisis and Commitment* (Delacorte Press, New York 1972).
J.-C. Brisville: *Camus* (Gallimard 1959).
J.-J. Brochier: *Albert Camus, Philosophe pour Classes Terminales* (Balland 1970).
Camus (Collection Génies et Réalités, Hachette 1964).
Ilone Coombs: *Camus, Homme de Théâtre* (Nizet 1968).
Alain Costes: *Albert Camus ou la Parole Manquante* (Payot 1973).
John Cruickshank: *Albert Camus and the Literature of Revolt* (OUP 1959).
Raymond Guy-Crozier: *Les Envers d'un Échec, Étude sur le Théâtre d'Albert Camus* (Lettres Modernes 1967).
Jean Grenier: *Albert Camus* (Gallimard 1968).
Donald Lazere: *The Unique Creation of Albert Camus* (Yale University Press 1973).
Herbert Lottman: *Albert Camus, a Biography* (Doubleday, New York 1979).
C. C. O'Brien: *Camus* (Fontana/Collins London 1970).
Jean Onimus: *Camus* (Desclée de Brouwer, Bruges 1965).
Emmett Parker: *Albert Camus, the Artist in the Arena* (University of Wisconsin Press, Madison 1965).
Roger Quilliot: *La Mer et les Prisons, Essai sur Albert Camus* (Gallimard 1956).
Jean Sarocchi: *Camus* (Presses Universitaires de France 1968).
Philip Thody: *Albert Camus 1913–1960* (Macmillan, New York 1962).
Claude Treil: *L'Indifférence dans l'Oeuvre d'Albert Camus* (Editions Cosmos, Montreal, 1971).
Fred H. Willhoite: *Beyond Nihilism, Albert Camus' Contribution to Political Thought* (Louisiana State University Press, Baton Rouge, 1968).

The following magazines devoted special numbers to Camus after his death:
Nouvelle Revue Française March 1960.
Preuves April 1960.
Revue d'Histoire du Théâtre December 1960.
Révolution Prolétarienne February 1960.
Simoun (Oran) no 31 *Camus l'Algérien.*
La Table Ronde February 1960.
Témoins March 1960.

Books by or about French Algerians
Paul Achard: *L'Homme de Mer* (Editions de France 1931)
Gabriel Audisio: *Jeunesse de la Méditerranée* (Gallimard 1935); *L'Opéra Fabuleux* (Julliard 1970)
Louis Bertrand: *Pépète et Balthasar* (Plon 1925); *Devant l'Islam* (Plon 1926)
Pierre Beysade: *La Guerre d'Algérie* (Editions Planète 1968)
Yves Courrière: *La Guerre d'Algérie* 4 volumes (Fayard 1969)
Jacques Duchemin: *Histoire du FLN* (La Table Ronde 1962)
Aimé Dupuy: *L'Algérie dans les Lettres d'Expression Française* (Editions universitaires 1956)

Max-Pol Fouchet: *Un Jour Je m'en Souviens* (Mercure de France 1968); *Max-Pol Fouchet, Poètes d'Aujourd'hui* (Seghers 1964 edited by Jean Quéval) Claude De Fréminville: *A la Vue de la Méditerranée* (Charlot Algiers 1938); *Buñoz* (Charlot, Paris 1946)
Mouloud Feraoun: *Lettres à ses Amis* (Seuil 1969); *Journal 1955–1962* (Seuil 1962)
Ahmed Taleb Ibrahimi: *De la Décolonisation à la Révolution Culturelle* (Société nationale, Algiers, 1973)
Mohammed Lebjaoui: *Vérités sur la Révolution Algérienne* (Gallimard 1970)
Jacqueline Lévi-Valensi and André Abbou: *Notes et Introduction* to *Fragments d'un Combat* (Gallimard 1978)
André Nouschi: *La Naissance du Nationalisme Algérien* (Editions de minuit 1962)
Amar Ouzegane: *Le Meilleur Combat* (Julliard 1962)
Robert Randau: *Les Colons* (Albin-Michel 1926 edition)
Emmanuel Roblès: *L'Action* (Soubiron, Algiers, 1938)
Jules Roy: *La Guerre d'Algérie* (Julliard 1960)
Emmanuel Sivan: *Communism and Nationalism in Algeria (1920–1960)* Thesis for the Hebrew University of Jerusalem, consulted at the Institut Maurice Thorez.
The following newspapers and magazines, published in Algiers, are useful in studying the young Camus and pre-1939 Algeria:
Alger-Républicain and *Soir-Républicain* 1938–40.
Jeune Méditerranée, (April and May 1937).
Echo d'Alger
Lutte Sociale
Revue Algérienne 1936–39
Sud 1931–33.

Books about Camus' 'French' period
Raymond Aron: *L'Opium des Intellectuels* (Calmann-Lévy 1955)
Simone de Beauvoir: *Mémoires – Mémoires d'une Jeune Fille Rangée, La Force de l'Age* and *La Force des Choses* (Gallimard 1958–1963)
Claude Bourdet: *L'Aventure Incertaine* (Stock 1975)
R.-L. Bruckberger: *Tu Finiras sur l'Échafaud* (Flammarion 1978)
Maria Casarès: *Résidente Privilégiée* (Fayard 1980)
Jean Daniel: *Le Temps qui Reste* (Stock 1973); *Le Refuge et la Source* (Grasset 1977)
J.-M. Domenach: *Le Retour au Tragique* (Esprit 1963)
Marie Granet et Henri Michel: *Combat* (Presses universitaires de France 1977)
Arthur Koestler: *The Yogi and the Commissar* (Macmillan 1945); *The Invisible Writing* (Collins-Hamish Hamilton 1954)
Jean Grenier: *Les Iles* (Gallimard 1933); *Inspirations Méditerranéennes* (Gallimard 1941); *Essai sur l'Esprit de l'Orthodoxie* (Gallimard 1938)
Gabriel Marcel: *L'Heure Théâtrale* (Plon 1959)
Emmanuel Mounier: *L'Espoir des Désespérés* (Seuil 1953)
Albert Ollivier: *Fausses Sorties* (La Jeune Parque 1946)

Claude Roy: *Mémoires – Moi Je*, *Nous* and *Somme toute* (Gallimard 1969–1976)
J.-P. Sartre: *Situations* vol. 1–4 (Gallimard 1947–1964)

The following newspapers and magazines are useful for studying certain aspects of this period:
Action 1947–48.
Combat 1941–1948.
L'Express 1955–1956.
Témoins 1955–60.
Les Temps Modernes 1945–1952.

Index

Aron, Raymond, 221, 222, 254, 257
Artaud, Antonin, 261 and n., 263–5
Article 330, L' (Courteline), 88, 102
Asphyxie, L' (Leduc), 234
Astruc, Alexandre, 201 and n., 221, 227n., 277
Audisio, Gabriel, 68, 69, 97, 100
Augustine, St., 64, 65, 163, 177, 181, 219, 276, 281; Camus' treatise on, 71–3
Auribeau labourers, trial of the, 115–17
Aymés, Marcel, 256

Bab-el-Oued, 24; grammar school, 12, 16–17, 31, 36–7, 325; fighting in (1962), 324
Bakunin, Mikhail, 249, 253
Balain, Blanche, 99–100, 121, 124, 125, 165, 172, 174–5, 248
Balazard, Paul, 112, 125, 170, 275
Barrault, Jean-Louis, 178, 233, 242, 261, 263, 265, 278
Barthes, Roland, 228, 229
Baudelaire, Charles Pierre, 37, 41, 248, 249, 272
Beauvoir, Simone de, 170, 177, 184, 194, 195, 198, 204–6, 258, 287, 291, 296–7, 323; on Camus, 182–3, 183n.; and *Combat*, 200, 201, 221; on *Caligula*, 211; and *Les Justes*, 244; and *La Chute*, 289
Beckett, Samuel, 6, 151, 157, 263, 292, 327
Belamich, André, 36–9, 43, 78, 86, 293
Belcourt, Camus' youth in, 10, 12–15, 27
Bell, Marie, 181
Ben Badis, 57, 58
Ben Bella, Ahmed, 286
Ben Saddock, trial of, 296
Bénisti, Louis, 23, 26–9, 35, 36, 38, 63, 72, 75, 78, 82, 93, 165, 167, 202, 204; work for Camus' theatre, 87, 88; and *Alger-Républicain*, 105; designs monument to Camus, 324
Berbers, the, 47

Bergson, Henri, 32, 35, 72
Berlin congress for cultural freedom (1950), 246
Bernanos, Georges, 180
Bernard, Jacqueline, 188, 189, 196, 219, 220, 222, 313
Bertrand, Louis, and the influence of his writings, 64–9; and the Arabs, 64–6, 160, 279, 304
Blake, Patricia, 216
Blanchar, Pierre, 314, 323
Blin, Roger, 315
Bloch-Michel, Jean, 200, 213, 222, 241, 321
Blum, Léon, 52, 53, 91, 113–16
Blum-Viollette plan, 56–8, 84, 91, 107
Bost, Jacques, 200, 234
Bougie, La (Ponge), 187
Bourdet, Claude, 180, 188, 189, 222 and n., 277, 288
Bourgeois, Léon, 80, 81
Brasillach, Robert, 214
Brasseur, Pierre, 242
Brazil, Camus visits, 243, 244
Breton, André, 41, 108, 109, 223, 235, 248, 249, 254, 255
Brothers Karamazov, The (Dostoevsky), 100, 103, 104, 179
Bruckberger, Father R.-L., 180–1, 183, 219, 229, 234, 311
Bugeaud, General, 46
Buñoz (de Fréminville), 132
Burmese Days (Orwell), 70, 219
Butor, Michel, 326
Buzzati, Dino, 275

Calderón, Pedro, adaptation by Camus, 267, 270–1
Caliban, magazine, 236
Caligula, play by Camus, 6, 29, 101, 112, 114, 129–31, 143–6, 211, 260–1; its production, 211; Angers production, 291; revival, 328
Camus, Albert: birth, 10; death of his father, 11; boyhood at Belcourt, 12–13; at elementary school, 14–16; grammar school,

274–82, 294–7, 300–2, 305, 317, 324, 325, 327

Force Ouvrière, Socialist trade union, 241, 242

Fouchet, Max-Pol, 22–9, 33–5, 38, 45, 46, 51, 60, 63, 75, 78–80, 100, 152, 190, 205, 253, 297, 325; and Simone Hié, 23, 41–4; and left wing groups, 24–6, 29, 34–43; quarrel with Camus, 43

Franco, General, 79, 167, 194, 268, 279

Franc-Tireur, 176

Fréminville, Claude de, 36–9, 43, 45, 72, 80, 87, 92, 96, 98, 100, 135, 155, 210, 314, 316; and the Communist Party, 38, 75, 93; *Buñoz*, 132

Frenay, Henri, 188

Front de la Libération Nationale, *see* FLN

Galindo, Christiane, 110; intimacy with Camus, 98–9, 165

Galindo, Pierre, 110–11

Gallimard, Anne, 320, 321

Gallimard, Claude, 294, 296

Gallimard, Gaston, 30, 178, 179, 180, 296, 321, 322

Gallimard, Janine, 320, 321

Gallimard, Michel, 180, 183, 210, 211, 234, 237, 244, 292, 294, 296, 299, 311, 317, 320; and Camus' fatal accident, 320–1; dies in hospital, 323

Gallimard publishing house, 31, 80, 181, 189, 199, 202, 204, 207, 210, 213, 231, 276, 293, 296, 317, 323; Camus works for, 178–81, 189, 211–12, 232–4, 237, 242, 247, 258, 289, 292, 296, 314; factions in the firm, 296

Germain, Louis, Camus' teacher, 15–16, 27, 129, 137, 279

Gernet, dean of Algiers University, 39, 77

Gide, André, 17, 26, 30, 32–4, 37–9, 79, 83, 95, 102, 121, 139, 179, 184, 190, 193, 194, 199, 204, 238,

245, 289; and the *NRF*, 30–1; and Communism, 54, 94; in Algiers, 190, 209; returns to Paris, 209; meetings with Camus, 209–10

Gide, Catherine, 245

Gilson, Etienne, 72

Gimond, Marcel, 199, 222

Girard, Maurice, 90, 93

Giraudoux, Jean, 121

GLI (Groupe de Liaison Internationale), 241–2, 246, 253

Gnostics, the, 72, 73

Gorki, Maxim, 54, 87, 91

Greene, Graham, 245

Grenier, Jean, 20, 21, 31–7, 39, 40, 43, 60, 64, 71, 72, 77, 79, 83, 95, 100, 143, 147, 175, 233, 234, 279, 312; influence on Camus, 10, 11, 32–4, 107, 137; and the NRF, 32; and the Communists, 75; advice to Camus, 75, 93–4; and *Combat*, 213; and *L'Express*, 277; Camus' preface for him, 316–17; and Camus' death, 321

Groupe de Liaison Internationale, *see* GLI

Guerre d'Algérie, La (Roy), 301

Guilloux, Louis, 11, 233, 241, 303, 322

Guitton, Jean, 71, 72

Heart of Darkness (Conrad), 303

Heart of the Matter, The (Greene), 245

Hegel, G. W. F., and Hegelianism, 232, 248, 249, 251, 256

Heidegger, Martin, 40, 186

Hemingway, Ernest, 153, 202; Camus and his techniques, 155–6

Herrand, Marcel, 192, 193, 195, 238, 268; death, 271

Hervé, Pierre, 254, 277

Heurgon, Jacques, professor of history, 39, 40, 88, 97, 124, 190, 209; lectures on the Augustan age, 144

Hié, Simone, 12, 45, 47–9, 73–5, 142, 164, 193, 238; girlfriend of Fouchet, 23, 41–4; marriage to

138–45, 147, 154, 155, 157–60, 267, 304; published after his death, 138
Mouches, Les (Sartre), 182, 185
Mounier, Emmanuel, 29 and n.
Muets, Les, short story (Camus), 269, 303, 304, 307
Muphti of Algiers, murder of, 116–18
Mur, Le (Sartre), 123, 185
Mussolini, Benito, 66, 68
Mythe de Sisyphe, Le, philosophical essay by Camus, 40, 63, 70, 101, 121, 129–31, 137, 143, 145–54, 161, 162, 167, 169, 171, 177, 183, 187, 203, 249–51; popularity in the 40s, 154

Namia, Robert, 126, 210, 277
Nasser, General Abdel, 279
National Committee of Writers, 187
NATO, 257
Nausée, La (Sartre), 123, 153, 183, 185, 326
Ni Victimes, ni Bourreaux, Camus' series for *Combat*, 220; republished, 236, 237
Nietzsche, Friedrich, 30, 31, 40, 182, 213, 232, 248, 249
Nimier, Roger, 296
Nizan, Paul, 121–2
Nobel Prize awarded to Camus, 7, 222, 292–5, 311, 312, 315, 323
Noces, essays by Camus, 8, 68, 69, 100, 101, 136–9, 171, 209, 274
Nourritures Terrestres, Les (Gide), 30
Nouvel Observateur, Le, 49, 126, 327
Nouvelle Revue Française, La (N.R.F.), 23, 27, 30–3, 37, 67, 68, 75, 94, 101, 138, 147, 178, 184, 204, 207, 211, 214, 233, 254, 278; in wartime, 178–9

OAS, 324, 325
O'Brien, Conor Cruise, 160, 161, 298n.

Occampo, Vittoria, 243
Occupation of France, 171, 174, 176, 192, 194, 195, 199, 202
Oettly, Paul, 211
Ollivier, Albert, 199, 211, 220–2
Oran, 37, 164–6, 169–72, 325
Oran-Républicain, 110
Orléansville: earthquake and rebuilding, 275, 322; Centre Albert Camus, 322; 1980 earthquake, 322
Ortiz, pied-noir leader, 283, 284
Orwell, George, 70, 219, 241, 252, 264
Ouzegane, Amar, 55, 59, 65, 82; and the Communists, 92, 93; and the Algerian rebellion and War, 277, 280, 282, 284, 285, 287; Camus testifies for him, 297

Palle, Albert, 200–1
Paquebot Tenacity, Le (Vildrac), 99, 102
Paris-Soir, 128, 199, 204; Camus works for, 166–9; deal with Laval, 168; moves to Clermont-Ferraud and Lyons, 168–9
Parti Populaire Algérien (PPA), 91–2
Parti Pris des Choses, Le (Ponge), 186, 187
Pasternak, Boris, 95
Paulham, Jean, 31, 179, 207, 233
PCA (Parti Communiste Algérien), 55–7, 75–8, 82–4, 90, 104, 119, 120, 122, 126, 175, 177, 182, 203; formation, 55; Camus and, 89–97, 110; political split, 91–3; relations with Arabs, break down, 92; and *Alger-Républicain*, 105; and Algerian War, 277, 286
PCF (Parti Communist Français) (and PC), 54 and n., 55, 56 and n., 91, 212, 246–7, 257, 258, 277, 282; organises PCA, 55
Peck, Marcel, 175, 188
Pépète et Balthazar (Bertrand), 64
Perrin, Maurice, 288, 329
Peste, La (Camus), 6, 8, 18, 28, 148,

About the Author

PATRICK MCCARTHY was born in Wales of Irish parents in 1941, and was educated at Oxford and Harvard. Mr. McCarthy has taught politics and literature at Cambridge, Cornell, and at Johns Hopkins University's Bologna Center, and is currently an associate professor at Haverford College. He is the author of a study of Céline which appeared in the United States in 1977, and is currently writing a biography of André Gide.